ELEMENTS

OF

INTERNATIONAL LAW:

WITH

A SKETCH

OF THE

HISTORY OF THE SCIENCE.

BY

HENRY WHEATON, LL. D.

RESIDENT MINISTER FROM THE UNITED STATES IN AMERICA TO THE
COURT OF BERLIN;

Member of the American Philosophical Society of Philadelphia; of the Royal Asiatic Society of London; and of the Scandinavian Literary Society of Copenhagen.

THE LAWBOOK EXCHANGE, LTD.
Clark, New Jersey

ISBN 9781584771708 (hardcover)
ISBN 9781616192693 (paperback)

Lawbook Exchange edition 2002, 2012

The quality of this reprint is equivalent to the quality of the original work.

THE LAWBOOK EXCHANGE, LTD.

33 Terminal Avenue
Clark, New Jersey 07066-1321

Please see our website for a selection of our other publications
and fine facsimile reprints of classic works of legal history:
www.lawbookexchange.com

Library of Congress Cataloging-in-Publication Data

Wheaton, Henry, 1785-1848.
    Elements of international law : with a sketch of the history of the science /
       by Henry Wheaton. p. cm.
    Originaliy published: Philadelphia: Carey, Lea & Blanchard, 1836.
    Includes bibliographical references.
    ISBN 1-58477-170-4 (cloth: alk. paper)
    1. International law. I. Title.

KZ2495.A3 E44 2001
341—dc2l   00-066335

Printed in the United States of America on acid-free paper

ELEMENTS

OF

INTERNATIONAL LAW:

WITH

A SKETCH

OF THE

HISTORY OF THE SCIENCE.

———

BY

HENRY WHEATON, LL. D.

RESIDENT MINISTER FROM THE UNITED STATES IN AMERICA TO THE
COURT OF BERLIN;
*Member of the American Philosophical Society of Philadelphia; of the Royal Asiatic Society
of London; and of the Scandinavian Literary Society of Copenhagen.*

———

PHILADELPHIA:

CAREY, LEA & BLANCHARD.
——
1836.

GRIGGS & CO., PRINTERS.

ADVERTISEMENT.

THE object of the Author in the following attempt to collect the rules and principles which govern, or are supposed to govern, the conduct of States in their mutual intercourse in peace and in war, and which have therefore received the name of International Law, has been to compile an elementary work for the use of persons engaged in diplomatic and other forms of public life, rather than for mere technical lawyers, although he ventures to hope that it may not be found wholly useless even to the latter. The great body of the rules and principles which compose this Law is commonly deduced from examples of what has occurred, or been decided in the practice and intercourse of nations. These examples have been greatly multiplied in number and interest during the long period which has elapsed since the publication of Vattel's highly appreciated work: a portion of human history abounding in fearful transgressions of that Law of Nations which is supposed to be founded on the higher sanction of the Natural Law, (more properly called the Law of God,) and at the same time rich in instructive discussions in cabinets, courts of justice, and legislative assemblies, respecting the nature and extent of the obligations between the independent societies of men called States. The principal aim of the Author has been to glean from these sources the general principles which may fairly be considered to have received the assent of most civilized and Christian nations, if not as invariable rules of conduct, at least as rules which they cannot disregard without general obloquy and the hazard of provoking the hostility of other communities who may be injured by their violation. Experience shows that these motives, even in the worst times, do really afford a considerable security for the ob-

servance of justice between States, if they do not furnish the perfect
sanction annexed by the lawgiver to the observance of the municipal code of any particular State. The knowledge of this science
has, consequently, been justly regarded as of the highest importance
to all who take an interest in political affairs. The Author cherishes
the hope that the following attempt to illustrate it will be received
with indulgence, if not with favour, by those who know the difficulties of the undertaking.

BERLIN,
Jan. 1, 1836.

CONTENTS.

PART FIRST.

CHAPTER I.

SOURCES AND SUBJECTS OF INTERNATIONAL LAW.

CHAPTER II.

SOVEREIGN STATES.

Part Second.

Absolute International Rights of States.

CHAPTER I.

RIGHT OF SELF-PRESERVATION.

CHAPTER II.

RIGHTS OF INDEPENDENCE.

CHAPTER III.

RIGHTS OF EQUALITY.

CHAPTER IV.

RIGHTS OF PROPERTY.

Part Third.

INTERNATIONAL RIGHTS OF STATES IN THEIR PACIFIC RELATIONS.

CHAPTER I.

RIGHTS OF LEGATION.

CHAPTER II.

RIGHTS OF NEGOTIATION AND TREATIES.

PART FOURTH.

INTERNATIONAL RIGHTS OF STATES IN THEIR HOSTILE RELATIONS.

CHAPTER I.

COMMENCEMENT OF WAR, AND ITS IMMEDIATE EFFECTS.

CHAPTER II.

RIGHTS OF WAR AS BETWEEN ENEMIES.

CHAPTER III.

RIGHTS OF WAR AS TO NEUTRALS.

CHAPTER IV.

TREATY OF PEACE.

SKETCH

OF THE

HISTORY OF INTERNATIONAL LAW.

SKETCH

HISTORY OF INTERNATIONAL LAW.

THE classic nations of antiquity had very imperfect notions of international justice. With the Greeks and Romans,
" foreigner" and "*barbarian*," or " enemy," were synonymous
in language and in fact. By their rude theory of public law,
the persons of aliens were doomed to slavery, and their property to confiscation, the moment they passed the bounds of
one petty state and touched the confines of another. Nothing but some positive compact gave them any exemption
from this unsocial principle. Piracy was unblushingly practised by the most civilized nations which then existed. The
peaceful merchant was liable to be plundered both on sea
and land, by men with whom he and his country had no
quarrel; and even the philosopher, who visited foreign countries to enrich his native land with the merchandise of science
and art, was exposed to be captured and sold as a slave to
some barbarian master. As to these barbarians themselves,
the acutest of the Grecian philosophers gravely asserts that
they were intended by nature to be the slaves of the Greeks,
and that it was lawful to make them so by all possible means.[1]

Aristot. Polit. lib. i. c. 8. The Greeks termed those who were connected with them by compact 'Ενσπονδοι, literally those with whom they had

Thucydides has correctly stated the leading political maxim of his countrymen,—" that to a king or commonwealth, nothing is unjust which is useful." The same idea is openly avowed by the Athenians, in their reply to the people of Melos. Aristides distinguished in this respect between public and private morality, holding that the rules of justice were to be sacredly observed between individuals, but as to public and political affairs, a very different conduct was to be followed. He accordingly scrupled not to invoke upon his own head the guilt and punishment of a breach of faith, which he advised the people to commit in order to promote their national interests.[2]

If such were what may be called the *pacific* relations of the Grecian states with each other, and with the rest of mankind, we may easily imagine that the rights of *war* must have been exerted with extreme rigour. To reduce to slavery prisoners taken in war, was the universal practice of the ancient world. But the cold-blooded cruelty with which the Athenians could deliberately devote, by a public decree, to mutilation or death those whom they ought, even in compliance with their own national prejudices, to have regarded as brethren, is a striking proof how lamentably deficient was their theory and practice of international justice. The institutions of Lycurgus imparted a still more stern and unrelenting character to the savage people for whom he undertook to legislate. The Lacedemonian government was the patron of the aristocratic faction throughout all Greece; and as the popular interests in the different republics naturally looked up to the democracy of Athens for support, and there

poured out libations to the gods. Those who were not entitled to claim the benefit of this sort of alliance, were called 'Εκσπονδοι, that is, what we should term outlaws. The able, but often too systematic and prejudiced historian of Greece, observes, that " it appears to have been very generally held among the Greeks of that age, that men were bound to no duties to each other without an express compact." He furnishes, among other instances, a practical example of this rule in the cruel conduct of the Spartans to their prisoners taken upon the surrender of Platæa.—*Mitford's Hist. of Greece*, vol. i. c. 15, s. 7.

[2] Theophrastus ap. Plutarch. in Aristide.

was no supreme federal authority adequate to check and
control them, these rival powers kept every other state in
continual commotion and furious disorders, which reduced
them to misery, and thinned their population by proscrip-
tions, banishments, and massacres.[3]

Cicero's theory of justice in the intercourse of states seems
to have been more liberal than that of the Grecian statesmen and philosophers, though the practice of his countrymen varied as much from that theory as their religious notions differed from his sublime conceptions of the Divine attributes. But neither had any correct or adequate notion of
a science of international law, as understood in modern times.
The intercourse of the Romans with foreign nations was but
too conformable with their domestic discipline. Their ill-
adjusted constitution fluctuated in perpetual mutations, but
always preserved the character impressed upon it by Rome's
martial founder of a state, the very law of whose being
was perpetual war, and whose unceasing occupation was
the conquest and colonization of foreign countries. For more
than seven centuries the Romans pursued a scheme of aggrandizement, conceived in deep policy, and prosecuted with
inflexible pride and pertinacity, at the expense of all the

---

[3] A learned modern writer has enumerated the following points as constituting the rude outlines of public law observed among the Greek states:—
1. The rites of sepulture were not to be denied to those slain in battle. 2.
After a victory, no durable trophy was to be erected. 3. When a city was
taken, those who took refuge in the temples could not lawfully be put to
death. 4. Those guilty of sacrilege were to be left unburied. 5. All the
Greeks were allowed to resort to the public games, and the temples, and to
sacrifice there without molestation. These rules were enforced by the
council of the Amphictyons, which was a religious rather than a political institution, and, as such, took cognizance of offences against the laws and customs which had been sanctioned by the national superstition.—Saint-Croix,
Gouvernemens Fédératifs.

" We find it difficult to comprehend and believe," says Niebuhr, " in the
existence of the spirit with which the ancient oligarchies maintained the
power they at all times abused: that spirit, however, is sufficiently manifested in the oath they exacted in some of the Greek states from their members, to bear malice towards the commonalty, and to devise all possible harm
against it."—*Niebuhr, Römische Geschichte*, 2 band.

useful pursuits and charities of private life. All solicitude for the fate of their fellow-citizens made captive in war was disdained by their stern and crafty policy.

> " Hoc caverat mens provida Reguli
> Dissentientis conditionibus
> Fædis, et exemplo trahenti
> Perniciem veniens in ævum,
> Si non periret immiserabilis
> Captiva pubes."

The institution of the Fecial law, with a college of heralds to expound it, which they borrowed from the Etruscans, is the only symptom of a recognition by these *Barbarians*, as the Greeks called them, of an international code, distinct from their own municipal law. This mere formal institution strongly contrasts with their oppressive conduct towards their allies, and their unjust and cruel treatment of their vanquished enemies. "Victory," in their expressive, metaphorical language, "made even the *sacred* things of the enemy *profane*;" confiscated all his property, moveable and immoveable, public and private; doomed him and his posterity to perpetual slavery; and dragged his kings and generals at the chariot-wheels of the conqueror.[4]

[4] No professed treatise of international law has been left us by any ancient writer. Neither the work of Aristotle upon the laws of war, nor the institutes of the Roman fecial law, have descended to modern times. "When the Romans called their fecial law the law of nations, we are not to understand from hence that it was a positive law, established by the consent of all nations. It was in itself only a civil law of their own : they called it a law of nations, because the design of it was to direct them how they should conduct themselves towards other nations in the hostile intercourse of war; and not because all nations were obliged to observe it." (*Rutherforth, Nat. Law*, b. ii. c. 9, § 10.) And the incidental notices which may be collected from the writers on the Roman law, of what they call the *jus gentium*, concur in showing, that the idea associated with this term was not that of a positive rule governing the intercourse of states, but what has been since called natural law, or the rule of conduct that exists, or ought to exist, amongst mankind, independent of positive compact and institution. Hence it is always contrasted by these writers with the municipal law, *jus civile*, and even with the constitutional code, *jus publicum*, which regulated the government of the city.—Ompteda, Litteratur des Volkerrechts, tom. i. pp. 142—161.

Though the Romans had a· very imperfect knowledge of international law as a science, and little regard for it as a practical rule of justice between states, yet their municipal code has essentially contributed to construct the edifice of public law in modern Europe. The stern spirit of the Stoic philosophy was breathed into the Roman law, and contributed to form the character of the most highly gifted, virtuous, and accomplished aristocracy the world ever saw. There is a calm and placid dignity in the pictures drawn by the classic writers of the private manners of the Roman patricians, strongly contrasting with the harsher features of their public conduct, but which blended together to form a character admirably fitting them to perform the dignified office of consultation in the laws.

> "Romæ dulce diu fuit et solemne, reclusa
> Mane domo vigilare, clienti promere jura."

Theirs was for a long time the exclusive prerogative of administering justice. The usage insensibly grew up of certain families devoting their peculiar attention to the study and practice of jurisprudence, and transmitting the knowledge thus gained, as a private inheritance and most valuable instrument of political power. These circumstances essentially contributed to the perfection of the science in a state, where any other liberal pursuit, except the study of philosophy, was for a long time thought unworthy of its ingenuous citizens. In performing the duty of interpreting the laws to their clients and fellow-citizens, they invented a sort of judicial legislation, which was improved from age to age by the long line of jurisconsults, following each other in regular and unbroken succession from the foundation of the republic to the fall of the empire. The consequence was, that civil law, which seems never to have grown up to be a science in any of the Grecian republics, became one very early at Rome, and was thence diffused over the civilized world.[5] The mighty fame and fortune of the Roman people, in this respect, cannot be

[5] Smith's Wealth of Nations. b. v. c. 1. Part III.

contemplated without emotion. Its martial glory has long
since departed, but the " Eternal City" still continues to rule
the greatest part of the civilized and Christian world, through
the powerful influence of her civil codes. The acute research and unrivalled sagacity of an illustrious German civilian of the present day, have laboriously collected and happily combined the multiplied proofs, scattered in many a
worm-eaten volume, that the Roman law, so far from having
been buried in the ruins of the Roman empire, survived
throughout the middle age, and continued to form an integral portion of European legislation long before the period
of the pretended discovery of the Pandects of Justinian at
Amalfi, in the beginning of the twelfth century. The vanquished Roman provincials were neither extirpated nor deprived of their personal freedom, nor was their entire property confiscated, by the Gothic invaders, as we are commonly taught to believe. The conquered people were not
only permitted to retain a large portion of their lands, and
the personal laws by which they had been previously governed ; but the municipal constitutions of the Roman cities were
preserved, so that the study and practice of the Roman law
could never have been entirely abandoned, even during what
has been called the midnight darkness of the middle age.[6]
Accordingly, we find that in every civilized country of Europe, the Scandinavian nations and England excepted, the
Roman civil law either formed the original basis of the municipal jurisprudence, or constitutes a suppletory code of
"written reason," appealed to where the local legislation is
silent, or imperfect, or requires the aid of interpretation to
explain its ambiguities.

The foundation of the modern science of international law
may be traced to a period nearly coincident to that memorable epoch in the history of mankind—the revival of letters,
the discovery of the new world, and the reformation of religion. The Roman law infused its spirit into the ecclesiastical

[6] Geschichte des Rœmischen Rechts in Mittelallter, von Dr. C. von Savig-
ny, 4 tom. Heidelberg, 1814—1826.

code of the Romish Church; and it may be considered a favourable circumstance for the revival of civilization in Europe, that the interests of the priesthood, in whom all the
moral power and knowledge of the age were concentrated,
induced them to cherish a certain respect for the immutable
rules of justice. The spiritual monarchy of the Roman pon-
tiffs was founded upon the want of some moral power to tem-
per the rude disorders of society during the middle age. The
influence of the papal authority was then felt as a blessing to
mankind: it rescued Europe from total barbarism; it afforded the only shelter from feudal oppression. The compilation
of the canon law, under the patronage of Pope Gregory the
IX., contributed to diffuse a knowledge of the rules of justice
among the Catholic clergy; whilst the art of casuistry, invented by them to aid in performing the duties of auricular
confession, opened a wide field for speculation, and brought
them in view of the true science of ethics. The universities
of Italy and Spain produced, in the sixteenth century, a succession of labourers in this new field. Among these were
Francis de Victoria, who flourished as a professor at Sala-
manca about 1546, and Dominic Soto, who was the pupil
and successor of Victoria at the same seat of learning,
(which Johnson said he loved for its noble decision upon the
Spanish conquests in America,) and published, in 1560, an
elaborate treatise " Of Justice and Law," the subject-matter
of his lecture delivered there, which he dedicated to the un-
fortunately celebrated Don Carlos. Both Victoria and Soto
condemned, with honest boldness and independence, the cruel
wars of avarice carried on by their countrymen in the new
world, under the pretext of propagating what was called
Christianity in that age. Soto was the arbiter appointed by
the emperor Charles V. to decide between Sepulveda, the
advocate of the Spanish-American colonists, and Las Casas,
the champion of the unhappy natives, as to the lawfulness of
enslaving the latter. The edict of reform of 1543 was
founded upon his decision in their favour. It is said that
Soto did not stop here, but condemned in the most unmea-
sured terms the African slave-trade, then beginning to be

carried on by the Portuguese. But I do not understand that Soto reprobated slavery in general, or even the slave-trade itself, so long as it was confined to that unfortunate portion of the inhabitants of Africa who had been doomed to servitude from time immemorial, or had been enslaved by conquest in war, in that age universally regarded as giving a legitimate title to property in human beings *jure gentium;* but only that he condemned that system of kidnapping, by which the Portuguese traders seduced the natives to the coast, under fraudulent pretences, and forced them by violence on board their slave-ships.[7]

Long before the appearance of the labourers in the new field of natural jurisprudence, the genius of commerce, ever

[7] " If the report," says Soto, "which has lately prevailed, be true, that Portuguese traders entice the wretched natives of Africa to the coast by amusements and presents, and every species of seduction and fraud, and compel them to embark in their ships as slaves,—neither those who have taken them, nor those who buy them from the takers, nor those who possess, can have safe conscience, until they manumit these slaves, however unable they may be to pay ransom."—*Soto, de Justitia et Jure,* lib. iv. quæst. ii. art. 2.

To the above names may be added that of Francisco Suarez, another casuist, who flourished in the same century, and of whom Grotius says that he had hardly an equal, in point of acuteness, among philosophers and theologians. Some parts of his theory of private morals are justly reprobated by Pascal in the *Lettres Provinciales;* but this Spanish Jesuit has the merit of having clearly conceived and expressed, even at that early day, in his treatise *De Legibus ac Deo Legislatore,* the distinction between what is called the law of nature and the conventional rules of intercourse observed among nations. " He first saw that international law was composed, not only of the simple principles of justice applied to the intercourse between states, but of those usages long observed in that intercourse by the European race, which have since been more exactly distinguished as the consuetudinary law acknowledged by the Christian nations of Europe and America." (*Mackintosh, Progress of Ethical Philosophy*, sect. 3, p. 51.) A number of practical treatises on the laws of war were also written about this period by Spanish and Italian authors, several of whom are cited by Grotius; and it is remarked by Sir J. Mackintosh, that Spain, under Charles V. and Philip II., having become the first military and political power in Europe, maintaining large armies and carrying on long wars, was likely to be the first that felt the want of that more practical part of the law of nations which reduces war to some regularity.

favourable to the improvement and happiness of mankind, had reduced to a written text the long-established customs and usages of the maritime nations bordering on the shores of the Mediterranean Sea. Spain and Italy mutually contest with each other the honour of compiling the *Consolato del Mare*. This code embraces a great mass of civil commercial regulations, with a few chapters on the subject of maritime captures in war, which show that the leading principles of prize-law, as since practised by the maritime states of Europe, had been settled and generally adopted at this early period. The first printed edition of this curious monument of commercial legislation is nearly coeval with the art of printing itself, and was published in the Catalonian dialect, at Barcelona, in 1494. There is no question that it was collected long previous to that period; but at what particular epoch, and by which of the numerous commercial republics with which the Mediterranean coasts were studded during the middle age, is matter of great uncertainty. The question of its origin has exercised the learning and ingenuity of various critics, whose zeal in exploring this dark recess of legal antiquities has been stimulated by national vanity and rivalship. Many of the provisions of this antique code have been incorporated into the more modern ordinances of the different European states, and especially into that beautiful model of legislation, the marine ordinance of Louis XIV. Its decisions are in general dictated by a spirit of justice and equity which recommends them to adoption, even at the present day; and they unquestionably attest the general sense of Christian Europe at the period when they were collected, respecting the commercial relations of its different states.[8]

[8] A beautiful edition of the *Consolato* was published at Madrid, in 1791, by Don Antonio Capmany, in the Catalonian, with a Spanish translation. The commentary of Valin upon the marine ordinance of Louis XIV., of 1681, contains a most valuable body of maritime law, from which the English writers and judges, especially Lord Mansfield, have borrowed very freely. Valin also published a separate *Traité des Prises*, in 1763, which contains a collection of the French prize ordinances down to that period.

Albericus Gentilis was the forerunner of Grotius in the
science whose history we are reviewing. He was born in
the March of Ancona, about the middle of the sixteenth century, of an ancient and illustrious family. His father, being
one of the few Italians who openly embraced the doctrines of
the Reformation, was compelled to fly with his family into
Germany, whence he sent his son *Alberico* to England, where
he found, not only freedom of conscience, but patronage and
favour, and was elected to fill the chair of jurisprudence at
Oxford. He did not confine his attention to the Roman law,
the only system then thought worthy of being taught in a
scientific manner, (the municipal code being abandoned to the
barbarous discipline of the inns of court, of which Sir Henry
Spelman has left us so feeling an account;) but investigated
the principles of natural jurisprudence, and of the consuetudinary law then governing the intercourse of Christian nations. His attention was especially directed to this last, by
the circumstance of his being retained as the advocate of
Spanish claimants in the English courts of prize. The fruits
of his professional labours were given to the world in the
earliest reports of judicial decisions on maritime law published in Europe. His more scholastic and academical stu-
dies produced the first regular treatise upon the law of war,
considered as a branch of international law, which appeared
in modern times. This work served as a light to guide the
path of the illustrious Grotius, when he entered upon and
pursued the same track of investigation in the following century.[9]

Gentilis also wrote a treatise on embassies, which he dedicated to his friend and patron, the gallant and accomplished

[9] The title of *Alberico Gentili*, to be considered as the father of the modern science of natural and international law, is asserted by his countryman
Lampredi. "He first explained the rules of war and peace, which probably
suggested to Grotius the idea of writing his own work—worthy to be remembered, among other things, for having contributed to augment the glory
of his native Italy, where he drew his knowledge of the Roman law, and
proved her to be the earliest teacher of natural jurisprudence, as she had
been the restorer and patroness of all liberal arts and learning."

Sir Philip Sidney, whose "high thoughts were seated in a heart of courtesy," who was the generous protector of persecuted genius in that stormy and tumultuous age. In this work, Gentilis defends the moral tendency of Machiavelli's *Prince*, commonly supposed to have been intended as a manual of tyranny, but which he insists is a disguised satire upon the vices of princes, and a full and calm exposition of the arts of tyrants, for the admonition and instruction of the people; written by a man always actually engaged on the popular side in the factions of his own country, and almost a fanatical admirer of the ancient republicans and regicides. Whatever may be thought of this long-disputed question as to Machiavelli's motives in writing, his work certainly presents to us a gloomy picture of the state of public law and European society in the beginning of the sixteenth century:— one mass of dissimulation, crime, and corruption, which called loudly for a great teacher and reformer to arise, who should speak the unambiguous language of truth and justice to princes and people, and stay the ravages of this moral pestilence.

Such a teacher and reformer was Hugo Grotius, who was born in the latter part of the same century, and flourished in the beginning of the seventeenth. That age was peculiarly fruitful in great men, but produced no one more remarkable for genius and for variety of talents and knowledge, or for the important influence his labours exercised upon the subsequent opinions and conduct of mankind. Almost equally distinguished as a scholar and man of business, he was at the same time an eloquent advocate, a scientific lawyer, classical historian, patriotic statesman, and learned theologian. His was one of those powerful minds which have paid the tribute of their assent to the truth of Christianity. His great abilities were devoted to the service of his country, and of mankind. He vindicated the freedom of the seas, as the common property of all nations, against the extravagant pretensions of Great Britain and Portugal.[10] His ungrateful

---

[10] The *Mare Liberum* of Grotius appeared in 1634 ; and Archbishop Laud immediately engaged the learned Selden to answer it, in a treatise entitled *Mare Clausum,* in which he not only maintained the national claim of sove-

country rewarded his virtues and services with exile, and
would have extended her injustice to perpetual imprisonment
or death, but for the courageous contrivance and self-devo-
tion of his wife. Involved in the persecution of the Pensionary Barnevelt and the other Arminians, he was shut
up in the fortress of Louvestein, in the year 1619. He was,
however, allowed the society of his books, and of his accomplished and heroic wife, who contrived to deceive his guards,
and induce them to carry him out in a chest, while she remained thus voluntarily exposed to the vengeance of his
enemies. Grotius escaped into France, and in his banish-
ment returned good for evil by rendering the most important
services to his countrymen; and even his persecutor, Prince
Maurice of Nassau, is treated with perfect fairness and impartiality in his Belgic history. In an age peculiarly infected
with party animosity, Grotius preserved himself pure from
the taint of bigotry; and though actively engaged in the
contention between the religious factions of the Gomarists
and Arminians, his expansive toleration embraced every sect,
whether Catholic or Protestant;—a degree of liberality almost unexampled in those times. When he could no longer
be useful in active life, he laboured to win men to the love
of peace and justice by the publication of his great work,
which made a deep impression upon all the liberal-minded
princes and ministers of that day, and contributed essentially
to influence their public conduct. Alexander carried the
Iliad of Homer in a golden casket, to inflame his love of conquest; whilst Gustavus Adolphus slept with the Treatise on
the Laws of War and Peace under his pillow, in that heroic
war which he waged in Germany for the liberties of Protestant Europe. It is difficult to decide which presents the
most striking contrast—the poet of Greece and the philosopher
of Holland, or the two heroes who imbibed such different and
opposite sentiments from their pages.[11]

reignty over the British seas, but the obnoxious claim of ship-money, which
it was at that time the object of Charles I. and his councillors to establish.

[11] The treatise *De Jure Belli ac Pacis* was composed during the author's
exile in France, and published at Paris in 1625. A very interesting sum-

Nor was this the only immediate practical effect of this publication. Its enlightened and benevolent doctrines so forcibly struck the mind of that liberal sovereign, the Elector Palatine, Charles Lewis, that he founded at Heidelberg the first professorship of the law of nature and nations instituted in Europe, and bestowed the chair upon the celebrated Puffendorf, who used the treatise of Grotius as his text-book.[12] Grotius thus became the creator of a new school of political philosophy, which laid the foundation for all those important improvements in the science of government, political economy, and legislation, which have marked the two last centuries as an era in the progress of mankind. His work was illustrated by a crowd of commentators in the universities of Holland and Germany, and within forty years after his death obtained an honour which had been exclusively reserved, by the learned world, for the classical writers of antiquity : it was edited *cum commentariis variorum*. His Latin style is sometimes obscured by an imitation of the sententious brevity of Tacitus; and the work sins against the prevailing taste of the present age, in being adorned with a profusion of illustrations from the writers of sacred and heathen antiquity. Yet it should be remembered, that these are so many different witnesses summoned to attest the concurring sentiments and usages of mankind among all ages and nations, and that their testimony was much more revered by the cotemporaries of Grotius than the unsupported authority or reasonings of any individual writer of their own time.[13]

mary of the life of Grotius was published in 1826, by that venerable lawyer and excellent man, the late Charles Butler.

[12] Puffendorf's principal work, *De Jure Naturæ et Gentium*, was first published in 1672, and subsequently abridged by the author, in a smaller treatise, entitled *De Officio Hominis et Civis*. The reputation of Puffendorf seems to have been founded more upon the fact of his having no cotemporary competitor, than upon his real merit either as an inventor or compiler. Leibnitz calls him, *Vir parum jurisconsultus, et minime philosophus.*

[13] "I have used," says Grotius, "in proof of this law, the testimony of philosophers, historians, poets, and, lastly, even of orators. Not that they are indiscriminately to be relied on as impartial authority, since they often bend to the prejudices of their sect, the nature of their argument, or the interest

The great treatise of Grotius on the *Law of Peace and War*, defective as it confessedly is in scientific arrangement and distinctiveness of aim, produced a wonderful impression on the public mind of Christian Europe, and gradually wrought a most salutary change in the practical intercourse of nations in favour of humanity and justice. This new science of natural jurisprudence, developed by the disciples of Grotius, and applied in the first instance to ascertain those rules of justice which ought to regulate the conduct of individuals in the social state, was subsequently adopted to determine the like rules which govern, or ought to govern, the conduct of independent nations and states, considered as moral beings living in a social state, independent of positive human institution. This gave rise to the mixed science of the law of nature and nations, which soon came to form an indispensable part of education all over Europe. Whatever defects may have been justly imputed to the works of the more eminent publicists, considered as scientific, expository treatises, it would be difficult to name any writers who have contributed so much to promote the progress of civilization as " these illustrious authors—these friends of human nature—these kind instructers of human errors and frailties—these benevolent spirits, who held up the torch of science to a benighted world." If the international intercourse of Europe, and the nations of European descent, has been since marked by superior humanity, justice, and liberality, in comparison with the usages of the other members of the human family, they are mainly indebted for this glo-

of their cause; but where many minds of different ages and countries concur in affirming the same sentiment, this general concurrence must be referred to some general cause; which, in the questions we have undertaken to examine, can be no other than a right induction from the principles of natural justice, or some common consent. The former indicates the law of nature, the latter the law of nations: which difference is not to be understood from the terms alone which these authors use, (for they often confound the law of nature with that of nations,) but from the nature of the subject in question. For if a certain maxim, which cannot be inferred as a corollary from the principles of natural justice, is nevertheless found to be generally observed, we must attribute its origin to the general consent of nations."—*Proleg.* § xli.

rious superiority to these private teachers of justice, to whose
moral authority sovereigns and states are often compelled to
bow, and whom they acknowledge as the ultimate arbiters of
their controversies in peace; whilst the same authority contributes to give laws even to war itself—mitigating its fero-
city, and limiting the range of its operations within the
narrowest possible bounds, consistent with its purposes and
objects.

Protestant Germany was the field where the science of
natural and international jurisprudence was first cultivated
with most assiduity and success. The scientific writers of
that intellectual land had not yet learned to use freely their
native Teutonic tongue. That rich, copious, and expressive
dialect—for scientific purposes clearly and decidedly superior
to any other, except Greek alone—was almost entirely ne-
glected by her scholars and men of science. They wrote in
the dead language of Rome, to instruct the living men of
their own age and country. In Germany more than any
other country, (and *then* even more than *now*,) scientific and
and active life stand detached from each other like two separate worlds. Their mutual intercourse, at this period, was
kept up through the medium of the learned or fashionable
language, common to both. Leibnitz wrote mostly in Latin
or French, and Wolf, his disciple, almost exclusively in Latin.
Leibnitz, so justly compared by Gibbon to those conquerors
whose empire has been lost in the ambition of universal conquest, comprised both the philosophy of law and the details
of practical jurisprudence within the vast circle of his at-
tainments. Wolf gleaned after Puffendorf in the field of
natural jurisprudence; he entitled himself to the credit of
first separating the law which prevails or ought to prevail,
between nations, from that part of the science which teaches
the duties of individuals; and of reducing the law of nations to
a full and systematic form, as derived from a suitable application of the rules of natural justice to the conduct of independent sovereigns and states. The slumber of his once
celebrated work, in nine ponderous tomes, is probably not
now often disturbed; especially as all that is really valuable
in their contents has been incorporated into the treatise of

Vattel—"a diffuse, unscientific, and superficial, but clear and
liberal writer, whose work still maintains its place as the
most convenient abridgment of a part of knowledge which,"
in the words of Mackintosh, "calls for the skill of a new
builder."[14]

Previously to these writers, Bynkershoek had selected for
discussion the particular questions deemed the most important, and of most frequent occurrence in the practical intercourse of nations, instead of undertaking, after the example of his predecessors in the school of Grotius, an entire
system of natural and public law. In precision and practical
utility, he excels all the other publicists. It should be observed, however, as detracting not a little from his merits,
that his pages are stained with ferocious sentiments respecting
the rights of war, unworthy of a writer who flourished in the
commencement of the eighteenth century: holding every
thing lawful against an enemy—that he may be destroyed,
though unarmed and defenceless, and even by poison, or any
kind of weapons. It might be supposed that an author who
sets out with such notions as these would write a very com-
pendious treatise upon the laws of war: yet Bynkershoek
proceeds to unfold, in a very clear and vigorous, though somewhat dogmatic and arrogant style, the principles of this
branch of the science; from which we learn that there are
many modes of hostility which the mitigated usage of nations, operating with the force of law, has prohibited between
enemies, and in which the respective rights of belligerents
and neutrals are expounded in a more critical and satisfactory
manner than by any other elementary writer.[15]

[14] Christiani Wolfii Jus Naturæ Methodo Scientifica Pertractatum, in 9
tomos distributum. *Francof.* 1740. Vattel, Droit des Gens ou Principes
de la Loi Naturelle. *Neufchatel,* 1758.

[15] Quæstiones Juris Publici. *Lugd. Batav.* 1737. Bynkershoek had
previously published his treatise De Dominio Maris, in 1702, and that De
Foro Legatorem, in 1721. The latter was translated into French, and published with valuable notes by Barbeyrac at the Hague, 1724, Amsterd. 1730,
1741, 1746. An elegant and accurate translation into English of the first
book of Bynkershoek's *Questiones Juris Publici,* enriched with valuable
notes, was published by Mr. Duponceau at Philadelphia in 1810, under the
title of the *Law of War.*

PART FIRST.

SOURCES AND SUBJECTS OF INTERNATIONAL LAW.

PART FIRST.

SOURCES AND SUBJECTS OF INTERNATIONAL LAW.

CHAPTER I.

SOURCES OF INTERNATIONAL LAW.

THE leading object of Grotius, and of his immediate disciples and successors, in the science of which he was the
founder, seems to have been, *First*, to lay down those rules
of justice which would be binding on men living in a social
state, independently of any positive laws of human institution ; or, as is commonly expressed, living together in *a state
of nature :* and,

§ 1.
Natural
Law de-
fined.

Secondly, To apply those rules, under the name of Natural
Law, to the mutual relations of separate communities living
in a similar state with respect to each other.

With a view to the first of these objects, *Grotius* sets out
with refuting the doctrine of those ancient sophists who
wholly denied the reality of moral distinctions, and that of
some modern theologians, who asserted that these distinctions
are created entirely by the arbitrary and revealed will of
God, in the same manner as certain political writers (such
as Hobbes) afterwards referred them to the positive institution of the civil magistrate. For this purpose, Grotius labours to show that there is a law audible in the voice of
conscience, enjoining some actions, and forbidding others, according to their respective suitableness or repugnance to the
reasonable and social nature of man. " Natural law," says
he, " is the dictate of right reason, pronouncing that there

is in some actions a moral obligation, and in other actions a
moral deformity, arising from their respective suitableness or
repugnance to the rational and social nature, and that, consequently, such actions are either forbidden or enjoined by
God, the Author of nature. Actions which are the subject
of this exertion of reason, are in themselves lawful or unlawful, and are, therefore, as such, necessarily commanded
or prohibited by God."[1]

§ 2.
Natural
Law iden-
tical with
the law of
God, or Di-
vine Law.

The term Natural Law is here evidently used for those
rules of justice which ought to govern the conduct of men,
as moral and accountable beings, living in a social state, independently of positive human institutions, (or, as is commonly expressed, living in a state of nature,) and which may
more properly be called the law of God, or the divine law,
being the rule of conduct prescribed by him to his rational
creatures, and revealed by the light of reason, or the sacred
Scriptures.

§ 3.
Natural
Law ap-
plied to the
intercourse
of States.

As independent communities acknowledge no common superior, they may be considered as living in a state of nature
with respect to each òther: and the obvious inference
drawn by the disciples and successors of Grotius was, that
the disputes arising among these independent communities
must be determined by what they called the Law of Nature.
This gave rise to a new and separate branch of the science,
called the Law of Nations, *jus gentium.*[2]

---

[1] De Jur. Bel. ac Pac. lib. i. cap. 1, § x.

[2] This law was termed *Jus inter Gentes,* by Dr. Zouch, an English civilian,
distinguished in the celebrated controversy during the reign of Charles II.
between the civilians and common lawyers, as to the extent of the Admiralty
jurisdiction. He introduced this term as more appropriate to express the
real scope and object of that rule of conduct which obtains between nations.
An equivalent term in the French language was afterwards proposed by
Chancellor D'Aguesseau, as better adapted to express the idea properly annexed to the system of jurisprudence, commonly called *Droit des Gens,* but
which, according to him, ought rather to be termed *Droit entre les Gens.*
(Œuvres de d'Aguesseau, tom. ii. p. 337, ed. 1773, 12mo. The term *International Law* has since been proposed by Mr. Bentham as calculated to

Grotius distinguished the law of nations from the natural §4. law by the different nature of its origin and obligation, which Law of Nations he attributed to the general consent of nations. In the in- distin- troduction to his great work, he says, " I have used in favour guished from Na- of this law, the testimony of philosophers, historians, poets, tural Law. and even of orators: not that they are indiscriminately to be relied on as impartial authority; since they often bend to the prejudices of their respective sects, the nature of their argu- ment, or the interest of their cause; but because where many minds of different ages and countries concur in the same sentiment, it must be referred to some general cause. In the subject now in question, this cause must be either a just deduction from the principles of natural justice, or uni- versal consent. The first discovers to us the natural law, the second the law of nations. In order to distinguish these two branches of the same science, we must consider, not merely the terms which authors have used to define them, (for they often confound the terms natural law and law of nations,) but the nature of the subject in question. For if a certain maxim which cannot be fairly inferred from admitted principles is, nevertheless, found to be every where observed, there is reason to conclude that it derives its origin from positive institution." Again he says, " As the laws of each particular state are designed to promote its advantage, the consent of all, or at least the greater number of states, may have produced certain laws between them. And, in fact, it appears that such laws have been established, tending to pro- mote the utility, not of any particular state, but of the great body of these communities. This is what is termed the Law of Nations, when it is distinguished from Natural Law."[3]

express in our language, in "a more significant manner, that branch of ju- risprudence which commonly goes under the name of *Law of Nations*, a denomination so uncharacteristic, that, were it not for the force of custom, it would seem rather to refer to internal or municipal jurisprudence." (*Morals and Legislation*, vol. ii. ed. 1823.) The term International Law has now taken root in the English language, and is familiarly used in all discussions connected with the science.

[3] Prolegom. §§ xlii. xviii.

§ 5.
Law of
Nature
and Law
of Nations
asserted to
be identi-
cal, by
Hobbes
and Puf-
fendorf.

Hobbes, who appeared after Grotius, and before Puffendorf, asserted that the general principles of natural law and the law of nations are one and the same, and that the distinction between them is merely verbal. Thus he says, " The natural law may be divided into the natural law of men, and the natural law of states, commonly called the law of nations. The precepts of both are the same; but since states, when they are once instituted, assume the personal qualities of individual men, that law, which when speaking of individual men, we call the Law of Nature, is called the Law of Nations when applied to whole states, nations, or people."[4] To this opinion *Puffendorf* implicitly subscribes, declaring that there is no other voluntary or positive law of nations properly invested with a true and legal force, and binding as the command of a superior power." In conformity with this opinion, Puffendorf contents himself with laying down the general principles of natural law, leaving it to the reader to apply it as he might find it necessary to private individuals or to independent societies.[5]

§ 6.
How far
the Law of
Nations is
a positive
law de-
rived from
the posi-
tive con-
sent of
nations.

Grotius, on the other hand, considers the law of nations as a positive institution, deriving its authority from the positive consent of all, or the greater part of nations, which he supposes to be united in a social compact for this purpose. But one of his commentators (Rutherforth) infers that there can be no such positive law of nations, because there is no such social union among nations as that supposed by Grotius. He concludes that the same law which is called the law of nature when applied to separate and unconnected individuals, becomes the law of nations when it is applied to the collective bodies of civil societies, considered as moral agents, or to the several members of civil societies, considered not as distinct agents, but as parts of these collective bodies. At the same time, he admits that the natural law is not the only measure of the obligations that nations may be under to one

[4] De Cive, cap. 14. § 4.
[5] De Jure Naturæ et Gentium, lib. ii. cap. 3. § 23.

another. When considered as moral agents, they become
capable, as individuals are, of binding themselves to each
other by particular compacts to do or avoid what the law of
nature has neither commanded nor forbidden. But these obligations neither arise from a positive law of nations, nor produce such a law. They arise from an immediate and direct
consent, and extend no farther than to the nations, which by
their own act of immediate and direct consent have made
themselves parties to them. The only foundation then, according to this writer, of international law, so far as it differs
from the law of nature, is the general consent of mankind to
consider each separate civil society as a distinct moral being.
He contends that no evidence of a positive international law
can be collected from usage, because there is no immemorial,
constant, uniform practice among nations from which such a
law can be collected. But if the law of nations, instead of
being merely positive, is only the law of nature applied in
consequence of a positive agreement among mankind to the
collective bodies of civil societies as moral agents, and to the
several members of such societies as parts of these bodies,
the dictates of this law may be ascertained by the same means
that we use in searching for the law of nature. The history
of what has passed from time to time among the several nations of the world may likewise be of some use in this inquiry: not because any constant and uninterrupted practice in
matters which are indifferent by the law of nature can be
collected from thence; but because we shall there find what
has been generally approved, and what has been generally
condemned in the variable and contradictory practice of nations. "There are two ways," says Grotius, (lib. i. cap. 1, §
xii.) "of investigating the law of nature: we ascertain this
law, either by arguing from the nature and circumstances of
mankind, or by observing what has been generally approved
by all nations, or at least by all civilized nations. The former is the more certain of the two: but the latter will lead
us, if not with the same certainty, yet with a high degree of
probability, to the knowledge of this law. For such a universal approbation must arise from some universal principle;

and this principle can be nothing else but the common sense or reason of mankind. Since, therefore, the general law of nature may be investigated in this manner, the same law as it is applied particularly to nations as moral agents, and hence called the law of nations, may be investigated in the same manner." Hence his commentator infers, that if we understand what the law of nature is, when it is applied to individual persons in a state of natural equality, we shall seldom be at a loss to judge what it is, when applied to nations, considered as collective persons in a like state of equality.[6]

§ 7.
Law of
Nations
derived
from rea-
son and
usage.

Bynkershoek, (who wrote after Puffendorf, and before Wolf and Vattel,) derives the law of nations from reason and usage (ex ratione et usu,) and founds usage on the evidence of treaties and ordinances (pacta et edicta,) with the comparison of examples frequently recurring. In treating on the law of contraband, he says, " The law of nations on this subject is to be drawn from no other source than reason and usage. Reason commands me to be equally friendly to two of my friends who are enemies to each other, and hence it follows that I am not to prefer either in war. Usage is shown by the constant, and as it were, perpetual custom which sovereigns have observed of making treaties and ordinances upon this subject, for they have often made such regulations by treaties to be carried into effect in case of war, and by laws enacted after the commencement of hostilities. I have said *by, as it were, a perpetual custom;* because one, or perhaps two treaties, which vary from the general usage, do not alter the law of nations."[7]

In treating of the question as to the competent judicature in cases affecting ambassadors, he says: " The ancient jurisconsults assert, that the law of nations is that which is observed, in accordance with the light of reason, between nations, if not among all, at least certainly among the greater part, and those the most civilized. According to my opinion

---

[6] Rutherforth's Inst. of Natural Law, b. i. c. 9, §§ 1—6.

[7] Quæstiones Jur. Pub. cap. 10.

we may safely follow this definition, which establishes two distinct bases of this law; namely, reason and custom. But in whatever manner we may define the law of nations, and however we may argue upon it, we must come at last to this conclusion, that what reason dictates to nations, and what nations observe between each other, as a consequence of the collation of cases frequently recurring, is the only law of those who are not governed by any other—(unicum jus sit eorum, qui alio jure non reguntur.) If all men are men, that is to say, if they make use of their reason, it must counsel and command them certain things which they ought to observe as if by mutual consent, and which being afterwards established by usage, impose upon nations a reciprocal obligation; without which law, we can neither conceive of war, nor peace, "nor alliances, nor embassies, nor commerce."[8]— Again, he says, treating the same question: "The Roman and pontifical law can hardly furnish a light to guide our steps: the entire question must be determined by reason and the usage of nations. I have alleged whatever reason can adduce for or against the question: but we must now see what usage has approved, for that must prevail, since the law of nations is thence derived."[9]   In a subsequent passage of the same treatise, he says: "It is nevertheless most true, that the States General of Holland alleged in 1651, that according to the law of nations, an ambassador cannot be arrested, though guilty of a criminal offence; and equity requires that we should observe that rule unless we have previously renounced it. The law of nations is only a presumption founded upon usage, and every such presumption ceases the moment the will of the party who is affected by it is expressed to the contrary. Huberus asserts that ambassadors cannot acquire or preserve their rights by prescription; but he confines this to the case of subjects who seek an asylum in the house of a foreign minister against the will of their own sovereign. I hold the rule to be general as to every privilege of ambassadors, and that there is no one they can

---

[8] De Foro Legatorum, cap. 3, § xii.   [9] Ibid. cap. 7, § viii.

pretend to enjoy against the express declaration of the sovereign, because an express dissent excludes the supposition
of a tacit consent, and there is no law of nations except
between those who voluntarily submit to it by tacit convention."[10]

§ 8.
The law of
nations is
not merely
the law of
nature ap-
plied to
sovereign
states.

Without refining too much upon this subject, it may be
properly observed that international law is something more
and other than merely the natural law (the law of God) applied to the conduct of independent states considered as moral beings. In order to determine what is the rule to be observed among nations in any particular case, it is not sufficient to inquire what would be the natural law in a similar
case, when applied to individual persons supposed to be living
in a state of social union, independently of positive human
institutions for their government. "The application of a
rule," says *Vattel*, "cannot be reasonable and just, unless
it is made in a manner suitable to the subject. We are not
to believe that the law of nations is precisely and in every
case the same as the law of nature, the subjects of them only
excepted, so that we need only substitute nations for individuals. A civil society or state is a subject very different
from an individual of the human race; whence, in many
cases, there follow, in virtue of the law of nature itself, very
different obligations and rights; for the same general rule,
applied to two subjects, cannot produce exactly the same
decisions when the subjects are different; since a particular
rule, that is very just with respect to one subject, may not
be applicable to another. There are many cases, then, in
which the law of nature does not determine between state
and state as it would between man and man. We must
therefore know how to accommodate the application of it to
different subjects; and it is the art of applying it with a just-
ness founded on right reason, that renders the law of nations
a distinct science."[11]

[10] De Foro Legatorum, cap. 19, § vi.
[11] Vattel, Droit des Gens, Prelim. § 6. This modification of natural law, in
its application to the mutual relations of states, is attributed by Vattel him-

If states are moral beings capable of contracting by direct
and positive consent, and still more if their consent to consider each other as such moral beings may be implied from
the general acquiescence of mankind, they are equally capable of binding themselves by that tacit convention which is
fairly to be implied from the approved usage and practice of
nations, and their general acquiescence in certain positive
rules for the regulation of their mutual intercourse. But it
has been asserted that such an approved usage and general
acquiescence can only spring up among nations of the same
class or family, united by the ties of similar origin, manners,
and religion. *Grotius* states that the *jus gentium* acquires its
obligatory force from the positive consent of all nations, or *at
least of several*. " I say of several, for except the natural
law, which is also called the *jus gentium*, there is no other
law which is common to all nations. It often happens, too,
that what is the law of nations in one part of the world is not
so in another, as we shall show in the proper place in respect
to prisoners of war and the *jus postliminii*."[12] So also Bynkershoek, in the passage before cited, says that " the law of
nations is that which is observed, in accordance with the
light of reason, between nations, if not among all, *at least certainly among the greater part, and those the most civilized*."
Montesquieu says, that " the law of nations is naturally founded

self to Wolf. (See Pref. p. xx.) " A great part of the law of nations," says
Lord Stowell, " stands upon the usage and practice of nations. It is introduced, indeed, by general principles, but it travels with those general principles only to a certain extent; and if it stops there, you are not at liberty
to go further, and say that mere general speculation would bear you out in
a further progress. For instance, on mere general principles, it is lawful to
destroy your enemy; and mere general principles make no great difference
as to the manner in which it is to be effected; but the conventional law of
mankind, which is evidenced in their practice, does make a distinction, and
allows some and prohibits other modes of destruction; and a belligerent is
bound to confine himself to those modes which the common practice of mankind has employed, and to relinquish those which the same practice has not
brought within the ordinary exercise of war, however sanctioned by its
principles and purposes."—*Robinson's Adm. Rep.* vol. i. p. 140. The
Flad Oyen.

[12] De Jur. Bel. ac Pac. lib. i. cap. 1, § xiv. 4.

upon the principle that all nations ought to do to each other in peace as much good, and in war as little injury, as possible, consistently with their true interests. The object of war s victory; that of victory is conquest; that of conquest is self-preservation. From this and the former principle ought to be derived those laws which form the law of nations." After thus stating the principles on which the law of nations *ought to be founded,* he proceeds to say, that " every nation has a law of nations—even the Iroquois, who eat their prisoners, have one. They send and receive ambassadors; they know the laws of war and peace; the evil is, that their law of nations is not founded upon true principles."[13]

§ 9.
There is
no univer-
sal law of
nations.

There is then, according to these writers, no universal, immutable law of nations, binding upon the whole human race—which all mankind in all ages and countries, ancient and modern, savage and civilized, Christian and pagan, have recognised in theory or in practice, have professed to obey, or have in fact obeyed;—no law of nations similar to that law of right reason of which Cicero speaks, " which is congenial to the feelings of nature, diffused among all men, uniform, eternal, commanding us to our duty and prohibiting every violation of it;—one eternal and immortal law, which can neither be repealed nor derogated from, addressing itself to all nations and all ages, deriving its authority from the common Sovereign of the universe, seeking no other lawgiver and interpreter, carrying home its sanctions to every breast by the inevitable punishment he inflicts on its transgressors." If there be any such universal law acknowledged by all nations, it must be that of reciprocity, of amicable or vindictive retaliation, as the case may require the application of either. The ordinary *jus gentium* is only a particular law, applicable to a distinct set or family of nations, varying at different times with the change in religion, manners, government, and other

[13] Esprit des Lois, liv. i. ch. 3. Montesquieu deduces the peculiar law of nations prevailing among different races from their peculiar moral and physical circumstances, in the same philosophical spirit with which he traces the origin and history of the civil laws of different nations.

institutions, among every class of nations. Hence the international law of the civilized, Christian nations of Europe and America, is one thing; and that which governs the intercourse of the Mohammedan nations of the East with each other, and with Christians, is another and a very different thing. The international law of Christendom began to be fixed about the time of Grotius, when the combined influence of religion, chivalry, the feudal system, and commercial and literary intercourse, had blended together the nations of Europe into one great family. This law does not merely consist of the principles of natural justice applied to the conduct of states considered as moral beings. It may, indeed, have a remote foundation of this sort; but the immediate visible basis on which the public law of Europe, and of the American nations which have sprung from the European stock, has been erected, are the customs, usages, and conventions observed by that portion of the human race in their mutual intercourse.[14]

Many examples of the practical application of this theory will be found in the intercourse actually subsisting between Turkey and the Barbary states on the one hand, and the Christian nations of Europe and America on the other; in which the latter have been sometimes content to take the law from the Mohammedans, and in others to modify the Christian code in its application to them. Instances of this are to be found in the cases of the ransom of prisoners, the rights of ambassadors, and many others which will readily occur to the intelligent reader. On some points the Mohammedans are considered entitled to a very relaxed application of the principles established by long usage between the states of Christendom holding an intimate and constant intercourse with each other. Thus a formal sentence of condemnation by a Court of Admiralty is not held necessary to transfer the property in a vessel captured by the Algerines, and subsequently sold to a Christian purchaser *bonœ fidei*. It is deemed sufficient if the confiscation takes place by a public

§ 10. International law between Christian and Mohammedan nations.

---

[14] Ward's History of the Law of Nations in Europe, *passim*.

act of the competent authority, according to the established
custom of that part of the world.[15]   On the other hand, the
merchants of the African states are not exempted from the
observance of the law of blockade, though on some points
they may be entitled to a more relaxed application of the
European law of nations.   " The law of nations," says the
same enlightened civilian just quoted, " is a law made up of
a good deal of complex reasoning, although derived from
very simple rules, and altogether composing a pretty artificial
system, which is not familiar to their knowledge or their observance.   But on a point like this—the breach of a blockade, one of the most universal and simple operations of war
in all ages and countries, excepting such as are merely savage—no such indulgence can be shown.   It must not be understood by them that if a European army or fleet is blockading a town or port, they are at liberty to trade with that
port.   If that could be maintained, it would render the obligation of a blockade perfectly nugatory.   They, in common with all other nations, must be subject to this first and
elementary principle of blockade—that persons are not to
carry into the blockaded port supplies of any kind.   It is not
a new operation of war ; it is almost as old and general as
war itself.   The subjects of the Barbary states could not be
ignorant of the general rules applying to a blockaded port,
so far as concerns the interests and duties of neutrals."[16]

§ 11.
Definition
of interna-
tional law.
The law of nations, or international law, as understood
among civilized, Christian nations, may be defined as consisting of those rules of conduct which reason deduces, as con-
sonant to justice, from the nature of the society existing
among independent nations; with such definitions and modifications as may be established by general consent.

§ 12.
In what
sense the
A distinguished writer upon the science of law has questioned how far the rules which have been adopted for the

[15] Robinson's Adm. Rep. vol. iv. p. 3.   The Helena.
[16] Sir W. Scott (Lord Stowell) in Robinson's Adm. Rep. vol. iii. p. 324.
The Hurtige Hane.

conduct of independent societies of men, or sovereign states, rules of conduct between states are called laws.
in their mutual relations with each other, can with strict propriety be called *laws*.[17] And one of his disciples has observed, that " *laws* (properly so called) are commands proceeding from a determinate rational being, or a determinate body of rational beings, to which is annexed an eventual evil as the sanction. Such is the law of nature, more properly called the law of God, or the divine law; and such are political human laws, prescribed by political superiors to persons in a state of subjection to their authority. But laws imposed by general opinion are styled *laws* by an analogical extension of the term. Such are the *laws of honour*, which are rules of conduct imposed by opinions current in the fashionable world, and enforced by appropriate sanctions. Such also are the laws which regulate the conduct of independent political societies in their mutual relations, and which are called the law of nations, or international law. This law obtaining between nations, is not positive law; for every positive law is prescribed by a given superior or sovereign to a person or persons in a state of subjection to its author. The rule regarding the conduct of sovereign states, considered as related to each other, is termed *law* by its analogy to positive law, being imposed upon nations or sovereigns, not by the positive command of a superior authority, but by opinions generally current among nations. The duties which it imposes are enforced by moral sanctions: by fear on the part of nations, or by fear on the part of sovereigns, of provoking general hostility, and incurring its probable evils, in case they should violate maxims generally received and respected."[18]

International law is commonly divided into two branches:— § 13. Divisions of international law.
I. What is termed the Natural Law of Nations, consisting of the rules of justice applicable to the conduct of those independent societies of men called states.

II. The Positive Law of Nations, which is again subdivided into three branches:—

---

[17] Bentham, Morals and Legislation, vol. ii. p. 256, ed. 1823.
[18] Austin, Province of Jurisprudence determined, pp. 147-8, 207-8.

1. The Voluntary Law of Nations, derived from the presumed consent of nations arising out of their general usage and consent.

2. The Conventional Law of Nations, derived from the express consent of nations, as evidenced in treaties and other international compacts.

3. The Customary Law of Nations, derived from the tacit consent of particular nations establishing a peculiar usage between themselves.[19]

§ 14.
Sources of
interna-
tional law.

The various sources of international law in these different branches, are the following:—

1. The rules of conduct which ought to be observed between nations, as deduced by reason from the nature of the society existing among independent states.

2. Text writers of authority showing what is the approved usage of nations, or the general opinion respecting their mutual conduct, with the definitions and modifications introduced by general consent.

3. The adjudications of international tribunals, such as boards of arbitration and courts of prize.

In the present imperfect state of positive international law, which acknowledges no permanent authorized judicial expositor of its principles and rules, resort must necessarily be had to the precedents collected from the decisions of the boards of arbitration specially constituted to determine controversies between particular states, or of the courts of prize established in every country to judge of the validity of captures made in war. Greater weight is justly attributable to the judgments of the mixed tribunals, appointed by the joint consent of the two nations between whom they are to decide, than to those of admiralty courts established by and dependent on the instructions of one nation only. It is said indeed to be the duty of these courts, though established in the belligerent country, to administer with indifference that justice which the law of nations holds out, without distinction, to independent states, some happening to be neutral and some

---

[19] Vattel, Droit des Gens, Prelim.

to be belligerent. The seat of judicial authority is locally in the belligerent country, according to the known law and practice of nations; but the law itself has no locality. It is the duty of the person who sits there to determine the questions that arise exactly as he would determine the same questions if sitting in the neutral country whose rights are to be adjudicated upon.[20] Such is the theory of judicial duty, as expounded by one of the greatest of maritime judges. How far the practice of recent times, or of any times, has corresponded with this theory, will always be a matter of doubt with those whose rights and interests are affected by the adjudications of these *ex parte* tribunals. This will be more especially the case with respect to a great maritime country, depending on the encouragement of its navy for its glory and safety, where the national bias is so strong in favour of the captor, that the judge must, unconsciously, feel its influence. On this account, it becomes the more necessary to investigate rigidly the principles on which these adjudications are founded, and the reasonings by which they are supported.[21] With this caution, the books of admiralty reports may become an instructive source of information respecting the practical administration of prize law.

4. Ordinances of particular states, prescribing rules for the conduct of their commissioned cruisers and prize tribunals.

5. The history of the wars, negotiations, treaties of peace, and other transactions relating to the public intercourse of nations.

6. Treaties of peace, alliance, and commerce, declaring, modifying, or defining the pre-existing international law.

Though the binding force of express compacts between nations may not depend upon positive law, still these compacts constituting a rule between the contracting parties, are familiarly called *laws* by analogy to the proper use of that term. The effect of treaties and conventions between na-

[20] Sir W. Scott (Lord Stowell) in the case of the Swedish Convoy, Robinson's Adm. Rep. vol. i. p. 34.

[21] Mr. Chief Justice Marshall, in the case of the ship Venus, Cranch's Rep. vol. viii. p. 253.

tions, is not necessarily restricted, as Rutherforth has supposed, to those states who are direct parties to these compacts. They cannot, indeed, modify the original and pre-
existing international law to the disadvantage of those states
who are not direct parties to the particular treaty in question. But if such a treaty relaxes the rigour of the primitive
law of nations in their favour, or is merely declaratory of the
pre-existing law, or furnishes a more definite rule in cases
where the practice of different states has given rise to conflicting pretensions, the conventional law thus introduced is
not only obligatory as between the contracting parties, but
constitutes a rule to be observed by them towards all the
rest of the world.[22]

What has commonly been called the positive or practical
law of nations may also be inferred from treaties; for though
one or two treaties varying from the general usage and custom of nations cannot alter the international law, yet an almost perpetual succession of treaties establishing a particular
rule will go very far towards proving what that law is upon
a disputed point. Some of the most important modifications
and improvements in the modern law of nations have thus
originated in treaties.[23]

[22] See "Substance of a Speech delivered by Lord Grenville in the House
of Lords, Nov. 13, 1801," upon the maritime convention of June, 1801, between Great Britain and Russia.

[23] Bynkershoek, Quæst. Jur. Pub. lib. i. cap. 10.

CHAPTER II.

SOVEREIGN STATES.

THE subjects of international law are separate political societies of men living independently of each other, and especially those called Sovereign States. **§ 1. Sovereign states defined.**

A sovereign state is generally defined to be any nation or people, whatever may be the form of its internal constitution, which governs itself independently of foreign powers.[1]

This definition, unless taken with great qualifications, cannot be admitted as entirely accurate. Some states are completely sovereign, and independent, acknowledging no superior but the supreme Ruler and Governor of the universe. The sovereignty of other states is limited and qualified in various degrees. **§ 2. Limited sovereignty.**

All independent states are equal in the eye of international law, whatever may be their relative power. The co-ordinate sovereignty of a particular state is not impaired by its occasional obedience to the commands of other states, or even the habitual influence exercised by them over its councils. It is only when this obedience, or this influence, assumes the form of express compact, that the sovereignty of the state, inferior in power, is legally affected by its connexion with the other. Treaties of equal alliance, freely contracted between independent states, do not impair their sovereignty. Treaties of unequal alliance, guarantee, mediation, and protection, may have a different effect. **Equality of states.**

Still the sovereignty of the inferior ally or protected state remains, though limited and qualified by the stipulations of the treaties of alliance and protection.[2]

[1] Vattel, Droit des Gens, liv. i. c. 1. § 4.
[2] Vattel, liv. i. c. 1. §§ 5, 6.

52 SOVEREIGN STATES.

City of Cracow. Thus the city of Cracow in Poland, with its territory, was declared by the congress of Vienna to be a free, independent, and neutral state, under the protection of Russia, Austria, and Prussia.[3] This state may be occasionally obedient to the commands of these great powers, or its councils may be habitually influenced by them, but its sovereignty still remains, except so far as it is affected by the protectorate which may be lawfully asserted over it in pursuance of the treaties of Vienna.

§ 3. Tributary and vassal states. So also tributary states, and states having a feudal relation to each other, are still considered as sovereign so far as their sovereignty is not affected by this relation. Thus it is evident that the tribute formerly paid by the principal maritime powers of Europe to the Barbary states, did not at all affect the sovereignty and independence of the former; whilst that paid by the principalities of Walachia and Moldavia to the Ottoman Porte under the mediation of Russia, can hardly be considered as leaving them any thing more than a shadow of sovereignty. So also the king of Naples has been a nominal vassal of the Papal see ever since the eleventh century: but this feudal dependence, now abolished, was never considered as impairing the sovereignty of the kingdom of Naples.[4]

§ 4. Single or united states. Sovereign states may be either single, or may be united together under a common sovereign, or by a federal compact.

§ 5. Personal union under the same sovereign. 1. If this union under a common sovereign is not an incorporate union, that is to say, if it is only *personal* in the reigning sovereign, or even if it is *real*, yet if the different component parts are united with a perfect equality of rights, the sovereignty of each state remains unimpaired.[5]

Thus the kingdom of Hanover is held by the King of the

[3] Acte du Congrès de Vienne du 9 Juin, 1815, Art. 6, 9, 10.
[4] Ward's Hist. of the Law of Nations, vol. ii. p. 69.
[5] Grotius, de Jur. Bel. ac Pac. lib. ii. cap. 9, §§ 8, 9. Kluber, Droit des Gens Moderne de l'Europe, pt. i. c. 1. § 27.

United Kingdom of Great Britain and Ireland separately from
his insular dominions. Hanover and the United Kingdom are
subject to the same prince, without any dependence on each
other, both kingdoms retaining their respective national rights
of sovereignty.

The union of the different states composing the Austrian § 6.
monarchy is a *real* union. The hereditary dominions of the *Real* union under the
house of Austria, the kingdoms of Hungary and Bohemia, same sove-
the Lombardo-Venetian kingdom, and other states, are all reign.
indissolubly united under the same sceptre, but with distinct
fundamental laws and other political institutions.

It appears to be an intelligible distinction between the union
of the Austrian states, and all other unions which are not
merely *personal* under the same crowned head, that though
the separate sovereignty of each state may still subsist inter-
nally in respect to its co-ordinate states, and in respect to the
imperial crown, yet the sovereignty of each is merged in the
general sovereignty of the empire, as to their international
relations with foreign powers.

2. An *incorporate* union is such as that which subsists be- § 7.
tween Scotland and England, and between Great Britain and incorpo-
Ireland, forming out of the three kingdoms an empire united rate union.
under one crown and one legislature, although each may
have distinct laws and a separate administration. The sovereignty of each original kingdom is completely merged in the
United Kingdom thus formed by their successive unions.

3. The union established by the congress of Vienna, be- § 8.
tween the empire of Russia and the kingdom of Poland, is Union be-
of a more anomalous character. By the Final Act of the sia and Po-
congress, the duchy of Warsaw was reunited to the Russian land.
empire, and it was stipulated that it should be irrevocably
connected with that empire by its constitution, to be possessed by His Majesty the emperor of all the Russias, his heirs
and successors in perpetuity, with the title of King of Poland;
His Majesty reserving the right to give to this state, enjoying
a distinct administration, such interior extension as he should

judge proper: and that the Poles subject respectively to Russia, Austria, and Prussia, should obtain a representation and national institutions, regulated according to that mode of political existence which each government to whom they belong should think useful and proper to grant.[6]

[6] "Le Duché de Varsovie, à l'exception des provinces et districts, dont il a été autrement disposé dans les articles suivans, est réuni à l'Empire de Russie. Il y sera lié irrévocablement par sa Constitution, pour être possédé par S. M. l'Empereur de toutes les Russies, ses héritiers et ses successeurs à perpétuité. Sa Majesté Imperiale se reserve de donner à cet état, jouissant d'une administration distincte, l'extension intérieure qu'elle jugera convenable. Elle prendra, avec ses autres titres celui de Czar, Roi de Pologne, conformément au protocole usité et consacré par les titres attachés à ses autres possessions.

"Les Polonais, sujets respectifs de la Russie, de l'Autriche, et de la Prusse, obtiendront une représentation et des institutions nationales, réglées d'après la mode d'existence politique que chacun des Gouvernemens auxquelles ils appartiennent jugera utile et convenable de leurs accorder."—*Art.* 1.

In consequence of the revolution and reconquest of Poland by Russia, a manifesto was issued by the Emperor Nicholas, on the 26th of February, 1832, by which the kingdom of Poland was declared to be perpetually united (*réuni*) to the Russian empire, and to form an integral part thereof; the coronation of the emperors of Russia and kings of Poland hereafter to take place at Moscow by one and the same act; Poland to be separately administered, and to preserve its civil and criminal code, subject to alteration and revision by the council of the Russian empire; and consultative provincial states to be established in the different Polish provinces. It is understood that Great Britain and France have protested against the measure of the Russian government as an infraction of the spirit, if not of the letter, of the treaties of Vienna. And it may be stated that so far as the disturbance of the general balance of European power consequent upon the partition of Poland, was meant to be corrected by the above stipulations, they have entirely failed of their effect, either in consequence of the contracting parties not concurring in their actual intentions, or failing to express them with the requisite clearness. Such is the intrinsic imperfection of all human language, that it frequently becomes impossible from the mere words alone of any writing, to ascertain the meaning of the parties. When to this intrinsic defect of every known tongue, is superadded that studied ambiguity, which almost justifies the maxim of a celebrated statesman, an active agent in these transactions, that "language was given to man to conceal his thoughts"—it becomes still more difficult to ascertain the real meaning of words selected to express the result of a compromise between opposite and almost irreconcilable interests and views. At the Congress of Vienna, Great Britain and

4. Sovereign states permanently united together by a fede-   § 9.
ral compact, either form a *system of confederated states* (pro-   Federal union.
perly so called) or a *supreme federal government*, which has
been sometimes called a *composite state.*

France avowedly wished to restore the nationality of Poland, with its ancient
boundaries as they existed before the first partition of 1772; Austria professed
herself not unwilling to sacrifice her share of the dismembered provinces
which she had reluctantly received as an equivalent for the inevitable aggrandizement of the other two partitioning states; and Prussia would doubtless have consented to a similar sacrifice for adequate equivalents: but Russia,
on the other hand, far from being inclined to give up Lithuania and the other
Polish provinces annexed to her empire at the first and second partitions,
claimed the Duchy of Warsaw as acquired by right of conquest in war with
France.   Under these circumstances, the British and French cabinets were
induced to consent to relinquish the absolute restoration of Poland as an independent state, in return for the creation of the kingdom of that name to
be possessed by the Russian sovereign, by a title distinct from his imperial
crown,—to be governed by its separate constitution and laws, and capable of
being extended by the addition of the other Polish provinces which had
been incorporated in the Russian empire; and also in return for the other
stipulations in favour of the Poles inhabiting the Prussian and Austrian portions of their former territory, and also for the acknowledgment of the independence of the free city of Cracow, the ancient capital of Poland.   Without pretending to scrutinize the various motives which may have influenced
the different powers, parties to this arrangement, it must be admitted that
nothing is more difficult than to maintain, or regulate the relations between
a sovereign nation, and a dependent, or even a co-ordinate state, by means
of foreign interference, which must always assume a character offensive to the
superior government.   If any of the parties to the treaties of Vienna really
intended to reserve to the Polish nation the consoling hope of ultimate restoration, and in the mean time to secure to them distinct institutions and
privileges as a compensation for the temporary loss of their national independence, and to prevent their being entirely absorbed in the partitioning
states,—it must be admitted that this intention has been very inadequately
expressed in the text of those treaties—and that it must be sought for in the
spirit by which their stipulations were dictated,—which, as already observed,
was that of a compromise among the discordant views of all the contracting
parties.   This compromise has evidently failed of its effect since the Polish
revolution of 1830; and the parties to the stipulations in question who seek
to avoid the consequences of that event, must go behind the treaty itself,
and reverting to the original idea of a complete restoration of Polish independence, must seek to realize that idea by means which are adequate to
the end,—by remodelling those stipulations so as to guaranty the existence
of Poland with its original extent, as a state independent of any connexion
with other powers.

§ 10.
Confede-
rated
states, each
retaining
its own so-
vereignty.

In the first case, the several states are connected together by a compact which does not essentially differ from an ordinary treaty of equal alliance. Consequently the sovereignty of each member of the union remains unimpaired; the resolutions of the federal body being enforced, not as laws directly binding on the private individual subjects, but through the agency of each separate government, adopting them, and giving them the force of law within its own jurisdiction.

§ 11.
Supreme
federal go-
vernment
or compo-
site state.

In the second case, the federal government created by the act of union, is sovereign and supreme within the sphere of the powers granted to it by that act, and the sovereignty of each several state is impaired both by the powers thus granted to the federal government, and the limitations thus imposed on the several states' governments.

§ 12.
Germanic
confedera-
tion.

1. Thus the sovereign princes and free cities of Germany, including the Emperor of Austria and the King of Prussia, in respect to their possessions which formerly belonged to the German empire, the King of Denmark for the duchy of Holstein, and the King of the Netherlands for the grand duchy of Luxembourg, are united in a perpetual league, under the name of the Germanic Confederation.

From the extremely complicated constitution of this league, it may at first sight appear doubtful to which of these two classes of federal compacts it properly belongs, and consequently how far the sovereignty of each member of the union is affected or impaired by its regulations.

The object of this union is declared to be the preservation of the external and internal security of Germany, the independence and inviolability of the confederated states. All the members of the confederation, as such, are entitled to equal rights. New states may be admitted into the union, by the unanimous consent of the members.[7]

The affairs of the union are confided to a federative diet, which sits at Frankfort on the Main, in which the respective

[7] Acte Final du Congrès de Vienne, art. 53, 54, 55. Deutche Bundes Acte, vom 8 Juni, 1815, art. 1. Wiener Schluss Acte, vom 15 Mai, 1820, art. 1, 6.

states are represented by their ministers, and are entitled to the following votes in what is called the *Ordinary Assembly* of the diet:

	Votes.
Austria	1
Prussia	1
Bavaria	1
Saxony	1
Hanover	1
Wurtemburg	1
Baden	1
Electoral Hesse	1
The Grand Duchy of Hesse	1
Denmark (for Holstein)	1
The Netherlands (for Luxemburg)	1
The Grand Ducal and Ducal Houses of Saxony	1
Brunswick and Nassau	1
Mecklenburg-Schwerin and Strelitz	1
Oldenburg, Anhalt, and Schwartzburg	1
Hohenzollern, Lichtenstein, Reuss, Schaumburg, Lippe, Waldeck, and Hesse Homburg	1
The free cities of Lubeck, Frankfort, Bremen, and Hamburg	1
	Total 17

Austria presides in the diet, but each state has a right to propose any measure for deliberation.

The diet is formed into what is called a *General Assembly*, (Plenum,) for the decision of certain specific questions. The votes *in pleno* are distributed as follows:

	Votes.
Austria	4
Prussia	4
Saxony	4
Bavaria	4
Hanover	4
Wurtemburg	4
Baden	3
Electoral Hesse	3
	Carried forward 30

		Votes.
Brought forward		30
The Grand Duchy of Hesse		3
Holstein		3
Luxemburg		3
Brunswick		2
Mecklenburg-Schwerin		2
Nassau		2
Saxe Weimar		1
Gotha		1
Coburg		1
Meinengen		1
Hilburghausen		1
Mecklenburg-Strelitz		1
Oldenburg		1
Anhalt-Dessau		1
Anhalt-Bernburg		1
Anhalt-Coethen		1
Schwartzburg-Sondershausen		1
Schwartzburg-Rudolstadt		1
Hohenzollern-Hechingen		1
Lichtenstein		1
Hohenzollern-Sigmaringen		1
Waldeck		1
Reuss (elder branch)		1
Reuss (younger branch)		1
Schaumburg-Lippe		1
Lippe		1
Hesse-Homburg		1
The free city of Lubeck		1
Frankfort		1
Bremen		1
Hamburg		1
Total		70

Every question to be submitted to the general assembly of the diet is first discussed in the ordinary assembly, where it is decided by a majority of votes. But in the general assembly (*in pleno*) two-thirds of all the votes are necessary to a decision. The ordinary assembly determines what subjects are to be submitted to the general assembly. But all questions concerning the adoption or alteration of the fundamental laws of the confederation, or organic regulations establishing permanent institutions as means of carrying into effect the declared objects of the union, or the admission of new members, or concerning the affairs of religion, must be submitted to the general assembly; and in all these cases absolute unanimity is necessary to a final decision.[8]

The diet has power to establish fundamental laws for the confederation, and organic regulations as to its foreign, military, and internal relations.[9]

All the states guaranty to each other the possession of their respective dominions within the union, and engage to defend, not only entire Germany, but each individual state in case of attack. When war is declared by the confederation, no state can negotiate separately with the enemy, nor conclude peace or an armistice without the consent of the rest. Each member of the confederation may contract alliances with other foreign states, provided they are not directed against the security of the confederation, or the individual states of which it is composed. No state can make war upon another member of the union, but all the states are bound to submit their differences to the decision of the diet. This body is to endeavour to settle them by mediation; and if unsuccessful, and a juridical sentence becomes necessary, resort is to be had to an *Austrëgal* proceeding, (Austrägal-Instanz,) to which the litigating parties are bound to submit without appeal.[10]

Each country of the confederation is entitled to a local constitution of states.[11] The diet may guaranty the constitution established by any particular state upon its application, and thereby acquires the right of settling the differences which may arise respecting its interpretation or execution, either by mediation or judicial arbitration, unless such con-

[8] Acte Final art. 58. Wiener Schluss Acte, art. 12—15.

[9] Acte Final, art. 62.

[10] Acte Final, art. 63.

[11] Bundes Acte, art. 13. In allen Bundestaaten wird eine landesständische Verfassung Statt finden.

stitution shall have provided other means of determining
controversies of this nature.[12]

In case of rebellion or insurrection, or imminent danger
thereof in several states of the confederation, the diet may
interfere to suppress such insurrection or rebellion, as threatening the general safety of the confederation. And it may
in like manner interfere on the application of any one state,
or, if the local government is prevented by the insurgents
from making such application, upon the notoriety of the fact
of the existence of such insurrection, or imminent danger
thereof, to suppress the same by the common force of the
confederation.[13]

In case of the denial or unreasonable delay of justice by
any state to its subjects, or others, the aggrieved party may
invoke the mediation of the diet; and if the suit between
private individuals involves a question respecting the conflicting rights and obligations of different members of the union,
and it cannot be amicably arranged by compromise, the diet
may submit the controversy to the decision of an Austrëgal
tribunal.[14]

The decrees of the diet are executed by the local governments of the particular states of the confederation, on application to them by the diet for that purpose, excepting in
those cases where the diet interferes to suppress an insurrection or rebellion in one or more of the states; and even in
these instances, the execution is to be enforced, so far as practicable, in concert with the local government against whose
subjects it is directed.[15]

The subjects of each member of the union have the right
of acquiring and holding real property in any other state of
the confederation; of migrating from one state to another;
of entering into the military or civil service of any one of
the confederated states, subject to the paramount claim of

---

[12] Wiener Schluss Acte, art. 60.
[13] Ibid. art. 25—28.   [14] Ibid. art. 29, 30.
[15] Wiener Schluss Acte, art. 32.

their own native sovereign; and of exemption from every
droit de retraction, or other similar tax on removing their effects from one state to another, unless where particular reciprocal compacts have stipulated to the contrary. The diet
has power to establish uniform laws relating to the freedom
of the press, and to secure to authors the copyright of their
works throughout the confederation.[16]

The different Christian sects throughout the confederation
are entitled to an equality of civil and political rights; and
the diet is empowered to take into consideration the means of
ameliorating the civil condition of the Jews, and of securing
to them in all the states of the confederation the full enjoyment of civil rights, upon condition that they submit themselves to all the obligations of other citizens. In the mean
time, the privileges granted to them by any particular state
are to be maintained.[17]

The diet has also power to regulate the commercial intercourse between the different states, and the free navigation
of the rivers belonging to the confederation, as secured by
the treaty of Vienna.[18]

Notwithstanding the great mass of powers thus given to
the diet, and the numerous restraints imposed upon the exercise of sovereignty by the individual states of which the
union is composed, it does not appear that the Germanic confederation can be distinguished from an ordinary equal alliance between independent sovereigns, except by its perma-
nence, and the greater number and complication of the
objects it is intended to embrace. The several states of the
confederation do not form by their union one composite state,
nor are they subject to a common sovereign. Though what
are called the fundamental *laws* of the confederation are
framed by the diet, which has also power to make organic
regulations respecting its external, internal, and military relations; these regulations are not, in general, enforced as laws
directly binding on the private individual subjects, but only

[16] Bundes Acte, art. 18.   [17] Bundes Acte, art. 16.
[18] Ibid. art. 19.   Acte Final, art. 108—117.

through the agency of each separate government adopting
them, and giving them the force of laws within its own local
jurisdiction.   If there be cases where the diet may rightfully
enforce its own resolutions directly against the individual
subjects, or the body of subjects within any particular state
of the confederation, without the agency of the local governments, (and there appear to be some such cases,) then
these cases, when they occur, form an exception to the general character of the union, which then so far becomes a
composite state, or supreme federal government.   But the
occasional obedience of the diet, and through it of the several
states, to the commands of the two great preponderating
members of the confederation, or even the habitual influence
exercised by them over its councils, and over the councils
of its several states, does not, in legal contemplation, impair
their sovereignty, or change the legal character of their
union.

Very important modifications were introduced into the
Germanic constitution by an act of the diet of the 28th of
June, 1832.   By the 1st article of this Act, it is declared,
that whereas, according to the 57th article of the Final Act
of the Congress of Vienna, the powers of the state ought to
remain in the hands of its chief, and the sovereign ought not
to be bound by the local constitution to require the co-operation of the chambers, except as to the exercise of certain
specified rights, the sovereigns of Germany, as members of
the confederation, have not only the right of rejecting the petitions of the chambers contrary to this principle, but the object of the confederation makes it their duty to reject such
petitions.

Art. 2. Since, according to the spirit of the said 57th article
of the Final Act, and its inductions as expressed in the 58th
article, the chambers cannot refuse to any German sovereign
the necessary means of fulfilling his federal obligations, and
those imposed by the local constitution, the cases in which
the chambers endeavour to make their consent to the taxes
necessary for these purposes depend upon the assent of the
sovereign to their propositions upon any other subject, are to

be classed among those cases to which are to be applied the 25th and 26th articles of the Final Act, relating to resistance of the subjects against the government.

Art. 3. The interior legislation of the states belonging to the Germanic confederation, cannot prejudice the object of the confederation as expressed in the 2d article of the original act of confederation, and in the 1st article of the Final Act: nor can this legislation obstruct in any manner the accomplishment of the federal obligations of the state, and especially the payment of the taxes necessary to fulfil them.

Art. 4. In order to maintain the rights and dignity of the confederation, and of the assembly representing it, against usurpations of every kind, and at the same time to facilitate to the states which are members of the confederation the maintenance of the constitutional relations between the local governments and the legislative chambers, there shall be appointed by the diet, in the first instance for the term of six years, a commission charged with the supervision of the deliberations of the chambers, and with directing their attention to the propositions and resolutions which may be found in opposition to the federal obligations, or to the rights of sovereignty, guarantied by the compacts of the confederation. This commission is to report to the diet, which, if it finds the matter proper for further consideration, will put itself in relation with the local government concerned. After the lapse of six years a new arrangement is to be made for the prolongation of the commission.

Art. 5. Since, according to the 59th article of the Final Act, in those states where the publication of the deliberations of the chambers is secured by the constitution, the free expression of opinion, either in the deliberations themselves, or in their publication through the medium of the press, cannot be so extended as to endanger the tranquillity of the state itself, or of the confederation in general, all the governments belonging to it mutually bind themselves, as they are already bound by their federal relations, to adopt and maintain such measures as may be necessary to prevent and punish every attack against the confederation in the local chambers.

Art, 6. Since the diet is already authorized by the 17th article of the Final Act, for the maintenance of the true meaning of the original act of confederation, to give its provisions such an interpretation as may be consistent with its object, in case doubts should arise in this respect, it is understood that the confederation has the exclusive right of interpreting, so as to produce their legal effect, the original act of the confederation and the Final Act, which right it exercises by its constitutional organ, the diet.

Further modifications of the federal constitution were introduced by the act of the diet of the 30th of October, 1834, in consequence of the diplomatic conferences held at Vienna in the same year by the representatives of the different states of Germany.

By the 1st article of this last-mentioned act, it is provided, that in case of differences arising between the government of any state and the legislative chambers, either respecting the interpretation of the local constitution, or upon the limits of the co-operation allowed to the chambers in carrying into effect certain determinate rights of the sovereign, and especially in case of the refusal of the necessary supplies for the support of government conformably to the constitution and the federal obligations of the state, after every legal and constitutional means of conciliation have been exhausted, the differences shall be decided by a federal tribunal of arbitrators appointed in the following manner.

2. The representatives, each holding one of the seventeen votes in the ordinary assembly of the diet, shall nominate, once in every three years, within the states represented by them, two persons distinguished by their reputation and length of service in the judicial and administrative service. The vacancies which may occur, during the said term of three years, in the tribunal of arbitrators thus constituted, shall be in like manner supplied as often as they may occur.

3. Whenever the case mentioned in the first article arises, and it becomes necessary to resort to a decision by this tribunal, there shall be chosen from among the thirty-four, six judges arbitrators, of whom three are to be selected by the

government, and three by the chambers. This number may
be reduced to two, or increased to eight, by the consent of
the parties: and in case of the neglect of either to name
judges, they may be appointed by the diet.

4. The arbiters thus designated shall elect an additional
arbiter as an umpire, and in case of an equal division of votes,
the umpire shall be appointed by the diet.

5. The documents respecting the matter in dispute shall
be transmitted to the umpire, by whom they shall be referred
to two of the judges arbitrators to report upon the same, the
one to be selected from among those chosen by the government, the other from among those chosen by the chambers.

6. The judges arbitrators, including the umpire, shall then
meet at a place designated by the parties, or in case of disagreement, by the diet, and decide by a majority of voices
the matter in controversy according to their conscientious
conviction.

7. In case they require further elucidations before proceeding to a decision, they shall apply to the diet, by whom the
same shall be furnished.

8. Unless in case of unavoidable delay under the circumstances stated in the preceding article, the decision shall be
pronounced within the space of four months at farthest from
the nomination of the umpire, and be transmitted to the diet,
in order to be communicated to the government of the state
interested.

9. The sentence of the judges arbitrators shall have the
effect of an austrëgal judgment, and shall be carried into execution in the manner prescribed by the ordinances of the
confederation.

In the case of disputes more particularly relating to the
financial budget, the effect of the arbitration extends to the
period of time for which the same may have been voted.

10. The costs and expenses of the arbitration are to be exclusively borne by the state interested, and in case of disputes respecting their payment, they shall be levied by a
decree of the diet.

11. The same tribunal shall decide upon the differences and disputes, which may arise, in the free towns of the confederation, between the senate and the authorities established by the burghers in virtue of their local constitutions. This provision is not to be construed to make any alteration in the 46th article of the act of the congress of Vienna of 1815, relating to the constitution of the free town of Frankfort.

12. The different members of the confederation may resort to the same tribunal of arbitration to determine the controversies arising between them; and whenever the consent of the states respectively interested is given for that purpose, the diet shall take the necessary measures to organize the tribunal according to the preceding articles.

§ 13.
United
States of
America.
The constitution of the United States of America is of a very different nature from that of the Germanic confederation. It is not merely a league of sovereign states for their common defence against external and internal violence, but a supreme federal government, or composite state, acting not only upon the sovereign members of the union, but directly upon all its citizens in their individual and corporate capacities. It was established, as the constitutional act expressly declares, by "the people of the United States, in order to form a more perfect union, establish justice, ensure domestic tranquillity, provide for the common defence, promote the general welfare, and secure the blessings of liberty to them and their posterity." The legislative power of the union is vested in a congress, consisting of a senate, the members of which are chosen by the local legislatures of the several states, and a house of representatives, elected by the people in each state. This congress has power to levy taxes and duties, to pay the debts, and provide for the common defence and general welfare of the union; to borrow money on the credit of the United States; to regulate commerce with foreign nations, among the several states, and with the Indian tribes; to establish a uniform rule of naturalization, and uniform laws on the subject of bankruptcy throughout the union; to coin money, and fix the standard of weights and measures;

to establish post-offices and post-roads; to secure to authors
and inventors the exclusive right to their writings and discoveries; to punish piracies and felonies on the high seas, and
offences against the law of nations; to declare war, grant
letters of marque and reprisal, and regulate captures by sea
and land; to raise and support armies; to provide and maintain a navy; to make rules for the government of the land
and naval forces; to exercise exclusive civil and criminal
legislation over the district where the seat of the federal
government is established, and over all forts, magazines, ar-
senals, and dockyards belonging to the union; and to make
all laws necessary and proper to carrry into execution all
these and the other powers vested in the federal government
by the constitution.   To give effect to this mass of sovereign
authorities, the executive power is vested in a President of
the United States, chosen by electors appointed in each state
in such manner as the legislature thereof may direct.   The
judicial power extends to all cases in law and equity arising
under the constitution, laws, and treaties of the union, and is
vested in a supreme court, and such inferior tribunals as congress may establish.   The federal judiciary exercises under
this grant of power the authority to examine the laws passed
by the congress and the several state legislatures, and, in
cases proper for judicial determination, to decide on the constitutional validity of such laws.   The treaty-making power
is vested exclusively in the president and senate, all treaties
negotiated with foreign states being subject to their ratification.   No state of the union can enter into any treaty, alliance, or confederation; grant letters of marque and reprisal; coin money; emit bills of credit; make any thing but
gold and silver coin a tender in the payment of debts; pass
any bill of attainder, *ex post facto* law, or law impairing the
obligation of contracts; grant any title of nobility; lay any
duties on imports or exports, except such as are necessary
to execute its local inspection laws, the produce of which
must be paid into the national treasury, and such laws as are
subject to the revision and control of the congress.   Nor can
any state, without the consent of congress, lay any tonnage

duty; keep troops or ships of war in time of peace; enter
into any agreement or compact with another state, or with a
foreign power ; or engage in war, unless actually invaded, or
in such imminent danger as does not admit of delay.   The
union guaranties to every state a republican form of government, and engages to protect each of them against invasion,
and on application of the legislature, or of the executive
(when the legislature cannot be convened,) against domestic
violence.

§ 14.
Swiss con-
federation.
The Swiss confederation, as remodelled by the federal pact
of 1815, consists of a union between the twenty-two cantons
of Switzerland, the object of which is declared to be the preservation of their freedom, independence, and security against
foreign attack, and of domestic order and tranquillity.   The
several cantons guaranty to each other their respective constitutions and territorial possessions.   The confederation has a
common army and treasury, supported by levies of men and
contributions of money in certain fixed proportions among
the different cantons.   In addition to these contributions,
the military expenses of the confederation are defrayed by
duties on the importation of foreign merchandise, collected
by the frontier cantons, according to the tariff established by
the diet, and paid into the common treasury.   The diet consists of one deputy from every canton, each having one vote,
and assembles every year, alternately at Berne, Zurich, and
Lucern, which are called the directing cantons (*vororte.*)   The
diet has the exclusive power of declaring war, and concluding
treaties of peace, alliance, and commerce, with foreign states.
A majority of three-fourths of the votes is essential to the validity of these acts; for all other purposes, a majority is sufficient.   Each canton may conclude separate military capitulations and treaties relating to economical matters and objects
of police with foreign powers, provided they do not contravene the federal pact nor the constitutional rights of the other
cantons.   The diet provides for the internal and external security of the confederation; directs the operations and ap-
points the commanders of the federal army ; and names the

ministers deputed to other foreign states. Beside the powers exercised by the directing canton, or *vorort*, previous to the year 1798, the diet may delegate to the same special full powers, under extraordinary circumstances, to be exercised when the diet is not in session; adding, when it thinks fit, federal representatives to assist the *vorort* in the direction of the affairs of the confederation. In case of internal or external danger, each canton has a right to require the aid of the other cantons; in which case notice is to be immediately given to the *vorort*, in order that the diet may be assembled to provide the necessary measures of security.[19]

[19] Bundesvertrag zwischen den zwey und zwanzig Cantonen der Schweitz Martens, nouveau Recueil, tom. viii. p. 173.

The above compact is plainly nothing more than a mere league, or system of confederated states, not differing essentially from a treaty of perpetual alliance between independent communities, in which each member of the Union retains its own sovereignty unimpaired. After the French revolution of July, 1830, various changes had taken place in the internal constitutions of the different cantons tending to give them a more democratic character. A plan for the revision of the national pact of 1815, which in various particulars tended to heighten its federal features, and to give to the central authority more of the character of a supreme federal government, or one composite state, was drawn up by a committee of the ordinary Swiss diet assembled at Lucern in 1832. This plan encountered very decided opposition on the part of the cantons of Neufchâtel, Uri, Underwalden, Schweitz, Bâle, Valais, and Tessin,—which had formed a sort of separate confederation, called the league of Sarnen, insisting upon the conditions of the pact of 1815, and the exclusion of the two new cantons of *Bâle-Compagne* and what are called the *exterior districts* of Schweitz,—which had declared themselves independent of the cantons from which they had separated. The plan of revision was submitted to the deliberations of an extraordinary diet assembled at Zurich in 1833, in which sixteen of the principal cantons were represented, and which again modified essentially the proposed plan upon entire federal principles. It retained, however, the most important feature of reform proposed by the diet at Lucern, by which the central executive power was to be vested in four councillors, with a president under the title of Landamman, elected for the term of four years. This council was to be divided into four departments of the Interior, Foreign Affairs, Finances, and War,—each councillor being charged with the duties of a department. The plan thus modified, was submitted to the legislative councils of the several cantons, by some of which it was rejected; by others, accepted, either unconditionally, or subject to an appeal to the people in their primary assemblies: whilst the dissentient cantons, ad-

§ 15.   Sovereignty is acquired by a state either at the origin of
Sovereign-
ty, when the civil society of which it consists, or when it separates
acquired. itself lawfully from the community of which it previously
formed a part, and on which it was dependent.[20]

§ 16.   The identity of a state consists in its having the same origin
Identity of
a state. or commencement of existence; and its difference from all
other states consists in its having a different origin or commencement of existence.   A state, as to the individual members of which it is composed, is a fluctuating body; but in
respect to the society, it is one and the same body, of which
the existence is perpetually kept up by a constant succession
of new members.   This existence continues until it is interrupted by some change affecting the being of the state.[21]

How af-   If this change be an internal revolution, merely altering the
fected by
internal re- municipal constitution and form of government, the state revolution. mains the same; it neither loses any of its rights, nor is discharged from any of its obligations.[22]

hering to the league of Sarnen, continued to protest against any alteration
in the original pact of 1815. The ordinary diet convened at Zurich in July,
1833, adopted measures for recognising the separation of *Bâle-Compagne*
from the ancient cantons,—and for dissolving the league of Sarnen, and
compelling the dissentient cantons to send deputies to the national diet. At
a subsequent session of the diet at the same place in 1834, in which all the
cantons were represented, the question of the revision of the federal pact
was again taken up, and considered as to the manner in which it should be
effected.   Three different modes were proposed for this purpose: that of a
constituent assembly representing the whole Swiss nation; a free conference
among the different cantons; or by the diet itself under special instructions
from the constituents represented in that body. Neither of these propositions obtained a majority of votes, so that Switzerland remains still subject
to the federal constitution, established in 1815 under the mediation of the
allied powers, and guarantied by the Congress of Vienna. (Acte Final
du Congrès de Vienne, art. 74. Annexæ, No. XI. Martens, Supplement au
Recueil, tom. VI.)

[20] Kluber, Droit des Gens Modernes de l'Europe, pt. i. ch. i. § 23.

[21] Grotius, de Jur. Bel. ac Pac. lib. ii. cap. 9, § iii.   Rutherforth's Inst. b.
ii. c. 10, §§ 12, 13.

[22] Grotius, § viii. Rutherforth, § 14. Puffendorf, de Jur. Nat. et Gent. lib.
viii. cap. 12, §§ 1—3.

Until the revolution is consummated, whilst the civil war involving a contest for the government continues, other states may remain indifferent spectators of the controversy, still continuing to treat the ancient government as sovereign, and the government *de facto* as a society entitled to the rights of war against its enemy; or may espouse the cause of the party which they believe to have justice on its side. In the first case, the foreign state fulfils all its obligations under the law of nations; and neither party has any right to complain, provided it maintains an impartial neutrality. In the latter, it becomes, of course, the enemy of the party against whom it declares itself, and the ally of the other; and as the positive law of nations makes no distinction, in this respect, between a just and an unjust war, the intervening state becomes entitled to all the rights of war against the opposite party.[23]

[margin: Conduct of foreign states towards another nation involved in civil war.]

If the foreign state professes neutrality, it is bound to allow impartially to both belligerent parties the free exercise of those rights which war gives to public enemies against each other; such as the right of blockade, and of capturing contraband and enemy's property. But the exercise of those rights, on the part of the revolting colony or province against the metropolitan country, may be modified by the obligation of treaties previously existing between that country and foreign states.[24]

[margin: Parties to civil war entitled to rights of war against each other.]

If, on the other hand, the change be effected by external violence, as by conquest, confirmed by treaties of peace, its effects upon the being of the state are to be determined by the stipulations of those treaties. The conquered and ceded country may be a portion only, or the whole of the vanquished state. If the former, the original state still continues; if the latter, it ceases to exist. In either case, the conquered territory may be incorporated into the conquering state as a province, or it may be united to it as a co ordinate state with equal sovereign rights.

[margin: § 17. Identity of a state, how affected by external violence.]

[23] Vattel, Droit des Gens, liv. ii. ch. 4, § 56. Martens, Précis du Droit des Gens, liv. iii. ch. 2, §§ 79—82.
[24] See Part IV. ch. 3, § 3.

§ 18.
By the
joint effect
of internal
and exter-
nal vio-
lence con-
firmed by
treaty.
Such a change in the being of a state may also be produced by the conjoint effect of internal revolution and foreign conquest, subsequently confirmed, or modified and adjusted by international compacts. Thus the House of Orange was expelled from the Seven United Provinces of the Netherlands, in 1797, in consequence of the French Revolution and the progress of the arms of France, and a democratic republic substituted in the place of the ancient Dutch constitution. At the same time the Belgic provinces, which had long been united to the Austrian monarchy as a co-ordinate state, were conquered by France, and annexed to the French republic by the treaties of Campo Formio and Luneville. On the restoration of the Prince of Orange, in 1813, he assumed the title of Sovereign Prince, and afterwards King, of the Netherlands; and by the treaties of Vienna, the former Seven United Provinces were united with the Austrian Low Countries into one state, under his sovereignty.[25]

Here is an example of two states incorporated into one, so as to form a new state, the independent existence of each of the former states entirely ceasing in respect to the other; whilst the rights and obligations of both still continue in respect to other foreign states, except so far as they may be affected by the compacts creating the new state.

In consequence of the revolution which took place in Belgium in 1830, this country was again severed from Holland, and its independence as a separate kingdom acknowledged and guarantied by the five great powers—Austria, France, Great Britain, Prussia, and Russia. Prince Leopold of Saxe-Cobourg having been subsequently elected king of the Belgians by the national congress, the terms and conditions of the separation were stipulated by the treaty concluded on the 15th of November, 1831, between those powers and Belgium, which was declared by the conference of London to constitute the invariable basis of the separation, independence, neutrality, and state of territorial possession of Belgium, subject to such modifications as might be the result of direct negotiation between that kingdom and the Netherlands.

[25] Acte Final du Congrès de Vienne, Art. 65, 72, 73.

If the revolution in a state be effected by a province or co- §19.
lony shaking off its sovereignty, so long as the independence Province
of the new state is not acknowledged by other powers, it may or colony
seem doubtful, in an international point of view, whether its asserting
sovereignty can be considered as complete, however it may how consi-
be regarded by its own government and citizens. It has al- dered by
ready been stated, that whilst the contest for the sovereignty eign states.
continues, and the civil war rages, other nations may either
remain passive, allowing to both contending parties all the
rights which war gives to public enemies, or may acknowledge the independence of the new state, forming with it
treaties of amity and commerce; or may join in alliance with
one party against the other. In the first case, neither party
has any right to complain so long as other nations maintain
an impartial neutrality, and abide the event of the contest.
The two last cases involve questions which seem to belong
rather to the field of politics than of law; but the practice
of nations, if it does not furnish an invariable rule for the solution of these questions, will at least shed some light upon
them. The memorable examples of the Swiss cantons and
of the Seven United Provinces of the Netherlands, which so
long levied war, concluded peace, contracted alliances, and
performed every other act of sovereignty, before their independence was finally acknowledged,—that of the first by the
German empire, and that of the latter by Spain,—go far to
show the general sense of mankind on this subject.

The acknowledgment of the independence of the United
States of America by France, coupled with the assistance
secretly rendered by the French court to the revolted colonies,
was considered by Great Britain as an unjustifiable aggression, and, under the circumstances, it probably was so.[27] But
had the French court conducted itself with good faith, and
maintained an impartial neutrality between the two belligerent parties, it may be doubted whether the treaty of com-

[27] *See* Memoire Justificatif pour servir de Réponse à l'Exposé des Motifs
de la Conduite du Roi de France relative à l'Angleterre. Gibbon's Miscell.
Works, vol. iv. p. 246.

merce, or even the eventual alliance between France and the
United States, could have furnished any just ground for a
declaration of war against the former by the British government. The more recent example of the acknowledgment of
the independence of the Spanish American provinces by the
United States, Great Britain, and other powers, whilst the
parent country still continues to withhold her assent, also
concurs to illustrate the general understanding of nations,
that where a revolted province or colony has declared, and
shown its ability to maintain its independence, the recognition
of its sovereignty by other foreign states is a question of policy and prudence only.

Recogni-
tion of its
indepen-
dence by
other for-
eign states.
This question must be determined by the sovereign legislative or executive power of these other states, and not by
any subordinate authority, or by the private judgment of
their individual subjects. Until the independence of the new
state has been acknowledged, either by the foreign state
where its sovereignty is drawn in question, or by the government of the country of which it was before a province,
courts of justice and private individuals are bound to consider the ancient state of things as remaining unaltered.[28]

§ 20.
Interna-
tional ef-
fects of a
change in
the person
of the so-
vereign or
in the in-
ternal con-
stitution of
the state.
The international effects produced by a change in the
person of the sovereign or in the form of government of any
state, may be considered:—

I. As to its treaties of alliance and commerce.

II. Its public debts.

III. Its public domain and private rights of property.

IV. Its responsibility for wrongs done to the governments
or subjects of another state.

Treaties.
I. Treaties are divided by the text writers into *personal*
and *real*. The former relate exclusively to the persons of
the contracting parties, such as family alliances and treaties
guarantying the throne to a particular sovereign and his

[28] Vesey's Ch. Rep. vol. ix. p. 347. The City of Berne *v.* the Bank of
England. Edwards's Adm. Rep. vol. i. p. 1. The Manilla, Appendix IV.
Note. D. Wheaton's Rep. vol. iii. p. 324. Hoyt *v.* Gelston, p. 634. The
United States *v.* Palmer.

family. They expire, of course, on the death of the king or the extinction of his family. The latter relate solely to the subject matters of the convention, independently of the persons of the contracting parties. They continue to bind the state, whatever intervening changes may take place in its internal constitution, or in the persons of its rulers. The state continues the same, notwithstanding such change, and consequently the treaty relating to national objects remains in force so long as the nation exists as an independent state. The only exception to this general rule, as to *real* treaties, is where the convention relates to the form of government itself, and is intended to prevent any such change in the internal constitution of the state.[29]

II. As to public debts—whether due to or from the revolutionized state—a mere change in the form of government, or in the person of the ruler, does not affect their obligation. The essential form of the state, that which constitutes it an independent community, remains the same; its accidental form only is changed. The debts being contracted in the name of the state, by its authorized agents, for its public use, the nation continues liable for them, notwithstanding the change in its internal constitution.[30]

Public debts.

III. As to the public domain and private rights of property. If the revolution be successful, and the internal change in the constitution of the state is finally confirmed by the event of the contest, the public domain passes to the new government; and this mutation is not necessarily attended with any alteration whatever in private rights of property. But it may be attended by such a change: it is competent for the national authority to work a transmutation, total or partial, of the property belonging to the vanquished party; and if actually confiscated, the fact must be taken for right. But to work such a transfer of proprietary rights, some positive and unequivocal act of confiscation is essential.

Public domain and private rights of property.

[29] Vattel, Droit des Gens, liv. ii. ch. 12, §§ 183—197.

[30] Grotius, de Jur. Bel. ac Pac. lib. ii. cap. 9, § viii. 1—3. Puffendorf, de Jur. Nat. et Gent. lib. viii. cap. 12, §§ 1, 2, 3.

If, on the other hand, the revolution in the government of
the state is followed by a restoration of the ancient order of
things, both public and private property, not actually confiscated, revert to the original proprietor on the restoration of
the legitimate government, as in the case of conquest they
revert to the former owners on the evacuation of the territory occupied by the public enemy.   The national domain,
not actually alienated by any intermediate act of the state,
returns to the sovereign along with the sovereignty.   Private
property, temporarily sequestrated, returns to the former
owner, as in the case of such property recaptured from an
enemy in war on the principle of the *jus postliminii.*

But if the national domain has been alienated, or the private property confiscated by some intervening act of the
state, the question as to the validity of such transfer becomes
more difficult of solution.

Even the lawful sovereign of a country may, or may not,
by the particular municipal constitution of the state, have the
power of alienating the public domain.   The general presumption, in mere internal transactions with his own subjects, is,
that he is not so authorized.[31]   But in the case of international
transactions, where foreigners and foreign governments are
concerned, the authority is presumed to exist, and may be
inferred from the general treaty-making power, unless there
be some express limitation in the fundamental laws of the
state.   So also where foreign governments and their subjects
treat with the actual head of the state, or the government
de facto, recognised by the acquiescence of the nation, for
the acquisition of any portion of the public domain or of private confiscated property, the acts of such government must,
on principle, be considered valid by the lawful sovereign on
his restoration, although they were the acts of him who is
considered by the restored sovereign as a usurper.[32]   On
the other hand, it seems that such alienations of public or
private property, to the subjects of the state, may be an-

---

[31] Puffendorf, de Jur. Nat. et Gent. lib. viii. cap. 12. §§ 1—3.

[32] Grotius, de Jur. Bel. ac Pac. lib. ii. cap. 14. § 16.

nulled or confirmed, as to their internal effects, at the will of
the restored legitimate sovereign, guided by such motives of
policy as may influence his councils, reserving the legal rights
of *bonœ fidei* purchasers under such alienation to be indemnified for ameliorations.[33]

Where the price or equivalent of the property sold or exchanged has accrued to the actual use and profit of the state,
the transfer may be confirmed, and the original proprietors
indemnified out of the public treasury, as was done in respect
to the lands of the emigrant French nobility, confiscated and
sold during the revolution. So also the sales of the national
domains situate in the German and Belgian provinces, united
to France during the revolution, and again detached from the
French territory by the treaties of Paris and Vienna in 1814
and 1815, or in the countries composing the Rhenish confederation, in the kingdom of Italy, and the Papal States,
were, in general, confirmed by these treaties by the Germanic
diet, or by the acts of the respective restored sovereigns.
But a long and intricate litigation ensued before the Germanic diet in respect to the alienation of the domains in the
countries composing the kingdom of Westphalia. The elector of Hesse Cassel and the duke of Brunswick refused to
confirm these alienations in respect to their territory, whilst
Prussia, which power had acknowledged the king of Westphalia, also acknowledged the validity of his acts in the countries annexed to the Prussian dominions by the treaties of
Vienna.[34]

IV. As to wrongs done to the government or subjects of
another state—it seems, that on strict principle, the nation
continues responsible to other states for the damages incurred
by such wrongs, notwithstanding an intermediate change
in the form of its government, or in the persons of its rulers.
This principle was applied in all its rigour by the victorious
allied powers in their treaties of peace with France in 1814
and 1815. More recent examples of its practical application

[33] Kluber, Droit des Gens. sec. ii. ch. 1, § 258.
[34] See the German Conversations Lexikon, art. *Domainenverkauf*.

have occurred in the negotiations between the United States and France, Holland, and Naples, relating to the spoliations committed on American commerce under the imperial government of Napoleon and his vassal kings. The responsibility of the restored government of France for these acts of its predecessors, was hardly denied by it even during the reigns of the Bourbon Kings of the elder branch, Louis XVIII. and Charles X., and was expressly admitted by the present ruler of that country in the treaty of indemnities concluded with the United States in 1831. The application of the principle to the measures of confiscation, adopted by the usurped government of Murat in furtherance of the views and policy of Napoleon, was contested by Naples—but the protracted discussions which ensued were at last terminated in the same manner by a treaty of indemnities concluded.

PART SECOND.

ABSOLUTE INTERNATIONAL RIGHTS OF STATES.

PART SECOND.

ABSOLUTE INTERNATIONAL RIGHTS OF STATES.

CHAPTER I.

RIGHT OF SELF-PRESERVATION.

Every state has certain sovereign rights, to which it is entitled as an independent moral being; in other words, because it is a state. These rights may be called the *absolute* international rights of states.

§ 1.
Absolute international rights.

The rights to which sovereign states are entitled, under particular circumstances, in their relations with others, may be termed their *conditional* international rights. These may arise from international relations existing either in peace or in war.

§ 2.
Conditional international rights.

Of the *absolute* international rights of states, one of the most essential and important, and that which lies at the foundation of all the rest, is the right of self-preservation. It is not only a right with respect to other states, but a duty with respect to its own members, and the most solemn and important which the state owes to them. This right necessarily involves all other incidental rights which are essential as means to give effect to the principal end.

§ 3.
Right of self-preservation.

Among these is the right of self-defence. This again involves the right to require the military service of all its people, to levy troops, and maintain a naval force, to build fortifications, and to impose and collect taxes for all these purposes.

Right of self-defence modified by the equal rights of

other
states, or
by treaty.

It is evident that the exercise of these absolute sovereign rights can be controlled only by the equal correspondent rights of other states, or by special compacts freely entered into with others to modify the exercise of these rights.

Thus the absolute right to erect fortifications within the territory of the state has sometimes been modified by treaties, where the erection of such fortifications has been deemed to threaten the safety of other communities, or where such a concession has been extorted in the pride of victory by a power strong enough to dictate the conditions of peace to its enemy. Thus by the treaty of Utrecht between Great Britain and France, confirmed by that of Aix-la-Chapelle in 1748, and of Paris in 1763, the French government engaged to demolish the fortifications of Dunkirk. This stipulation, so humiliating to France, was effaced in the treaty of peace concluded between the two countries in 1783, after the war of the American revolution. By the treaty signed at Paris in 1815, between the allied powers and France, it was stipulated that the fortifications of Huningen, within the French territory, which had been constantly a subject of uneasiness to the city of Basle in the Helvetic confederation, should be demolished, and should never be renewed or replaced by other fortifications at a distance of less than three leagues from the city of Basle.[1]

§ 4.
Right of
interven-
tion.

The right of every independent state to increase its national dominions, wealth, population, and power, by all innocent and lawful means, such as the pacific acquisition of new territory, the discovery and settlement of new countries, the extension of its navigation and fisheries, the improvement of its revenues, arts, agriculture, and commerce, the increase of its military and naval force, is an incontrovertible right of sovereignty, generally recognised by the usage and opinion of nations. It can be limited in its exercise only by the equal correspondent rights of other states growing out of the same primeval right of self-preservation. Where the exercise of this right by any of these means directly affects the security

[1] Martens, Recueil des Traités, tom. ii. p. 469.

of others, as where it immediately interferes with the actual
exercise of the sovereign rights of other states, there is no difficulty in assigning its precise limits. But where it merely
involves a supposed contingent danger to the safety of others,
arising out of the undue aggrandizement of a particular state,
or the disturbance of what has been called the balance of
power, questions of the greatest difficulty arise, which belong
rather to the science of politics than of public law. Each
member of the great society of nations being entirely independent of every other, and living in what has been called a
state of nature in respect to others, acknowledging no common sovereign arbiter, or judge; the law which prevails between nations being deficient in those external sanctions by
which the laws of civil society are enforced among individuals; and the performance of the duties of international law
being compelled by moral sanctions only, by fear on the
part of nations of provoking general hostility, and incurring
its probable evils in case they should violate this law; an apprehension of the possible consequences of the undue aggrandizement of any one nation upon the independence and
safety of others has induced the states of modern Europe to
observe, with systematic vigilance, every material disturbance
in the equilibrium of their respective forces. This preventive
policy has been the pretext of the most bloody and destructive wars waged in modern times, some of which have certainly originated in well-founded apprehensions of peril to the
independence of weaker states, but the greater part have
been founded upon insufficient reasons, disguising the real motives by which princes and cabinets have been influenced.
Wherever the spirit of encroachment has really threatened
the general security, it has commonly broken out in such
overt acts as not only plainly indicated the ambitious purpose,
but also furnished substantive grounds in themselves sufficient
to justify a resort to arms by other nations. Such were the Wars of
grounds of confederacies created, and the wars undertaken the Refor-
to check the aggrandizement of Spain and the house of Austria, under Charles V. and his successors;—an object finally
accomplished by the treaty of Westphalia, which so long

constituted the written public law of Europe. The long and
violent struggle between the religious parties engendered by
the Reformation in Germany spread throughout Europe, and
became closely connected with political interests and ambition. The great Catholic and Protestant powers mutually
protected the adherents of their own faith in the bosom of
rival states. The repeated interference of Austria and Spain
in favour of the Catholic faction in France, Germany, and
England, and of the Protestant powers to protect their persecuted brethren in Germany, France, and the Netherlands,
gave a peculiar colouring to the political transactions of the
age. This was still more heightened by the conduct of Catholic France under the ministry of Cardinal Richelieu, in
sustaining, by a singular refinement of policy, the Protestant
princes and people of Germany against the house of Austria,
whilst she was persecuting with unrelenting severity her own
subjects of the reformed faith. The balance of power adjusted by the peace of Westphalia was once more disturbed by
the ambition of Louis XIV., which compelled the Protestant
states of Europe to unite with the house of Austria against
the encroachments of France herself, and induced the allies
to patronise the English revolution of 1688, whilst the French
monarch interfered to support the pretensions of the Stuarts.
These great transactions furnish numerous examples of intervention by the European states in the affairs of each other,
where the interests and security of the intervening powers
were supposed to be seriously affected by the domestic transactions of other nations, which can hardly be referred to any
fixed and definite principle of international law, or furnish a
general rule fit to be observed in other apparently analogous
cases.*

---

* The idea of a systematic arrangement for securing to states, within the
same sphere of political action, the undisturbed possession of their existing
territories and other rights, is supposed by Robertson to have originated
among the princes and republics of modern Italy. (Hist. Charles V. Vol. I.
§ 2.) But Hume had before attempted to show that the system of the balance of power, if not theoretically understood, was at least practically adopted, by the ancient states of Greece and the neighbouring nations. (Essays,

The same remarks will apply to the more recent, but not § 5. less important events, growing out of the French Revolution. They furnish a strong admonition against attempting to re- duce to a rule, and to incorporate into the code of nations, a principle so indefinite and so peculiarly liable to abuse in its practical application. The successive coalitions formed by the great European monarchies against France, subsequent to her first revolution of 1789, were avowedly designed to check the progress of her revolutionary principles and the extension of her military power. The efforts of these coali- tions ultimately resulted in the formation of an alliance, in- tended to be permanent, between the four great powers of Russia, Austria, Prussia, and Great Britain, to which France subsequently acceded, at the Congress of Aix-la-Chapelle, in 1818, constituting a sort of superintending authority in these powers over the international affairs of Europe, the precise extent and objects of which were never very accurately de- fined. As interpreted by those of the contracting powers who were also the original parties to the compact called the Holy Alliance, this union was intended to form a perpetual system of intervention among the European states, adapted to pre- vent any such change in the internal forms of their respective governments as might endanger the existence of the monar- chical institutions which had been re-established under the legitimate dynasties of their respective reigning houses. This general right of interference was sometimes defined so as to be applicable to every case of popular revolution, where the

Vol. I. pt. 2. Essay 7.) The leading idea of the system is distinctly stated by Polybius, (Hist. lib. I. cap. 83,) and the speeches of Demosthenes fre- quently refer his countrymen to the policy of maintaining that equilibrium among the different states of Greece which was disturbed by the growing power of Macedon. Still it must be admitted that the first practical appli- cation of the theory of the balancing system to that constant supervision now exercised over the relative forces of European states may be distinctly traced to the developemnts their policy received soon after the invasion of Italy by Charles VIII., which period is also coincident with the establishment of permanent diplomatic mission appointed to exercise the right of mutual in- spection.

Wars of the French Revolu- tion.

Alliance of the five great Eu- ropean powers.

change in the form of government did not proceed from the
voluntary concession of the reigning sovereign, or was not
confirmed by his sanction, given under such circumstances as
to remove all doubt of his having freely consented. At others,
it was extended to every revolutionary movement pronounced
by these powers to endanger, in its consequences, immediate
or remote, the social order of Europe, or the particular safety
of neighbouring states.

§ 6.
Congress
of Trop-
pau and of
Laybach.

The measures adopted by Austria, Russia, and Prussia, at
the congress of Troppau and of Laybach, in respect to the
Neapolitan revolution of 1820, were founded upon principles adapted to give the great powers of the European continent a perpetual pretext for interfering in the internal concerns of its different states. The British government expressly dissented from these principles, not only upon the ground
of their being, if reciprocally acted on, contrary to the fundamental laws of Great Britain, but such as could not safely
be admitted as part of a system of international law. In the
circular despatch addressed on this occasion to all its diplomatic agents, it was stated, that though no government could
be more prepared than the British government was, to up-
hold the right of any state or states to interfere, where their
own immediate security or essential interests are seriously
endangered by the internal transactions of another state, it
regarded the assumption of such a right as only to be justified
by the strongest necessity, and to be limited and regulated
thereby ; and did not admit that it could receive a general
and indiscriminate application to all revolutionary move-
ments, without reference to their immediate bearing upon
some particular state or states, or that it could be made pros-
pectively the basis of an alliance. The British government
regarded its exercise as an exception to general principles of
the greatest value and importance, and as one that only properly grows out of the special circumstances of the case; but
it at the same time considered, that exceptions of this description never can, without the utmost danger, be so far reduced

to rule as to be incorporated into the ordinary diplomacy of states, or into the institutes of the law of nations.[2]

The British government also declined being a party to the §7. proceedings of the congress held at Verona in 1822, which Congress of Verona. ultimately led to an armed interference by France, under the sanction of Austria, Russia, and Prussia, in the internal affairs of Spain, and the overthrow of the Spanish constitution of the Cortes. The British government disclaimed for itself, and denied to other powers, the right of requiring any changes in the internal institutions of independent states, with the menace of hostile attack in case of refusal. It did not consider the Spanish revolution as affording a case of that direct and imminent danger to the safety and interests of other states, which might justify a forcible interference. The original alliance between Great Britain and the other principal European powers, was specifically designed for the reconquest and liberation of the European continent from the military dominion of France; and, having subverted that dominion, it took the state of possession, as established by the peace, under the joint protection of the alliance. It never was, however, intended as a union for the government of the world, or for the superintendence of the internal affairs of other states. No proof had been produced to the British government of any design on the part of Spain to invade the territory of France; of any attempt to introduce disaffection among her soldiery; or of any project to undermine her political institutions; and so long as the struggles and disturbances of Spain should be confined within the circle of her own territory, they could not be admitted by the British government to afford any plea for foreign interference. If the end of the last, and the beginning of the present century, saw all Europe combined against France, it was not on account of the internal changes which France thought necessary for her own political and civil reformation; but because she attempted to propagate,

[2] Lord Castlereagh's Circular Despatch, Jan. 19, 1821. Annual Register, vol. lxii. pt. ii. p. 737.

first, her principles, and afterwards her dominion, by the sword.[3]

§ 8.
War between
Spain and
her American colonies.

Both Great Britain and the United States, on the same occasion, protested against the right of the allied powers to interfere by forcible means in the contest between Spain and her revolted American colonies. The British government declared its determination to remain strictly neutral, should the war be unhappily prolonged; but that the junction of any foreign power, in an enterprise of Spain against the colonies, would be viewed by it as constituting an entirely new question, and one upon which it must take such decision as the interests of Great Britain might require. That it could not enter into any stipulation binding itself either to refuse or delay its recognition of the independence of the colonies, nor wait indefinitely for an accommodation between Spain and the colonies; and that it would consider any foreign interference by force or by menace, in the dispute between them, as a motive for recognising the latter without delay.[4]

The United States government declared that it should consider any attempt on the part of the allied European powers, to extend their peculiar political system to the American continent, as dangerous to the peace and safety of the United States. With the existing colonies or dependencies of any European power, they had not interfered, and should not interfere; but with the governments whose independence they had recognised, they could not view any interposition for the purpose of oppressing them, or controlling in any other manner their destiny, in any other light than as a manifestation of an unfriendly disposition towards the United States. They had declared their neutrality in the war between Spain and

---

[3] Confidential Minute of Lord Castlereagh on the Affairs of Spain, communicated to the Allied Courts in May, 1823. Annual Register, vol. lxv.; *Public Documents*, p. 93. Mr. Secretary Canning's Letter to Sir C. Stuart, 28 Jan. 1823, p. 114. Same to the Same, 31 March, 1823, p. 141.

[4] Memorandum of Conference between Mr. Secretary Canning and Prince Polignac, 9 Oct. 1823. Annual Register, vol. lxvi. p. 99. *Public Documents*.

those new governments at the time of their recognition, and
to this neutrality they should continue to adhere, provided
no change should occur which in their judgment should make
a correspondent change on the part of the United States indispensable to their own security. The late events in Spain
and Portugal showed that Europe was still unsettled. Of
this important fact no stronger proof could be adduced, than
that the allied powers should have thought it proper, on any
principle satisfactory to themselves, to have interposed by
force in the internal concerns of Spain. To what extent
such interpositions might be carried on the same principle,
was a question, on which all independent powers, whose
governments differed from theirs, were interested ; even those
most remote, and none more so than the United States.

The policy of the American government in regard to Europe, adopted at an early stage of the war which had so
long agitated that quarter of the globe, nevertheless remained
the same. This policy was not to interfere in the internal
concerns of any of the European powers ; to consider the
government, *de facto*, as the legitimate government for them ;
to cultivate friendly relations with it, and to preserve those
relations by a frank, firm, and manly policy ; meeting in all
instances the just claims of every power—submitting to injuries from none. But with regard to the American continents, circumstances were widely different. It was impossible that the allied powers should extend their political system
to any portion of these continents, without endangering the
peace and happiness of the United States. It was therefore
impossible that the latter should behold such interposition in
any form with indifference.[5]

Great Britain had limited herself to protesting against the
interference of the French government in the internal affairs
of Spain, and had refrained from interposing by force to prevent the invasion of the peninsula by France. The consti-

§ 9.
British in-
terference
in the af-
fairs of
Portugal
in 1826.

[5] President's Message to Congress, 2 Dec. 1823. Annual Register, vol.
xv. *Public Documents*, p. 193.

tution of the Cortes was overturned, and Ferdinand VII. restored to absolute power. These events were followed by
the death of John VI. King of Portugal in 1825. The constitution of Brazil had provided that its crown should never
be united on the same head with that of Portugal ; and Don
Pedro resigned the latter to his infant daughter Donna Maria,
appointing a regency to govern the kingdom during her minority, and at the same time granting a constitutional charter to the European dominions of the house of Braganza. The
Spanish government, restored to the plenitude of its absolute
authority, and dreading the example of the peaceable establishment of a constitutional government in the neighbouring
kingdom, countenanced the pretensions of Don Miguel to the
Portuguese crown, and supported the efforts of his partisans
to overthrow the regency and the charter. Hostile inroads
into the territory of Portugal were concerted in Spain, and
executed with the connivance of the Spanish authorities by
Portuguese troops belonging to the party of the Pretender,
who had deserted into Spain, and were received and suc-
coured by the Spanish authorities on the frontiers. Under
these circumstances the British government received an application from the regency of Portugal, claiming, in virtue of
the ancient treaties of alliance and friendship subsisting between the two crowns, the military aid of Great Britain
against the hostile aggression of Spain. In acceding to that
application, and sending a corps of British troops for the defence of Portugal, it was stated by the British minister that
the Portuguese constitution was admitted to have proceeded
from a legitimate source, and it was recommended to Eng-
lishmen by the ready acceptance which it had met with from
all orders of the Portuguese people. But it would not be, for
the British nation to force it on the people of Portugal if they
were unwilling to receive it; or if any schism should exist
among the Portuguese themselves, as to its fitness and conge-
niality to the wants and wishes of the nation. They went to
Portugal in the discharge of a sacred obligation contracted under ancient and modern treaties. When there, nothing would
be done by them to enforce the establishment of the constitu-

tion, but they must take care that nothing was done by others to prevent it from being fairly carried into effect. The hostile aggression of Spain, in countenancing and aiding the party opposed to the Portuguese constitution, was in direct violation of repeated solemn assurances of the Spanish cabinet to the British government, engaging to abstain from such interference. The sole object of Great Britain was to obtain the faithful execution of those engagements. The former case of the invasion of Spain by France, having for its object to overturn the Spanish constitution, was essentially different in its circumstances. France had given to Great Britain cause of war by that aggression upon the independence of Spain. The British government might lawfully have interfered on grounds of political expediency; but they were not bound to interfere, as they were now bound to interfere, on behalf of Portugal by the obligations of treaty. War might have been their free choice, if they had deemed it politic in the case of Spain: interference on behalf of Portugal was their duty, unless they were prepared to abandon the principles of national faith and national honour.[6]

The interference of the Christian powers of Europe in favour of the Greeks, who, after enduring ages of cruel oppression, had shaken off the Ottoman yoke, affords a further illustration of the principles of international law authorizing such an interference, not only where the interests and safety of the other powers are immediately affected by the internal transactions of a particular state, but where the general interests of humanity are infringed by the excesses of a barbarous and despotic government. These principles are fully recognised in the treaty for the pacification of Greece, signed at London on the 6th of July, 1827. The preamble of this treaty sets forth that the three contracting parties were "penetrated with the necessity of putting an end to the sanguinary contest, which, by delivering up the Greek provinces and the isles of the Archipelago, to all the disorders of anar-

§ 10. Interference of the Christian powers of Europe in favour of the Greeks.

[6] Mr. Canning's Speech in the House of Commons, 11 Dec. 1826. Annual Register, vol. lxviii. p. 192.

chy, produces daily fresh impediments to the commerce of
the European states, and gives occasion to piracies, which
not only expose the subjects of the high contracting parties
to considerable losses, but besides, render necessary burden-
some measures of protection and repression." It then states
that the British and French governments, having received a
pressing request from the Greeks to interpose their mediation with the Porte, and being, as well as the emperor of
Russia, animated by the desire of stopping the effusion of
blood, and of arresting the evils of all kinds which might arise
from the continuance of such a state of things, had resolved
to unite their efforts, and to regulate the operations thereof
by a formal treaty, with the view of re-establishing peace
between the contending parties, by means of an arrangement,
which was called for as much by humanity, as by the interest of the repose of Europe. The treaty then provides, (art.
1,) that the three contracting powers should offer their mediation to the Porte by a joint declaration of their ambassadors at Constantinople; and that there should be made, at
the same time, to the two contending parties, the demand of
an immediate armistice as a preliminary condition indispensable to opening any negotiation. Article 2d provides the
terms of the arrangement to be made, as to the civil and
political condition of Greece, in consequence of the principles
of a previous understanding between Great Britain and Russia. By the 3d article it was agreed that the details of this
arrangement, and the limits of the territory to be included
under it, should be settled in a separate negotiation between
the high contracting powers and the two contending parties.
To this public treaty, an additional and secret article was
added, stipulating that the high contracting parties would
take immediate measures for establishing commercial relations with the Greeks, by sending to them and receiving from
them consular agents, so long as there should exist among
them authorities capable of maintaining such relations. That
if, within the term of one month, the Porte did not accept
the proposed armistice, or if the Greeks refused to execute
it, the high contracting parties should declare to that one of

the two contending parties that should wish to continue hostilities, or to both, if it should become necessary, that the
contracting powers intended to exert all the means, which
circumstances might suggest to their prudence, to give immediate effect to the armistice, by preventing, as far as might
be in their power, all collision between the contending parties; and, in fact, would conjointly employ all their means in
the accomplishment of the object thereof, without, however,
taking any part in the hostilities of the contending parties;
and would transmit eventual instructions for that purpose to
the admirals commanding their squadrons in the Levant.
That if these measures did not suffice to induce the Ottoman
Porte to adopt the propositions made by the high contracting
powers, or if, on the other hand, the Greeks should renounce
the conditions stipulated in their favour, the contracting parties would nevertheless continue to prosecute the work of
pacification on the basis agreed upon between them; and in
consequence they authorized, from that time forward, their
representatives in London to discuss and determine the ul-
terior measures to which it might become necessary to resort.

The Greeks accepted the proffered mediation of the three
powers, which the Turks rejected, and instructions were
given to the commanders of the allied squadrons to compel
the cessation of hostilities. This was effected by the result
of the battle of Navarino, with the occupation of the Morea
by French troops: and the independence of the Greek state
was ultimately recognised by the Ottoman Porte, under the
mediation of the contracting powers. If, as some writers
have supposed, the Turks belong to a family or set of nations which is not bound by the general international law of
Christendom, they have still no right to complain of the measures which the Christian powers thought proper to adopt for
the protection of their religious brethren oppressed by the
Mohammedan rule. In a ruder age the nations of Europe,
impelled by a generous and enthusiastic feeling of sympathy,
inundated the plains of Asia to recover the holy sepulchre
from the possession of infidels, and to deliver the Christian pil-

grims from the merciless oppressions practised by the Sara-
cens. The Protestant princes and states of Europe, during
the sixteenth and seventeeth centuries, did not scruple to
confederate and wage war in order to secure the freedom of
religious worship for the votaries of their faith in the bosom
of Catholic communities to whose subjects it was denied.
Still more justifiable was the interference of the Christian
powers of Europe to rescue a whole nation, not merely from
religious persecution, but from the cruel alternative of being
transported from their native land into Egyptian bondage, or
exterminated by their merciless oppressors.   The rights of
human nature, wantonly outraged by this cruel warfare, prosecuted for six years against a civilized and Christian people,
to whose ancestors mankind are so largely indebted for the
blessings of arts and of letters, were but tardily and imper-
fectly vindicated by this measure; but its principle was fully
justified by the great paramount law of self-preservation.
"Whatever a nation may lawfully defend for itself, it may
defend for another people, if called upon to interpose."   The
interference of the Christian powers to put an end to this
bloody contest might therefore have been safely rested upon
this ground alone, without appealing to the interest of commerce and of the repose of Europe, which, as well as the
interests of humanity, are alluded to in the treaty as the determining motives of the high contracting parties.[7]

[7] Another treaty was concluded at London between the same three powers
on the 7th of May, 1832, by which the election of Prince Otho of Bavaria,
as King of Greece was confirmed, and the sovereignty and independence of
the new kingdom guarantied by the contracting parties, according to the
terms of the protocol signed by them on the 3d of February, 1830, and accepted by Greece and the Ottoman Porte.

CHAPTER II.

RIGHTS OF INDEPENDENCE.

EVERY state, as a distinct moral being independent of every other, may freely exercise all its sovereign rights in any manner not inconsistent with the equal rights of other states. Among these is that of establishing, altering, or abolishing its own municipal constitution of government. No foreign state can lawfully interfere with the exercise of this right, unless such interference is authorized by some special compact, or by such a clear case of necessity as immediately affects its own independence, freedom, and security.[1]

§ 1. Independence of the state in respect to its internal government.

The approved usage of nations authorizes the proposal by one state of its good offices or mediation for the settlement of the intestine dissensions of another state. When such offer is accepted by the contending parties, it becomes a just title for the interference of the mediating power.

Such a title may also grow out of positive compact previously existing, such as treaties of mediation and guarantee. Of this nature was the guarantee by France and Sweden of the Germanic constitution at the peace of Westphalia in 1648, the result of the thirty years' war waged by the princes and states of Germany for the preservation of their civil and religious liberties, against the ambition of the house of Austria.

The republic of Geneva was connected by an ancient alliance with the Swiss cantons of Berne and Zurich, in consequence of which they united with France, in 1738, in offering the joint mediation of the three powers to the contending political parties by which the tranquillity of the re-

§ 2. Mediation of other foreign states for the settlement of its internal dissensions.

[1] Vide ante, pt. ii. ch. 1, § 4.

public was disturbed. The result of this mediation was the settlement of a constitution, which giving rise to new disputes in 1768, they were again adjusted by the intervention of the mediating powers. In 1782, the French government once more united with these cantons and the court of Sardinia in mediating between the aristocratic and democratic parties; but it appears to be very questionable how far these transactions, especially the last, can be reconciled with the respect due, on the strict principles of international law, to the just rights and independence of the smallest, not less than to those of the greatest, states.[2]

The present constitution of the Helvetic confederation was also adjusted in 1813 by the mediation of the great allied powers, and subsequently recognised by them at the congress of Vienna as the basis of the federative pact of Switzerland. By the same act the united Swiss cantons guaranty their respective local constitutions of government.[3]

So also the local constitutions of the different states composing the Germanic confederation may be guarantied by the diet on the application of the particular state in which the constitution is established; and this guarantee gives the diet the right of determining all controversies respecting the interpretation and execution of the constitution thus established and guarantied.[4]

And the constitution of the United States of America guaranties to each state of the federal union a republican form of government, and engages to protect each of them against invasion, and, on application of the local authorities, against domestic violence.[5]

§ 3.
Indepen-
dence of

This perfect independence of every sovereign state, in respect to its political institutions, extends to the choice of the

---

[2] Flassan, Histoire de la Diplomatie Francaise, tom. v. p. 78, tom. vii. pp. 27, 297.

[3] Acte Final du Congrès de Vienne, art. 74.

[4] Wiener Schluss-Acte vom 15 Mai, 1820, art. 60. Corpus Juris Germanici von Mayer, tom. ii. p. 196.

[5] Constitution of the United States, Art. 3.

supreme magistrate and other rulers, as well as to the form every state of government itself. In hereditary governments, the suc- $\begin{smallmatrix}\text{in respect}\\\text{to the}\end{smallmatrix}$ cession to the crown being regulated by the fundamental choice of laws, all disputes respecting the succession are rightfully set- its rulers. tled by the nation itself, independently of the interference or control of foreign powers. So also in elective governments, the choice of the chief or other magistrates ought to be freely made, in the manner prescribed by the constitution of the state, without the intervention of any foreign influence or authority.[6]

The only exceptions to the application of these general rules §4. arise out of compact, such as treaties of alliance, guarantee, $\begin{smallmatrix}\text{Excep-}\\\text{tions grow-}\end{smallmatrix}$ and mediation, to which the state itself whose concerns are ing out of in question has become a party ; or formed by other powers $\begin{smallmatrix}\text{compact or}\\\text{other just}\end{smallmatrix}$ in the exercise of a supposed right of intervention growing right of in- out of a necessity involving their own particular security, or tervention. some contingent danger affecting the general security of na- tions. Such, among others, were the wars relating to the Spanish succession in the beginning of the eighteenth century, and to the Bavarian and Austrian successions in the latter part of the same century. The history of modern Europe also affords many other examples of the actual interference of foreign powers in the choice of the sovereign or chief ma- gistrate of those states where this choice was constitutionally determined by popular election, or by an elective council, such as in the cases of the head of the Germanic empire, the king of Poland, and the Roman pontiff; but in these cases no argument can be drawn from the fact to the right. In the particular case, however, of the election of the pope, who is the supreme pontiff of the Roman Catholic church, as well as a temporal sovereign, the emperor of Austria, and the kings of France and Spain, have, by very ancient usage, each a right to exclude one candidate.[7]

[6] Vattel, Droit des Gens, liv. i. ch. 5, §§ 66, 67.

[7] Kluber, Droit des Gens Moderne de l'Europe, pt. ii. tit. 1, ch. 2, § 48.

§ 5.
Exclusive
power of
civil and
criminal
legislation.

The supreme, exclusive power of civil and criminal legislation is also an essential right of every independent state.

This sovereign right extends, with the exceptions hereafter mentioned, to the regulation of all the real (or immoveable) and personal (or moveable) property within the territory, whether held by a feudal or allodial tenure, and whether it belongs to subjects or foreigners.

Lex loci
rei sitæ.

The law of the place, where real (or immoveable) property is situate, governs in every thing relating to the tenure, the title, and the forms of conveyance of such property. Hence it is that a deed or will of real property executed in a foreign country must be executed with the formalities required by the local laws of the state where the land lies.[8]

Lex domi-
cilii.

With respect to personal (or moveable) property, the same rule generally prevails, except that the law of the place where the person to whom it belonged was domiciled at the time of his decease governs the succession *ab intestato* to his personal effects.[9] So also the law of the place where any instrument relating to personal property is executed by a party domiciled in that place, governs, as to the external form, the interpretation and effect of the instrument: *Locus regit actum:* Thus a testament of personal property, if executed according to the formalities required by the law of the place where it is made, and where the party making it was domiciled, is valid in every other country, and is to be interpreted and given effect to according to the *lex loci.*[10]

8 Vattel, liv. ii. ch. 8, § 111.

9 Huberus, Prælect. tom. ii. lib. ii. tit. 3, *de Conflictu Legum*, §§ 14, 15. Merlin, Répertoire de Jurisprudence, tit. *Loi*, §§ 6, 3. Bynkershoek, Quæst. Jur. Pub. lib. i. cap. 16. See also an opinion given by Grotius as counsel in 1613. Henry's Foreign Law, Appendix, p. 196. Yet it has been recently doubted how far a British subject can, by changing his native domicil for a foreign domicil without the British empire, change the rule of succession to his personal property in Great Britain; though it is admitted that a change of domicil within the empire, as from England to Scotland, would have that effect. Per Sir J. Nicholl, in Curling *v.* Thornton, Addams' Eccles. Rep. vol. ii. p. 17.

10 This principle, laid down by all the text writers, was recently recognised in England, in a case where a native of Scotland domiciled in India, but

The municipal laws of most countries prohibit foreigners from holding real (or immoveable) property within the territory of the state. During the prevalence of the feudal system in Europe, the acquisition of land involved the notion of allegiance to the prince within whose dominions it lay, which might be inconsistent with that which the proprietor owed to his native sovereign. It was also during the same rude ages that the *jus albinatus,* or *droit d'aubaine,* was established, by which all the property of a deceased foreigner (moveable and immoveable) was confiscated to the use of the state, to the exclusion of his heirs, whether claiming *ab intestato,* or under a will of the decedent. In the progress of civilization, this barbarous and inhospitable usage has been by degrees almost entirely abolished. This improvement has been accomplished either by municipal regulations, or by international compacts founded upon the basis of reciprocity. Previous to the French revolution, the *droit d'aubaine* had been either abolished or modified by treaties between France and other states, and it was entirely abrogated by a decree of the constituent assembly in 1791, with respect to all nations. This concession

§ 6. Droit d'Aubaine.

who possessed heritable bonds in Scotland, as well as personal property there, and also in India, having executed a will in India ineffectual to convey Scottish heritage; and a question having arisen whether his heir at law (who claimed the heritable bonds as heir) was also entitled to a share of the moveable property as legatee under the will, it was held by Lord Chancellor *Brougham,* in delivering the judgment of the House of Lords, affirming that of the court below, that the construction of the will, and the legal consequences of that construction, must be determined by the law of the land where it was made, and where the testator had his domicil, namely, India, *i. e.* by the law of England prevailing in that country ; and this, although the will was made the subject of judicial inquiry in the tribunals of Scotland, for these courts also are bound to decide according to the law of the place where the will was made.—Trotter *v.* Trotter, 3 Wilson & Shaw's Rep. on Appeal Cases in the House of Lords, pp. 407—414. But it ought to be observed that the precedents respecting the operations of a will of personal property, executed according to the law of the place where it is made, but wanting the formalities required in the country where the property lies, have been considered by very high judicial authority as rather applying between different co-ordinate states of the same empire governed by distinct laws, than as between countries entirely independent of each other.—Addams' Eccles. Rep. vol. i. p. 21, Curling *v.* Thornton.

was retracted, and the subject placed on its original footing
of reciprocity, by the Code Napoléon in 1803 ; but this part
of the civil code was again repealed by the ordinance of the
14th July, 1819, admitting foreigners to the right of possessing both moveable and immoveable property in France, and of
taking by succession *ab intestato*, or by will, in the same manner with native subjects. The analogous usage of the *droit
de retraction*, or *droit de retrait* (jus detractus) by which a tax
was levied upon the removal from one state to another of
property acquired by succession or by testamentary disposition, has also been reciprocally abolished in most civilized
countries.[11]

§ 7.
Personal
status.

The sovereign power of municipal legislation also extends
to the regulation of the personal rights of the subjects of the
state within its territory, to every thing affecting their civil
state and condition.

It extends (with certain exceptions) to the supreme police
over all persons within the territory, whether subjects or not,
and to all criminal offences committed by them within the
same.

Some of these arise from the positive law of nations, others
are the effect of special compact.

There are also certain cases where the municipal laws of
the state, civil and criminal, operate beyond its territorial jurisdiction. These are,

Laws re-
lating to
state and
capacity
of persons
may ope-
rate extra-
territori-
ally.

I. Laws relating to the state and capacity of persons.

In general the laws of the state applicable to the civil condition and personal capacity of its citizens operate upon them
even when resident in a foreign country.

Such are those universal personal qualities which take effect either from birth, such as citizenship, legitimacy, and
illegitimacy ; at a fixed time after birth, as minority and majority ; or at an indeterminate time after birth, as idiocy and
lunacy, bankruptcy, marriage, and divorce, ascertained by

---

[11] Vattel, liv. ii. ch. 8, §§ 112—114. Kluber, Droit des Gens Moderne de
l'Europe, pt. 2. tit. 1, ch. 2, §§ 32, 33. Von Mayer, Corpus Juris Con-
fœderationis Germanicæ, tom. ii. p. 17. Merlin, Repértoire, tit. *Aubaine*.

the judgment of a competent tribunal. The laws of the state affecting all these personal qualities of its subjects travel with them wherever they go, and attach to them in whatever country they are resident.[12]

This general rule is, however, subject to the following exceptions :—

1. To the right of every independent sovereign state to naturalize foreigners, and to confer upon them the privileges of their acquired domicil.

Even supposing a natural-born subject of one country cannot throw off his primitive allegiance, so as to cease to be responsible for criminal acts against his native country, it has been determined, both in Great Britain and the United States, that he may become by residence and naturalization in a foreign state entitled to all the commercial privileges of his acquired domicil and citizenship. Thus by the treaty of 1794, between the United States and Great Britain, the trade to the countries beyond the Cape of Good Hope within the limits of the East India Company's charter, was opened to American citizens, whilst it still continued prohibited to British subjects: it was held by the Court of King's Bench that a natural-born British subject might become a citizen of the United States, and be entitled to all the advantages of trade conceded between his native country and that foreign country; and that the circumstance of his returning to his native country for a mere temporary purpose would not deprive him of those advantages.[13]

2. The sovereign right of every independent state to regulate the property within its territory constitutes another exception to the rule.

Thus the personal capacity to contract a marriage as to age, consent of parents, &c., is regulated by the law of the state of which the party is a subject; but the effects of a nuptial contract upon real (or immoveable) property in another state are determined by the *lex loci rei sitæ*. Huberus,

Marginal note: Naturalization conferring commercial privileges.

---

[12] Pardessus, Droit Commercial, pt. vi. tit. 7, ch. 2, § 1.

[13] Term Rep. vol. viii. p. 31. Bos. & Pull. Rep. vol. i. p. 43, Wilson *v.* Marryatt,

indeed, lays down the contrary doctrine, upon the ground
that the foreign law, in this case, does not affect the territory
immediately, but only in an incidental manner, and *that* by
the implied consent of the sovereign, for the benefit of his
subjects, without prejudicing his or their rights. But the
practice of nations is certainly different, and therefore no such
consent can be implied to waive the local law which has impressed certain indelible qualities upon immoveable property
within the territorial jurisdiction.[14]

Effect of
bankrupt
discharge
and title of
assignees
in another
country.

By the general international law of Europe and America,
a certificate of discharge obtained by a bankrupt in the country of which he is a subject, and where the contract was
made and the parties domiciled, is valid to discharge the
debtor in every other country ; but the opinions of jurists
and the practice of nations have been much divided upon the
question how far the title of his assignees or syndics will control his personal property situate in a foreign country, and
prevent its being attached and distributed under the local
laws in a different course from that prescribed by the bankrupt code of his own country. According to the law of most
European countries, the proceeding which is prior in point of
time is deemed prior in point of right, and draws to itself the
right to take and distribute the property. The rule thus
established is rested upon the general principle that personal
(or moveable) property is, by a legal fiction, considered as
situate in the country where the bankrupt had his domicil.
The international bankrupt law of America considers the
lex loci rei sitæ as prevailing over the *lex domicilii* in respect
to creditors, and that the laws of other states cannot be permitted to have an extra-territorial operation to the prejudice
of the authority, rights, and interests of the state where the
property lies. The supreme court of the United States has
therefore determined that both the government under its prerogative priority, and private creditors attaching under the
local laws, are to be preferred to the claim of the assignees
for the benefit of the general creditors under a foreign bank-

[14] Kent's Commentaries on American Law, vol. ii. pp. 183, 184, Note.

rupt law, although the debtor was domiciled and the contract made in a foreign country.[15]

3. The general rule as to the application of personal statutes yields in some cases to the operation of the *lex loci contractus.*

Thus a bankrupt's certificate under the laws of his own country cannot operate in another state, to discharge him from his debts contracted with foreigners in a foreign country. And though the personal capacity to enter into the nuptial contract as to age, consent of parents, and prohibited degrees of affinity, &c. is generally to be governed by the law of the state of which the party is a subject, the marriage ceremony is always regulated by the law of the place where it is celebrated; and if valid there, it is considered as valid every where else, unless made in fraud of the laws of the country of which the parties are domiciled subjects.

II. The municipal laws of the state may also operate beyond its territorial jurisdiction, where a contract made within the territory comes either directly or incidentally in question in the judicial tribunals of a foreign state. §8. Lex loci contractus.

A contract, valid by the law of the place where it is made, is, generally speaking, valid every where else. The general comity and mutual convenience of nations has established the rule that the law of that place governs in every thing respecting the form, interpretation, obligation, and effect of the contract, wherever the authority, rights, and interests of other states and their citizens are not thereby prejudiced.

This qualification of the rule suggests the exceptions which arise to its application. And, Exceptions to its operation.

1. It cannot apply to cases properly governed by the *lex loci rei sitæ,* (as in the case before put of the effect of a nuptial contract upon real property in a foreign state,) or by the laws

[15] Bell's Commentaries on the Law of Scotland, vol. ii. pp. 681—687. Rose's Cases in Bankruptcy, vol. i. p. 462. Kent's Commentaries on American Law, vol. ii. pp. 393, 404—408, 459. Cranch's Rep. vol. v. p. 289, Harrison *v.* Sterry. Wheaton's Rep. vol. xii. pp. 153—163, Ogden *v.* Saunders.

of another state relating to the personal state and capacity
of its citizens.

2. It cannot apply where it would injuriously conflict with
the laws of another state relating to its police, its public
health, its commerce, its revenue, and generally its sovereign
authority, and the rights and interests of its citizens.

Thus if goods are sold in a place where they are not prohibited, to be delivered in a place where they are prohibited,
although the trade is perfectly lawful by the *lex loci contractus*, the price cannot be recovered in the state where the
goods are deliverable, because to enforce the contract there
would be to sanction a breach of its own commercial laws.
But the tribunals of one country do not take notice of, or enforce, either directly or incidentally, the laws of trade or revenue of another state, and therefore an insurance of prohibited
trade may be enforced in the tribunals of any other country
than that where it is prohibited by the local laws.[16]

Foreign marriages.   A marriage contracted in a foreign country, by a fraudulent evasion of the laws of the state to which the parties belong, might seem, on principle, to be void in the country of
their domicil, though valid under the laws of the place where
the marriage is contracted.   Such are marriages contracted
in a foreign state, and according to its laws, by persons who
are minors, or otherwise incapable of contracting, by the
law of their own country.   These cases seem to form exceptions to the general operation of the *lex loci contractus*, which
no state is bound to admit where it injuriously affects its
sovereign authority, or the rights and interests of its citizens.
But according to the international marriage law of the British empire, a clandestine marriage in Scotland, of parties
originally domiciled in England, who resort to Scotland for
the sole purpose of evading the English marriage act, requiring the consent of parents or guardians, is considered valid
in the English ecclesiastical courts.   This jurisprudence is

[16] Pardessus, Droit Commercial, pt. vi. tit. 7, ch. 2, § 3.   Emerigon,
Traité d'Assurance, tom. i. pp. 212—215.   Park on Insurance, p. 341.
Sixth Ed.   The moral equity of this rule has been strongly questioned by
Bynkershoek and Pothier.

said to have been adopted upon the ground of its being a part of the general law and practice of Christendom, and that infinite confusion and mischief would ensue, with respect to legitimacy, succession, and other personal and proprietary rights, if the validity of the marriage contract was not to be determined by the law of the place where it was made. The same principle has been recognised between the different states of the American Union, upon similar grounds of public policy.[17]

On the other hand, the age of consent required by the French civil code is considered by the law of France as a personal quality of French subjects, following them where-ver they remove; and consequently, a marriage, by a Frenchman, within the required age, will not be regarded as valid by the French tribunals, though the parties may have been above the age required by the law of the place where it was contracted.[18]

3. As every sovereign state has the exclusive right of re-gulating the proceedings in its own courts of justice, the *lex loci contractus* of another country cannot apply to such cases as are properly to be determined by the *lex fori* of that state where the contract is brought in question.

§ 9.
Lex fori.

Thus, if a contract made in one country is attempted to be enforced, or comes incidentally in question, in the judicial tribunals of another, every thing relating to the forms of pro-ceeding, the rules of evidence, and of limitation (or prescrip-tion) is to be determined by the law of the state where the suit is pending, not of that where the contract was made.[19]

III. The municipal institutions of a state may also operate beyond the limits of its territorial jurisdiction, in the follow-ing cases:—

§ 10.
Foreign sovereign, his ambas-sador,

[17] Haggard's Consist. Rep. vol. ii. pp. 428—433.   Kent's Commentaries, vol. ii. p. 93.
[18] Merlin, Repértoire, tit. *Loi*, § 6.   Toullier, Droit Français, tom. i. No. 118, 576.
[19] Kent's Commentaries, vol. ii. p. 462,   Second Ed.

army, or
fleet, with-
in the terri-
tory of ano-
ther state.

1. The person of a foreign sovereign going into the territory of another state is, by the general usage and comity of nations, exempt from the ordinary local jurisdiction. Representing the power, dignity, and all the sovereign attributes of his own nation, and going into the territory of another state under the permission which (in time of peace) is implied from the absence of any prohibition, he is not amenable to the civil or criminal jurisdiction of the country where he temporarily resides.[20]

2. The person of an ambassador, or other public minister, whilst within the territory of the state to which he is delegated, is also exempt from the local jurisdiction. His residence is considered as a continued residence in his own country, and he retains his national character unmixed with that of the country where he locally resides.[21]

3. A foreign army, or fleet, marching through, sailing over, or stationed in the territory of another state with whom the foreign sovereign is in amity, are also in like manner exempt from the civil and criminal jurisdiction of the place.[22]

If there be no express prohibition, the ports of a friendly state are considered as open to the public armed and commissioned ships belonging to another nation with whom that state is at peace. Such ships are exempt from the jurisdiction of the local tribunals and authorities, whether they enter the ports under the license implied from the absence of any prohibition, or under an express permission, stipulated by treaty. But the private vessels of one state entering the ports of another, are not exempt from the local jurisdiction, unless by express compact, and to the extent provided by such compact. Nor does the exemption of foreign public ships, coming into the waters of a neutral state, from the local jurisdiction, extend to their prize ships or goods captured by armaments fitted out in its ports in violation of its neutrality.[23]

[20] Bynkershoek, de Foro Legat. cap. iii. § 13. cap. ix. § 10.

[21] Vide infra, pt. iii. ch. 1.

[22] Casaregis, Disc. 136—174.

[23] Vattel, liv. i. ch. 19, § 216. Cranch's Rep. vol. vii. p. 116. The Exchange.

4. Both the public and private vessels of every nation, on the high seas, and out of the territorial limits of any other state, are subject to the jurisdiction of the state to which they belong.

§ 11. Jurisdiction of the state over its public and private vessels on the high seas.

Vattel says that the domain of a nation extends to all its just possessions, and by its possessions we are not only to understand its territory, but all the rights (droits) it enjoys. And he also considers the vessels of a nation on the high seas as portions of its territory, though he admits the right of search for contraband and enemy's property. *Grotius* holds that sovereignty may be acquired over a portion of the sea, *ratione personarum, ut si classis qui maritimis est exercitus, aliquo in loco maris se habeat.* But, as one of his commentators has observed, though there can be no doubt about the jurisdiction of a nation over the persons which compose its fleets when they are out at sea, it does not follow that the nation has jurisdiction over any portion of the ocean itself. It is not a permanent property which it acquires, but a mere temporary right of occupancy in a place which is common to all mankind to be successively used by all as they have occasion.[24]

This jurisdiction which the nation has over its public and private vessels on the high seas, is exclusive only so far as respects offences against its own municipal laws. Piracy and other offences against the law of nations, being crimes not against any particular state, but against all mankind, may be punished in the competent tribunal of any country where the offender may be found, or into which he may be carried, although committed on board a foreign vessel on the high seas.[25]

Though these offences may be tried in the competent court of any nation having, by lawful means, the custody of the offenders, yet the right of visitation and search does not exist in time of peace. This right cannot be employed for the purpose of executing upon foreign vessels and persons on

---

[24] Vattel, liv. ch. 19, § 216. liv. ii. ch. 7, § 80. Grotius, de Jur. Bel. ac Pac. lib. ii. cap. iii. § 13. Rutherforth's Inst. vol. ii. b. 2, ch. 9, §§ 8, 19.

[25] Sir L. Jenkins' Works, vol. i. p. 714.

the high seas the prohibition of a traffic, which is neither
piratical, nor contrary to the law of nations, (such, *e. g.* as
the slave trade,) unless the visitation and search be expressly permitted by international compact.[26]

Every state has an incontestable right to the service of all
its members in the national defence, but it can only give effect
to this right by lawful means.   Its right to reclaim the military service of its citizens can only be exercised within its
own territory, or in some place not subject to the jurisdiction of any other nation.   The ocean is such a place, and any
state may unquestionably there exercise, on board its own
vessels, its right of compelling the military or naval services
of its subjects.   But whether it may exercise the same right,
in respect to the vessels of other nations, is a question of
more difficulty.

In respect to public commissioned vessels belonging to the
state, their entire immunity from every species and purpose
of search is generally conceded.   As to private vessels belonging to the subjects of a foreign nation, the right to search
them on the high seas, for deserters and other persons liable
to military and naval service, has been uniformly asserted
by Great Britain, and as constantly denied by the United
States.   This litigation between the two nations, who by the
identity of their origin and language are the most deeply
interested in the question, formed one of the principal objects
of the late war between them.   It is to be hoped that the
sources of this controversy may be dried up by the substitu-
tion of a registry of seamen, and a system of voluntary enlistment with limited service, for the odious practice of im-
pressment which has hitherto prevailed in the British navy,
and which can never be extended, even to the private ships
of a foreign nation, without provoking hostilities on the part
of any maritime state capable of resisting such a pretension.[27]

[26] Dodson's Adm. Rep. vol. ii. p. 238.   The Louis.   Wheaton's Rep. vol.
x, pp. 122, 123.   The Antelope.

[27] Edinburgh Review, vol. xi. art. 1.   Mr. Canning's Letter to Mr. Mon-
roe, Sept. 23, 1827.   American State Papers, vol. vi. p. 103.

IV. The municipal laws and institutions of any state may operate beyond its own territory, and within the territory of another state, by special compact between the two states. §12. Consular jurisdiction.

Such are the treaties by which the consuls and other commercial agents of one nation are authorized to exercise, over their own countrymen, a jurisdiction within the territory of the state where they reside. The nature and extent of this peculiar jurisdiction depends upon the stipulations of the treaties between the two states. Among Christian nations it is generally confined to the decision of controversies in civil cases arising between the merchants, seamen, and other subjects of the state in foreign countries; to the registering of wills, contracts, and other instruments executed in presence of the consul; and to the administration of the estates of their fellow-subjects deceased within the territorial limits of the consulate. The resident consuls of the Christian powers in Turkey, the Barbary States, and other Mohammedan countries, exercise both civil and criminal jurisdiction over their countrymen, to the exclusion of the local magistrates and tribunals. This jurisdiction is subject, in civil cases, to an appeal to the superior tribunals of their own country. The criminal jurisdiction is usually limited to the infliction of pecuniary penalties, and in offences of a higher grade, the consular functions are similar to those of a police magistrate, or *juge d'instruction.* He collects the documentary and other proofs, and sends them, together with the prisoner, home to his own country for trial.[28]

Every sovereign state is independent of every other in the exercise of its judicial power. §13. Independence of

This general position must, of course, be qualified by the exceptions to its application arising out of express compact, such as conventions with foreign states and acts of confederation, by which the state may be united in a league with other states for some common purpose. By the stipulations of these compacts it may part with certain portions of its the state as to its judicial power,

---

[28] De Steck, Essai sur les Consuls, sect. vii. §§ 30—40. Pardessus, Droit Commercial, pt. vi. tit. 6, ch. 2, § 2. ch. 4. §§ 1, 2, 3.

judicial power, or may modify its exercise with a view to the attainment of the object of the treaty or act of union.

Subject to these exceptions, the judicial power of every state is coextensive with its legislative power. At the same time it does not embrace those cases in which the municipal institutions of another nation operate within the territory. Such are the cases of a foreign sovereign, or his public minister, fleet or army, coming within the territorial limits of another state, which, as already observed, are, in general, exempt from the operation of the local laws.[29]

§ 14.
Extent of
the judicial
power over
criminal of-
fences.

I. The judicial power of every independent state, then, extends, with the qualifications mentioned,—

1. To the punishment of all offences against the municipal laws of the state, by whomsoever committed, within the territory.

2. To the punishment of all such offences, by whomsoever committed, on board its public and private vessels on the high seas, and on board its public vessels in foreign ports.

3. To the punishment of all such offences by its subjects, wheresoever committed.

4. To the punishment of piracy and other offences against the law of nations, by whomsoever and wheresoever committed.

It is evident that a state cannot punish an offence against its municipal laws committed within the territory of another state, unless by its own citizens; nor can it arrest the persons or property of the supposed offender within that territory; but it may arrest its own citizens in a place which is not within the jurisdiction of any other nation, as the high seas, and punish them for offences committed within such a place, or within the territory of a foreign state.

Laws of
trade and
navigation.

Laws of trade and navigation cannot affect foreigners beyond the territorial limits of the state, but they are binding upon its citizens wherever they may be. Thus offences against the laws of a state prohibiting or regulating any par-

[29] Vide ante, § 10.

ticular traffic may be punished by its tribunals when committed by its citizens, in whatever place ; but if committed by foreigners, such offences can only be thus punished when committed within the territory of the state, or on board of its vessels in some place not within the jurisdiction of any other state.

And the laws of treason, which are binding on all persons resident within the territory, since such persons owe a temporary allegiance to the state, may be applied to foreigners if committed within its territory ; but these laws may be applied to citizens, in whatever place the offence is committed, since their allegiance travels with them wherever they go. Laws of treason.

A distinction is to be noticed respecting the operation of laws of trade upon citizens resident in a foreign country, that where it is a mere commercial regulation permitting or prohibiting a certain trade, the party resident abroad may have the benefit of his commercial domicil, so far as to exempt him from the operation of the municipal law of his own country, whilst his former allegiance still continues.   But if the statute creates a criminal offence, and visits it with personal penalties expressly applicable to all the subjects of the state, it will apply to such offences committed by them when domiciled in a foreign country, by the laws of which the act constituting the crime is not prohibited. Commercial domicil.

No sovereign state is bound, unless by special compact, to deliver up persons, whether its own subjects or foreigners, charged with or convicted of crimes committed in another country, upon the demand of a foreign state or its officers of justice.   The extradition of persons charged with or convicted of criminal offences affecting the general peace and security of society is, however, voluntarily practised by certain states as a matter of general convenience and comity.[30] Extradition of criminals.

The delivering up by one state of deserters from the military or naval service of another also depends entirely upon

---

[30] Vattel, liv. ii. ch. 6, § 76.   Martens, Précis du Droit des Gens Moderne de l'Europe, liv. iii. ch. 3, § 101.

mutual comity, or upon special compact between different nations.[31]

§ 15.
Extra-ter-
ritorial
operation
of a crimi-
nal sen-
tence.

A criminal sentence pronounced under the municipal law in one state can have no direct legal effect in another. If it is a sentence of conviction, it cannot be executed without the limits of the state in which it is pronounced upon the person or property of the offender ; and if he is convicted of an infamous crime, attended with civil disqualifications in his own country, such a sentence can have no legal effect in another independent state.[32]

But a valid sentence, whether of conviction or acquittal, pronounced in one state, may have certain indirect and collateral effects in other states. If pronounced under the municipal law in the state where the supposed crime was committed, or to which the supposed offender owed allegiance, the sentence, either of conviction or acquittal, would, of course, be an effectual bar (*exceptio rei judicatæ*) to a prosecution in any other state. If pronounced in another foreign state than that where the offence is alleged to have been committed, or to which the party owed allegiance, the sentence would be a nullity, and of no avail to protect him against a prosecution in any other state having jurisdiction of the offence.

It follows as a corollary from these principles, that the practice of delinquents flying from one jurisdiction into another, for the purpose of obtaining a milder punishment or an acquittal in the tribunals of the country where they seek refuge, is wholly unsanctioned by international law and the approved usage of nations.[33]

§ 16.
Piracy
under the
law of na-
tions.

The judicial power of every state extends to the punishment of certain offences against the law of nations, among which is piracy.

[31] Bynkershoek, Quæst. Jur. Pub. lib. i. cap. 22. Note to Duponceau's Transl. p. 174.

[32] Martens, Précis, &c., liv. iii. ch. 3, § 86. Kluber, Droit des Gens Moderne de l'Europe, pt. ii. tit. 1, ch. 2, §§ 64, 65.

[33] Henry on Foreign Law, pp. 46, 47.

Piracy is defined by the text writers to be the offence of depredating on the seas, without being authorized by any sovereign state, or with commissions from different sovereigns at war with each other.[34]

The officers and crew of an armed vessel, commissioned against one nation, and depredating upon another, are not liable to be treated as pirates in thus exceeding their authority. The state by whom the commission is granted, being responsible to other nations for what is done by its commissioned cruisers, has the exclusive jurisdiction to try and punish all offences committed under colour of its authority.[35]

The offence of depredating under commissions from different sovereigns at war with each other is clearly piratical, since the authority conferred by one is repugnant to the other; but it has been doubted how far it may be lawful to cruise under commissions from different sovereigns allied against a common enemy. The better opinion, however, seems to be, that although it might not amount to the crime of piracy, still it would be irregular and illegal, because the two co-belligerents may have adopted different rules of conduct respecting neutrals, or may be separately bound by engagements unknown to the party.[36]

Pirates being the common enemies of all mankind, and all nations having an equal interest in their apprehension and punishment, they may be lawfully captured on the high seas by the armed vessels of any particular state, and brought within its territorial jurisdiction for trial in its tribunals.[37]

[34] See authorities cited in Note to the case of United States *v.* Smith, Wheaton's Rep. vol. v. p. 157.

[35] Bynkershoek, Quæst. Jur. Pub. lib. i. cap. 17. Rutherforth's Inst. vol. ii. p. 595.

[36] Bynkershoek, Quæst. Jur. Pub. lib. i. cap. 17, Duponceau's Transl. p. 130. Valin, Commentaire sur l'Ord. de la Marine. "The law," says Sir L. Jenkins, "distinguishes between a pirate who is a highwayman, and sets up for robbing, either having no commission at all, or else hath two or three, and a lawful man of war that exceeds his commission."—*Works,* vol. ii. p. 714.

[37] "Every man, by the usage of our European nations, is *justiciable* in the place where the crime is committed: so are pirates, being reputed out of

Distinction
between
piracy by
the law of
nations
and piracy
under mu-
nicipal sta-
tutes.

This proposition, however, must be confined to piracy as defined by the law of nations, and cannot be extended to offences which are made piracy by municipal legislation. Piracy under the law of nations may be tried and punished in the courts of justice of any nation, by whomsoever and wheresoever committed; but piracy created by municipal statute can only be tried by that state within whose territorial jurisdiction, and on board of whose vessels, the offence thus created was committed. Thus the crimes of murder and robbery committed by foreigners, on board of a foreign vessel, on the high seas, are not justiciable in the tribunals of another country than that to which the vessel belongs; but if committed on board of a vessel not at the time belonging, in fact as well as right, to any foreign power or its subjects, but in possession of a crew acting in defiance of all law, and acknowledging obedience to no flag whatsoever, these crimes may be punished as piracy under the law of nations in the courts of any nation having custody of the offenders.[38]

§ 17.
Slave
trade, whe-
ther prohi-
bited by
the law of
nations.

The slave trade, though prohibited by the municipal laws of most nations, and declared to be piracy by the statutes of Great Britain and the United States, is not such by the general international law, and its interdiction cannot be enforced by the exercise of the ordinary right of visitation and search. That right does not exist in time of peace, independently of special compact.[39]

The African slave trade, once considered not only a lawful, but desirable branch of commerce, a participation in which was made the object of wars, negotiations, and treaties between different European states, is now denounced as an odious crime by the almost universal consent of nations. This branch of commerce was successively prohibited by the municipal laws of Denmark, the United States, and Great

the protection of all laws and privileges, and to be tried in what ports soever they may be taken."—*Sir L. Jenkins' Works*, ib.

[38] Wheaton's Rep. vol. v. pp. 144, 184.   United States *v.* Clintock, United States *v.* Pirates.

[39] Dodson's Adm. Rep. vol. ii. p. 210.   Le Louis.   Wheaton's Rep. vol. x. p. 66.   La Jeune Eugenie.

Britain, to their own subjects. Its final abolition was stipulated by the treaties of Paris, Kiel, and Ghent, in 1814, confirmed by the declaration of the Congress of Vienna of the 8th of February, 1815, and reiterated by the additional article annexed to the treaty of peace concluded at Paris on the 20th November, 1815. The accession of Spain and Portugal to the principle of the abolition was finally obtained by the treaties between Great Britain and those powers of the 23rd September, 1817, and the 22nd January, 1815. And by a convention concluded with Brazil in 1826, it was made piratical for the subjects of that country to be engaged in the trade after the year 1830.

This general concert of nations to extinguish the traffic has given rise to the opinion, that, though once tolerated, and even protected and encouraged by the laws of every maritime country, it ought henceforth to be considered as interdicted by the international code of Europe and America. This opinion Decisions of British and American courts of justice. first received judicial countenance from the authority of the judgment of the Lords of Appeal in prize causes, pronounced by *Sir W. Grant* in the case of an American vessel, the trade having been previously abolished by the laws of the United States as well as of Great Britain. The trade having been thus prohibited by the laws of both countries, and having been declared to be contrary to the principles of justice and humanity, the court deemed itself authorized to assert that it could not, abstractedly speaking, have a legitimate existence, and was, *primâ facie*, illegal, upon principles of universal law. The entire burden of proof was thus thrown upon the claimant to show that by the municipal law of his own country he was entitled to carry on this traffic. No claimant could " be heard in an application to a court of prize for the restitution of human beings carried unjustly to another country for the purpose of disposing of them as slaves."[40]

The principle of this decision was subsequently questioned by *Sir W. Scott* (Lord Stowell) in the case of the *Louis*, a French vessel, captured by the British cruiser as having been engaged in the slave trade. In this case it was held that the

[40] Acton's Rep. vol. i. p. 240. The Amadie.

trade could not be considered as contrary to the law of nations. A court of justice, in the administration of law, could
not impute criminality to an act where the law imputes none.
It must look to the legal standard of morality—a standard
which, upon a question of this nature, must be found in the
law of nations, as fixed and evidenced by general, ancient,
and admitted practice, by treaties, and by the general tenor
of the laws, ordinances, and formal transactions of civilized
states; and looking to these authorities, the learned judge
found a difficulty in maintaining that the transaction was legally criminal. The slave trade, on the contrary, had been
carried on by all nations, including Great Britain, until a very
recent period, and was still carried on by Spain and Portugal,
and not yet absolutely prohibited by France. It was not,
therefore, a criminal traffic by the consuetudinary law of nations; and every nation, independently of special compact,
retained a legal right to carry it on. No one nation had a
right to force the way to the liberation of America, by tram-
pling on the independence of other states, or to procure an
eminent good by means that were unlawful; or to press forward to a great principle, by breaking through other great
principles that stood in the way.[41]

A similar course of reasoning was adopted by the supreme
court of the United States in the case of Spanish and Portuguese vessels captured by American cruisers whilst the trade
was still tolerated by the laws of Spain and Portugal. It
was stated, in the judgment of the court, that it could hardly
be denied that the slave trade was contrary to the law of
nature. That every man had a natural right to the fruits of
his own labour, was generally admitted; and that no other
person could rightfully deprive him of those fruits, and appropriate them against his will, seemed to be the necessary
result of this admission. But from the earliest times war had
existed, and war conferred rights in which all had acquiesced.
Among the most enlightened nations of antiquity, one of these

---

[41] Dodson's Adm. Rep. vol. ii. p. 238. See also the case of Madrazo v.
Willes, determined in the Court of King's Bench in 1820. Barnwell and
Alderson's Rep. vol. iii. p. 353.

rights was, that the victor might enslave the vanquished. That which was the usage of all nations could not be pronounced repugnant to the law of nations, which was certainly to be tried by the test of general usage. That which had received the assent of all must be the law of all.

Slavery, then, had its origin in force; but as the world had agreed that it was a legitimate result of force, the state of things which was thus produced by general consent could not be pronounced unlawful.

Throughout Christendom this harsh rule had been exploded, and war was no longer considered as giving a right to enslave captives. But this triumph had not been universal. The parties to the modern law of nations do not propagate their principles by force; and Africa had not yet adopted them. Throughout the whole extent of that immense continent, so far as we know its history, it is still the law of nations that prisoners are slaves. The question then was, could those who had renounced this law be permitted to participate in its effects by purchasing the human beings who are its victims?

Whatever might be the answer of a moralist to this question, a jurist must search for its legal solution in those principles which are sanctioned by the usages, the national acts, and the general assent, of that portion of the world, of which he considers himself a part, and to whose law the appeal is made. If we resort to this standard as the test of international law, the question must be considered as decided in favour of the legality of the trade. Both Europe and America embarked in it; and for nearly two centuries, it was carried on without opposition, and without censure. A jurist could not say that a practice thus supported was illegal, and that those engaged in it might be punished, either personally, or by deprivation of property.

In this commerce, thus sanctioned by universal assent, every nation had an equal right to engage. No principle of general law was more universally acknowledged, than the perfect equality of nations. Russia and Geneva have equal rights. It results from this equality, that no one can rightfully impose

a rule on another. Each legislates for itself, but its legislation can operate on itself alone. A right, then, which was
vested in all by the consent of all, could be divested only by
consent; and this trade, in which all had participated, must
remain lawful to those who could not be induced to relinquish
it. As no nation could prescribe a rule for others, no one
could make a law of nations; and this traffic remained lawful to those whose governments had not forbidden it.

If it was consistent with the law of nations, it could not
in itself be piracy. It could be made so only by statute; and
the obligation of the statute could not transcend the legislative power of the state which might enact it.

If the trade was neither repugnant to the law of nations,
nor piratical, it was almost superfluous to say in that court
that the right of bringing in for adjudication in time of peace,
even where the vessel belonged to a nation which had prohibited the trade, could not exist. The courts of justice of
no country executed the penal laws of another; and the
course of policy of the American government on the subject
of visitation and search, would decide any case against the
captors in which that right had been exercised by an American cruiser, on the vessel of a foreign nation, not violating
the municipal laws of the United States. It followed that a
foreign vessel engaged in the African slave trade, captured on
the high seas in time of peace, by an American cruiser, and
brought in for adjudication, would be restored to the original
owners.[42]

§ 18.
Extent of
the judicial
power as to
property
within the
territory.

II. The judicial power of every State extends to all civil
proceedings, *in rem*, relating to real or personal property
within the territory.

This follows, in respect to real property, as a necessary
consequence of the rule relating to the application of the *lex
loci rei sitæ*. As every thing relating to the tenure, title,
and transfer of real property (or immoveables) is regulated
by the local law, so also the proceedings in courts of justice
relating to that species of property, such as the rules of evi-

---

[42] Wheaton's Rep. vol. x. p. 66. The Antelope.

dence and of prescription, the forms of action and pleadings, must necessarily be governed by the same law.

A similar rule applies to all civil proceedings *in rem*, respecting personal property (or moveables) within the territory, which must also be regulated by the local law, with this qualification, that foreign laws may furnish the rule of decision in cases where they apply, whilst the forms of process, and rules of evidence and prescription, are still governed by the *lex fori*. Thus the *lex domicilii* forms the law in respect to a testament of personal property or succession *ab intestato*, if the will is made, or the party on whom the succession devolves resides in a foreign country; whilst at the same time the *lex fori* of the state in whose tribunals the suit is pending determines the forms of process and the rules of evidence and prescription.

§ 19. Distinction between the rule of decision and the rule of procedure as affecting cases *in rem.*

Though the distribution of the personal effects of an intestate is to be made according to the law of the place where the deceased was domiciled, it does not therefore follow that the distribution is in all cases to be made by the tribunals of that place to the exclusion of those of the country where the property is situate. Whether the tribunal of the state where the property lies is to decree distribution, or to remit the property abroad, is a matter of judicial discretion to be exercised according to circumstances. It is the duty of every government to protect its own citizens in the recovery of their debts and other just claims; and in the case of a solvent estate it would be an unreasonable and useless comity to send the funds abroad, and the resident creditor after them. But if the estate be insolvent, it ought not to be sequestered for the exclusive benefit of the subjects of the state where it lies. In all civilized countries, foreigners, in such a case, are entitled to prove their debts and share in the distribution.[43]

Succession to personal property *ab intestato.*

Though the forms in which a testament of personal property made in a foreign country is to be executed, are regulated by the local law, such a testament cannot be carried

Foreign will, how carried into effect in another country.

[43] Kent's Commentaries on American Law, 2nd ed. vol. ii. pp. 432—434, and the cases there cited.

into effect in the state where the property lies, until, in the language of the law of England, *probate* has been obtained in the proper tribunal of such state, or, in the language of the civilians, it has been *homologated*, or registered, in such tribunal.[44]

So also a foreign executor, constituted such by the will of the testator, cannot exercise his authority in another state without taking out letters of administration in the proper local court. Nor can the administration of a successor *ab intestato*, appointed *ex officio* under the laws of a foreign state, interfere with the personal property in another state belonging to the succession without having his authority confirmed by the local tribunal.

§ 20.
Conclu-
siveness of
foreign
sentences
in rem.

The judgment or sentence of a foreign tribunal of competent jurisdiction proceeding *in rem*, such as the sentences of Prize Courts under the law of nations, or Admiralty and Exchequer, or other revenue courts, under the municipal law, are conclusive as to the proprietary interest in, and title to, the thing in question, wherever the same comes incidentally in controversy in another state.

Whatever doubts may exist as to the conclusiveness of foreign sentences in respect of facts collaterally involved in the judgment, the peace of the civilized world, and the general security and convenience of commerce, obviously require that full and complete effect should be given to such sentences, wherever the title to the specific property, which has been once determined in a competent tribunal, is again drawn in question in any other court or country.

Transfer of
property
under fo-
reign bank-
rupt pro-
ceedings.

How far a bankruptcy declared under the laws of one country will affect the real and personal property of the bankrupt situate in another state, is, (as we have already seen,) a question of which the usage of nations, and the opinions of civilians, furnish no satisfactory solution. Even as between co-ordinate states, belonging to the same common empire, it has been doubted how far the assignment under the bankrupt laws of one country will operate a transfer of pro-

[44] Wheaton's Rep. vol. xii. p. 169.   Code Civil, liv. iii. tit. 2, art. 1000.

perty in another. In respect to real property, which generally has some indelible characteristics impressed upon it by the local law, these difficulties are enhanced in those cases where the *lex loci rei sitæ* requires some formal act to be done by the bankrupt, or his attorney, especially constituted, in the place where the property lies, in order to consummate the transfer. In those countries where the theory of the English bankrupt system, that the assignment transfers all the property of the bankrupt, wherever situate, is admitted in practice, the local tribunals would probably be ancillary to the execution of the assignment by compelling the bankrupt, or his attorney, to execute such formal acts as are required by the local laws to complete the conveyance.[45]

The practice of the English court of chancery in assuming jurisdiction incidentally of questions affecting the title to lands in the British colonies, in the exercise of its jurisdiction *in personam*, where the party resides in England, and thus compelling him, indirectly, to give effect to its decrees as to real property situate out of its local jurisdiction, seems very questionable on principle, unless where it is restrained to the case of a party who has fraudulently obtained an undue advantage over other creditors by judicial proceedings instituted without personal notice to the defendant.

But whatever effect may, in general, be attributed to the assignment in bankruptcy as to property situate in another state, it is evident that it cannot operate where one creditor has fairly obtained by legal diligence a specific lien and right of preference, under the laws of the country where the property is situate.[46]

III. The judicial power of every state may be extended to all controversies respecting personal rights and contracts, or injuries to the person or property, when the party resides

§ 21.
Extent of the judicial power over

---

[45] See Lord Eldon's observations in Selkrigg *v.* Davis, Rose's Cases in Bankruptcy, vol. ii. p. 311. Vesey's Rep. vol. ix. p. 77. Banfield *v.* Solomon.

[46] Kent's Comment. on American Law, vol. ii. pp. 405—408. Second ed.

foreigners
residing
within the
territory.

within the territory, wherever the cause of action may have originated.

This general principle is entirely independent of the rule of decision which is to govern the tribunal. The rule of decision may be the law of the country where the judge is sitting, or it may be the law of a foreign state in cases where it applies; but that does not affect the question of jurisdiction, which depends, or may be made to depend, exclusively upon the residence of the party.

Depends
upon mu-
nicipal re-
gulations.

The operation of the general rule of international law as to civil jurisdiction, extending to all persons, who owe even a temporary allegiance to the state, may be limited by the positive institutions of any particular country. It is the duty as well as the right of every nation to administer justice to its own citizens; but there is no uniform and constant practice of nations as to taking cognizance of controversies between foreigners. It may be assumed or declined, at the discretion of each state, guided by such motives as may influence its juridical policy. All real and possessory actions may be brought, and indeed must be brought, in the place where the property lies: but the law of England, and of other countries

Law of
England
and Ame-
rica.

where the English common law forms the basis of the local jurisprudence, considers all personal actions, whether arising *ex delictu* or *ex contractu*, as transitory; and permits them to be brought in the domestic forum, whoever may be the parties, and wherever the cause of action may originate. This rule is supported by a legal fiction, which supposes the injury to have been inflicted, or the contract to have been made, within the local jurisdiction. In the countries which have modelled their municipal jurisprudence upon the Roman civil law, the maxim of that code, *Actor sequitur forum rei*, is generally followed, and personal actions must therefore be brought in the tribunals of the place where the defendant has acquired a fixed domicil.

French
law.

By the law of France, foreigners who have established their domicil in the country by special license (*autorisation*) of the king are entitled to all civil rights, and, among others, to that of suing in the local tribunals as French subjects.

Under other circumstances, these tribunals have jurisdiction where foreigners are parties in the following cases only:—

1. Where the contract is made in France, or elsewhere, between foreigners and French subjects.

2. In commercial matters, on all contracts made in France, with whomsoever made, where the parties have elected a domicil, in which they are liable to be sued, either by the express terms of the contract, or by necessary implication resulting from its nature.

3. Where foreigners voluntarily submit their controversies to the decision of the French tribunals, by waiving a plea to the jurisdiction.

In all other cases where foreigners, not domiciled in France by special license of the king, are concerned, the French tribunals decline jurisdiction, even when the contract is made in France.[47]

The practice which prevails in some countries of proceeding against absent parties, who are not only foreigners, but have not acquired a domicil within the territory, by means of some formal public notice, like that of the *viis et modis* of the Roman civil law, without actual personal notice of the suit, cannot be reconciled with the principles of international justice. So far indeed as it merely affects the specific property of the absent debtor within the territory, attaching it for the benefit of a particular creditor, who is thus permitted to gain a preference by superior diligence, or for the general benefit of all the creditors who come in within a certain fixed period, and claim the benefit of a rateable distribution, such a practice may be tolerated, and in the administration of international bankrupt law is frequently allowed to give a preference to the attaching creditor against the law of what is termed the *locus concursûs creditorum*, which is the place of the debtor's domicil.

[47] Code Civil, art. 13, 14, 15. Code de Commerce, art. 631. Discussions sur le Code Civil. tom. i. p. 48. Pothier, Procédure Civile, partie i. ch. 1, p. 2. Valin, sur l'Ord. de la Marine, tom. i. pp. 113, 253, 254. Pardessus, Droit Commercial, pt. vi. tit. 7, ch. 1, § 1.

§ 22.
Distinction
between
the rule of
decision
and rule of
proceeding
in cases of
contract.

Where the tribunal has jurisdiction, the rule of decision is the law applicable to the case, whether it be the municipal or a foreign code; but the rule of proceeding is generally determined by the *lex fori* of the place where the suit is pending. But it is not always easy to distinguish the rule of decision from the rule of proceeding. It may, however, be stated in general, that whatever belongs to the obligation of the contract is regulated by the *lex domicilii* or the *lex loci contractus*, and whatever belongs to the remedy for enforcing the contract is regulated by the *lex fori*.

Obligation
and reme-
dy.

If the tribunal is called upon to apply to the case, the law of the country where it sits, as between persons domiciled in that country, no difficulty can possibly arise. As the obligation of the contract and the remedy to enforce it are both derived from the municipal law, the rule of decision and the rule of proceeding must be sought in the same code. In other cases it is necessary to distinguish with accuracy between the obligation and the remedy.

The obligation of the contract, then, may be said to consist of the following parts:—

1. The personal capacity of the parties to contract.

2. The will of the parties expressed as to the terms and conditions of the contract.

3. The external form of the contract.

The personal capacity of parties to contract depends upon those personal qualities which are annexed to their civil condition by the municipal law of their own state, and which travel with them wherever they go, and attach to them in whatever foreign country they are temporarily resident. Such are the privileges and disabilities conferred by the *lex domicilii* in respect to majority and minority, marriage and divorce, sanity or lunacy, and which determine the capacity or incapacity of parties to contract independently of the law of the place where the contract is made, or that of the place where it is sought to be enforced.

It is only those universal personal qualities, which the laws of all civilized nations concur in considering as essentially affecting the capacity to contract, which are exclusively regulated by the *lex domicilii*, and not those particular prohibitions or disabilities which are arbitrary in their nature and founded upon local policy, such as the prohibition in some countries of noblemen and ecclesiastics from engaging in trade and forming commercial contracts. The quality of a major or minor, of a married or single woman, &c., are universal personal qualities, which, with all the incidents belonging to them, are ascertained by the *lex domicilii*, but which are also every where recognised as forming essential ingredients in the capacity to contract.[48]

How far bankruptcy ought to be considered as a privilege or disability of this nature, and thus be restricted in its operation to the territory of that state under whose bankrupt code the proceedings take place, is, as already stated, a question of difficulty, in respect to which no constant and uniform usage prevails among nations. Supposing the bankrupt code of any country to form a part of the obligation of every contract made in that country with its citizens, and that every such contract is subject to the implied condition that the debtor may be discharged from his obligation in the manner prescribed by the bankrupt laws, it would seem on principle that a certificate of discharge ought to be effectual in the tribunals of any other state where the creditor may bring his suit. If, on the other hand, the bankrupt code merely forms a part of the remedy for a breach of the contract, it belongs to the *lex fori*, which cannot operate extra-territorially within the jurisdiction of any other state having the exclusive right of regulating the proceedings in its own courts of justice; still less can it have such an operation where it is a mere partial modification of the remedy, such as an exemption from arrest and imprisonment of the debtor's person on a *cessio bonorum*. Such an exemption being strictly local in its nature, and to be administered in all its details by the tribunals of the state creating it, cannot form a law for those of any foreign state. But if the exemption from arrest and imprisonment, instead of being merely contingent upon the

Bankrupt-cy.

[48] Pardessus, Droit Commercial, pt. vi. tit. 7, ch. 2, § 1.

failure of the debtor to perform his obligation through insol‑ vency, enters into and forms an essential ingredient in the original contract itself by the law of the country where it is made, it cannot be enforced in any other state by the prohi‑ bited means. Thus by the law of France, and other coun‑ tries where the *contrainte par corps* is limited to commercial debts, an ordinary debt contracted in that country by its sub‑ jects cannot be enforced by means of personal arrest in any other state, although the *lex fori* may authorize imprisonment for every description of debts.[49]

The obligation of the contract consists, secondly, of the will of the parties expressed as to its terms and conditions.

The interpretation of these depends, of course, upon the *lex loci contractus*, as do also the nature and extent of those im‑ plied conditions which are annexed by the local law or usage to the contract. Thus the rate of interest, unless fixed by the parties, is allowed by the law as damages for the deten‑ tion of the debt, and the proceeding to recover these da‑ mages may strictly be considered as a part of the remedy. The rate of interest is, however, regulated by the law of the place where the contract is made, unless, indeed, it appears that the parties had in view the law of some other country. In that case, the lawful rate of interest of the place of pay‑ ment, or to which the loan has reference by security being taken upon property there situate, will control the *lex loci contractus.*[50]

3. The external form of the contract constitutes an essen‑ tial part of its obligation.

This must be regulated by the law of the place of contract, which determines whether it must be in writing, or under seal, or executed with certain formalities before a notary or other public officer, and how attested. A want of compliance with these requisites renders the contract void *ab initio,* and being void by the law of the place, it cannot be carried into effect in any other state. But a mere fiscal regulation does not

---

[49] Bosanquet and Puller's Rep. vol. i. p. 131. Melan *v.* the Duke of Fitz‑ James.

[50] Kent's Comm. on American Law, vol. ii. p. 460. Second edit.

operate extra-territorially; and therefore the want of a stamp required by the local law to be impressed on an instrument, cannot be objected where it is sought to be enforced in the tribunals of another country.

There is an essential difference between the form of the contract and the extrinsic evidence by which the contract is to be proved. Thus the *lex loci contractus* may require certain contracts to be in writing, and attested in a particular manner, and a want of compliance with these forms will render them entirely void. But if these forms are actually complied with, the extrinsic evidence by which the existence and terms of the contract are to be proved in a foreign tribunal is regulated by the *lex fori*.

The same reasons which have induced states to give an international effect to testaments, contracts, and other acts *inter vivos* or *causa mortis*, have also induced them to give a similar effect to the judicial proceedings of every state where they are drawn in question in the tribunals of another country. But as *res adjudicata* in one country can have, *per se*, no effect in another, the conclusiveness of foreign sentences and judgments in personal actions is more or less restrained by the usage of different nations, or by special compact between them. §23. Conclusiveness of foreign sentences in personal actions.

By the law of England, the judgment of a foreign tribunal of competent jurisdiction is conclusive where the same matter comes incidentally in controversy between the same parties, and full effect is given to the *exceptio rei judicatæ* where it is pleaded in bar of a new suit for the same cause of action. A foreign judgment is *primâ facie* evidence where the party claiming the benefit of it applies to the English courts to enforce it, and it lies on the defendant to impeach the justice of it, or to show that it was irregularly obtained. If this is not shown, it is received as evidence of a debt, for which a new judgment is rendered in the English court, and execution awarded. But if it appears by the record of the proceedings on which the original judgment was founded, that it was unjustly or fraudulently obtained, without actual personal notice Law of England.

to the party affected by it; or if it is clearly and unequivocally shown, by extrinsic evidence, that the judgment has manifestly proceeded upon false premises or inadequate reasons, or upon a palpable mistake of local or foreign law; it will not be enforced by the English tribunals."[51]

American law. The same jurisprudence prevails in the United States of America, in respect to judgments and decrees rendered by the tribunals of a state foreign to the union. As between the different states of the union itself, a judgment obtained in one state has the same credit and effect in all the other states, which it has by the laws of that state where it was obtained; *i. e.* it has the conclusive effect of a domestic judgment.[52]

Law of France. The law of France restrains the operation of foreign judgments within still narrower limits. Judgments obtained in a foreign country against French subjects are not conclusive, either where the same matter comes again incidentally in controversy, or where a direct suit is brought to enforce the judgment in the French tribunals. And this want of comity is even carried so far, that where a French subject commences a suit in a foreign tribunal, and judgment is rendered against him, the exception of *lis finita* is not admitted as a bar to a new action by the same party in the tribunals of his own country. If the judgment in question has been obtained against a foreigner, subject to the jurisdiction of the tribunal where it was pronounced, it is conclusive in bar of a new action in the French tribunals between the same parties. But the party who seeks to enforce it must bring a new suit upon it, in which the judgment is *primâ facie* evidence only, the defendant being permitted to contest the merits, and to show not only that it was irregularly obtained, but that it is unjust and illegal.[53]

[51] Knapp's Rep. in the Privy Council, vol. i. p. 274. Frankland *v.* M'Gusty. Barnwell and Adolphus' Rep. vol. ii. p. 757. Novelli *v.* Ross, vol, iii. p. 951. Becque *v.* M'Carthy.

[52] Cranch's Rep. vol. vii. pp. 481—484. Mills *v.* Duryee. Wheaton's Rep. vol. iii. p. 234. Hampton *v.* M'Connell.

[53] Code Civil, art. 2123, 2128. Code de Procédure Civil, art. 546. Pardessus, Droit Commercial, pt. vi. tit. 7, ch. 2, § 2, No. 1488. Merlin, Ré-

A decree of divorce, obtained in a foreign country by a Foreign
fraudulent evasion of the laws of the state to which the par- divorces.
ties belong, would seem, on principle, to be clearly void in
the country of their domicil where the marriage took place,
though valid under the laws of the country where the divorce
was obtained. Such are divorces obtained by parties going
into another country for the sole purpose of obtaining a dissolution of the nuptial contract for causes not allowed by the
laws of their own country, or where those laws do not permit a divorce à vinculo for any cause whatever. This subject has been thrown into almost inextricable confusion by the
contrariety of decisions between the tribunals of England and
Scotland, the courts of the former refusing to recognise divorces à vinculo pronounced by the Scottish tribunals between
English subjects who had not acquired a bonâ fide, permanent
domicil in Scotland; whilst the Scottish courts persist in granting such divorces in cases where, by the law of England, Ireland, and the colonies connected with the United Kingdom,
the authority of parliament alone is competent to dissolve the
marriage, so as to enable either party, during the lifetime of
the other, again to contract lawful wedlock.[54]

pertoire, tom. vi. tit. *Jugement.* Questions de Droit, tom. iii. tit. *Jugement.*
Toullier, Droit Civil Français, tom. x. Nos. 76—86.

[54] Dow's Parliament. Cases, vol. i. p. 117. Torey *v.* Lindsay; p. 124. Lol-
ly's case. See Fergusson's Reports of Decisions in the Consistorial Courts
of Scotland, *passim.*

CHAPTER III.

RIGHTS OF EQUALITY.

§ 1.
Natural
equality of
states mo-
dified by
compact
and usage.
THE natural equality of sovereign states may be modified by positive compact, or by consent implied from constant usage, so as to entitle one state to superiority over another in respect to certain external objects, such as rank, titles, and other ceremonial distinctions.

§ 2.
Royal ho-
nours.
Thus the international law of Europe has attributed to certain states what are called *royal honours*, which are actually enjoyed by every empire or kingdom in Europe, by the pope, the grand duchies in Germany, and the Germanic and Swiss confederations. They were also formerly conceded to the German empire, and to some of the great republics, such as the United Netherlands and Venice.

These *royal honours* entitle the states by whom they are possessed to precedence over all others who do not enjoy the same rank, with the exclusive right of sending to other states public ministers of the first rank, as ambassadors, together with certain other distinctive titles and ceremonies.[1]

§ 3.
Prece-
dence
among
princes
and states
enjoying
royal ho-
nours.
Among the princes who enjoy this rank, the Catholic powers concede the precedency to the pope, or sovereign pontiff; but Russia, and the Protestant states of Europe consider him as bishop of Rome only, and a sovereign prince in Italy, and such of them as enjoy royal honours refuse him the precedence.

The emperor of Germany, under the former constitution of the empire, was entitled to precedence over all other tem-

[1] Vattel, Droit des Gens, tom. i. liv. ii. ch. 3, § 38. Martens, Précis du Droit des Gens Moderne de l'Europe, liv. iii. ch. 2, § 129. Kluber, Droit des Gens Moderne, pt. ii. tit. 1 ch. 3, §§ 91, 92.

poral princes, as the supposed successor of Charlemagne and
of the Cæsars in the empire of the west; but since the dissolution of the late Germanic constitution, and the abdication
of the titles and prerogatives of its head by the emperor of
Austria, the precedence of this sovereign over other princes
of the same rank may be considered questionable.[2]

The various contests between crowned heads for precedence are matter of curious historical research, as illustrative
of European manners at different periods; but the practical
importance of these discussions has been greatly diminished
by the progress of civilization, which no longer permits the
serious interests of mankind to be sacrificed to such vain pretensions.

The text writers commonly assigned to what were called
the great republics, who were entitled to royal honours, a
rank inferior to crowned heads of that class; and the United
Netherlands, Venice, and Switzerland, certainly did formerly
yield the precedence to emperors and reigning kings, though
they contested it with the electors and other inferior princes
entitled to royal honours. But disputes of this sort have
commonly been determined by the relative power of the contending parties, rather than by any general rule derived from
the form of government. Cromwell knew how to make the
dignity and equality of the English commonwealth respected
by the crowned heads of Europe; and in the different treaties
between the French republic and other powers, it was expressly stipulated that the same ceremonial as to rank and
etiquette should be observed between them and France
which had subsisted before the revolution.[3]

Those monarchical sovereigns who are not crowned heads,
but who enjoy royal honours, concede the precedence on all
occasions to emperors and kings.

Monarchical sovereigns who do not enjoy royal honours
yield the precedence to those princes who are entitled to
these honours.

[2] Martens, § 132. Kluber, § 95.
[3] Treaty of Campio Formio, art. 23, and of Luneville, art. 17, with Austria. Treaties of Basle with Prussia and Spain.

Demi-sovereign or dependent states rank below sovereign states.[4]

These different points respecting the relative rank of sovereigns and states have never been determined by any positive regulation or international pact: they rest on usage and general acquiescence. An abortive attempt was made at the congress of Vienna to classify the different states of Europe, with a view to determine their relative rank. At the sitting of the 10th December, 1814, the plenipotentiaries of the eight powers who signed the treaty of peace at Paris named a committee to which this subject was referred. At the sitting of the 9th February, 1815, the report of the committee, which proposed to establish three classes of powers, relatively to the rank of their respective ministers, was discussed by the congress; but doubts having arisen respecting this classification, and especially as to the rank assigned to the great republics, the question was indefinitely postponed, and a regulation established determining the relative rank of the diplomatic agents of crowned heads.[5]

§ 4.
Usage of the *alternat.*

Where the rank between different states is equal or undetermined, different expedients have been resorted to for the purpose of avoiding a contest, and at the same time reserving the respective rights and pretensions of the parties. Among these is what is called the usage of the *alternat*, by which the rank and places of different powers is changed from time to time, either in a certain regular order, or one determined by lot. Thus, in drawing up public treaties and conventions, it is the usage of certain powers to *alternate*, both in the preamble and the signatures, so that each power occupies, in the copy intended to be delivered to it, the first place. The regulation of the congress of Vienna, above referred to, provided that in acts and treaties between those powers which admit the *alternat*, the order to be observed by the different ministers shall be determined by lot.[6]

[4] Kluber, § 98.
[5] Kluber, Acten des Wiener Congresses, tom. viii. pp. 98, 102, 108, 116.
[6] Annexe, xvii. à l'Acte du Congrès de Vienne, art. 7.

Another expedient which has frequently been adopted to avoid controversies respecting the order of signatures to treaties and other public acts, is that of signing in the order assigned by the *French* alphabet to the respective powers represented by their ministers.[7]

The primitive equality of nations authorizes each nation to make use of its own language in treating with others, and this right is still in a certain degree preserved in the practice of some states. But general convenience early suggested the use of the Latin language in the diplomatic intercourse between the different nations of Europe. Towards the end of the fifteenth century, the preponderance of Spain contributed to the general diffusion of the Castilian tongue as the ordinary medium of political correspondence. This, again, has been superseded by the language of France, which, since the age of Louis XIV., has become the almost universal diplomatic idiom of the civilized world. Those states which still retain the use of their national language in treaties and diplomatic correspondence usually annex to the papers transmitted by them a translation in the language of the opposite party, wherever it is understood that this comity will be reciprocated. Such is the usage of the Germanic confederation, of Spain, and the Italian courts. Those states which have a common language generally use it in their transactions with each other. Such is the case between the Germanic confederation and its different members, and between the respective members themselves ; between the different states of Italy ; and between Great Britain and the United States of America.

§ 5. Language used in diplomatic intercourse.

All sovereign princes or states may assume whatever titles of dignity they think fit, and may exact from their own subjects these marks of honour. But their recognition by other states is not a matter of strict right, especially in the case of

§ 6. Titles of sovereign princes and states,

[7] Kluber, Uebersicht der diplomatischen Verhandlungen des Wiener Congresses, § 164.

new titles of higher dignity assumed by sovereigns. Thus the royal title of King of Prussia, which was assumed by Frederick I. in 1701, was first acknowledged by the emperor of Germany, and subsequently by the other princes and states of Europe. It was not acknowledged by the Pope until the reign of Frederick William II. in 1786, and by the Teutonic knights until 1792, this once famous military order still retaining the shadow of its antiquated claims to the duchy of Prussia until that period.[8] So also the title of Emperor of all the Russias, which was taken by the Czar Peter the Great, in 1701, was successively acknowledged by Prussia, the United Netherlands, and Sweden in 1723, by Denmark in 1732, by Turkey in 1739, by the emperor and the empire in 1745-6, by France in 1745, by Spain in 1759, and by the republic of Poland in 1764. In the recognition of this title by France, a reservation of the right of precedence claimed by that crown was insisted on, and a stipulation entered into by Russia in the form of a *Réversale*, that this change of title should make no alteration in the ceremonies observed between the two courts. On the accession of the Empress Catherine II. in 1762, she refused to renew this stipulation in that form, but *declared* that the imperial title should make no change in the ceremonial observed between the two courts. This declaration was answered by the court of Versailles in a counter-declaration, renewing the recognition of that title, upon the express condition that if any alteration should be made by the court of St. Petersburg in the rules previously observed by the two courts as to rank and precedence, the French crown would resume its ancient style, and cease to give the title of Imperial to that of Russia.[9]

The title of emperor, from the historical associations with which it is connected, was formerly considered the most eminent and honourable among all sovereign titles; but it was never regarded by other crowned heads as conferring, except

[8] Ward's History of the Law of Nations, vol. ii. pp. 245—248. Kluber, Droit des Gens Moderne de l'Europe, pte. ii. tit. 1, ch. 2, § 107, note *c*.

[9] Flassan, Histoire de la Diplomatie Française, tom. vi. liv. iii. pp. 329—364.

in the single case of the emperor of Germany, any prerogative or precedence over those princes.

The usage of nations has established certain maritime ce-
remonials to be observed, either on the ocean or those parts
of the sea over which a sort of supremacy is claimed by a
particular state.

§ 7.
Maritime
ceremo-
nials.

Among these is the salute by striking the flag or the sails,
or by firing a certain number of guns, on approaching a fleet
or ship of war, or entering a fortified port or harbour.

Every sovereign state has the exclusive right, in virtue of
its independence and equality, to regulate the maritime ceremonial to be observed by its own vessels, towards each other,
or towards those of another nation, on the high seas, or
within its own territorial jurisdiction. It has a similar right
to regulate the ceremonial to be observed within its own exclusive jurisdiction by the vessels of all nations, as well with
respect to each other, as towards its own fortresses and ships
of war, and the reciprocal honours to be rendered by the
latter to foreign ships. These regulations are established
either by its own municipal ordinances, or by reciprocal treaties with other maritime powers.[10]

Where the dominion claimed by the state is contested by
foreign nations, as in the case of Great Britain in the Narrow Seas, the maritime honours to be rendered by its flag
are also the subject of contention. The disputes on this subject have not unfrequently formed the motives or pretexts for
war between the powers asserting these pretensions and those
by whom they were resisted. The maritime honours required by Denmark, in consequence of the supremacy claimed
by that power over the Sound and Belts, at the entrance of
the Baltic Sea, have been regulated and modified by different treaties with other states, and especially by the convention of the 15th of January, 1829, between Russia and Denmark, suppressing most of the formalities required by former

[10] Bynkershoek, de Dominio Maris, cap. 2, 4. Martens, Précis du Droit
des Gens Moderne de l'Europe, liv. iv. ch. 4, § 159. Kluber, Droit des
Gens Moderne de l'Europe, pte. ii. tit. 1, ch. 3, §§ 117—122.

treaties. This convention is to continue in force until a
general regulation shall be established among all the maritime powers of Europe, according to the protocol of the Congress of Aix la Chapelle, signed on the 9th November, 1818,
by the terms of which it was agreed by the ministers of the
five great powers, Austria, France, Great Britain, Prussia,
and Russia, that the existing regulations observed by them
should be referred to the ministerial conferences at London,
and that the other maritime powers should be invited to communicate their views of the subject in order to form some
such general regulation.[11]

[11] J. H. W. Schlegel, Staats Recht des Konigreichs Dänemark, 1 Theil,
p. 412. Martens, Nouveau Recueil, tom. viii. p. 73.

CHAPTER IV.

RIGHTS OF PROPERTY.

THE exclusive right of every independent state to its terri- §1. tory and other property is founded upon the title originally National acquired by occupancy, and subsequently confirmed by the tary rights. presumption arising from the lapse of time, or by treaties and other compacts with foreign states.

The things belonging to the nation include its public pro- §2. perty or domain, and those things belonging to private indi- Property of the viduals or bodies corporate within the territory. state.

This national proprietary right, so far as it excludes that §3. of other nations, is *absolute*; but in respect to the members of domain. the state it is *paramount* only, and forms what is called the eminent domain.[1]

The writers on natural law have questioned how far that §4. peculiar species of presumption arising from the lapse of time tion. which is called *prescription* is justly applicable as between nation and nation; but the constant and approved practice of nations shows that, by whatever name it be called, the uninterrupted possession of territory or other property, for a certain length of time, by one state, excludes the claim of every other, in the same manner as by the law of nature and the municipal code of every civilized nation, a similar posses- sion by an individual excludes the claim of every other per- son to the article of property in question. This rule is founded upon the supposition, confirmed by constant experience, that

[1] Vattel, Droit des Gens, liv. i. ch. 20, §§ 235, 244.   Rutherforth's Inst. of Natural Law, vol. ii. ch. 9, § 6.

every person will naturally seek to enjoy that which belongs
to him, and the inference fairly to be drawn from his silence
and neglect, of the original defect of his title or his intention
to relinquish it.[2]

§ 5.
Conquest
and disco-
very con-
firmed by
compact
and the
lapse of
time.

The title of almost all the nations of Europe to the territory now possessed by them in that quarter of the world was
originally derived from conquest, which has been subsequently confirmed by international compacts to which all the
European states have successively become parties. Their
claim to the possessions held by them in the New World discovered by Columbus and other adventurers, and to the
territories which they have acquired on the continents and
islands of Africa and Asia, was originally derived from discovery or conquest and colonization, and has since been confirmed in the same manner by positive compact. Independently of these sources of title, the general consent of mankind
has established the principle that long and uninterrupted
possession by one nation excludes the claim of every other.
Whether this general consent be considered as an implied
contract or as positive law, all nations are equally bound by
it, since all are parties to it ; since none can safely disregard
it without impugning its own title to its possessions ; and
since it is founded upon mutual utility, and tends to promote
the general welfare of mankind.

The Spaniards and Portuguese took the lead among the
nations of Europe in the splendid maritime discoveries in the
East and the West, during the fifteenth and sixteenth centuries. According to the European ideas of that age, the heathen nations of the other quarters of the globe were the lawful spoil and prey of their civilized conquerors, and as between the Christian powers themselves, the Sovereign Pontiff was the supreme arbiter of conflicting claims. Hence
the famous bull issued by Pope Alexander VI. in 1493, by
which he granted to the united crowns of Castille and Arra-

[2] Grotius, de Jur. Bel. ac Pac. lib. ii. cap. 4. Puffendorf, Jus Naturæ et
Gentium, lib. iv. cap. 12. Vattel, Droit des Gens, tom. i. liv. ii. ch. 11.
Rutherforth's Inst. of Natural Law, vol. i. ch. 8, vol. ii. ch. 9, §§ 3, 6.

gon all lands discovered, and to be discovered, beyond a line drawn from pole to pole, one hundred leagues west from the Azores, or Western Islands, under which Spain has since claimed to exclude all other European nations from the possession and use, not only of the lands, but of the seas, in the New World west of that line. Independent of this papal grant, the right of prior discovery was the foundation upon which the different European nations, by whom conquests and settlements were successively made on the American continent, rested their respective claims to appropriate its territory to the exclusive use of each nation. Even Spain did not found her pretensions solely on the papal grant. Portugal asserted a title derived from discovery and conquest to a portion of South America, taking care to keep to the eastward of the line traced by the Pope, by which the globe seemed to be divided between these two great monarchies. On the other hand, Great Britain, France, and Holland, disregarded the pretended authority of the papal see, and pushed their discoveries, conquests, and settlements, both in the East and the West Indies, until conflicting with the paramount claims of Spain and Portugal, they produced bloody and destructive wars between the different maritime powers of Europe. But there was one thing in which they all agreed, that of almost entirely disregarding the right of the native inhabitants of these regions. Thus the bull of Pope Alexander VI. reserved from the grant to Spain, all lands which had been previously occupied by any other *Christian* nation: and the patent granted by Henry VII. of England to John Cabot and his sons authorized them " to seek out and discover all islands, regions, and provinces whatsoever that may belong to heathens and infidels," and " to subdue, occupy, and possess these territories, as his vassals and lieutenants." In the same manner the grant from Queen Elizabeth to Sir Humphrey Gilbert empowers him to " discover such remote heathen and barbarous lands, countries, and territories, not actually possessed of any Christian prince or people, and to hold, occupy, and enjoy the same with all their commodities, jurisdictions, and royalties." It thus became a maxim of policy and of law that the right of the native Indians was subordinate to that of the first Christian discoverer, whose paramount claim excluded that of every other civilized nation, and gradually extinguished that of the natives. In the various wars, treaties, and negotiations, to which the conflicting pretensions of the different states of Christendom to territory on the American continent have given rise, the primitive title of the Indians has been entirely overlooked, or left to be disposed of by the states within whose limits they happened to fall by the stipulations of the treaties between the different European powers. Their title has thus been almost entirely extinguished by force of arms, or by voluntary compact, as the progress of cultivation gràdually compelled the savage tenant of the forest to yield to the superior power and skill of his civilized invader.

Dispute between Great Britain and Spain relating to Nootka Sound.

In the dispute which took place in 1790, between Great Britain and Spain, relative to Nootka Sound, the latter claimed all the north-western coast of America as far north as Prince William's Sound, in latitude 61°, upon the ground of prior discovery and long possession, confirmed by the eighth article of the treaty of Utrecht, referring to the state of possession in the time of his Catholic Majesty Charles II. This claim was contested by the British government, upon the principle that the earth is the common inheritance of mankind, of which each individual and each nation has a right to appropriate a share by occupancy and cultivation. This dispute was terminated by a convention between the two powers, stipulating that their respective subjects should not be disturbed in their navigation and fisheries in the Pacific Ocean or the South Seas, or in landing on the coasts of those seas, not already occupied, for the purpose of carrying on their commerce with the natives of the country, or of making setttlements there, subject to the following provisions:—

1. That the British navigation and fishery should not be made the pretext for illicit trade with the Spanish settlements, and that British subjects should not navigate or fish within the space of ten marine leagues from any part of the coasts already occupied by Spain.

2. That with respect to the eastern and western coasts of South America and the adjacent islands, no settlement should be formed thereafter by the respective subjects in such parts of those coasts as are situated to the south of those parts of the same coasts, and of the adjacent islands already occupied by Spain; provided that the respective subjects should retain the liberty of landing on the coasts and islands so situated, for the purposes of their fishery, and of erecting huts and other temporary buildings, for those purposes only.[3]

By a ukase of the emperor Alexander of Russia, of the 4-16th September, 1821, an exclusive territorial right on the north-west coast of America was asserted as belonging to the Russian empire, from Behring's Straits to the 51st degree of north latitude, and in the Aleutian islands, on the east coast of Siberia, and the Kurile islands from the same straits to the South Cape in the island of Ooroop, in 45°. 51' north latitude. The navigation and fishery of all other nations was prohibited in the islands, ports, and gulfs within the above limits; and every foreign vessel was forbidden to touch at any of the Russian establishments above enumerated, or even to approach them within a less distance than 100 Italian miles, under penalty of confiscation of the cargo. The proprietary rights of Russia to the extent of the north-west coast of America specified in this decree, were rested upon the three bases said to be required by the general law of nations and immemorial usage:—that is, upon the title of first discovery; upon the title of first occupation; and, in the last place, upon that which results from a peaceable and uncontested possession of more than half a century. It was added that the extent of sea, of which the Russian possessions on the continents of Asia and America form the limits, comprehended all the conditions which were ordinarily attached to shut seas (mers fermées;) and the Russian government might consequently deem itself authorized to exercise upon this sea the right of sovereignty, and especially that of entirely interdicting the entrance of foreigners. But

Conven- tion be- tween the United States and Russia re- specting the North- western Coast of America.

[3] Annual Register for 1790, (State Papers,) pp. 285—305; 1791, pp. 208—214, 222—227.

it preferred only asserting its essential rights by measures adapted to prevent contraband trade within the chartered limits of the American Russian Company.

All these grounds were contested, in point of fact as well as right, by the government of the United States, and the question became the subject of negotiation between the two countries.

This negotiation was terminated by a convention signed at Petersburgh on the 5-17th of April, 1824, in which it was stipulated that the citizens and subjects of the two powers should not be disturbed in their navigation and fishery, or in the faculty of resorting to the coasts, upon points not already occupied, in any part of the Pacific Ocean, subject to the following conditions:—

1. That the citizens or subjects of the two powers should not resort to any point where the other has an establishment, without special permission.

2. That neither the government nor citizens of the United States should form any establishment upon the north-west coast of America, or any of the adjacent islands *to the north* of 54 degrees and 40 minutes of north latitude; nor should the Russian government or subjects form any establishment *south* of the same parallel. But the ships of both powers, or those belonging to their citizens or subjects, may frequent the interior seas, gulfs, harbours, and creeks upon the coast, for the purpose of fishing and trading with the natives, excepting in spirituous liquors, fire-arms, other arms, and munitions of war of every description.[4]

§ 6.
Maritime
territorial
jurisdic-
tion.

The maritime territory of every state extends to the ports, harbours, bays, mouths of rivers, and adjacent parts of the sea enclosed by headlands belonging to the same state. The general usage of nations superadds to this extent of territorial jurisdiction a distance of a marine league, or as far as a cannon-shot will reach from the shore, along all the coasts of the state. Within these limits, its rights of property

[4] Annual Register, vol. lxiv. pp. 576—584. Correspondence between M. de Poletica and Mr. Adams.

and territorial jurisdiction are absolute, and exclude those of every other nation.[5]

The term " coasts" includes the natural appendages of the territory which rise out of the water, although these islands are not of sufficient firmness to be inhabited or fortified; but it does not properly comprehend all the shoals which form sunken continuations of the land perpetually covered with water. The rule of law on this subject is *terræ dominium finitur, ubi finitur armorum vis;* and since the introduction of fire-arms, that distance has usually been recognised to be about three miles from the shore. In a case before Sir W. Scott (Lord Stowell) respecting the legality of a capture alleged to be made within the neutral territory of the United States, at the mouth of the river Mississippi, a question arose as to what was to be deemed the shore, since there are a number of little mud islands, composed of earth and trees drifted down by the river, which form a kind of portico to the main land. It was contended that these were not to be considered as any part of the American territory—that there were a sort of " no man's land," not of consistency enough to support the purposes of life, uninhabited, and resorted to only for shooting and taking birds' nests. It was argued that the line of territory was to be taken only from the Balise, which is a fort raised on made land by the former Spanish possessors. But the learned judge was of a different opinion, and determined that the protection of the territory was to be reckoned from these islands, and that they are the natural appendages of the coast on which they border, and from which indeed they were formed. Their elements were derived immediately from the territory, and on the principle of alluvium and increment, on which so much is to be found in the books of law, *Quod vis fluminis de tuo prædio detraxerit, et vicino prædio at-*

§ 7.
Extent of the term *coasts* or *shore.*

---

[5] Grotius, de Jur. Bel. ac Pac. lib. ii. cap. 3, § x. Bynkershoek, Quæst. Jur. Pub. lib. i. cap. 8. De Dominio Maris, cap. 2. Vattel, liv. i. ch. 23, § 289. Valin, Comm. sur l'Ordonnance de la Marine, liv. v. tit. 1. Azuni, Diritto Marit. pt. i. cap. 2, art. 3, § 15. Galiani, dei Doveri dei Principi Neutrali in Tempo di Guerra, liv. i. Life and Works of Sir L. Jenkins, vol. ii. p. 780.

tulerit, palam tuum remanet, even if it had been carried over to an adjoining territory. Whether they were composed of earth or solid rock would not vary the right of dominion, for the right of dominion does not depend upon the texture of the soil.[6]

The King's Chambers. The exclusive territorial jurisdiction of the British crown over the enclosed parts of the sea along the coasts of the island of Great Britain has immemorially extended to those bays called the *King's Chambers; i. e.* portions of the sea cut off by lines drawn from one promontory to another. A similar jurisdiction is also asserted by the United States over the Delaware Bay and other bays and estuaries forming portions of their territory. It appears from Sir Leoline Jenkins, that both in the reigns of James I. and of Charles II. the security of British commerce was provided for by express prohibitions against the roving or hovering of foreign ships of war so near the neutral coasts and harbours of Great Britain as to disturb or threaten vessels homeward or outward bound; and that captures by such foreign cruisers, even of their enemies' vessels, would be restored by the Court of Admiralty if made within the King's Chambers. So also the British "hovering act," passed in 1736, (9 Geo. II. cap. 35,) assumes, for certain revenue purposes, a jurisdiction of four leagues from the coasts, by prohibiting foreign goods to be transshipped within that distance without payment of duties. A similar provision is contained in the revenue laws of the United States; and both these provisions have been declared by judicial authority, in each country, to be consistent with the law and usage of nations.[7]

§ 8. Claim to contiguous portions of Such regulations can only be justified on the ground of their being essentially necessary to the security and interests of the state. They are not intended to assert an exclu-

---

[6] Robinson's Adm. Reports, vol. v. p. 385 (*c.*) The Anna.

[7] Life and Works of Sir. L. Jenkins, vol. ii. pp. 727, 728, 780. Opinion of the United States Attorney-General on the capture of the British ship Grange in the Delaware Bay, 1793. Waite's American State Papers, vol. i. p. 75. Dodson's Adm. Reports, vol. ii. p. 245. Le Louis Cranch's Reports, vol. ii. p. 187. Church *v.* Hubbard. Vattel, Droit des Gens, liv. i. ch. 22, § 288.

sive right of sovereignty and domain over such extensive the sea for special portions of the sea. Even a claim to contiguous portions is purposes. not to be viewed with much indulgence, it is to be strictly construed, and clearly made out. " It is," says Sir *W. Scott*, " a claim of private and exclusive property, over a subject where a general, or at least a common, use is to be presumed ; it is a claim which can only arise on portions of the sea, or on rivers flowing through different states. In the sea, out of the reach of common shot, universal use is presumed : in rivers flowing through conterminous states, a common use to the different states is presumed. Yet, in both of these, there may, by legal possibility, exist a peculiar property, excluding the universal or the common use. Portions of the sea are prescribed for ; so are rivers flowing through contiguous states : the banks on one side may have been first settled, by which the possession and property may have been acquired, or cessions may have taken place upon conquests or other events. But the general presumption certainly bears strongly against such exclusive rights, and the title is a matter to be established on the part of those claiming under it, in the same manner as all other legal demands are to be substantiated,—by clear and competent evidence."[8]

Besides those bays, gulfs, straits, mouths of rivers, and § 9. estuaries which are enclosed by capes and headlands belong- Claims to portions of ing to the territory of the state, a jurisdiction and right of the sea upon the property over certain other portions of the sea have been ground of claimed by different nations, on the ground of immemorial prescrip- use. Such, for example, was the sovereignty formerly tion. claimed by the republic of Venice over the Adriatic. The maritime supremacy claimed by Great Britain over what are called the Narrow Seas has generally been asserted merely by requiring certain honours to the British flag in those seas, which have been rendered or refused by other nations according to circumstances, but the claim itself has never been sanctioned by general acquiescence.[9]

[8] Robinson's Adm. Reports, vol. iii. p. 339. The Twee Gebroeders.

[9] Vattel, Droit des Gens, liv. i. ch. 23, § 289. Martens, Précis du Droit des

The Black Sea.

So long as the shores of the Black Sea were exclusively possessed by Turkey, that sea might with propriety be considered as *mare clausum;* and there seems no reason to question the right of the Ottoman Porte to exclude other nations from navigating the passage which connects it with the Mediterranean, both shores of this passage being at the same time portions of the Turkish territory ; but since the territorial acquisitions made by Russia, and the commercial establishments formed by her on the shores of the Euxine, both that empire and other maritime powers have become entitled to participate in the commerce of the Black Sea, and consequently to the free navigation of the Dardanelles and the Bosphorus. This right was expressly recognised by the seventh article of the treaty of Adrianople, concluded in 1829, between Russia and the Porte, both as to Russian vessels and those of other European states in amity with Turkey.[10]

By the 12th article of the treaty of peace concluded on the 5th of January, 1809, between Great Britain and the Porte, it is declared that as it had " been at all times prohibited to vessels of war to enter the canal of Constantinople, that is to say in the Strait of the Dardanelles, and in that of the Black Sea ; and as this ancient rule of the Ottoman Empire ought in like manner to be observed in future in time of peace towards every power whatsoever, the British court promises also to conform itself to this principle."

By the treaty of alliance concluded on the 8th July, 1833, at Hoonkiar Skelessi, between Russia and Turkey, it was stipulated in favour of Russia that the Porte should shut the Dardanelles on the side of the Mediterranean against foreign armed vessels in time of war. Some complaint has been made of the partial effect of this stipulation in its operation as against other powers ; but as the *casus fœderis* only applies to a state of war, no practical question can arise respecting it until some power at war with Russia attempts to force the passage of the Dardanelles.

Gens Moderne de l'Europe, liv. ii. ch. 1, § 42.   Edinburgh Review, vol. xi. art. 1, pp. 17—19.

[10] Martens, Nouveau Recueil; tom. viii. p. 143.

The supremacy asserted by the king of Denmark over the Baltic Sea. Sound and the two belts which form the outlet of the Baltic Sea into the ocean, is rested by the Danish publicists upon immemorial prescription, sanctioned by a long succession of treaties with other powers. According to these writers, the Danish claim of sovereignty has been exercised from the earliest times beneficially for the protection of commerce against pirates and other enemies by means of guard-ships, and against the perils of the seas by the establishment of lights and land-marks. The Danes continued for several centuries masters of the coasts on both sides of the Sound, the province of Scania not having been ceded to Sweden until the treaty of Roeskild in 1658, confirmed by that of 1660, in which it was stipulated that Sweden should never lay claim to the Sound tolls in consequence of the cession, but should content herself with a compensation for keeping up the light-houses on the coast of Scania. The exclusive right of Denmark was recognised as early as 1368, by a treaty with the Hanseatic republics, and by that of 1490 with Henry VII. of England, which forbids English vessels from passing the Great Belt as well as the Sound, unless in case of unavoidable necessity; in which case they were to pay the same duties at Wyborg as if they had passed the Sound at Elsinore. The treaty concluded at Spires in 1544, with the emperor Charles V., which has commonly been referred to as the origin, or at least the first recognition, of the Danish claim to the Sound tolls, merely stipulates, in general terms, that the merchants of the Low Countries frequenting the ports of Denmark should pay the same duties as formerly. The rates of the tariff were first definitely ascertained by the treaty of Christianopel, in 1645, with the Dutch, and this has since served as the standard for the duties payable by other nations *privileged* by treaty. Those not privileged pay according to a more ancient tariff on the specified articles, and one and a quarter per cent. on unspecified articles.[11]

[11] Schlegel, Staats-Recht des Königreichs Danemark, 1 Theil, cap. 7, §§ 27—29.

Qu. Whe-
ther the
Baltic Sea
is *mare*
clausum?

The Baltic Sea is considered by the maritime powers bordering on its coasts as *mare clausum* against the exercise of
hostilities upon its waters by other powers whilst the Baltic
powers are at peace. This principle was proclaimed in the
treaties of armed neutrality in 1780 and 1800, and by the
treaty of 1794 between Denmark and Sweden, guarantying
the tranquillity of that sea. In the Russian declaration of
war against Great Britain of 1807, the inviolability of that
sea and the reciprocal guarantees of the powers that border
upon it (guarantees said to have been contracted with the
knowledge of the British government) were stated as aggra-
vations of the British proceedings in entering the Sound and
attacking the Danish capital in that year. In the British
answer to this declaration, it was denied that Great Britain
had at any time acquiesced in the principles upon which the
inviolability of the Baltic is maintained; however she might,
at particular periods, have forborne, for special reasons in-
fluencing her conduct at the time, to act in contradiction to
them. Such forbearance never could have applied but to a
state of peace and real neutrality in the north; and she could
not be expected to recur to it after France had been suffered,
by the conquest of Prussia, to establish herself in full sovereignty along the whole coast, from Dantzic to Lubeck.[12]

§ 10.
Controver-
sy respect-
ing the do-
minion of
the seas.

The controversy how far the open sea or main ocean, beyond the immediate vicinity of the coasts, may be appropriated by one nation to the exclusion of others, which once
exercised the pens of the ablest European jurists, can hardly
be considered open at this day. *Grotius*, in his treatise on
the Law of Peace and War, hardly admits more than the
possibility of appropriating the waters immediately contiguous, though he adduces a number of quotations from ancient
authors, showing that a broader pretension has been sometimes sanctioned by usage and opinion. But he never intimates that any thing more than a limited portion could be
thus claimed; and he uniformly speaks of " *pars*," or " *portus*

[12] Annual Register, vol. xlix. (State Papers,) p. 773.

muris," always confining his view to the effect of the neighbouring land in giving a jurisdiction and property of this sort.[13] He had previously taken the lead in maintaining the common right of mankind to the free navigation, commerce, and fisheries of the Atlantic and Pacific Oceans, against the exclusive claims of Spain and Portugal, founded on the right of previous discovery, confirmed by possession and the papal grants. The treatise *De Mare Libero* was published in 1609. The claim of sovereignty asserted by the kings of England over the British seas was supported by *Albericus Gentilis,* in his *Advocatio Hispanica,* in 1613. In 1635, *Selden* published his *Mare Clausum,* in which the general principles maintained by Grotius are called in question, and the claim of England more fully vindicated than by Gentilis. The first book of Selden's celebrated treatise is devoted to the proposition that the sea may be made property, which he attempts to show, not by reasoning, but by collecting a multitude of quotations from ancient authors, in the style of Grotius, but with much less selection. He no where grapples with the arguments by which such a vague and extensive dominion is shown to be repugnant to the law of nations. And in the second part, which indeed is the main object of his work, he has recourse only to proofs of usage and of positive compact, in order to show that Great Britain is entitled to the sovereignty of what are called the *Narrow Seas.*[14] Father *Paul Sarpi,* the celebrated historian of the council of Trent, also wrote a vindication of the claim of the republic of Venice to the sovereignty of the Adriatic.[15] *Bynkershoek* examined the general question, in the earliest of his published works, with the vigour and acumen which distinguish all his writings. He admits that certain portions of the sea may be susceptible of exclusive dominion, though he denies the claim of the English crown to the British seas on the ground of the want of uninterrupted possession. He asserts that there was

[13] De Jur. Bel. ac Pac. lib. ii. cap. 3, §§ 8—13.

[14] Edinburgh Review, vol. xi. art. 1, p. 16.

[15] Paola Sarpi, Del Dominio del Mare Adriatico e sue Reggioni per il *Jus Belli* della Serenissima Rep. de Venezia, *Venet.* 1676, 12°.

no instance, at the time when he wrote, in which the sea
was subject to any particular sovereign, where the surrounding territory did not belong to him.[16]   *Puffendorf* lays it down,
that in a narrow sea the dominion belongs to the sovereigns
of the surrounding land, and is distributed, where there are
several such sovereigns, according to the rules applicable to
neighbouring proprietors on a lake or river, supposing no
compact has been made, " as is pretended," he says, " by
Great Britain ;" but he expresses himself with a sort of in-
dignation at the idea that the main ocean can ever be appropriated.[17]   The authority of *Vattel* would be full and explicit
to the same purpose, were it not weakened by the concession, that though the exclusive right of navigation or fishery in the sea cannot be claimed by one nation on the ground
of immemorial use, nor lost to others by non-user, on the
principle of prescription, yet it may be thus established where
the non-user assumes the nature of a consent or tacit agreement, and thus becomes a title in favour of one nation against
another.[18]

§ 11.
Rivers
forming
part of the
territory of
the state.

The territory of the state includes the lakes, seas, and
rivers entirely enclosed within its limits. The rivers which
flow through the territory also form a part of the domain,
from their sources to their mouths, or as far as they flow
within the territory, including the bays or estuaries formed
by their junction with the sea. Where a navigable river
forms the boundary of conterminous states, the middle of the
channel, or *Thalweg*, is generally taken as the line of separation between the two states, the presumption of law being
that the right of navigation is common to both ; but this presumption may be destroyed by actual proof of prior occupancy, and long undisturbed possession giving to one of the
riparian proprietors the exclusive title to the entire river.[19]

16 De Dominio Maris, Opera Minora, Dissert. V. first published in 1702.
17 De Jure Naturæ et Gentium, lib. iv. cap. 5, § 7.
18 Droit des Gens, liv. i. ch. 23, §§ 279—286.
19 Vattel, Droit des Gens, liv. i. ch. 22, § 266. Martens, Précis du Droit
des Gens Moderne de l'Europe, liv. ii. ch. 1, § 39.

Things of which the use is inexhaustible, such as the sea and running water, cannot be so appropriated as to exclude others from using these elements in any manner which does not occasion a loss or inconvenience to the proprietor. This is what is called an *innocent use.* Thus we have seen that the jurisdiction possessed by one nation over sounds, straits, and other arms of the sea, leading through its own territory to that of another, or to other seas common to all nations, does not exclude others from the right of innocent passage through these communications. The same principle is applicable to rivers flowing from one state through the territory of another into the sea, or into the territory of a third state. The right of navigating, for commercial purposes, a river which flows through the territories of different states, is common to all the nations inhabiting the different parts of its banks; but this right of innocent passage being what the text writers call an *imperfect right,* its exercise is necessarily modified by the safety and convenience of the state affected by it, and can only be effectually secured by mutual convention regulating the mode of its exercise.[20]

§ 12. Right of innocent passage on rivers flowing through different states.

It seems that this right draws after it the incidental right of using all the means which are necessary to the secure enjoyment of the principal right itself. Thus the Roman law, which considered navigable rivers as public or common property, declared that the right to the use of the shores was incident to that of the water; and that the right to navigate a river involved the right to moor vessels to its banks, to lade and unlade cargoes, &c. The publicists apply this principle of the Roman civil law to the same case between nations, and infer the right to use the adjacent land for these purposes as means necessary to the attainment of the end for which the free navigation of the water is permitted.[21]

§ 13. Incidental right to use the banks of the rivers.

[20] Grotius, de Jur. Bel. ac Pac lib. ii. cap. 2, §§ 12—14; cap. 3, §§ 7—12. Vattel, Droit des Gens, liv. ii. ch. 9, §§ 126—130; ch. 10, §§ 132—134 Puffendorf, de Jur. Naturæ et Gentium, lib. iii. cap. 3, §§ 3—6.

[21] Grotius, de Jur. Bel. ac Pac. lib. ii. cap. 2, § 15. Puffendorf, de Jur. Naturæ et Gentium, lib. iii. cap. 3, § 8. Vattel, Droit des Gens, liv. ii. ch. 9, § 129.

§ 14.
These
rights *im-*
perfect in
their na-
ture.

The incidental right, like the principal right itself, is im-perfect in its nature, and the mutual convenience of both parties must be consulted in its exercise.

§ 15.
Modifica-
tion of
the serights
by com-
pact.

Those who are interested in the enjoyment of these rights may renounce them entirely, or consent to modify them in such manner as mutual convenience and policy may dictate. A remarkable instance of such a renunciation is found in the treaty of Westphalia, confirmed by subsequent treaties, by which the navigation of the river Scheldt was closed to the Belgic provinces, in favour of the Dutch. The forcible open-ing of this navigation by the French on the occupation of Bel-gium by the arms of the French Republic in 1792, in viola-tion of these treaties, was one of the principal ostensible causes of the war between France on one side, and Great Britain and Holland on the other. By the treaties of Vienna, the Belgic provinces were united to Holland, under the same sovereign, and the navigation of the Scheldt was placed on the same footing of freedom with that of the Rhine and other great European rivers.

§ 16.
Treaties of
Vienna re-
specting
the great
European
rivers.

By the treaty of Vienna in 1815, the commercial naviga-tion of rivers, which separate different states, or flow through their respective territories, was declared to be entirely free in their whole course, from the point where each river be-comes navigable to its mouth; provided that the regulations relating to the police of the navigation should be observed, which regulations were to be uniform, and as favourable as possible to the commerce of all nations.[22]

By the *Annexe* xvi. to the final act of the congress of Vi-enna, the free navigation of the Rhine is confirmed " in its whole course, from the point where it becomes navigable to the sea, ascending or descending;" and detailed regulations are provided respecting the navigation of that river, and the Neckar, the Mayn, the Moselle, the Meuse, and the Scheldt, which are declared in like manner to be free from the point

[22] Acte Final du Congrès de Vienne, art. 14, 96, 109.

where each of these rivers becomes navigable to its mouth. Similar regulations respecting the free navigation of the Elbe were established among the powers interested in the commerce of that river, by an act signed at Dresden the 12th December, 1821. And the stipulations between the different powers interested in the free navigation of the Vistula and other rivers of ancient Poland contained in the treaty of the 3d May, 1815, between Austria and Russia, and of the same date between Russia and Prussia, to which last Austria subsequently acceded, are confirmed by the final act of the congress of Vienna. The same treaty also extends the general principles adopted by the congress relating to the navigation of rivers to that of the Po.[23]

The interpretation of these stipulations respecting the free navigation of the Rhine gave rise to a controversy between the kingdom of the Netherlands and the other states interested in the commerce of that river. The Dutch government claimed the exclusive right of regulating and imposing duties upon the trade, within its own territory, at the places where the different branches into which the Rhine divides itself fall into the sea. The expression in the treaties of Paris and Vienna "*jusqu' à la mer*," to the sea, was said to be different in its import from the term " into the sea :" and besides, it was added, if the upper states insist so strictly upon the terms of the treaties, they must be contented with the course of the proper Rhine itself. The mass of waters brought down by that river, dividing itself a short distance above Nimiguen, is carried to the sea through three principal channels, the *Waal*, the *Leck*, and the *Yssel :* the first descending by Gorcum, where it changes its name for that of the *Meuse ;* the second approaching the sea at Rotterdam ; and the third, taking a northerly course by Zutphen and Deventer, empties itself into Zuyderzee. None of these channels, however, is called the Rhine ; that name is preserved to a small stream which leaves the Leck at Wyck, takes its course by the

§ 17. Navigation of the Rhine.

[23] Mayer, Corpus Juris Germanici, tom. ii. p. 224—239, 298. Acte Final, art. 14, 118, 96.

learned retreats of Utrecht and Leyden, gradually dispersing
and losing its waters among the sandy downs at Kulwyck.
The proper Rhine being thus useless for the purposes of
navigation, the Leck was substituted for it by common consent of the powers interested in the question; and the government of the Netherlands afterwards consented that the Waal,
as being better adapted to the purposes of navigation, should
be substituted for the Leck. But it was insisted by that
government that the Waal terminates at Gorcum, to which
the tide ascends, and where consequently the Rhine terminates; all that remains of that branch of the river from Gorcum to Helvoetsluys and the mouth of the Meuse is an arm
of the sea, enclosed within the territory of the kingdom, and
consequently subject to any regulations which its government
may think fit to establish.

On the other side, it was contended by the powers interested in the navigation of the river, that the stipulations in
the treaty of Paris in 1814, by which the sovereignty of the
House of Orange over Holland was revived, with an accession of territory, and the navigation of the Rhine was, at the
same time, declared to be free, " from the point where it becomes navigable to the sea," were inseparably connected in
the intentions of the allied powers who were parties to the
treaty. The intentions thus disclosed were afterwards carried into effect by the congress of Vienna, which determined
the union of Belgium to Holland, and confirmed the freedom
of navigation of the Rhine, as a condition annexed to this
augmentation of territory which had been accepted by the
government of the Netherlands. The right to the free navigation of the river, it was said, draws after it, by necessary
implication, the innocent use of the different waters which
unite it with the sea; and the expression " to the sea" was in
this respect equivalent to the term " into the sea," since the
pretension of the Netherlands to levy unlimited duties upon
its principal passages into the sea would render wholly useless
to other states the privilege of navigating the river within
the Dutch territory.[24]

[24] Annual Register for 1826, vol. lxviii. p. 259—263.

After a long and tedious negotiation, this question was finally settled by the convention concluded at Mayence the 31st of March, 1831, between all the ripuarian states of the Rhine, by which the navigation of the river was declared free from the point where it becomes navigable into the sea, (*bis in die See,*) including its two principal outlets or mouths in the kingdom of the Netherlands, the *Leck* and the *Waal,* passing by Rotterdam and Briel through the first-named watercourse, and by Dortrecht and Helvoetsluys through the latter, with the use of the artificial communication by the canal of Voorne with Helvoetsluys. By the terms of this treaty, the government of the Netherlands stipulates, in case the passages by the main sea by Briel or Helvoetsluys should at any time become innavigable, through natural or artificial causes, to indicate other watercourses for the navigation and commerce of the ripuarian states, equal in convenience to those which may be open to the navigation and commerce of its own subjects. The convention also provides minute regulations of police and fixed toll-duties on vessels and merchandise passing through the Netherlands territory to or from the sea, and also by the different ports of the upper ripuarian states on the Rhine.[25]

§ 18. Navigation of the Mississippi.

By the treaty of peace concluded at Paris in 1763, between France, Spain, and Great Britain, the province of Canada was ceded to Great Britain by France, and that of Florida to the same power by Spain, and the boundary between the French and British possessions in North America was ascertained by a line drawn through the middle of the river Mississippi from its source to the Iberville, and from thence through the latter river and the lakes Maurepas and Pontchartrain to the sea. The right of navigating the Mississippi was at the same time secured to the subjects of Great Britain from its source to the sea, and the passages in and out of its mouth, without being stopped or visited, or the payment of any duty whatsoever. The province of Louisiana was soon afterwards ceded by France to Spain; and by the

[25] Martens, Nouveau Recueil, tom. ix. p. 252.

treaty of Paris, 1783, Florida was retroceded to Spain by
Great Britain. The independence of the United States was
acknowledged, and the right of navigating the Mississippi was
secured to the citizens of the United States and the subjects
of Great Britain by the separate treaty between these powers.
But Spain having become thus possessed of both banks of the
Mississippi at its mouth, and a considerable distance above
its mouth, claimed its exclusive navigation below the point
where the southern boundary of the United States struck the
river. This claim was resisted, and the right to participate
in the navigation of the river from its source to the sea was
insisted on by the United States, under the treaties of 1763
and 1783, as well as the law of nature and nations. The
dispute was terminated by the treaty of San Lorenzo el Real,
in 1795, by the 4th article of which his Catholic Majesty
agreed that the navigation of the Mississippi, in its whole
breadth, from its source to the ocean, should be free to the
citizens of the United States: and by the 22nd article, they
were permitted to deposite their goods at the port of New Orleans, and to export them from thence, without paying any
other duty than the hire of the warehouses. The subsequent
acquisition of Louisiana and Florida by the United States
having included within their territory the whole river from its
source to the Gulf of Mexico, and the stipulation in the treaty
of 1783, securing to British subjects a right to participate in
its navigation, not having been renewed by the treaty of
Ghent in 1814, the right of navigating the Mississippi is now
vested exclusively in the United States.

The right of the United States to participate with Spain in
the navigation of the river Mississippi was rested by the American government on the sentiment written in deep characters
on the heart of man, that the ocean is free to all men, and
its rivers to all their inhabitants. This natural right was found
to be universally acknowledged and protected in all tracts of
country, united under the same political society, by laying the
navigable rivers open to all their inhabitants. When these
rivers enter the limits of another society if the right of the
upper inhabitants to descend the stream was in any case ob-

structed, it was an act of force by a stronger society against a weaker, condemned by the judgment of mankind. The then recent case of the attempt of the emperor Joseph II. to open the navigation of the Scheldt from Antwerp to the sea was considered as a striking proof of the general union of sentiment on this point, as it was believed that Amsterdam had scarcely an advocate out of Holland, and even there her pretensions were advocated on the ground of treaties, and not of natural right. This sentiment of right in favour of the upper inhabitants must become stronger in the proportion which their extent of country bears to the lower. The United States held 600,000 square miles of inhabitable territory on the Mississippi and its branches, and this river with its branches afforded many thousands of miles of navigable waters penetrating this territory in all its parts. The inhabitable territory of Spain below their boundary and bordering on the river, which alone could pretend any fear of being incommoded by their use of the river, were not the thousandth part of that extent. This vast portion of the territory of the United States had no other outlet for its productions, and these productions were of the bulkiest kind. And, in truth, their passage down the river might not only be innocent, as to the Spanish subjects on the river, but would not fail to enrich them far beyond their actual condition. The real interests, then, of all the inhabitants, upper and lower, concurred in fact with their respective rights.

If the appeal was to the law of nature and nations, as expressed by writers on the subject, it was agreed by them, that even if the river, where it passes between Florida and Louisiana, were the exclusive right of Spain, still an innocent passage along it was a natural right in those inhabiting its borders above. It would indeed be what those writers call an imperfect right, because the modification of its exercise depends, in a considerable degree, on the conveniency of the nation through which they were to pass. But it was still a right as real as any other right however well defined; and were it to be refused, or so shackled by regulations not necessary for the peace or safety of the inhabitants, as to render its use impracticable to us, it would then be an injury, of which we should be entitled to demand redress. The right of the upper inhabitants to use this navigation was the counterpart to that of those possessing the shores below, and founded in the same natural relations with the soil and water. And the line at which their respective rights met was to be advanced or withdrawn, so as to equalise the inconveniences resulting to each party from the exercise of the right by the other. This estimate was to be fairly made with a mutual disposition to make equal sacrifices, and the numbers on each side ought to have their due weight in the estimate. Spain held so very small a tract of habitable land on either side below our boundary, that it might in fact be considered as a strait in the sea; for though it was eighty leagues from our southern boundary to the mouth of the river, yet it was only here and there in spots and slips that the land rises above the level of the water in times of inundation. There were then, and ever must be, so few inhabitants on her part of the river, that the freest use of its navigation might be admitted to us without their annoyance.[26]

It was essential to the interests of both parties that the navigation of the river should be free to both, on the footing on which it was defined by the treaty of Paris, viz. through its whole breadth. The channel of the Mississippi was remarkably winding, crossing and recrossing perpetually from one side to the other of the general bed of the river. Within the elbows thus made by the channel there was generally an eddy setting upwards, and it was by taking advantage of these eddies, and constantly crossing from one to another of them, that boats were enabled to ascend the river. Without this right the navigation of the whole river would be impracticable both to the Americans and Spaniards.

It was a principle that the right to a thing gives a right to the means without which it could not be used, that is to say,

[26] The authorities referred to on this head were the following: Grotius, de Jur. Bel. ac Pac. lib. ii. cap. 2. §§ 11—13; c. 3, §§ 7—12. Puffendorf, lib. iii. cap. 3, §§ 3—6. Wolff's Inst. §§ 310—312. Vattel, liv. i. § 292; liv. ii. §§ 123—139.

that the means follow the end. Thus a right to navigate a river draws to it a right to moor vessels to its shores, to land on them in cases of distress, or for other necessary purposes, &c. This principle was founded in natural reason, was evidenced by the common sense of mankind, and declared by the writers before quoted.

The Roman law, which, like other municipal laws, placed the navigation of their rivers on the footing of nature, as to their own citizens, by declaring them public, declared also that the right to the use of the shores was incident to that of the water.[27] The laws of every country probably did the same. This must have been so understood between France and Great Britain at the treaty of Paris, where a right was ceded to British subjects to navigate the whole river, and expressly that part between the island of New Orleans and the western bank, without stipulating a word about the use of the shores, though both of them belonged then to France, and were to belong immediately to Spain. Had not the use of the shores been considered as incident to that of the water, it would have been expressly stipulated, since its necessity was too obvious to have escaped either party. Accordingly all British subjects used the shores habitually for the purposes necessary to the navigation of the river; and when a Spanish governor undertook at one time to forbid this, and even cut loose the vessels fastened to the shores, a British vessel went immediately, moored itself opposite the town of New Orleans, and set out guards with orders to fire on such as might attempt to disturb her moorings. The governor acquiesced, the right was constantly exercised afterwards, and no interruption ever offered.

This incidental right extends even beyond the shores, when circumstances render it necessary to the exercise of the principal right; as in the case of a vessel damaged, where the mere shore could not be a safe deposite for her cargo till she could be repaired, she may remove into safe ground off the river. The Roman law was here quoted too, because it

[27] Inst. liv. ii. t. 1. §§ 1   5.

gave a good idea both of the extent and the limitations of this right.[28]

§ 19.
Navigation
of the St.
Lawrence.
The relative position of the United States and Great Britain, in respect to the navigation of the great northern lakes and the river St. Lawrence, appears to be similar to that of the United States and Spain, previously to the cession of Louisiana and Florida, in respect to the Mississippi; the United States being in possession of the southern shores of the lakes and the river St. Lawrence to the point where their northern boundary line strikes the river, and Great Britain of the northern shores of the lakes and the river in its whole extent to the sea, as well as of the southern banks of the river, from the latitude 45° north to its mouth.

The claim of the people of the United States, of a right to navigate the St. Lawrence to and from the sea, has recently become the subject of discussion between the American and British governments.

On the part of the United States government, this right is rested on the same grounds of natural right and obvious necessity which had formerly been urged in respect to the river Mississippi. The dispute between different European powers respecting the navigation of the Scheldt in 1784, was also referred to in the correspondence on this subject, and the case of that river was distinguished from that of the St. Lawrence by its peculiar circumstances. Among others, it is known to have been alleged by the Dutch, that the whole course of the two branches of this river which passed within the dominions of Holland was entirely *artificial;* that it owed its existence to the skill and labour of Dutchmen; that its banks had been erected and maintained by them at a great expense. Hence, probably, the motive for that stipulation in the treaty of Westphalia, that the lower Scheldt, with the canals of Sas and Swin, and other mouths of the sea adjoining them, should be kept closed on the side belonging to Hol-

[28] Mr. Jefferson's Instructions to U. S. ministers in Spain, March 18, 1792. Waite's State Papers, vol. x. pp. 135—140.

land. But the case of the St. Lawrence was totally different, and the principles on which its free navigation was maintained by the United States had recently received an unequivocal confirmation in the solemn acts of the principal states of Europe. In the treaties concluded at the congress of Vienna, it had been stipulated that the navigation of the Rhine, the Neckar, the Meyn, the Moselle, the Maese, and the Scheldt, should be free to all nations. These stipulations, to which Great Britain was a party, might be considered as an indication of the present judgment of Europe upon the general question. The importance of the present claim might be estimated by the fact, that the inhabitants of at least eight states of the American union, besides the territory of Michigan, had an immediate interest in it, besides the prospective interests of other parts connected with this river and the inland seas through which it communicates with the ocean. The right of this great and growing population to the use of this, its only natural outlet to the ocean, was supported by the same principles and authorities which had been urged by Mr. *Jefferson* in the negotiation with Spain respecting the navigation of the river Mississippi. The present claim was also fortified by the consideration that this navigation was, before the war of the American revolution, the common property of all the British subjects inhabiting this continent, having been acquired from France by the united exertions of the mother country and the colonies in the war of 1756. The claim of the United States to the free navigation of the St. Lawrence was of the same nature with that of Great Britain to the navigation of the Mississippi, as recognised by the seventh article of the treaty of Paris, 1763, when the mouth and lower shores of that river were held by another power. The claim, whilst necessary to the United States, was not injurious to Great Britain, nor could it violate any of her just rights.[29]

On the part of the British government, the claim was considered as involving the question whether a *perfect* right to

[29] American Paper on the Navigation of the St. Lawrence. Congr Documents, Sessions 1827, 1828; No. 43, p. 34.

the free navigation of the river St. Lawrence could be maintained according to the principles and practice of the law of nations.

The liberty of passage to be enjoyed by one nation through the dominions of another was treated by the most eminent writers on public law as a qualified, occasional exception to the paramount rights of property. They made no distinction between the right of passage by a river, flowing from the possessions of one nation through those of another, to the ocean, and the same right to be enjoyed by means of any highway, whether of land or water, generally accessible to the inhabitants of the earth. The right of passage, then, must hold good for other purposes, besides those of trade,—for objects of war, as well as for objects of peace,—for all nations, no less than for any nation in particular, and be attached to artificial as well as to natural highways. The principle could not therefore be insisted on by the American government, unless it was prepared to apply the same principle by reciprocity, in favour of British subjects, to the navigation of the Mississippi and the Hudson, access to which from Canada might be obtained by a few miles of land-carriage, or by the artificial communications created by the canals of New York and Ohio. Hence the necessity which has been felt by the writers on public law, of controlling the operation of a principle so extensive and dangerous, by restricting the right of transit to purposes of *innocent* utility, to be exclusively determined by the local sovereign. Hence the right in question is termed by them an *imperfect* right. But there was nothing in these writers, or in the stipulations of the treaties of Vienna, respecting the navigation of the great rivers of Germany, to countenance the American doctrine of an absolute, natural right. These stipulations were the result of mutual consent, founded on considerations of mutual interest growing out of the relative situation of the different states concerned in this navigation. The same observation would apply to the various conventional regulations which had been at different periods applied to the navigation of the river Mississippi. As to any supposed right derived from the simultaneous acquisition of the St. Lawrence by the British and American people, it could not be allowed to have survived the treaty of 1783, by which the independence of the United States was acknowledged, and a partition of the British dominions in North America was made between the new government and that of the mother country.[30]

To this argument it has been replied, on the part of the United States, that if the St. Lawrence were regarded as a *strait* connecting navigable seas, as it ought properly to be, there would be less controversy. The principle on which the right to navigate straits depends, is, that they are accessorial to those seas which they unite, and the right of navigating which is not exclusive, but common to all nations; the right to navigate the seas drawing after it that of passing the straits. The United States and Great Britain have between them the exclusive right of navigating the lakes. The St. Lawrence connects them with the ocean. The right to navigate both (the lakes and the ocean) includes that of passing from one to the other through the natural link. Was it then reasonable or just that one of the two co-proprietors of the lakes should altogether exclude his associate from the use of a common bounty of nature, necessary to the full enjoyment of them? The distinction between the right of passage, claimed by one nation through the territories of another, on land, and that on navigable water, though not always clearly marked by the writers on public law, has a manifest existence in the nature of things. In the former case, the passage can hardly ever take place, especially if it be of numerous bodies, without some detriment or inconvenience to the state whose territory is traversed. But in the case of a passage on water no such injury is sustained. The American government did not mean to contend for any principle, the benefit of which, in analogous circumstances, it would deny to Great Britain. If, therefore, in the further progress of discovery, a connexion should be developed between the river Mississippi and Upper Canada, similar to that which exists between the

[30] British Paper on the Navigation of the St. Lawrence, Sessions 1827, 1828; No. 43, p. 41.

United States and the St. Lawrence, the American government would be always ready to apply, in respect to the Mississippi, the same principles it contended for in respect to the
St. Lawrence.   But the case of rivers, which rise and de-
bouche altogether within the limits of the same nation, ought
not to be confounded with those which, having their sources
and navigable portions of their streams in states above,
finally discharge themselves within the limits of other states
below.   In the former case, the question as to opening the
navigation to other nations, depended upon the same considerations which might influence the regulation of other commercial intercourse with foreign states, and was to be exclusively determined by the local sovereign.   But in respect to
the latter, the free navigation of the river was a natural
right in the upper inhabitants, of which they could not be
entirely deprived by the arbitrary caprice of the lower state.
Nor was the fact of subjecting the use of this right to treaty
regulations, as was proposed at Vienna to be done in respect
to the navigation of the European rivers, sufficient to prove
that the origin of the right was conventional, and not natural.
It often happened to be highly convenient, if not sometimes
indispensable, to avoid controversies, by prescribing certain
rules for the enjoyment of a natural right.   The law of nature, though sufficiently intelligible in its great outlines and
general purposes, does not always reach every minute detail
which is called for by the complicated wants and varieties of
modern navigation and commerce.   Hence the right of navigating the ocean itself, in many instances, principally incident
to a state of war, is subjected, by innumerable treaties, to
various regulations.   These regulations—the transactions at
Vienna, and other analogous stipulations—should be regarded
only as the spontaneous homage of man to the paramount
Lawgiver of the universe, by delivering his great works from
the artificial shackles and selfish contrivances to which they
have been arbitrarily and unjustly subjected.[31]

[31] Mr. Secretary Clay's Letter to Mr. Gallatin, June 19, 1826. Sessions
1827, 1828; No. 43, p. 18.

PART THIRD.

INTERNATIONAL RIGHTS OF STATES
IN THEIR PACIFIC RELATIONS.

PART THIRD.

INTERNATIONAL RIGHTS OF STATES IN THEIR PACIFIC RELATIONS.

CHAPTER I.

RIGHTS OF LEGATION.

THERE is no circumstance which marks more distinctly the progress of modern civilization than the institution of permanent diplomatic missions between different states. The rights of ambassadors were known and in some degree respected by the classic nations of antiquity. During the middle ages they were less distinctly recognised, and it was not until the seventeenth century that they were firmly established. The institution of resident permanent legations at all the European courts took place subsequently to the peace of Westphalia, and was rendered expedient by the increasing interest of the different states in each other's affairs growing out of more extensive commercial and political relations, and more refined speculations respecting the balance of power. Hence the rights of legation have become definitely ascertained, and incorporated into the international code. § 1.
Usage of
permanent
diplomatic
missions.

Every independent state has a right to send public ministers to, and receive ministers from, any other sovereign state with which it desires to maintain the relations of peace and amity. No state, strictly speaking, is obliged, by the positive law of nations, to send or receive public ministers, although the usage and comity of nations seem to have esta- § 2.
Right to
send, and
obligation
to receive,
public ministers.

blished a sort of reciprocal duty in this respect. It is evident, however, that this cannot be more than an imperfect obligation, and must be modified by the nature and importance of the relations to be maintained between different states by means of diplomatic intercourse.[1]

§ 3.
Rights of
legation,
to what
states be-
longing.

How far the rights of legation belong to dependent or semi-sovereign states, must depend upon the nature of their peculiar relation to the superior state under whose protection they are placed. Thus, by the treaty concluded at Kainardgi, in 1774, between Russia and the Porte, the provinces of Moldavia and Wallachia, placed under the protection of the former power, have the right of sending chargés d'affaires of the Greek communion to represent them at the court of Constantinople.[2]

So also of confederated states; their right of sending public ministers to each other, or to foreign states, depends upon the peculiar nature and constitution of the union by which they are bound together. Under the constitution of the former German empire, and that of the present Germanic confederation, this right is preserved to all the princes and states composing the federal union. Such was also the former constitution of the United Provinces of the Low Countries, and such is now that of the Swiss confederation. By the constitution of the United States of America every state is expressly forbidden from entering, without the consent of congress, into any treaty, alliance, or confederation, with any other state of the union, or with a foreign state, or from entering, without the same consent, into any agreement or compact with another state, or with a foreign power. The original power of sending and receiving public ministers is essentially modified, if it be not entirely taken away, by this prohibition.

[1] Vattel, Droit des Gens, liv. iv. ch. 5, §§ 55—65. Rutherforth's Institutes, vol. ii. b. ii. ch. 9, § 20. Martens, Précis du Droit des Gens Moderne de l'Europe, liv. vii. ch. 1, §§ 187—190.

[2] Vattel, liv. iv. ch. 5, § 60. Kluber, Droit des Gens Moderne de l'Europe, st. 2. tit. 2, ch. 3, § 175.

The question, to what department of the government be- §4. longs the right of sending and receiving public ministers, also How affected by depends upon the municipal constitution of the state. In civil war or monarchies, whether absolute or constitutional, this prerog- the sove- ative usually resides in the sovereign. In republics, it is reignty. vested either in the chief magistrate, or in a senate or coun- cil, conjointly with, or exclusive of such magistrate. In the case of a revolution, civil war, or other contest for the sovereignty, although, strictly speaking, the nation has the exclusive right of determining in whom the legitimate autho- rity of the country resides, yet foreign states must of neces- sity judge for themselves whether they will recognise the government *de facto,* by sending to, and receiving ambassa- dors from it, or whether they will continue their accustomed diplomatic relations with the prince whom they choose to re- gard as the legitimate sovereign, or suspend altogether these relations with the nation in question. So also where an em- pire is severed by the revolt of a province or colony de- claring and maintaining its independence, foreign states are governed by expediency in determining whether they will commence diplomatic intercourse with the new state, or wait for its recognition by the metropolitan country.[3]

For the purpose of avoiding the difficulties which might arise from a formal and positive decision of these questions, diplomatic agents are frequently substituted, who are clothed with the powers, and enjoy the immunities of ministers, though they are not invested with the representative character, nor entitled to diplomatic honours.

As no state is under a perfect obligation to receive minis- §5. ters from another, it may annex such conditions to their re- Condition- ception as it thinks fit; but when once received, they are in tion of fo- all other respects entitled to the privileges annexed by the reign mi- law of nations to their public character. Thus some govern- ments have established it as a rule not to receive one of their own native subjects as a minister from a foreign power; and

---

[3] Vide ante, pt. i. ch. 2, §§ 17, 18.

a government may receive one of its own subjects under the expressed condition that he shall continue amenable to the local laws and jurisdiction.   So also one court may refuse to receive a particular individual as minister from another court, alleging the motives on which such refusal is grounded.[4]

§ 6.
Classifica-
tion of pub-
lic minis-
ters.

The primitive law of nations makes no distinction between the different classes of public ministers: but the modern usage of Europe having introduced into the voluntary law of nations certain distinctions in this respect, which, for want of exact definition, became the perpetual source of controversies, a uniform rule was at last adopted by the congress of Vienna, and that of Aix la Chapelle, which put an end to those disputes.   By the rule thus established, public ministers are divided into the four following classes :—

1. Ambassadors, and papal legates or nuncios.

2. Envoys, ministers, or others accredited to sovereigns, (auprès des souverains.)

3. Ministers resident accredited to sovereigns.

4. Chargés d'Affaires accredited to the minister of foreign affairs.[5]

Ambassadors and other public ministers of the first class are exclusively entitled to what is called the *representative* character, being considered as peculiarly representing the sovereign or state by whom they are delegated, and entitled to the same honours to which their constituent would be entitled were he personally present.   This must, however, be taken in a general sense, as indicating the sort of honours to which they are entitled ; and the exact ceremonial to be observed towards this class of ministers depends upon usage, which has fluctuated at different periods of European history. There is a slight shade of difference between ambassadors ordinary and extraordinary ; the former designation being

[4] Bynkershoek, de Foro Competent. Legatorum, cap. 11, § 10.   Martens, Manuel Diplomatique, ch. 1, § 6.

[5] Récez du Congrès de Vienne du 19 Mars, 1815.   Protocol du Congrès d'Aix la Chapelle du 21 Novembre, 1818.   Martens, Manuel Diplomatique, ch. 4, § 38.

exclusively applied to those sent on permanent missions, the latter to those employed on a particular or extraordinary occasion, or residing at a foreign court for an indeterminate period.[6]

The right of sending ambassadors is exclusively confined to crowned heads, the 'great republics, and other states entitled to royal honours.[7]

All other public ministers are destitute of that peculiar character which is supposed to be derived from representing generally the person and dignity of the sovereign. They represent him only in respect to the particular business committed to their charge at the court to which they are accredited.[8]

Ministers of the second class are envoys, envoys extraordinary, ministers plenipotentiary, envoys extraordinary and ministers plenipotentiary, and internuncios of the pope.[9]

In the third class are included ministers, ministers resident, residents, and ministers chargés d'affaires accredited to sovereigns.[10]

Chargés d'affaires, accredited to the minister of foreign affairs of the court at which they reside, are either chargés d'affaires *ad hoc*, who are originally sent and accredited by their governments, or chargés d'affaires *par interim*, substituted in the place of the minister of their respective nations during his absence.[11]

According to the rule prescribed by the congress of Vienna, and which has since been generally adopted, public ministers take rank between themselves in each class according to the date of the official notification of their arrival at the court to which they are accredited.[12]

---

[6] Vattel, Droit des Gens, liv. iv. ch. 6, §§ 70—79. Martens, Précis du Droit des Gens Moderne de l'Europe, liv. vii. ch. 2, § 192. Martens, Manuel Diplomatique, ch. 1, § 9.

[7] Martens, Précis, &c. liv. vii. ch. 2, § 198. Vide ante, pt. ii. ch. 3, § 2.

[8] Martens, Manuel Diplomatique, ch. 1, § 10.

[9] Ibid.

[10] Martens, Précis, &c. liv. vii. ch. 2, § 194.

[11] Martens, Manuel Diplomatique, ch. 1, § 11.

[12] Recez du Congrès de Vienne du 19 Mars, 1815, art 4.

The same decision of the congress of Vienna has also abolished all distinctions of rank between public ministers arising from consanguinity, and family or political relations between their different courts.[13]

A state which has a right to send public ministers of different classes may determine for itself what rank it chooses to confer upon its diplomatic agents; but usage generally requires that those who maintain permanent missions near the government of each other should send and receive ministers of equal rank. One minister may represent his sovereign at different courts, and a state may send several ministers to the same court. A minister or ministers may also have full powers to treat with foreign states, as at a congress of different nations, without being accredited to any particular court.[14]

Consuls and other commercial agents, not being accredited to the sovereign or minister of foreign affairs, are not, in general, considered as public ministers; but the consuls maintained by the Christian powers of Europe and America near the Barbary States are accredited and treated as public ministers.[15]

§ 7.
Letters of
credence.
Every diplomatic agent, in order to be received in that character, and to enjoy the privileges and honours attached to his rank, must be furnished with a letter of credence. In the case of an ambassador, envoy, or minister of either of the three first classes, this letter of credence is addressed by the sovereign or other chief magistrate of his own state to the sovereign or state to whom the minister is delegated. In the case of a chargés d'affaires, it is addressed by the secretary, or minister of state charged with the department of foreign affairs, to the minister of foreign affairs of the other government. It may be in the form of a *cabinet letter*, but is

[13] Ib. art. 6.

[14] Martens, Précis, &c. liv. vii. ch. 2, §§ 199—204.

[15] Bynkershoek, de Foro Competent. Legat. cap. 10, §§ 4—6. Martens, Manuel Diplomatique, ch. 1, § 13. Vattel, liv. ii. ch. 2, § 34. Wicquefort, de l'Ambassadeur, liv. i. § 1, p. 63.

more generally in that of a *letter of council.* If the latter, it is signed by the sovereign, and sealed with the great seal of state. The minister is furnished with an authenticated copy, to be delivered to the minister of foreign affairs on asking an audience for the purpose of delivering the original to the sovereign or other chief magistrate of the state to whom he is sent. The letter of credence states the general object of his mission, and requests that full faith and credit may be given to what he shall say on the part of his court.[16]

The full power authorizing the minister to negotiate may be inserted in the letter of credence, but it is more usually drawn up in the form of letters patent. In general, ministers sent to a congress are not provided with a letter of credence, but only with a full power, of which they reciprocally exchange copies with each other, or deposite them in the hands of the mediating power or presiding minister.[17]   § 8. Full power.

The instructions of the minister are for his own direction only, and not to be communicated to the government to which he is accredited, unless he is ordered by his own government to communicate them *in extenso,* or partially, or in the exercise of his discretion, he deems it expedient to make such a communication.[18]   § 9. Instructions.

A public minister proceeding to his destined post, in time of peace, requires no other protection than a passport from his own government. In time of war, he must be provided with a safe-conduct, or passport, from the government of the state with which his own country is in hostility, to enable him to travel securely through its territories.[19]   § 10. Passport.

---

[16] Martens, Précis, &c. liv. vii. ch. 3, § 202. Wicquefort, de l'Ambassadeur, liv. i. § 15.

[17] Wicquefort, liv. i. § 16. Martens, Précis, &c. liv. vii. ch. 3, § 204. Manuel Diplomatique, ch. 2, § 17.

[18] Manuel Diplomatique, ch. 2, § 16.

[19] Vattel, liv. iv. ch. 7, § 85. Manuel Diplomatique, ch. 2, § 19. Flassan, Histoire de la Diplomatie Française, tom. v. p. 246.

§ 11.
Public
minister
passing
through
the terri-
tory of
another
state than
that to
which he
is accre-
dited.

A public minister, in passing through the territory of a friendly state, other than that of the government to which he is accredited, is entitled to respect and protection, though not invested with all the privileges and immunities which he enjoys within the dominions of the sovereign to whom he is sent. The extent of respect and protection due to a public minister within the territory of a foreign state other than that to which he is sent, is carried by *Vattel* further than seems to be warranted by reason, the usage of nations, or the authority of other text writers upon international law. The inviolability of ambassadors under that law is by *Grotius* and *Bynkershoek*, among others, understood as binding on those sovereigns only to whom they are sent; and *Wicquefort*, in particular, who has been ever considered as the stoutest champion of ambassadorial rights, determines that the assassination of the ministers of Francis I., referred to by Vattel, though an atrocious murder, was no breach of international law as to the privileges of ambassadors. It might be a violation of the right of innocent passage, aggravated by the circumstance of the dignified character of the persons on whom the crime was committed, and even a just cause of war against the emperor Charles V., without involving the question of protection as an ambassador, which arises exclusively from a legal implication which can only exist between the states from and to whom he is sent.[20]

§ 12.
Duties of
a public
minister on
arriving at
his post.

It is the duty of every public minister, on arriving at his destined post, to notify his arrival to the minister of foreign affairs. If the foreign minister is of the first class, this notification is usually communicated by a secretary of embassy or legation, or other person attached to the mission, who hands to the minister of foreign affairs a copy of the letter of credence, at the same time requesting an audience of the sovereign for his principal. Ministers of the second and third

[20] Vattel, liv. iv. ch. 7, § 84. Wicquefort, liv. i. § 29, pp. 433—439. Grotius, de Jur. Bel. ac Pac. lib. ii. cap. 18, § 5. Bynkershoek, de Foro Competent. Legat. cap. 9, § 7. Rutherforth's Instit. vol. ii. b. ii. ch. 9, § xx. Ward's Hist. of the Law of Nations, vol. ii. ch. 17, pp. 334—339.

classes generally notify their arrival by letter to the minister of foreign affairs, requesting him to take the orders of the sovereign as to the delivery of their letters of credence. Chargés d'affaires, who are not accredited to the sovereign, notify their arrival in the same manner, at the same time requesting an audience of the minister of foreign affairs for the purpose of delivering their letters of credence.

§ 13.
Audience of the sovereign or chief magistrate.

Ambassadors, and other ministers of the first class, are entitled to a *public* audience of the sovereign; but this ceremony is not necessary to enable them to enter on their functions, and, together with the ceremony of the *solemn entry*, which was formerly practised with respect to this class of ministers, is now usually dispensed with, and they are received in a *private* audience in the same manner as other ministers. At this audience, the letter of credence is delivered, and the minister pronounces a complimentary discourse, to which the sovereign replies. In republican states, the foreign minister is received in a similar manner, by the chief executive magistrate or council charged with the foreign affairs of the nation.[21]

§ 14.
Diplomatic etiquette.

The usage of civilized nations has established a certain etiquette to be observed by the members of the diplomatic corps resident at the same court towards each other, and towards the members of the government to which they are accredited. The duties which comity requires to be observed in this respect belong rather to the code of manners than of laws, and can hardly be made the subject of positive sanction: but there are certain established rules in respect to them, the non-observance of which may be attended with inconvenience in the performance of more serious and important duties. Such are the visits of etiquette which the diplomatic ceremonial of Europe requires to be rendered and reciprocated between public ministers resident at the same court.[22]

[21] Martens, Manuel Diplomatique, ch. 4, §§ 33—36.
[22] Manuel Diplomatique, ch. 4, § 37.

§ 15.
Privileges
of a public
minister.
From the moment a public minister enters the territory of the state to which he is sent, during the time of his residence, and until he leaves the country, he is entitled to an entire exemption from the local jurisdiction, both civil and criminal. Representing the rights, interests, and dignity of the sovereign or state by whom he is delegated, his person is sacred and inviolable. To give a more lively idea of this complete exemption from the local jurisdiction, the fiction of extra-territoriality has been invented, by which the minister, though actually in a foreign country, is supposed still to remain within the territory of his own sovereign. He continues still subject to the laws of his own country, which govern his personal *status* and rights of property, whether derived from contract, inheritance, or testament. His children born abroad are considered as natives. This exemption from the local laws and jurisdiction is founded upon mutual utility growing out of the necessity that public ministers should be entirely independent of the local authority, in order to fulfil the duties of their mission. The act of sending the minister on the one hand, and of receiving him on the other, amounts to a tacit compact between the two states that he shall be subject only to the authority of his own nation.[23]

The passports or safe conduct, granted by his own government in time of peace, or by the government to which he is sent in time of war, are sufficient evidence of his public character for this purpose.[24]

§ 16.
Exceptions to the
general
rule of
This immunity extends, not only to the person of the minister, but to his family and suite, secretaries of legation and other secretaries, his servants, moveable effects, and the house in which he resides.[25]

[23] Grotius, de Jur. Bel. ac Pac. lib. ii. cap. 18, § 1—6. Rutherforth's Inst. vol. ii. b. ii. ch. 9, § 20. Wicquefort, de l'Ambassadeur, liv. i. § 27. Bynkershoek, de Jure Competent. Legat. cap. 5, 8. Vattel, Droit des Gens, liv. iv. ch. 7, §§ 81—125. Martens, Précis, &c. liv. vii. ch. 5, §§ 214—218. Kluber, Droit des Gens Moderne de l'Europe, pt. ii. tit. 2, § 203.

[24] Vattel, liv. iv. ch. 7, § 83.

[25] Grotius, de Jur. Bel. ac Pac. lib. xviii. §§ 8, 9. Bynkershoek, de Foro Competent. Legat. cap. 13, § 5, cap. 15, 20. Vattel, liv. iv. ch. 8, § 113;

The minister's person is in general entirely exempt both exemption from the civil and criminal jurisdiction of the country where local juris- he resides. To this general exemption, there may be the fol- diction. lowing exceptions:

1. This exemption from the jurisdiction of the local tribunals and authorities does not apply to the *contentious* jurisdiction which may be conferred on those tribunals by the minister voluntarily making himself a party to a suit at law.[26]

2. If he is a citizen or subject of the country to which he is sent, and that country has not renounced its authority over him, he remains still subject to its jurisdiction. But it may be questionable whether his reception as a minister from another power, without any express reservation as to his previous allegiance, ought not to be considered as a renunciation of this claim, since such reception implies a tacit convention between the two states that he shall be entirely exempt from the local jurisdiction.[27]

3. If he is at the same time in the service of the power who receives him as a minister, as sometimes happens among the German courts, he continues still subject to the local jurisdiction.[28]

4. In case of offences committed by public ministers affecting the existence and safety of the state where they reside, if the danger is urgent, their persons and papers may be seized, and they may be sent out of the country. In all other cases, it appears to be the established usage of nations to request their recall by their own sovereign, which, if unreasonably refused by him, would unquestionably authorize the offended state to send away the offender. There may be other cases which might, under circumstances of sufficient aggravation, warrant the state thus offended in proceeding against an ambassador as a public enemy, or in inflicting punishment upon

ch. 9, §§ 117—123. Martens, Précis, &c. liv. vii. ch. 5, §§ 215—227; ch. 9, §§ 234—237.

[26] Bynkershoek, cap. 16, §§ 13—15. Vattel, liv. iv. ch. 8, § 111. Martens, Précis, &c. liv. vii. ch. 5, § 216.

[27] Bynkershoek, cap. 11. Vattel, liv. iv. ch. 8, § 112.

[28] Martens, Manuel Diplomatique, ch. 3, § 23.

his person if justice should be refused by his own sovereign. But the circumstances which would authorize such a proceeding are hardly capable of precise definition, nor can any general rule be collected from the examples to be found in the history of nations where public ministers have thrown off their public character and plotted against the safety of the state to which they were accredited. These anomalous exceptions to the general rule resolve themselves into the paramount right of self-preservation and necessity. *Grotius* distinguishes here between what may be done in the way of self-defence, and what may be done in the way of punishment. Though the law of nations will not allow an ambassador's life to be taken away as a punishment for a crime after it has been committed, yet this law does not oblige the state to suffer him to use violence without endeavouring to resist it.[29]

§ 17. Personal exemption extending to his family, secretaries, servants, &c. The wife and family, servants and suite, of the minister, participate in the inviolability attached to his public character. The secretaries of embassy and legation are especially entitled, as official persons, to the privileges of the diplomatic corps in respect to their exemption from the local jurisdiction.[30]

The municipal laws of some, and the usages of most nations, require an official list of the domestic servants of foreign ministers to be communicated to the secretary or minister of foreign affairs, in order to entitle them to the benefit of this exemption.[31]

It follows from the principle of the extra-territoriality of

[29] Grotius, de Jur. Bel. ac Pac. lib. ii. cap. 18, § 4. Rutherforth's Inst. vol. ii. b. ii. ch. 9, § 20. Bynkershoek, de Foro Competent. Legat. cap. 17, 18, 19. Vattel, liv. iv. ch. 7, §§ 94—102. Martens, Précis, &c. liv. vii. ch. 5, § 218. Ward's Hist. of the Law of Nations, vol. ii. ch. 17, pp. 291—334.

[30] Grotius, lib. ii. cap. 18, § 8. Bynkershoek, cap. 15, 20. Vattel, liv. iv. ch. 9, §§ 120—123. Martens, Précis, &c. liv. vii. ch. 5, § 219; ch. 9, §§ 234—237.

[31] Blackstone's Commentaries, vol. i. ch. 7. LL. of the United States, vol. i. ch. 9, § 26.

the minister, his family, and other persons attached to the legation or belonging to his suite, and their exemption from the local laws and jurisdiction of the country where they reside, that the civil and criminal jurisdiction over these persons rests with the minister, to be exercised according to the laws and usages of his own country. In respect to civil jurisdiction, both contentious and voluntary, this rule is, with some exceptions, followed in the practice of nations. But in respect to criminal offences committed by his domestics, although in strictness the minister has a right to try and punish them, the modern usage merely authorizes him to arrest and send them for trial to their own country. He may also, in the exercise of his discretion, discharge them from his service, or deliver them up for trial under the laws of the state where he resides, as he may renounce any other privilege to which he is entitled by the public law.[32]

The personal effects or moveables belonging to the minister, within the territory of the state where he resides, are entirely exempt from the local jurisdiction; so also of his dwelling-house; but any other real property, or immoveables, of which he may be possessed within the foreign territory, is subject to its laws and jurisdiction. Nor is the personal property of which he may be possessed as a merchant carrying on trade, or in a fiduciary character as an executor, &c., exempt from the operation of the local laws.[33] *§ 18. Exemption of the minister's house and property.*

His person and personal effects are not liable to taxation. He is exempt from the payment of duties on the importation of articles for his own personal use and that of his family. But this latter exemption is, at present, by the usage of most nations, limited to a fixed sum during the continuance of the mission. He is liable to the payment of tolls and postages. The hotel in which he resides, though exempt from the quar- *§ 19. Duties and taxes.*

[32] Bynkershoek, cap. 15, 20. Vattel, liv. iv. ch, 9, § 124. Rutherforth's Inst. vol. ii. b. ii. ch. 9, § 20. Kluber, pt. ii. tit. 2, §§ 212—214.

[33] Vattel, liv. iv. ch. 8, §§ 113—115. Martens, Précis, &c. liv. vii. ch. 8, § 217. Kluber, pt. ii. tit. 2, ch. 3, § 210.

tering of troops, is subject to taxation in common with the
other real property of the country, whether it belongs to him
or to his government. And though, in general, his house is
inviolable, and cannot be entered without his permission by
police, custom-house, or excise officers, yet the abuse of this
privilege, by which it was converted in some countries into
an asylum for fugitives from justice, has caused it to be very
much restrained by the recent usage of nations.[34]

§ 20.
Messen-
gers and
couriers.

The practice of nations has also extended the inviolability
of public ministers to the messengers and couriers sent with
despatches to or from the legations established in different
countries. They are exempt from every species of visitation
and search in passing through the territories of those powers
with whom their own government is in amity. For the purpose of giving effect to this exemption, they must be provided
with passports from their own government, attesting their official character; and in the case of despatches sent by sea,
the vessel or *aviso* must also be provided with a commission
or pass. In time of war, a special arrangement, by means
of a cartel or flag of truce, furnished with passports, not only
from their own government, but from its enemy, is necessary
for the purpose of securing these despatch vessels from interruption, as between the belligerent powers. But an ambassador or other public minister, resident in a neutral country
for the purpose of preserving the relations of peace and amity
between the neutral state and his own government, has a
right freely to send his despatches in a neutral vessel, which
cannot lawfully be interrupted by the cruisers of a power at
war with his own country.[35]

§ 21.
Freedom
of religious
worship.

A minister resident in a foreign country is entitled to the
privilege of religious worship in his own private chapel, according to the peculiar forms of his national faith, although

[34] Vattel, liv. iv. ch. 9, §§ 117, 118. Martens, Précis, &c. liv. vii. ch. 5,
§ 220. Manuel Diplomatique, ch. 3, §§ 30, 31.
[35] Vattel, liv. iv. ch. 9, § 123. Martens, Précis, &c. liv. vii. ch. 13, § 250.
Robinson's Adm. Rep. vol. vi. p. 466. The Caroline.

it may not be generally tolerated by the laws of the state where he resides. Ever since the epoch of the Reformation, this privilege has been secured by convention or usage between the Catholic and Protestant nations of Europe. It is also enjoyed by the public ministers and consuls from the Christian powers in Turkey and the Barbary States. The increasing spirit of religious freedom and liberality has gradually extended this privilege to the establishment, in most countries, of public chapels attached to the different foreign embassies, in which not only foreigners of the same nation, but even natives of the country of the same religion, are allowed the free exercise of their peculiar worship. This does not, in general, extend to public processions, the use of bells, or other external rites celebrated beyond the walls of the chapel.[36]

Consuls are not public ministers. Whatever protection they may be entitled to in the discharge of their official duties, and whatever special privileges may be conferred upon them by the local laws and usages, or by international compact, they are not entitled by the general law of nations to the peculiar immunities of ambassadors. No state is bound to permit the residence of foreign consuls, unless it has stipulated by convention to receive them. They are to be approved and admitted by the local sovereign, and, if guilty of illegal or improper conduct, are liable to have the *exequatur*, which is granted them, withdrawn, and may be punished by the laws of the state where they reside, or sent back to their own country, at the discretion of the government which they have offended. In civil and criminal cases, they are subject to the local law in the same manner with other foreign residents owing a temporary allegiance to the state.[37]

§ 22. Consuls, not entitled to the peculiar privileges of public ministers.

[36] Vattel, liv. iv. ch. 7, § 104.   Martens, Précis, &c. liv. vii. ch. 6, §§ 222—226.   Kluber, Droit des Gens Moderne de l'Europe, pt. ii. tit. 2, ch. 3, §§ 215—216.

[37] Wicquefort, de l'Ambassadeur, liv. i. § 5. Bynkershoek, cap. 10. Martens, Précis, &c. liv. iv. ch. 3, § 148.   Kent's Comment. on American Law, vol. i. pp. 43—45. 2nd Edit.

§ 23.
Termina-
tion of
public mis-
sion.

The mission of a foreign minister resident at a foreign court, or at a congress of ambassadors, may terminate during his life in one of the seven following manners :—

1. By the expiration of the period fixed for the duration of the mission; or, where the minister is constituted *ad interim* only, by the return of the ordinary minister to his post. In either of these cases, a formal recall is unnecessary.

2. When the object of the mission is fulfilled, as in the case of embassies of mere ceremony; or where the mission is special, and the object of the negotiation is attained or has failed.

3. By the recall of the minister.

4. By the decease or abdication of his own sovereign, or the sovereign to whom he is accredited. In either of these cases, it is necessary that his letters of credence should be renewed; which, in the former instance, is sometimes done in the letter of notification written by the successor of the deceased sovereign to the prince at whose court the minister resides. In the latter case, he is provided with new letters of credence; but where there is reason to believe that the mission will be suspended for a short time only, a negotiation already commenced may be continued with the same minister confidentially *sub spe rati.*

5. When the minister, on account of any violation of the law of nations, or any important incident in the course of his negotiation, assumes himself the responsibility of declaring his mission terminated.

6. When, on account of the minister's misconduct, or the measures of his government, the court at which he resides thinks fit to send him away without waiting for his recall.

7. By a change in the diplomatic rank of the minister.

When, by any of the circumstances above-mentioned, the minister is suspended from his functions, and in whatever manner his mission is terminated, he still remains entitled to all the privileges of his public character until his return to his own country.[38]

[38] Martens, Manuel Diplomatique, ch. 7, § 59; ch. 2, § 15. Précis, &c. liv. vii. ch. 9, § 239. Vattel, liv. iv. ch. 9, § 126.

A formal letter of recall must be sent to the minister by his government: 1. Where the object of his mission has been accomplished, or has failed. 2. Where he is recalled from motives which do not affect the friendly relations of the two governments. 3. On account of a misunderstanding between the two governments, or their ministers; as where the court at which the minister resides has demanded his recall, or the government from which he is sent considers its rights to have been violated, or determines to make use of reprisals. § 24. Letter of recall.

In the two first cases, nearly the same formalities are observed as on the arrival of the minister. He delivers a copy of his letter of recall to the minister of foreign affairs, and asks an audience of the sovereign for the purpose of taking leave. At this audience the minister delivers the original of his letter of recall to the sovereign, with a complimentary address adapted to the occasion.

If the minister is recalled on account of a misunderstanding between the two governments, the peculiar circumstances of the case must determine whether a formal letter of recall is to be sent to him, or whether he may quit the residence without waiting for it; whether the minister is to demand, and whether the sovereign is to grant him an audience of leave.

Where the diplomatic rank of the minister is raised or lowered, as where an envoy becomes an ambassador, or an ambassador has fulfilled his functions as such, and is to remain as a minister of the second or third class, he presents his letter of recall, and a letter of credence in his new character.

Where the mission is terminated by the death of the minister, his body is to be decently interred, or it may be sent home for interment; but the external religious ceremonies to be observed on this occasion depend upon the laws and usages of the place. The secretary of legation, or if there be no secretary, the minister of some allied power, is to place the seals upon his effects, and the local authorities have no right to interfere, unless in case of necessity. All questions respecting the succession *ab intestato* to the minister's moveable

property, or the validity of his testament, are to be determined by the laws of his own country. His effects may be
removed from the country where he resided without the payment of any *droit d'aubaine* or *detraction*.

Although in strictness the personal privileges of the minister expire with the termination of his mission by death,
the custom of nations entitles the widow and family of the
deceased minister, together with their domestics, to a continuance for a limited period of the same immunities which
they enjoyed during his lifetime.

It is the usage of certain courts to give presents to foreign
ministers on their recall, and on other special occasions.
Some governments prohibit their ministers from receiving
such presents. Such was formerly the rule observed by the
Venetian republic, and such is now the law of the United
States of America.[39]

[39] Martens, Précis, &c. liv. vii. ch. 10, §§ 240—245. Manuel Diplomatique,
ch. 7, §§ 60—65.

CHAPTER II.

RIGHTS OF NEGOTIATION AND TREATIES.

THE power of negotiating and contracting public treaties between nation and nation exists in full vigour in every sovereign state which has not parted with this portion of its sovereignty, or agreed to modify its exercise by compact with other states.

§ 1. Faculty of contracting by treaty, how limited or modified.

Semi-sovereign or dependent states have, in general, only a limited faculty of contracting in this manner; and even sovereign and independent states may restrain or modify this faculty by treaties of alliance or confederation with others. Thus the several states of the North American Union are expressly prohibited from entering into any treaty with foreign powers, or with each other, without the consent of the congress; whilst the sovereign members of the Germanic Confederation retain the power of concluding treaties of alliance and commerce not inconsistent with the fundamental laws of the confederation.[1]

The constitution or fundamental law of every particular state must determine in whom is vested the power of negotiating and contracting treaties with foreign powers. In absolute, and even in constitutional monarchies, it is usually vested in the reigning sovereign. In republics, the chief magistrate, senate, or executive council is intrusted with the exercise of this sovereign power.

There are certain compacts between nations which are concluded, not in virtue of any special authority, but in the exercise of a general implied power confided to certain public agents as incidental to their official stations. Such are the

§ 2. Cartels, truces, and capitulations.

---

[1] See pt. i: ch: 2, §§ 9—14.

official acts of generals and admirals, suspending or limiting
the exercise of hostilities within the sphere of their respective
military or naval commands, by means of special licenses to
trade, of cartels for the exchange of prisoners, of truces for
the suspension of arms, or capitulations for the surrender of a
fortress, city, or province. These conventions do not, in general, require the ratification of the supreme power of the
state, unless such a ratification be expressly reserved in the
act itself.[2]

§ 3.
Sponsions.

Such acts or engagements, when made without authority,
or exceeding the limits of the authority under which they
purport to be made, are called *sponsions*. These conventions
must be confirmed by express or tacit ratification. The
former is given in positive terms, and with the usual forms ;
the latter is implied from the fact of acting under the agreement as if bound by its stipulations. Mere silence is not sufficient to infer a ratification by either party, though good
faith requires that the party refusing it should notify its determination to the other party, in order to prevent the latter
from carrying its own part of the agreement into effect. If,
however, it has been totally or partially executed by either
party, acting in good faith upon the supposition that the agent
was duly authorized, the party thus acting is entitled to be
indemnified or replaced in his former situation.[3]

§ 4.
Full power
and ratifi-
cation.

As to other public treaties : in order to enable a public
minister or other diplomatic agent to conclude and sign a
treaty with the government to which he is accredited, he
must be furnished with a *full power*. Treaties and conventions thus negotiated and signed are, by the law of nature,
binding upon the state in whose name they are concluded,
in the same manner as any other contract made by a duly

[2] Grotius, de Jur. Bel. ac Pac. lib. iii. cap. 22, §§ 6—8. Vattel, Droit des
Gens, liv. ii. ch. 14, § 207.

[3] Grotius, de Jur. Bel. ac Pac. lib. ii. cap. 15, § 16; lib. iii. cap. 22, §§ 1
—3. Vattel, Droit des Gens, liv. ii. ch. 14, §§ 209—212. Rutherforth's
Inst. b. ii. ch. 9, § 21.

authorized agent binds his principal according to the general rules of civil jurisprudence. The question, how far, under the positive law of nations, ratification by the state, in whose name the treaty is made by its duly authorized plenipotentiaries, is essential to its validity, has been the subject of much doubt and discussion among institutional writers. It seems, however, to be the settled usage of nations to require a previous ratification; and this pre-requisite is usually reserved by the express terms of the treaty itself. Some writers hold that such ratification is not essential to the validity of the treaty, unless it be expressly reserved in the full power or in the treaty itself; from which they infer that it may be arbitrarily refused when it is thus reserved. Others maintain that it cannot with propriety be withheld, unless for strong and substantial reasons ; such, for example, as the minister having deviated from his instructions.[4]

The municipal constitution of every particular state determines in whom resides the authority to ratify treaties negotiated and concluded with foreign powers, so as to render them obligatory upon the nation. In absolute monarchies, it is the prerogative of the sovereign himself to confirm the act of his plenipotentiary by his final sanction. In certain limited or constitutional monarchies, the consent of the legislative power of the nation is, in some cases, required for that purpose. In some republics, as in that of the United States of America, the advice and consent of the senate is essential to enable the chief executive magistrate to pledge the national faith in this form. In all these cases it is, consequently, an implied condition in negotiating with foreign powers that the treaties concluded by the executive government shall be subject to ratification in the manner prescribed by the fundamental laws of the state.

§ 5.
The treaty making power dependent on the municipal constitution.

---

[4] Wicquefort, de l'Ambassadeur, liv. ii. § 15. Vattel, Droit des Gens, liv. ii. ch. 12, § 156; liv. iv. ch. 6, § 77. Martens, Précis du Droit des Gens, &c. liv. ii. ch. 2, § 49. Kluber, Droit des Gens Moderne, pt. ii. sect. 1, ch. 2, § 142.

§ 6.
Auxiliary
legislative
measures,
how far
necessary
to the va-
lidity of a
treaty.

The treaty, when thus ratified, is obligatory upon the contracting states, independently of the auxiliary legislative
measures which may be necessary on the part of either, in
order to carry it into complete effect.   Where, indeed, such
auxiliary legislation becomes necessary, in consequence of
some limitation upon the treaty-making power expressed in
the fundamental laws of the state, or necessarily implied
from the distribution of its constitutional powers—such, for
example, as a prohibition of alienating the national domain—
then the treaty may be considered as imperfect in its obligation, until the national assent has been given in the forms
required by the municipal constitution.   A general power
to make treaties of peace necessarily implies a power to decide the terms on which they shall be made ; and among
these may properly be included the cession of the public territory and other property, as well as of private property included in the eminent domain annexed to the national sovereignty.   If there be no limitation expressed in the fundamental laws of the state, or necessarily implied from the
distribution of its constitutional authorities, on the treaty-
making power in this respect, it necessarily extends to the
alienation of public and private property, when deemed necessary or expedient.[5]

Commercial treaties, which have the effect of altering the
existing laws of trade and navigation of the contracting parties, may require the sanction of the legislative power in each
state for their execution.   Thus the commercial treaty of
Utrecht, between France and Great Britain, by which the
trade between the two countries was to be placed on the footing of reciprocity, was never carried into effect, the British
parliament having rejected the bill which was brought in for
the purpose of modifying the existing laws of trade and navigation, so as to adapt them to the stipulations of the treaty.
In treaties requiring the appropriation of moneys for their

---

[5] Grotius, de Jur. Bel. ac Pac. lib. iii. cap. 20, § 7. Vattel, Droit des
Gens, liv. i. ch. 20, § 244; ch. 2, §§ 262—265. Kent's Comment. on Amer.
Law, vol. i. p. 165. 2d Ed.

execution, it is the usual practice of the British government to stipulate that the king will recommend to parliament to make the grant necessary for that purpose. Under the constitution of the United States, by which treaties made and ratified by the president, with the advice and consent of the senate, are declared to be " the supreme law of the land," it seems to be understood that the congress is bound to redeem the national faith thus pledged, and to pass the laws necessary to carry the treaty into effect.[6]

General compacts between nations may be divided into what are called *transitory conventions*, and *treaties* properly so termed. The first are perpetual in their nature, so that being once carried into effect, they subsist independent of any change in the sovereignty and form of government of the contracting parties; and although their operation may, in some cases, be suspended during war, they revive on the return of peace without any express stipulation. Such are treaties of cession, boundary, or exchange of territory, or those which create a permanent servitude in favour of one nation within the territory of another.[7]

§ 7. Transitory conventions perpetual in their nature.

Thus the treaty of peace of 1783, between Great Britain and the United States, by which the independence of the latter was acknowledged, prohibited future confiscations of property; and the treaty of 1794, between the same parties, confirmed the titles of British subjects holding lands in the United States, and of American citizens holding lands in Great Britain, which might otherwise be forfeited for alienage. Under these stipulations, the supreme court of the United States determined that the title both of British subjects and of corporations to lands in America was protected by the treaty of peace, and confirmed by the treaty of 1794, so that it could not be forfeited by any intermediate legislative act, or other proceeding, for alienage. Even supposing

---

[6] Kent's Comment. vol.   p. 286.   2d Ed.
[7] Vattel Droit des Gens, liv. ii. ch. 12, § 192.   Martens, Précis, &c. liv. ii. ch. 2, § 58.

the treaties were abrogated by the war which broke out between the two countries in 1812, it would not follow that the
rights of property already vested under those treaties could
be devested by supervening hostilities. The extinction of the
treaties would no more extinguish the title to real property
acquired or secured under their stipulations than the repeal
of a municipal law affects rights of property vested under its
provisions. But independent of this incontestable principle,
on which the security of all property rests, the court was not
inclined to admit the doctrine, that treaties become, by war
between the two contracting parties, *ipso facto* extinguished,
if not revived by an express or implied renewal on the return
of peace. Whatever might be the latitude of doctrine laid
down by elementary writers on the law of nations, dealing in
general terms in relation to the subject, it was satisfied that
the doctrine contended for was not universally true. There
might be treaties of such a nature, as to their object and
import, as that war would necessarily put an end to them;
but where treaties contemplated a permanent arrangement
of territory, and other national rights, or in their terms were
meant to provide for the event of an intervening war, it
would be against every principle of just interpretation to
hold them extinguished by war. If such were the law, even
the treaty of 1783, so far as it fixed the limits of the United
States, and acknowledged their independence, would be gone,
and they would have had again to struggle for both, upon
original revolutionary principles. Such a construction was
never asserted, and would be so monstrous as to supersede all
reasoning. The court, therefore, concluded that treaties
stipulating for permanent rights and general arrangements,
and professing to aim at perpetuity, and to deal with the
case of war as well as of peace, do not cease on the occurrence of war, but are, at most, only suspended while it lasts;
and unless they are waived by the parties, or new and repugnant stipulations are made, revive upon the return of
peace.[8]

[8] Wheaton's Rep. vol. viii. p. 464. The Society for the Propagation of
the Gospel in Foreign Parts, *v.* the Town of New Haven.

Treaties, properly so called, or *fœdera,* are those of friend- §8.
ship and alliance, commerce and navigation, which even if Treaties,
perpetual in terms, expire of course:— the opera-
tion of
1. In case either of the contracting parties loses its exist- which
ence as an independent state. certain
2. Where the internal constitution of government of either cases.
state is so changed as to render the treaty inapplicable under
circumstances different from those with a view to which it
was concluded.

Here the distinction laid down by institutional writers between *real* and *personal* treaties becomes important. The
first bind the contracting parties, independently of any change
of sovereignty or in the rulers of the state. The latter include only treaties of mere personal alliance, such as are expressly made with a view to the person of the actual ruler
or reigning sovereign, and though they bind the state during
his existence, expire with his natural life or his public connexion with the state.[9]

3. In case of war between the contracting parties; unless
such stipulations as are made expressly with a view to a rupture, such as the period of time allowed to the respective
subjects to retire with their effects, or other limitations of the
general rights of war. Such is the stipulation contained in
the 10th article of the treaty of 1794, between Great Britain
and the United States,—providing that private debts and
shares, or moneys in the public funds, or in public or private
banks belonging to private individuals, should never, in the
event of war, be sequestered or confiscated. There can be
no doubt that the obligation of this article would not be impaired by a supervening war, being the very contingency
meant to be provided for, and that it must remain in full
force until mutually agreed to be rescinded.[10]

Most international compacts, and especially treaties of §9.
peace, are of a mixed character, and contain articles of both Treaties
revived

[9] Vide ante, pt. i. ch. 2, § 20.
[10] Vattel, liv. iii. ch. 10, § 175. Kent's Comment. on American Law, vol.
i. p. 176. 2d Ed.

and con-
firmed on
the renew-
al of peace.
kinds, which renders it frequently difficult to distinguish between those stipulations which are perpetual in their nature,
and such as are extinguished by war between the contracting parties, or by such changes of circumstances as affect
the being of either party, and thus render the compact inapplicable to the new condition of things. It is for this reason, and from abundance of caution, that stipulations are
frequently inserted in treaties of peace, expressly reviving
and confirming the treaties formerly subsisting between the
contracting parties, and containing stipulations of a permanent character, or in some other mode excluding the conclusion that the obligation of such antecedent treaties is
meant to be waived by either party. The reiterated confir-
mations of the treaties of Westphalia and Utrecht, in almost
every subsequent treaty of peace or commerce between the
same parties, constituted a sort of written code of conventional law, by which the distribution of power and territory
among the principal European states was permanently settled,
until violently disturbed by the partition of Poland and the
wars of the French revolution. The arrangements of territory and political relations substituted by the treaties of
Vienna for the ancient conventional law of Europe, and
doubtless intended to be of a similar permanent character,
have already undergone very important modifications in consequence of the late French revolution 1830, by which the
alliance between the great powers has been broken into two
confederacies, repugnant in their origin and principles, and
continually threatening to disturb a settlement which has not
yet acquired that solidity which general acquiescence and
the lapse of time can alone give to such transactions.

§ 10.
Guaran-
tees.
The convention of guarantee is one of the most usual international contracts. It is an engagement by which one
state promises to aid another where it is interrupted, or threatened to be disturbed in the peaceable enjoyment of its rights
by a third power. It may be applied to every species of
right and obligation that can exist between nations ; to the
possession and boundaries of territories, the sovereignty of

the state, its constitution of government, the right of succession, &c.; but it is most commonly applied to treaties of peace. The guarantee may also be contained in a distinct and separate convention, or included among the stipulations annexed to the principal treaty intended to be guarantied. It then becomes an accessary obligation.[11]

The guarantee may be stipulated by a third power not a party to the principal treaty, by one of the contracting parties in favour of another, or mutually between all the parties. Thus by the treaty of peace concluded at Aix la Chapelle in 1748, the eight high contracting parties mutually guarantied to each other all the stipulations of the treaty.

The guarantying party is bound to nothing more than to render the assistance stipulated. If it prove insufficient, he is not obliged to indemnify the power to whom his aid has been promised. Nor is he bound to interfere to the prejudice of the just rights of a third party, or in violation of a previous treaty rendering the guarantee inapplicable in a particular case. Guarantees apply only to rights and possessions existing at the time they are stipulated. It was upon these grounds that Louis XV. declared in 1741 in favour of the elector of Bavaria against Maria Theresa, the heiress of the emperor Charles VI., although the court of France had previously guarantied the Pragmatic Sanction of that emperor, regulating the succession to his hereditary states. And it was upon similar grounds that France refused to fulfil the treaty of alliance of 1756 with Austria, in respect to the pretensions of the latter power upon Bavaria in 1778, which threatened to produce a war with Russia. Whatever doubts may be suggested as to the application of these principles to the above cases, there can be none respecting the principles themselves, which are recognised by all the text writers.[12]

These writers make a distinction between a *Surety* and a *Guarantee.* Thus Vattel lays it down, that where the mat-

[11] Vattel, Droit des Gens, liv. ii. ch. 16, §§ 235—239. Kluber, Droit des Gens Moderne de l'Europe, pt. ii. tit. 2, sect. 1, ch. 2, §§ 157, 158.

[12] Vattel, liv. ii. ch. 16, § 238. Flassan, Histoire de la Diplomatie Française, tom. vii. p. 195.

ter relates to things which another may do or give as well as he who makes the original promise, as for instance the payment of a sum of money, it is safer to demand a *surety* (caution) than a *guarantee* (garant.) For the surety is bound to make good the promise in default of the principal; whereas the guarantee is only obliged to use his best endeavours to obtain a performance of the promise from him who has made it.[13]

§ 11.
Treaties of alliance.

Treaties of alliance may be either defensive or offensive. In the first case, the engagements of the ally extend only to a war really and truly defensive; to a war of aggression first commenced, in point of fact, against the other contracting party. In the second, the ally engages generally to co-operate in hostilities against a specified power, or against any power with whom the other party may be engaged in war.

An alliance may also be both offensive and defensive.

§ 12.
Distinction between general alliance and treaties of limited succour and subsidy.

General alliances are to be distinguished from treaties of limited succour and subsidy. Where one state stipulates to furnish to another a limited succour of troops, ships of war, money, or provisions, without any promise looking to an eventual engagement in general hostilities, such a treaty does not necessarily render the party furnishing this limited succour the enemy of the opposite belligerent. It only becomes such so far as respects the auxiliary forces thus supplied; in all other respects it remains neutral. Such, for example, have long been the accustomed relations of the confederated cantons of Switzerland with the other European powers.[14]

§ 13.
Casus fœderis of a defensive alliance.

Grotius, and the other text writers, hold that the *casus fœderis* of a defensive alliance does not apply to the case of a war manifestly unjust, *i. e.* to a war of aggression on the part of the power claiming the benefit of the alliance. And it is even said to be a tacit condition annexed to every treaty

[13] Vattel, § 239.
[14] Vattel, Droit des Gens, liv. iii. ch. 6, §§ 79—82.

made in time of peace, stipulating to afford succours in time
of war, that the stipulation is applicable only to a just war.
To promise assistance in an unjust war would be an obligation to commit injustice, and no such contract is valid. But,
it is added, this tacit restriction in the terms of a general
alliance can be applied only to a manifest case of unjust
aggression on the part of the other contracting party, and
cannot be used as a pretext to elude the performance of a
positive and unequivocal engagement without justly exposing
the ally to the imputation of bad faith. In doubtful cases,
the presumption ought rather to be in favour of our confederate, and of the justice of his quarrel.[15]

The application of these general principles must depend
upon the nature and terms of the particular guarantees contained in the treaty in question. This will best be illustrated
by specific examples.

Thus the States-General of Holland were engaged, pre- Alliance
viously to the war of 1756, between France and Great Bri- between
tain, in three different guarantees and defensive treaties with tain and
the latter power. The first was the original defensive alli- Holland.
ance, forming the basis of all the subsequent compacts between the two countries, concluded at Westminster in 1678.
In the preamble to this treaty, the preservation of each
other's dominions was stated as the cause of making it; and
it stipulated a mutual guarantee of all they already enjoyed,
or might thereafter acquire by treaties of peace, " in Europe
only." They farther guarantied all treaties which were at
that time made, or might thereafter conjointly be made, with
any other power. They stipulated also to defend and preserve each other in the possession of all towns or fortresses
which did at that time belong, or should in future belong, to
either of them ; and, that for this purpose, when either nation
was attacked or molested, the other should immediately succour it with a certain number of troops and ships, and should

[30] Grotius, de Jur. Bel. ac Pac. lib. ii. cap. 15, § 13 ; cap. 25, § 4. Bynkershoek, Quæst. Jur. Pub. lib. i. cap. 9. Vattel, Droit des Gens, liv. ii. ch.
12, § 168. liv. iii. ch. 6, §§ 86—96.

he obliged to break with the aggressor in two months after the party that was already at war should require it; and that they should then act conjointly with all their forces, to bring the common enemy to a reasonable accommodation.

The second defensive alliance then subsisting between Great Britain and Holland was that stipulated by the treaties of barrier and succession of 1709 and 1713, by which the Dutch barrier on the side of Flanders was guarantied on the one part, and the Protestant succession to the British crown on the other: and it was mutually stipulated, that in case either party should be attacked, the other should furnish, at the requisition of the injured party, certain specified succours; and if the danger should be such as to require a greater force, the other ally should be obliged to augment his succours, and ultimately to act with all his power in open war against the aggressor.

The third and last defensive alliance between the same powers was the treaty concluded at the Hague in 1717, to which France was also a party. The object of this treaty was declared to be, the preservation of each other reciprocally, and the possession of their dominions, as established by the treaty of Utrecht. The contracting parties stipulated to defend all and each of the articles of the said treaty, as far as they relate to the contracting parties respectively, or each of them in particular; and they guaranty all the kingdoms, provinces, states, rights, and advantages, which each of the parties at the signing of that treaty possessed, confining this guarantee to Europe only. The succours stipulated by this treaty were similar to those above-mentioned; first, interposition of good offices, then a certain number of forces, and, lastly, declaration of war. This treaty was renewed by the quadruple alliance of 1718, and by the treaty of Aix la Chapelle, 1748.

It was alleged on the part of the British court that the States-General had refused to comply with the terms of these treaties, although Minorca, a possession *in Europe*, which had been secured to Great Britain by the treaty of Utrecht, was attacked by France.

Two answers were given by the Dutch government to the demand of the stipulated succours.

1. That Great Britain was the aggressor in the war; and that unless she had been first attacked by France, the *casus fœderis* did not arise.

2. That admitting that France was the aggressor in Europe, yet it was only in consequence of the hostilities previously commenced in America, which were expressly excepted from the terms of the guarantees.

To the first of these objections it was irresistibly replied by the elder Lord *Liverpool*, that although the treaties which contained these guarantees were called defensive treaties only, yet the words of them, and particularly that of 1678, which was the basis of all the rest, by no means expressed the point clearly in the sense of the objection, since they guarantied " all the rights and possessions," of both parties, against "all kings, princes, republics, and states ;" so that if either should " be attacked or molested by hostile act, or open war, or in any other manner disturbed in the possession of his states, territories, rights, immunities, and freedom of commerce," it was then declared what should be done in defence of these objects of the guarantee, by the ally who was not at war; but it was no where mentioned as necessary that the attack of these should be the first injury or attack. "Nor," continues Lord Liverpool, " doth this loose manner of expression appear to have been an omission or inaccuracy. They who framed these guarantees certainly chose to leave this question, without any farther explanation, to that good faith which must ultimately decide upon all contracts between sovereign states. It is not presumed that they hereby meant that either party should be obliged to support every act of violence or injustice which his ally might be prompted to commit through the views of interest or ambition; but, on the other hand, they were cautious of affording too frequent opportunities to pretend that the case of the guarantees did not exist, and of eluding thereby the principal intention of the alliance : both these inconveniences were equally to be avoided ; and they wisely thought fit to guard against the

latter, no less than the former. They knew that in every
war between civilized nations, each party endeavours to
throw upon the other the odium and guilt of the first act of
provocation and aggression; and that the worst of causes
was never without its excuse. They foresaw that this alone
would unavoidably give sufficient occasion to endless cavils
and disputes, whenever the infidelity of an ally inclined him
to avail himself of them. To have confined, therefore, the
case of the guarantee by a more minute description of it, and
under closer restrictions of form, would have subjected to
still greater uncertainty a point, which, from the nature of
the thing itself, was already too liable to doubt :—they were
sensible that the cases would be infinitely various; that the
motives to self-defence, though just, might not always be
apparent; that an artful enemy might disguise the most
alarming preparations ; and that an injured nation might be
necessitated to commit even a preventive hostility before the
danger which caused it could be publicly known. Upon such
considerations these negotiators wisely thought proper to give
the greatest latitude to this question, and to leave it open to
a fair and liberal construction, such as might be expected
from friends, whose interests these treaties were supposed
to have for ever united."[16]

His Lordship's answer to the next objection, that the hostilities commenced by France in Europe were only in consequence of hostilities previously commenced in America,
seems equally satisfactory, and will serve to illustrate the
good faith by which these contracts ought to be interpreted.
" If the reasoning on which this objection is founded was admitted, it would alone be sufficient to destroy the effects of
every guarantee, and to extinguish that confidence which
nations mutually place in each other on the faith of defensive alliances: it points out to the enemy a certain method
of avoiding the inconvenience of such an alliance ; it shows
him where he ought to begin his attack. Let only the first

---

[16] Discourse on the Conduct of the Government of Great Britain in respect
to Neutral Nations. By Charles, Earl of Liverpool. 1st Ed. 1757.

effort be made upon some place not included in the guarantee, and after that he may pursue his views against its very object without any apprehension of the consequence: let France first attack some little spot belonging to Holland in America, and her barrier would be no longer guarantied. To argue in this manner is to trifle with the most solemn engagements. The proper object of guarantees is the preservation of some particular country to some particular power. The treaties above-mentioned promise the defence of the dominions of each party in Europe, simply and absolutely, whenever they are *attacked* or *molested*. If in the present war the first attack was made out of Europe, it is manifest that long ago an attack hath been made in Europe; and that is beyond a doubt the case of these guarantees.

"Let us try, however, if we cannot discover what hath once been the opinion of Holland upon a point of this nature. It hath already been observed that the defensive alliance between England and Holland, of 1678, is but a copy of the twelve first articles of the French treaty of 1662. Soon after Holland had concluded this last alliance with France, she became engaged in a war with England. The attack then began, as in the present case, out of Europe, on the coast of Guinea; and the cause of the war was also the same—a disputed right to certain possessions out of the bounds of Europe, some in Africa, and others in the East Indies. Hostilities having continued for some time in those parts, they afterwards commenced also in Europe. Immediately upon this, Holland declared that the case of that guarantee did exist, and demanded the succours which were stipulated. I need not produce the memorials of their ministers to prove this: history sufficiently informs us that France acknowledged the claim, granted the succours, and entered even into open war in the defence of her ally. Here, then, we have the sentiments of Holland on the same article in a case minutely parallel. The conduct of France also pleads in favour of the same opinion, though her concession in this respect checked at that time her youthful monarch in the first essay of his ambition, delayed for some months his entrance into the Spanish provinces, and brought on him the enmity of England."[17]

Alliance between Great Britain and Portugal.

The nature and extent of the obligations contracted by treaties of defensive alliance and guarantee will be farther illustrated by the case of the treaties subsisting between Great Britain and Portugal, which has been before alluded to for another purpose.[18] The treaty of alliance, originally concluded between these powers in 1642, immediately after the revolt of the Portuguese nation against Spain and the establishment of the house of Braganza on the throne, was renewed in 1654 by the protector Cromwell, and again confirmed by the treaty of 1661 between Charles II. and Alfonzo VI., for the marriage of the former prince with Catharine of Braganza. This last-mentioned treaty fixes the aid to be given, and declares that Great Britain will succour Portugal "on all occasions when that country is attacked." By a secret article, Charles II., in consideration of the cession of Tangier and Bombay, binds himself " to defend the colonies and conquests of Portugal against all enemies, present or future." In 1703 another treaty of defensive and perpetual alliance was concluded at Lisbon between Great Britain and the States-General on the one side, and the king of Portugal on the other ; the guarantees contained in which were again confirmed by the treaties of peace at Utrecht, between Portugal and France, in 1713, and between Portugal and Spain, in 1715. On the emigration of the Portuguese royal family to Brazil, in 1807, a convention was concluded between Great Britain and Portugal, by which the latter kingdom is guarantied to the lawful heir of the house of Braganza, and the British government promises never to recognise any other ruler. By the more recent treaty between the two powers, concluded at Rio Janeiro in 1810, it was declared, " that the two powers have agreed on an alliance for defence and reciprocal guarantee against every hostile attack, conformably to the treaties already subsisting between them, the stipulations of which shall remain in full force, and are renewed by the

---

[17] Liverpool's Discourse, p. 86.
[18] Vide ante, pt. ii. ch. 1, § 9.

present treaty in their fullest and most extensive interpretation." This treaty confirms the stipulation of Great Britain to acknowledge no other sovereign of Portugal but the heir of the house of Braganza. The treaty of Vienna, of the 22d January, 1815, between Great Britain and Portugal, contains the following article :—" The treaty of alliance at Rio Janeiro, of the 19th February, 1810, being founded on temporary circumstances, which have happily ceased to exist, the said treaty is hereby declared to be of no effect ; without prejudice, however, to the ancient treaties of alliance, friendship, and guarantee, which have so long and so happily subsisted between the two crowns, and which are hereby renewed by the high contracting parties, and acknowledged to be of full force and effect."

Such was the nature of the compacts of alliance and guarantee subsisting between Great Britain and Portugal, at the time when the interference of Spain in the affairs of the latter kingdom compelled the British government to interfere for the protection of the Portuguese nation against the hostile designs of the Spanish court. In addition to the grounds stated in the British parliament to justify this counteracting interference, it was urged, in a very able article on the affairs of Portugal, contemporaneously published in the Edinburgh Review, that although, in general, an alliance for defence and guarantee does not impose any obligation, nor, indeed, give any warrant to interfere in intestine divisions, the peculiar circumstance of the case did constitute the *casus fœderis* contemplated by the treaties in question. A defensive alliance is a contract between several states, by which they agree to aid each other in their defensive (or, in other words, in their just) wars against other states. Morally speaking, no other species of alliance is just, because no other species of war can be just. The simplest case of defensive war is where our ally is openly invaded with military force, by a power to whom she has given no just cause of war. If France or Spain, for instance, had marched an army into Portugal to subvert its constitutional government, the duty

of England would have been too evident to render a statement of it necessary. But this was not the only case to
which the treaties were applicable. If troops were assembled, and preparations made, with the manifest purpose of
aggression against an ally ; if his subjects were instigated to
revolt, and his soldiers to mutiny ; if insurgents on his territory were supplied with money, with arms, and military
stores : if, at the same time, his authority were treated as a
usurpation, all participation in the protection granted to other
foreigners refused to the well-affected part of his subjects,
while those who proclaimed their hostility to his person were
received as the most favoured strangers ;—in such a combination of circumstances, it could not be doubted that the
case foreseen by defensive alliances would arise, and that he
would be entitled to claim that succour, either general or
specific, for which his alliances had stipulated. The wrong
would be as complete, and the danger might be as great, as
if his territory were invaded by a foreign force. The mode
chosen by his enemy might even be more effectual, and more
certainly destructive, than open war. Whether the attack
made on him be open or secret, if it be equally unjust, and
exposes him to the same peril, he is equally authorized to
call for aid. All contracts, under the law of nations, are
interpreted as extending to every case manifestly and certainly parallel to those cases for which they provide by express words. In that law, which has no tribunal but the
conscience of mankind, there is no distinction between the
evasion and the violation of a contract. It requires aid against
disguised as much as against avowed injustice ; and it does
not fall into so gross an absurdity as to make the obligation
to succour less where the danger is greater. The only rule
for the interpretation of defensive alliances seems to be, that
every wrong which gives to one ally a just cause of war,
entitles him to succour from the other ally. The right to aid
is a secondary right, incident to that of repelling injustice by
force. Wherever he may morally employ his own strength
for that purpose, he may with reason demand the auxiliary

strength of his ally.[19] Fraud neither gives nor takes away any right. Had France, in the year 1715, assembled squadrons in her harbours and troops on her coasts; had she prompted and distributed writings against the legitimate government of George I.; had she received with open arms battalions of deserters from his troops, and furnished the army of the earl of Mar with pay and arms when he proclaimed the pretender; Great Britain, after demand and refusal of reparation, would have had a perfect right to declare war against France, and, consequently, as complete a title to the succour which the States-General were bound to furnish by their treaties of alliance and guarantee of the succession of the house of Hanover, as if the pretended king, James III., at the head of the French army, were marching on London. The war would be equally defensive on the part of England, and the obligation equally incumbent on Holland. It would show a more than ordinary defect of understanding to confound a war defensive in its *principles* with a war defensive in its *operations*. Where attack is the best mode of providing for the defence of a state, the war is defensive in principle, though the operations are offensive. Where the war is unnecessary to safety, its *offensive* character is not altered, because the wrong-doer is reduced to defensive warfare. So a state, against which dangerous wrong is manifestly meditated, may prevent it by striking the first blow, without thereby waging a war in its principle offensive. Accordingly, it is not every attack made on a state that will entitle it to aid under a defensive alliance; for if that state had given just cause of war to the invader, the war would not be on its part defensive in principle.[20]

[19] Vattel's reasoning is still more conclusive in a case of guarantee:— " Si l'alliance défensive porte un garantic de toutes les terres que l'allié possède actuellement, le *casus fœderis* se deploie toutes les fois que ces terres sont envahies *ou menaçées d'invasion*."—Liv. iii. ch. 6, § 91.

[20] " Dans une alliance défensive le *casus fœderis* n'existe pas tout de suite que notre allié est attaqué. Il faut voir s'il n'a point donné à son ennemie un juste sujet de lui faire la guerre. S'il est dans le tort, il faut l'engager à donner une satisfaction raisonable."—*Vattel,* liv. iii. ch. 6, § 90.

§ 14.
Hostages
for the ex-
ecution of
treaties.

The execution of a treaty is sometimes secured by *hostages* given by one party to the other. The most recent and re-markable example of this practice occurred at the peace of Aix-la-Chapelle, in 1748, where the restitution of Cape Bre-ton in North America, by Great Britain to France, was se-cured by several British peers sent as hostages to Paris.[21]

§ 15.
Interpre-
tation of
treaties.

Public treaties are to be interpreted like municipal laws and private contracts. Such is the inevitable imperfection and ambiguity of all human language, that the mere words alone of any writing, literally expounded, will go a very little way towards explaining its meaning. Certain technical rules of interpretation have therefore been adopted by writers on ethics and public law, to explain the meaning of international compacts in cases of doubt. These rules are fully expounded by *Grotius* and his commentators, and the reader is referred especially to the principles laid down by *Vattel* and *Ruther-forth*, as containing the completest view of this important subject.[22]

§ 16.
Mediation.

Negotiations are sometimes conducted under the mediation of a third power, spontaneously tendering its good offices for this purpose, or upon the request of one or both of the liti-gating powers, or in virtue of a previous stipulation for that purpose. If the mediation is spontaneously offered, it may be refused by either party: but if it is the result of a previ-ous agreement between the two parties, it cannot be refused without a breach of good faith. When accepted by both parties, it becomes the right and the duty of the mediating power to interpose its advice, with a view to the adjustment of their differences. It thus becomes a party to the negotia-tion, but has no authority to constrain either party to adopt its opinion. Nor is it obliged to guaranty the performance

[21] Vattel, liv. ii. ch. 16, §§ 245—261.

[22] Grotius, de Jur. Bel. ac Pac. lib. ii. cap. 16. Vattel, liv. ii. ch. 17. Rutherforth's Inst. b. ii. ch. 7.

of the treaty concluded under its mediation, though, in point of fact, it frequently does so.[23]

The art of negotiation seems, from its very nature, hardly capable of being reduced to a systematic science. It depends essentially on personal character and qualities, united with a knowledge of the world and experience in business. These talents may be strengthened by the study of history, and especially the history of diplomatic negotiations; but the want of them can hardly be supplied by any knowledge derived merely from books. One of the earliest works of this kind is that commonly called *Le Parfait Ambassadeur*, originally published in Spanish by Don Antonio de Vera, long time ambassador of Spain at Venice, who died in 1658. It was subsequently published by the author in Latin, and different translations appeared in Italian and French. Wicquefort's book, published in 1679, under the title of *L'Ambassadeur et ses Fonctions*, although its principal object is to treat of the rights of legation, contains much valuable information upon the art of negotiation. Callieres, one of the French plenipotentiaries at the treaty of Ryswick, published in 1716 a work entitled *De la Manière de Négocier avec les Souverains*, which obtained considerable reputation. The Abbé Mably also attempted to treat this subject systematically, in an essay entitled *Principes des Négotiations*, which is commonly prefixed as an introduction to his *Droit Publique de l'Europe* in the various editions of the works of that author. A catalogue of the different histories which have appeared of particular negotiations would be almost interminable, but nearly all that is valuable in them will be found collected in the excellent work of M. Flassan, entitled *L'Histoire de la Diplomatie Française*. The late Count de Ségur's compilation from the papers of Favier, one of the principal secret agents employed in the double diplomacy of Louis XV., entitled *Politique de tous les Cabinets de l'Europe pendant les Règnes de Louis XV. et de*

§ 17. Diplomatic history.

[23] Kluber, Droit des Gens Moderne de l'Europe, pt. ii. tit. 2, § 1; ch. 2, § 160.

Louis XVI., with the notes of the able and experienced editor, is a work which also throws great light upon the history of French diplomacy. A history of treaties from the earliest times to the emperor Charlemagne, collected from the ancient Latin and Greek authors, and from other monuments of antiquity, was published by Barbeyrac in 1739. It had been preceded by the immense collection of Dumont, embracing all the public treaties of Europe from the age of Charlemagne to the commencement of the eighteenth century.[24] The best collections of the more modern European treaties are those published at different periods by Professor Martens, of Göttingen, including the most important public acts upon which the present conventional law of Europe is founded. To these may be added Koch's *Histoire abregée des Traités de Paix depuis la Paix de Westphalie*, continued by Schöll. A complete collection of the proceedings of the congress of Vienna has also been published in German, by Kluber.[25]

[24] Corps Universel Diplomatique du Droit des Gens, &c. 8 tomes fol. Amsterd. 1726—1731. Supplement au Corps Universel Diplomatique, 5 tomes fol. 1739.

[25] Acten des Wiener Congresses in den Jahren, 1814 und 1815; von J. L. Kluber, Erlangen, 1815 und 1816; 6 Bde. 8vo.

PART FOURTH.

INTERNATIONAL RIGHTS OF STATES
IN THEIR HOSTILE RELATIONS.

PART FOURTH.

INTERNATIONAL RIGHTS OF STATES IN THEIR HOSTILE RELATIONS.

CHAPTER I.

COMMENCEMENT OF WAR, AND ITS IMMEDIATE EFFECTS.

THE independent societies of men called states acknowledge no common arbiter or judge, except such as are constituted by special compact. The law by which they are governed, or profess to be governed, is deficient in those positive sanctions which are annexed to the municipal code of each distinct society. Every state has therefore a right to resort to force as the only means of redress for injuries inflicted upon it by others, in the same manner as individuals would be entitled to that remedy were they not subject to the laws of civil society. Each state is also entitled to judge for itself what are the nature and extent of the injuries which will justify such a means of redress.

§ 1. Redress by forcible means between nations.

Among the various modes of terminating the differences between nations, by forcible means short of actual war, are the following:—

1. By laying an embargo or sequestration on the ships and goods, or other property of the offending nation found within the territory of the injured state.

2. By taking forcible possession of the thing in controversy by securing to yourself by force, and refusing to the other nation, the enjoyment of the right drawn in question.

3. By exercising the right of vindictive retaliation, (*retorsio facti,*) or of amicable retaliation, (*retorsion de droit ;*) by which last the one nation applies, in its transactions with the other, the same rule of conduct by which that other is governed under similar circumstances.

4. By making reprisals upon the persons and things belonging to the offending nation, until a satisfactory reparation is made for the alleged injury.[1]

§ 2.
Reprisals.

This last seems to extend to every species of forcible means for procuring redress, short of actual war, and, of course, to include all the other above enumerated. Reprisals are *negative*, when a state refuses to fulfil a perfect obligation which it has contracted, or to permit another nation to enjoy a right which it claims; they are *positive*, when they consist in seizing the persons and effects belonging to the other nation, in order to obtain satisfaction.[2]

Reprisals are also either *general* or *special*. They are *general*, when a state which has received, or supposes it has received, an injury from another nation, delivers commissions to its officers and subjects to take the persons and property belonging to the other nation, wherever the same may be found. It is, according to present usage, the first step which is usually taken at the commencement of a public war, and may be considered as amounting to a declaration of hostilities, unless satisfaction is made by the offending state. *Special* reprisals are, where letters of marque are granted, in time of peace, to particular individuals who have suffered an injury from the government or subjects of another nation.[3]

Reprisals are to be granted only in case of a clear and open denial of justice. The right of granting them is vested in the sovereign or supreme power of the state, and in former times was regulated by treaties and by the municipal ordi-

[1] Vattel, liv. ii. ch. 18. Kluber, Droit des Gens Moderne de l'Europe, § 234.

[2] Kluber, § 234, Note (*c.*)

[3] Bynkershoek, Quæst. Jur. Pub. lib. i. Duponceau's Transl. p. 182, Note.

nances of different nations. Thus, in England, the statute 4 Hen. V. cap. 7, declares, "That if any subjects of the realm are oppressed in time of peace by any foreigners, the king will grant marque in due form to all that feel themselves grieved;" which form is specially pointed out, and directed to be observed in the statute. So also, in France, the celebrated marine ordinance of Louis XIV. of 1681, prescribed the forms to be observed for obtaining special letters of marque by French subjects against those of other nations. But these special reprisals in time of peace have almost entirely fallen into disuse.[4]

Any of these acts of reprisal, or resort to forcible means of redress between nations, may assume the character of war in case adequate satisfaction is refused by the offending state. "Reprisals," says *Vattel*, "are used between nation and nation, in order to do themselves justice when they cannot otherwise obtain it. If a nation has taken possession of what belongs to another, if it refuses to pay a debt, to repair an injury, or to give adequate satisfaction for it, the latter may seize something belonging to the former, and apply it to its own advantage till it obtains payment of what is due, together with interest and damages; or keep it as a pledge till the offended nation has refused ample satisfaction. The effects thus seized are preserved while there is any hope of obtaining satisfaction or justice. As soon as that hope disappears, they are confiscated, and then reprisals are accomplished. If the two nations, upon this ground of quarrel, come to an open rupture, satisfaction is considered as refused from the moment that war is declared, or hostilities commenced; and then, also, the effects seized may be confiscated."[5]

§ 3. Effect of reprisals.

Thus, where an embargo was laid on Dutch property in the ports of Great Britain, on the rupture of the peace of

§ 4. Embargo previous to

[4] Vattel, Droit des Gens, liv. ii. ch. 18, §§ 342–346. Bynkershoek, Quæst. Jur. Pub. lib. i. cap. 24. Martens, Précis du Droit des Gens Moderne de l'Europe, liv. viii. ch. 2, § 260.
[5] Vattel, Droit des Gens, liv. ii. ch. 18, § 342.

declaration
of hostili-
ties. Amiens in 1803, under such circumstances as were considered
by the British government as constituting a hostile aggression on the part of Holland, Sir *W. Scott*, (Lord Stowell,) in
delivering his judgment in this case, said, that "the seizure
was at first equivocal; and if the matter in dispute had terminated in reconciliation, the seizure would have been converted into a mere civil embargo, so terminated. Such would
have been the retroactive effect of that course of circumstances. On the contrary, if the transaction end in hostility,
the retroactive effect is exactly the other way. It impresses
the direct hostile character upon the original seizure; it is
declared to be no embargo; it is no longer an equivocal act,
subject to two interpretations; there is a declaration of the
animus by which it is done; that it was done *hostili animo*,
and is to be considered as a hostile measure *ab initio* against
persons guilty of injuries which they refuse to redeem by any
amicable alteration of their measures. This is the necessary
course, if no particular compact intervenes for the restitution
of such property taken before a formal declaration of hostilities."[6]

§ 5.
Right of
making
war, in
whom
vested. The right of making war, as well as of authorizing reprisals, or other acts of vindictive retaliation, belongs in every
civilized nation to the supreme power of the state. The exercise of this right is regulated by the fundamental laws or
municipal constitution in each country, and may be delegated
to its inferior authorities in remote possessions, or even to a
commercial corporation—such, for example, as the British
East India Company—exercising, under the authority of the
state, sovereign rights in respect to foreign nations.[7]

§ 6.
Public or
solemn
war. A contest by force between independent sovereign states
is called a public war. If it is declared in form, or duly
commenced, it entitles both the belligerent parties to all the
rights of war against each other. The voluntary or positive

[6] Robinson's Adm. Rep. vol. v. p. 246. The Boedes Lust.

[7] Vattel, liv. iii. ch. 1, § 4. Martens, Précis, &c. liv. viii. ch. 2, §§ 260, 264.

law of nations makes no distinction in this respect between a just and an unjust war. A war in form, or duly commenced, is to be considered, as to its effects, as just on both sides. Whatever is permitted, by the laws of war, to one of the belligerent parties, is equally permitted to the other.[8]

A *perfect* war is where one whole nation is at war with another nation, and all the members of both nations are authorized to commit hostilities against all the members of the other, in every case and under every circumstance permitted by the general laws of war. An *imperfect* war is limited as to places, persons, and things.[9]

§ 7. Perfect or imperfect war.

A civil war between the different members of the same society is what *Grotius* calls a *mixed* war; it is according to him *public* on the side of the established government, and *private* on the part of the people resisting its authority. But the general usage of nations regards such a war as entitling both the contending parties to all the rights of war as against each other, and even as respects neutral nations.[10]

A formal declaration of war to the enemy was once considered necessary to legalize hostilities between nations. It was uniformly practised by the ancient Romans, and by the states of modern Europe until about the middle of the seventeenth century. The latest example of this kind was the declaration of war by France against Spain, at Brussels, in 1635, by heralds at arms, according to the forms observed during the middle age. The present usage is to publish a manifesto, within the territory of the state declaring war, announcing the existence of hostilities and the motives for commencing them. This publication may be necessary for the instruction and direction of the subjects of the belligerent state in respect to their intercourse with the enemy, and regarding certain effects which the voluntary law of nations

§ 8. Declaration of war, how far necessary.

---

[8] Vattel, Droit des Gens, liv. iii. ch. 12. Rutherforth's Inst. b. ii. ch. 9, § 15.

[9] Such were the limited hostilities authorized by the United States against France in 1798. Dallas' Rep. vol. ii. p. 21; vol. iv. p. 37.

[10] Vide ante, pt. i. ch. 2, § 19.

attributes to war in form. Without such a declaration, it
might be difficult to distinguish in a treaty of peace those acts
which are to be accounted lawful effects of war, from those
which either nation may consider as naked wrongs, and for
which they may, under certain circumstances, claim reparation.[11]

§ 9.
Enemy's
property
found in
the territo-
ry on the
commence-
ment of
war, how
far liable
to confis-
cation.

As no declaration, or other notice to the enemy, of the existence of war, is necessary, in order to legalize hostilities,
and as the property of the enemy is, in general, liable to
seizure and confiscation as prize of war, it would seem to
follow as a consequence that the property belonging to him
and found within the territory of the belligerent state at the
commencement of hostilities is liable to the same fate with
his other property wheresoever situated. But there is a great
diversity of opinions upon this subject among institutional
writers, and the tendency of modern usage between nations
seems to be to exempt such property from the operations of
war.

One of the exceptions to the general rule, laid down by
the text writers, which subjects all the property of the enemy
to capture, respects property locally situated within the jurisdiction of a neutral state; but this exemption is referred
to the right of the neutral state, not to any privilege which
the situation gives to the hostile owner. Does reason, or the
approved practice of nations, suggest any other exception?

With the Romans, who considered it lawful to enslave, or
even to kill an enemy found within the territory of the state
on the breaking out of war, it would very naturally follow
that his property found in the same situation would become
the spoil of the first taker. *Grotius*, whose great work on
the laws of war and peace appeared in 1625, adopts, as the
basis of his opinion upon this question, the rules of the Roman
law, but qualifies them by the more humane sentiments

[11] Grotius, de Jur. Bel. ac Pac. lib. i. cap. 3, § 4. Bynkershoek, Quæst.
Jur. Pub. lib. i. cap. 2. Rutherforth's Inst: b: ii. ch: 9, § 10. Vattel, Droit
des Gens, liv. iv. ch. 4, § 56. Kluber, Droit des Gens Moderne de l'Europe,
§§ 238, 239.

which began to prevail in the intercourse of mankind at the time he wrote. In respect to debts, due to private persons, he considers the right to demand them as suspended only during the war, and reviving with the peace. *Bynkershoek,* who wrote about the year 1737, adopts the same rules, and follows them to all their consequences. He holds that, as no declaration of war to the enemy is necessary, no notice is necessary to legalize the capture of his property, unless he has by express compact reserved the right to withdraw it on the breaking out of hostilities. This rule he extends to things in action, as debts and credits, as well as to things in possession. He adduces, in confirmation of this doctrine, a variety of examples from the conduct of different states, embracing a period of something more than a century, beginning in the year 1556 and ending in 1657. But he acknowledges that the right had been questioned, and especially by the States-General of Holland; and he adduces no precedent of its exercise later than the year 1667, seventy years before his publication. Against the ancient examples cited by him, there is the negative usage of the subsequent period of nearly a century and a half previously to the wars of the French revolution. During all this period, the only exception to be found is the case of the Silesia loan in 1753. In the argument of the English civilians against the reprisals made by the king of Prussia in that case on account of the capture of Prussian vessels by the cruisers of Great Britain, it is stated that " it would not be easy to find an instance where a prince had thought fit to make reprisals upon a debt due from himself to private men. There is a confidence that this will not be done. A private man lends money to a prince upon an engagement of honour; because a prince cannot be compelled, like other men, by a court of justice. So scrupulously did England and France adhere to this public faith, that even during the war," (alluding to the war terminated by the peace of Aix-la-Chapelle,) " they suffered no inquiry to be made whether any part of the public debt was due to the subjects of the enemy, though it is certain many

English had money in the French funds, and many French had money in ours."[12]

Vattel, who wrote about twenty years after Bynkershoek, after laying down the general principle that the property of the enemy is liable to seizure and confiscation, qualifies it by the exception of real property (*les immeubles*) held by the enemy's subjects within the belligerent state, which having been acquired by the consent of the sovereign, is to be considered as on the same footing with the property of his own subjects, and not liable to confiscation *jure belli*. But he adds that the rents and profits may be sequestrated, in order to prevent their being remitted to the enemy. As to debts, and other things in action, he holds that war gives the same right to them as to the other property belonging to the enemy. He then quotes the example referred to by Grotius, of the hundred talents due by the Thebans to the Thessalians, of which Alexander had become master by right of conquest, but which he remitted to the Thessalians as an act of favour : and proceeds to state that " the sovereign has naturally the same right over what his subjects may be indebted to the enemy ; therefore he may confiscate debts of this nature, if the term of payment happen in time of war, or at least he may prohibit his subjects from paying while the war lasts. But at present, the advantages and safety of commerce have induced all the sovereigns of Europe to relax from this rigour. And as this custom has been generally received, he who should act contrary to it would injure the public faith; since foreigners have confided in his subjects only in the firm persuasion that the general usage would be observed. The state does not even touch the sums which it owes to the enemy; every where, in case of war, the funds

---

[12] Grotius, de Jur. Bel. ac Pac. lib. iii. cap. 20, § 16. Bynkershoek, Quæst. Jur. Pub. lib. i. cap. 2, 7. Letters of Camillus, by A. Hamilton, No. 20.

Vattel calls the Report of the English civilians " un excellent morceau de droit des gens," (liv. ii. ch. 7, § 34, Note *a ;*) and Montesquieu terms it "une reponse sans replique."—*Œuvres*, tom. vi. p. 445.

confided to the public, are exempt from seizure and confiscation." In another passage, Vattel gives the reason of this
exemption. "In reprisals, the property of subjects is seized,
as well as that belonging to the sovereign or state. Every
thing which belongs to the nation is liable to reprisals as soon
as it can be seized, provided it be not a deposite confided to
the public faith. This deposite being found in our hands only
on account of that confidence which the proprietor has re-
posed in our good faith, ought to be respected even in case of
open war. Such is the usage in France, in England, and
elsewhere, in respect to money placed by foreigners in the
public funds." Again he says : "The sovereign declaring
war can neither detain those subjects of the enemy who were
within his dominions at the time of the declaration, nor their
effects. They came into his country on the public faith : by
permitting them to enter his territories, and continue there,
he has tacitly promised them liberty and perfect security for
their return. He ought, then, to allow them a reasonable
time to retire with their effects, and if they remain beyond
the time fixed, he may treat them as enemies ; but only as
enemies disarmed."[13]

It appears, then, to be the established rule of international
usage that property of the enemy found within the territory
of the belligerent state, or debts due to his subjects by the
government or individuals, at the commencement of hostilities, are not liable to be seized and confiscated as prizes of
war. This rule is frequently enforced by treaty stipulations,
but unless it be thus enforced it cannot be considered as an
inflexible, though an established, rule. "The rule," as it
has been beautifully observed, "like other precepts of morality, of humanity, and even of wisdom, is addressed to the
judgment of the sovereign—it is a guide which he follows or
abandons at his will ; and although it cannot be disregarded
by him without obloquy, yet it may be disregarded. It is

---

[13] Vattel, Droit des Gens, liv. ii. ch. 18, § 344; liv. iii. ch. 4, § 63; ch. 5,
§§ 73—77.

not an immutable rule of law, but depends on political considerations, which may continually vary."[14]

§ 10.
Rule of reciprocity.
Among these considerations is the conduct observed by the enemy. If he confiscates property found within his territory, or debts due to our subjects on the breaking out of war, it would certainly be just, and it may, under certain circumstances, be politic, to retort upon his subjects by a similar proceeding. This principle of reciprocity operates in many cases of international law. It is stated by Sir *W. Scott* to be the constant practice of Great Britain, on the breaking out of war, to condemn property seized before the war, if the enemy condemns, and to restore if the enemy restores. "It is," says he, "a principle sanctioned by that great foundation of the law of England, Magna Charta itself, which prescribes, that at the commencement of a war, the enemy's merchants shall be kept and treated as our own merchants are kept and treated in their country."[15] And it is also stated in the report of the English civilians in 1753, before referred to, in order to enforce their argument, that the king of Prussia could not justly extend his reprisals to the Silesia loan, that "French ships and effects, wrongfully taken, after the Spanish war, and before the French war, have, during the heat of the war with France, and since, been restored by sentence of your Majesty's courts to the French owners. No such ships or effects ever were attempted to be confiscated as enemy's property, here, during the war; because, had it not been for the wrong first done, these effects would not have been in your Majesty's dominions."

§ 11.
Droits of Admiralty.
The ancient law of England seems thus to have surpassed in liberality its modern practice. In the recent maritime wars commenced by that country, it has been the constant usage to seize and condemn as droits of admiralty the property of the enemy found in its ports at the breaking out of

[14] Mr. Chief Justice Marshall in Brown *v.* the United States, Cranch's Rep. vol. viii.
[15] Robinson's Adm. Rep. vol. i. p. 64. The Santa Cruz.

hostilities, and this practice does not appear to have been influenced by the corresponding conduct of the enemy in that respect. As has been observed by an English writer, commenting on the judgment of Sir W. Scott in the case of the Dutch ships, "there seems something of subtlety in the distinction between the virtual and the actual declaration of hostilities, and in the device of giving to the actual declaration a retrospective efficacy, in order to cover the defect of the virtual declaration previously implied."[16]

In respect to debts due to an enemy previously to the commencement of hostilities, the law of Great Britain pursues a policy of a more liberal, or at least of a wiser character. A maritime power which has an overwhelming naval superiority may have an interest, or may suppose it has an interest, in asserting the right of confiscating enemy's property seized before an actual declaration of war; but a nation, which by the extent of its capital must generally be the creditor of every other commercial country, can certainly have no interest in confiscating debts due to an enemy, since that enemy might, in almost every instance, retaliate with much more injurious effect. Hence, though the prerogative of confiscating such debts, and compelling their payment to the crown, still theoretically exists, it is seldom or never practically exerted. The right of the original creditor to sue for the recovery of the debt is not extinguished: it is only suspended during the war, and revives in full force on the restoration of peace.[17]

§ 12. Debts due to the enemy.

Such, too, is the law and practice of the United States. The debts due by American citizens to British subjects before the war of the revolution, and not actually confiscated, were judicially considered as revived, together with the right to sue for their recovery, on the restoration of peace between the two countries. The impediments which had existed to

[16] Chitty's Law of Nations, ch. 3, p. 80.
[17] Bosanquet and Puller's Rep. vol. iii. p. 191. Furtado v. Rogers. Vesey, Jun. Rep. vol. xiii. p. 71, ex parte Boussmaker. Edward's Adm. Rep. p. 60. The Nuestra Senora de los Dolores.

the collection of British debts under the local laws of the different states of the confederation were stipulated to be removed by the treaty of peace in 1783; but this stipulation proving ineffectual for the complete indemnification of the creditors, the controversy between the two countries on this subject was finally adjusted by the payment of a sum *en bloc* by the government of the United States for the use of the British creditors. The commercial treaty of 1794 also contained an express declaration that it was unjust and impolitic that private contracts should be impaired by national differences, with a mutual stipulation that " neither the debts due from individuals of the one nation to individuals of the other, nor shares, nor moneys which they may have in the public or private banks, shall ever, in any event of war, or national differences, be sequestered or confiscated."[18]

On the commencement of hostilities between France and Great Britain in 1793, the former power sequestrated the debts and other property belonging to the subjects of her enemy, which decree was retaliated by a countervailing measure on the part of the British government. By the additional articles to the treaty of peace between the two powers, concluded at Paris in April, 1814, the sequestrations were removed on both sides, and commissaries were appointed to liquidate the claims of British subjects for the value of their property unduly confiscated by the French authorities, and also for the total or partial loss of the debts due to them, or other property unduly retained under sequestration subsequently to 1792. The engagement thus extorted from France may be considered as a severe application of the rights of conquest to a fallen enemy, rather than a measure of even-handed justice; since it does not appear that French property, seized in the ports of Great Britain and at sea, in anticipation of hostilities, and subsequently condemned as droits of admiralty, was restored to the original owners under this treaty on the return of peace between the two countries.[19]

---

[18] Dallas' Rep. vol. iii. pp. 4, 5, 199—285.

[19] Martens, Nouveau Recueil, tom. ii. p. 16.

So also, on the rupture between Great Britain and Denmark in 1807, the Danish ships and other property, which had been seized in the British ports and on the high seas before the actual declaration of hostilities, were condemned as droits of admiralty by the retrospective operation of the declaration. The Danish government issued an ordinance, retaliating this seizure by sequestrating all debts due from Danish to British subjects, and causing them to be paid into the Danish royal treasury. The English court of King's Bench determined that this ordinance was not a legal defence to a suit in England for such a debt, not being conformable to the usage of nations; the text writers having condemned the practice, and no instance having occurred of the exercise of the right, except the ordinance in question, for upwards of a century. The soundness of this judgment may well be questioned. It has been justly observed, that between debts contracted under the faith of laws, and property acquired on the faith of the same laws, reason draws no distinction; and the right of the sovereign to confiscate debts is precisely the same with the right to confiscate other property found within the country on the breaking out of the war. Both require some special act expressing the sovereign will, and both depend, not on any inflexible rule of international law, but on political considerations by which the judgment of the sovereign may be guided.[20]

One of the immediate consequences of the commencement of hostilities is the interdiction of all commercial intercourse between the subjects of the states at war, without the license of their respective governments. In Sir W. Scott's judgment, in the case of the *Hoop*, this is stated to be a principle of universal law, and not peculiar to the maritime jurisprudence of England. It is laid down by *Bynkershoek* as a universal principle of law. "There can be no doubt," says that writer, "that from the nature of war itself, all commercial intercourse ceases between enemies. Although there be no

§ 13. Trading with the enemy, unlawful on the part of subjects of the belligerent state.

[20] Maule & Selwyn's Rep. vol. vi. p. 92. Wolff *v.* Oxholm. Cranch's Rep. vol. viii. p. 110. Brown *v.* the United States.

special interdiction of such intercourse, as is often the case, commerce is forbidden by the mere operation of the law of war. Declarations of war themselves sufficiently manifest it, for they enjoin on every subject to attack the subjects of the other prince, seize on their goods, and do them all the harm in their power. The utility, however, of merchants, and the mutual wants of nations, have almost got the better of the law of war, as to commerce. Hence it is alternately permitted and forbidden in time of war, as princes think it most for the interests of their subjects. A commercial nation is anxious to trade, and accommodates the laws of war to the greater or lesser want that it may be in of the goods of others. Thus sometimes a mutual commerce is permitted generally; sometimes as to certain merchandises only, while others are prohibited; and sometimes it is prohibited altogether. But in whatever manner it may be permitted, whether generally or specially, it is always, in my opinion, so far a suspension of the laws of war; and in this manner, there is partly war and partly peace between the subjects of both countries."[21]

"It appears from these passages to have been the law of Holland. *Valin* states it to have been the law of France, whether the trade was attempted to be carried on in national or in neutral vessels; and it appears from a case cited (in the *Hoop*) to have been the law of Spain; and it may without rashness be affirmed to be a general principle of law in most of the countries of Europe."[22]

Sir *W. Scott* proceeds to state two grounds upon which this sort of communication is forbidden. The first is, that " by the law and constitution of Great Britain the sovereign alone has the power of declaring war and peace. He alone, therefore, who has the power of entirely removing the state of war, has the power of removing it in part, by permitting, where he sees proper, that commercial intercourse which is a partial suspension of the war. There may be occasions on which such an intercourse may be highly expedient; but it is not for individuals to determine on the expediency of such

[21] Bynkershoek, Quæst. Jur. Pub. lib. i. cap. 3.
[22] Valin, Comm. sur l'Ordonn. de la Marine, liv. iii. tit. 6, art. 3.

occasions, on their own notions of commerce merely, and possibly on grounds of private advantage not very reconcileable with the general interests of the state. It is for the state alone, on more enlarged views of policy, and of all circumstances that may be connected with such an intercourse, to determine when it shall be permitted, and under what regulations. No principle ought to be held more sacred than that this intercourse cannot subsist on any other footing than that of the direct permission of the state. Who can be insensible to the consequences that might follow, if every person in time of war had a right to carry on a commercial intercourse with the enemy, and, under colour of that, had the means of carrying on any other species of intercourse he might think fit? The inconvenience to the public might be extreme; and where is the inconvenience on the other side, that the merchant should be compelled, in such a situation of the two countries, to carry on his trade between them (if necessary) under the eye and control of the government charged with the care of the public safety?

" Another principle of law, of a less' politic nature, but equally general in its reception and direct in its application, forbids this sort of communication as fundamentally inconsistent with the relation existing between the two belligerent countries; and that is, the total inability to sustain any contract by an appeal to the tribunals of the one country, on the part of the subjects of the other. In the law of almost every country, the character of alien enemy carries with it a disability to sue, or to sustain, in the language of the civilians, a *persona standi in judicio*. A state in which contracts cannot be enforced cannot be a state of legal commerce. If the parties who are to contract have no right to compel the performance of the contract, nor even to appear in a court of justice for that purpose, can there be a stronger proof that the law imposes a legal inability to contract? To such transactions it gives no sanction—they have no legal existence; and the whole of such commerce is attempted without its protection, and against its authority. *Bynkershoek* expresses himself with force upon this argument, in his first book, chapter vii., where he lays down that the legality of commerce and the mutual use of courts of justice are inseparable. He says, that cases of commerce are undistinguishable from cases of any other species in this respect : ' But if the enemy be once permitted to bring actions, it is difficult to distinguish from what causes they may arise ; nor have I been able to observe that this distinction has ever been carried into practice.' "

Sir *W. Scott* then notices the constant current of decisions in the British courts of prize where the rule had been rigidly enforced in cases where acts of parliament had, on different occasions, been made to relax the navigation law and other revenue acts; where the government had authorized, under the sanction of an act of parliament, a homeward trade from the enemy's possessions, but had not specifically protected an outward trade to the same, though intimately connected with that homeward trade, and almost necessary to its existence ; were strong claims, not merely of convenience, but of necessity, excused it on the part of the individual ; where cargoes had been laden before the war, but the parties had not used all possible diligence to countermand the voyage after the first notice of hostilities; and where it had been enforced, not only against British subjects, but also against those of its allies in the war, upon the supposition that the rule was founded upon a universal principle, which states allied in war had a right to notice and apply mutually to each other's subjects.

Such, according to this eminent civilian, are the general principles of the rule under which the public law of Europe, and the municipal law of its different states, have interdicted all commerce with an enemy. It is thus sanctioned by the double authority of public and of private jurisprudence ; and is founded both upon the sound and salutary principle forbidding all intercourse with an enemy, unless by permission of the sovereign or state, and upon the doctrine that he who is *hostis*—who has no *persona standi in judicio*, no means of enforcing contracts, cannot make contracts unless by such permission.[23]

[23] Robinson's Adm. Rep. vol. i. p. 196.   The Hoop.

The same principles were applied by the American courts Decisions of the American courts. of justice to the intercourse of their citizens with the enemy on the breaking out of the late war between the United States and Great Britain. A case occurred in which a citizen had purchased a quantity of goods within the British territory, a long time previous to the declaration of hostilities, and had deposited them on an island near the frontier; upon the breaking out of hostilities, his agents had hired a vessel to proceed to the place of deposite, and bring away the goods; on her return she was captured, and, with the cargo, condemned as prize of war. It was contended for the claimant that this was not a trading within the meaning of the cases cited to support the condemnation; that, on the breaking out of war, every citizen had a right, and it was the interest of the community to permit its members, to withdraw property purchased before the war, and lying in the enemy's country. But the supreme court determined that whatever relaxation of the strict rights of war the more mitigated and mild practice of modern times might have established, there had been none on this subject. The universal sense of nations had acknowledged the demoralizing effects which would result from the admission of individual intercourse between the states at war. The whole nation is embarked in one common bottom, and must be reconciled to one common fate. Every individual of the one nation must acknowledge every individual of the other nation as his own enemy, because he is the enemy of his country. This being the duty of the citizen, what is the consequence of a breach of that duty? The law of prize is a part of the law of nations. By it a hostile character is attached to trade, independent of the character of the trader who pursues or directs it. Condemnation to the captor is equally the fate of the enemy's property, and of that found engaged in an anti-neutral trade. But a citizen or ally may be engaged in a hostile trade, and thereby involve his property in the fate of those in whose cause he embarks. This liability of the property of a citizen to condemnation as prize of war may likewise be accounted for on other considerations. Every thing that issues from a hostile country is, *primâ facie*, the property of the enemy; and it is incumbent upon the claimant to support the negative of the proposition. But if the claimant be a citizen, or an ally, at the same time that he makes out his interest, he confesses the commission of an offence, which, under a well known rule of the municipal law, deprives him of his right to prosecute his claim. Nor did this doctrine rest upon abstract reasoning only: it was supported by the practice of the most enlightened, perhaps it might be said, of all commercial nations: and it afforded the court full confidence in their judgment in this case, that they found, upon recurring to the records of the court of appeals in prize causes established during the war of the revolution, that in various cases it was reasoned upon as the established law of that court. Certain it was, that it was the law of England before the American revolution, and therefore formed a part of the admiralty and maritime jurisdiction conferred upon the United States courts by their federal constitution. Whether the trading, in that case, was such as in the eye of the prize law subjects the property to capture and confiscation, depended on the legal force of the term. If by *trading*, in the law of prize, were meant that signification of the term, which consists in negotiation or contract, the case would certainly not come under the penalty of the rule. But the object, policy, and spirit of the rule are intended to cut off all communication, or actual locomotive intercourse between individuals of the states at war. Negotiation or contract had therefore no necessary connexion with the offence. Intercourse, inconsistent with actual hostility, is the offence against which the rule is directed; and by substituting this term for that of *trading with the enemy*, an answer was given to the argument, that this was not a trading within the meaning of the cases cited. Whether, on the breaking out of war, a citizen has a right to remove to his own country with his property, or not, the claimant certainly had not a right to leave his own country for the purpose of bringing home his property from an enemy country. As to the claim for the vessel, it was held to be founded upon no pretext whatever;

for the undertaking was altogether voluntary and inexcusable.[24]

So also, where goods were purchased, some time before the war, by the agent of an American citizen in Great Britain, but not shipped until nearly a year after the declaration of hostilities, they were pronounced liable to confiscation. Supposing a citizen had a right, on the breaking out of hostilities, to withdraw his property, purchased before the war, from the enemy's country, (on which the court gave no opinion,) such right must be exercised with due diligence, and within a reasonable time after a knowledge of hostilities. To admit a citizen to withdraw property from a hostile country a long time after the commencement of war, upon the pretext of its having been purchased before the war, would lead to the most injurious consequences, and hold out temptations to every species of fraudulent and illegal traffic with the enemy. To such an unlimited extent the right could not exist.[25]

We have seen what is the rule of public and municipal law on this subject, and what are the sanctions by which it is guarded. Various attempts have been made to evade its operation, and to escape its penalties; but its inflexible rigour has defeated all these attempts. The apparent exceptions to the rule, far from weakening its force, confirm and strengthen it. They all resolve themselves into cases where the trading was with a neutral, or the circumstances were considered as implying a license, or the trading was not consummated until the enemy had ceased to be such. In all other cases, an express license from the government is held to be necessary to legalize commercial intercourse with the enemy.[26]

Not only is such intercourse with the enemy, on the part of the subjects of the belligerent state, prohibited and pun-

§ 14. Trade with the

[24] Cranch's Rep. vol. viii. p. 155. The Rapid.
[25] Cranch's Rep. vol. viii. p. 434. The St. Lawrence. Vol. ix. p. 120, S. C.
[26] Robinson's Adm. Rep. vol. vi. p. 127. The Franklin. Vol. iv. p. 195. The Madonna delle Grazie. Vol. v. p. 141. The Juffrow Catharina. P. 251. The Alby. Wheaton's Rep. vol. ii. Appendix, Note I. p. 34.

common ished with confiscation in the prize courts of their own coun-
enemy, un-
lawful on try, but, during a conjoint war, no subject of an ally can trade
the part of with the common enemy, without being liable to the forfeiture
allied sub-
jects. in the prize courts of the ally of his property engaged in such
trade. This rule is a corollary of the other, and is founded
upon the principle that such trade is forbidden to the subjects
of the co-belligerent by the municipal law of his own country, by the universal law of nations, and by the express or
implied terms of the treaty of alliance subsisting between
the allied powers. And as the former rule can be relaxed
only by the permission of the sovereign power of the state, so
this can be relaxed only by the permission of the allied nations according to their mutual agreement. A declaration of
hostilities naturally carries with it an interdiction of all commercial intercourse. Where one state only is at war, this interdiction may be relaxed as to its own subjects without injuring any other states; but when allied nations are pursuing
a common cause against a common enemy, there is an implied,
if not an express contract, that neither of the co-belligerent
states shall do any thing to defeat the common object. If one
state allows its subjects to carry on an uninterrupted trade with
the enemy, the consequence will be that it will supply aid and
comfort to the enemy which may be injurious to the common
cause. It should seem that it is not enough, therefore, to
satisfy the prize court of one of the allied states, to say that
the other has allowed this practice to its own subjects; it
should also be shown, either that the practice is of such a
nature as cannot interfere with the common operations, or
that it has the allowance of the other confederate state.[27]

§ 15.   It follows as a corollary from the principle, interdicting all
Contracts
with the commercial and other pacific intercourse with the public
enemy enemy, that every species of private contract made with his
prohibited. subjects during the war is unlawful. The rule thus deduced
is applicable to insurance on enemy's property and trade; to

[27] Bynkershoek, Quæst. Jur. Pub. lib. i. cap. 10.   Robinson's Adm. Rep.
vol. iv. p. 251; vol. vi. p. 403.   The Neptunus.

the drawing and negotiating of bills of exchange between subjects of the powers at war; to the remission of funds, in
money or bills, to the enemy's country; to commercial part-
nerships entered into between the subjects of the two countries after the declaration of war, or existing previous to the
declaration, which last are dissolved by the mere force and
act of the war itself, although as to other contracts it only
suspends the remedy.[28]

Grotius, in the second chapter of his third book, where he
is treating of the liability of the property of subjects for the
injuries committed by the state to other communities, lays
down that " by the law of nations, all the subjects of' the offending state, who are such from a permanent cause, whether
natives or emigrants from another country, are liable to reprisals, but not so those who are only travelling or sojourning
for a little time;—for reprisals," says he, " have been introduced as a species of charge imposed in order to pay the
debts of the public; from which are exempt those who are
only temporarily subject to the laws. Ambassadors and their
goods are, however, excepted from this liability of subjects,
but not those sent to an enemy." In the fourth chapter of
the same book, where he is treating of the right of killing
and doing other bodily harm to enemies, in what he calls
solemn war, he holds that this right extends, " not only to those
who bear arms, or are subjects of the author of the war, but
to all those who are found within the enemy's territory. In
fact, as we have reason to fear the hostile intentions even of
strangers who are within the enemy's territory at the time,
that is sufficient to render the right of which we are speaking applicable even to them in a general war. In which respect there is a distinction between war and reprisals, which
last, as we have seen, are a kind of contribution paid by the
subjects for the debts of the state."[29]

§ 16.
Persons
domiciled
in the
enemy's
country
liable to
reprisals.

[28] Bynkershoek, Quæst. Jur. Pub. lib. i. cap. 21. Duponceau's Trans. p.
165, Note. Kent's Commentaries on American Law, vol. i. p. 64.
[29] De Jur. Bel. ac Pac. lib. iii. cap. 2, § 7; cap. 4, § 6.

Barbeyrac, in a note collating these passages, observes, that "the late M. Cocceius, in a dissertation which I have already cited, *De Jure Belli in Amicos,* rejects this distinction, and insists that even those foreigners who have not been allowed time to retire ought to be considered as adhering to the enemy, and for that reason justly exposed to acts of hostility. In order to supply this pretended defect, he afterwards distinguishes foreigners who remain in the country, from those who only transiently pass through it, and are constrained by sickness or the necessity of their affairs. But this is alone sufficient to show that, in this place, as in many others, he criticised our author without understanding him. In the following paragraph, Grotius manifestly distinguishes from the foreigners of whom he has just spoken those who are permanent subjects of the enemy, by whom he doubtless understands, as the learned Gronovius has already explained, those who are *domiciled* in the country. Our author explains his own meaning in the second chapter of this book, in speaking of reprisals, which he allows against this species of foreigners, whilst he does not grant them against those who only pass through the country, or are temporarily resident in it."[30]

Whatever may be the extent of the claims of a man's native country upon his political allegiance, there can be no doubt that the natural-born subject of one country may become the citizen of another, in time of peace, for the purposes of trade, and may become entitled to all the commercial privileges attached to his acquired domicil. On the other hand, if war breaks out between his adopted country and his native country, or any other, his property becomes liable to reprisals in the same manner as the effects of those who owe a permanent allegiance to the enemy state.

§ 17.
Species of residence constitu- ting domi- cil.
As to what species of residence constitutes such a domicil as will render the party liable to reprisals, the text writers are deficient in definitions and details. Their defects are supplied by the precedents furnished by the British prize

[30] Grotius, par Barbeyrac, *in loc.*

courts, which, if they have not applied the principle with undue severity in the case of neutrals, have certainly not mitigated it in its application to that of British subjects resident in the enemy's country on the commencement of hostilities.

In the judgment of the lords of appeal in prize causes, upon the cases arising out of the capture of St. Eustatius by Admiral Rodney, delivered in 1785 by *Lord Camden*, he stated that "if a man went into a foreign country upon a visit, to travel for health, to settle a particular business, or the like, he thought it would be hard to seize upon his goods; but a residence, not attended with these circumstances, ought to be considered as a permanent residence." In applying the evidence and the law to the resident foreigners in St. Eustatius, he said, that "in every point of view, they ought to be considered resident subjects. Their persons, their lives, their industry, were employed for the benefit of the state under whose protection they lived; and if war broke out, they continuing to reside there, paid their proportion of taxes, imposts, and the like, equally with natural-born subjects, and no doubt come within that description."[31]

"Time," says Sir *W. Scott*, "is the grand ingredient in constituting domicil. In most cases, it is unavoidably conclusive. It is not unfrequently said, that if a person comes only for a special purpose, *that* shall not fix a domicil. This is not to be taken in an unqualified latitude, and without some respect to the time which such a purpose may or shall occupy; for if the purpose be of such a nature as *may probably*, or *does actually*, detain the person for a great length of time, a general residence might grow upon the special purpose. A special purpose may lead a man to a country, where it shall detain him the whole of his life. Against such a long residence, the plea of an original special purpose could not be averred; it must be inferred, in such a case, that other purposes forced themselves upon him, and mixed themselves with the original de-

[31] MS. Proceedings of the Commissioners under the Treaty of 1794, between Great Britain and the United States. Opinion of Mr. W. Pinkney in the case of the Betsey.

sign, and impressed upon him the character of the country
where he resided. Supposing a man comes into a belligerent
country at or before the beginning of a war, it is certainly
reasonable not to bind him too soon to an acquired character,
and to allow him a fair time to disentangle himself; but if he
continues to reside during a good part of the war, contribut-
ing by the payment of taxes and other means to the strength
of that country, he could not plead his special purpose with
any effect against the rights of hostility. If he could, there
would be no sufficient guard against the frauds and abuses of
masked, pretended, original and sole purposes of a long-con-
tinued residence. There is a time which will estop such a
plea; no rule can fix the time à priori, but such a rule there
must be. In proof of the efficacy of mere time, it is not im-
pertinent to remark that the same quantity of business, which
would not fix a domicil in a certain quantity of time, would
nevertheless have that effect if distributed over a larger space
of time. This matter is to be taken in the compound ratio
of the time and the occupation, with a great preponderance
on the article of time: be the occupation what it may, it
cannot happen, with but few exceptions, that mere length of
time shall not constitute a domicil."[32]

In the case of the *Indian Chief,* determined in 1800, Mr.
Johnson, a citizen of the United States domiciled in England,
had engaged in a mercantile enterprise to the British East
Indies, a trade prohibited to British subjects, but allowed to
American citizens under the commercial treaty of 1794, between the United States and Great Britain. The vessel
came into a British port on its return voyage, and was seized
as engaged in illicit trade. Mr. Johnson, having then left
England, was determined not to be a British subject at the
time of capture, and restitution was decreed. In delivering
his judgment in this case, Sir *W. Scott* said, "Taking it to be
clear that the national character of Mr. Johnson, as a British
merchant, was founded in residence only, that it was acquired by residence, and rested on that circumstance alone,

[32] Robinson's Adm. Rep. vol. ii. p. 324. The Harmony.

it must be held that from the moment he turned his back on the country where he resided, on his way to his own country, he was in the act of resuming his original character, and must be considered as an American. The character that is gained by residence, ceases by non-residence. It is an adventitious character, and no longer adheres to him from the moment he puts himself in motion, *bonâ fide*, to quit the country, *sine animo revertendi*."[33]

The native character easily reverts, and it requires fewer circumstances to constitute domicil, in the case of a native subject, than to impress the national character on one who is originally of another country. Thus the property of a Frenchman, who had been residing and was probably naturalized in the United States, but who had returned to St. Domingo, and shipped from thence the produce of that island to France, was condemned in the High Court of Admiralty.[34] *The native character easily reverts.*

In the *Indian Chief*, the case of Mr. Dutilth is referred to by the claimant's counsel, as having obtained restitution, though *at the time of sailing* he was resident in the enemy's country; but a decision of the lords of appeal, in 1800, is mentioned by Sir C. Robinson, in which Mr. Dutilth's property was condemned according to the circumstances of his residence at the time of capture. That decision is more particularly stated by Sir J. Nicholl, at the hearing of the case of the *Harmony* before the lords, July 7, 1803. " The case of Mr. Dutilth also illustrates the present. He came to Europe about the end of July, 1793, at a time when there was a great deal of alarm on account of the state of commerce. He went to Holland, then not only in a state of amity, but of alliance with this country; he continued there until the French entered. During the whole time he was there, he was without any establishment; he had no counting-house ; he had no contracts nor dealings with contractors there; he

[33] Robinson's Adm. Rep. vol. iii. p. 12. The Indian Chief.
[34] Robinson's Adm. Rep. vol. v. p. 99. La Virginie. The same rule is also adopted in the prize law of France, (Code des Prises, tom. i. pp. 92, 139, 303,) and by the American prize courts, (Wheaton's Rep. vol. ii. p. 76.) The Dos Hermanos.

employed merchants there to sell his property, paying them a commission.   Upon the French entering into Holland, he applied for advice to know what was left for him to do under the circumstances, having remained there on account of the doubtful state of mercantile credit, which not only affected Dutch and American, but English houses, who were all looking after the state of credit in that country.   In 1794, when the French came there, Mr. D. applied to Mr. Adams, the American minister, who advised him to stay until he could get a passport.   He continued there until the latter end of that year, and having wound up his concerns, came away. Some part of his property was captured before he came there.   That part which was taken before he came there was restored to him, (the Fair American, Adm. 1796,) but that part which was taken while he was there was condemned, and *that* because he was in Holland at the time of the capture."—(The Hannibal and Pomona, Lords, 1800.)[35]

The case of the *Diana*, determined by Sir W. Scott in 1803, is also full of instruction on this subject.   During the war which commenced in 1795 between Great Britain and Holland, the colony of Demerara surrendered to the British arms, and by the treaty of Amiens it was restored to the Dutch. That treaty contained an article allowing the inhabitants, of whatever country they might be, a term of three years, to be computed from the notification of the treaty, for the purpose of disposing of their effects acquired before or during the war, in which term they might have the free enjoyment of their property.   Previous to the declaration of war against Holland in 1803, the Diana and several other vessels, laden with colonial produce, were captured on a voyage from Demerara to Holland.   Immediately after the declaration, and before the expiration of the three years from the notification of the treaty of Amiens, Demerara again surrendered to Great Britain.   Claims to the captured property were filed by original British subjects, inhabitants of Demerara, some of whom had settled in the colony while it was in possession of Great

35 Wheaton's Rep. vol. ii. p. 56, Note.

Britain; others before that event. The cause came on for hearing after it had again become a British colony.

Sir *W. Scott* decreed restitution to those British subjects who had settled in the colony while in British possession, but condemned the property of those who had settled there before that time. He held that those of the first class by settling in Demerara while belonging to Great Britain, afforded a presumption of their intending to return if the island should be transferred to a foreign power, which presumption, recognised by the treaty, relieved those claimants from the necessity of proving such intention. He thought it reasonable that they should be admitted to their *jus postliminii,* and he held them entitled to the protection of British subjects. But he was clearly of opinion that " mere recency of establishment would not avail, if the intention of making a permanent residence there was fixed upon the party. The case of Mr. Whitehill fully established this point. He had arrived at St. Eustatius only a day or two before Admiral Rodney and the British forces made their appearance; but it was proved that he had gone to establish himself there, and his property was condemned. Here recency, therefore, would not be sufficient."

But the property of those claimants who had settled in Demerara before that colony came into the possession of Great Britain, was condemned. " Having settled without any faith in British possession, it cannot be supposed," he said, that they would have relinquished their residence because that possession had ceased. They had passed from one sovereignty with indifference; and if they may be supposed to have looked again to a connexion with this country, they must have viewed it as a circumstance that was in no degree likely to affect their intention of remaining there. On the situation of persons settled there previous to the time of British possession, I feel myself obliged to pronounce that they must be considered in the same light as persons resident in Amsterdam. It must be understood, however, that if there were among these any who were actually removing, and that fact is properly ascertained, their goods may be capable of restitution. All that I mean to express is, that there must be evidence of an intention to remove on the part of those who settled prior to British possession, the presumption not being in their favour."[36]

Case of persons removing from the enemy's country on the breaking out of war.
The case of the *Ocean*, determined in 1804, was a claim relating to British subjects settled in foreign states in time of amity, and taking early measures to withdraw themselves on the breaking out of war. It appeared that the claimant had been settled as a partner in a house of trade in Holland, but that he had made arrangements for the dissolution of the partnership, and was prevented from removing personally only by the violent detention of all British subjects who happened to be within the territories of the enemy at the breaking out of the war. In this case, Sir *W. Scott* said, " it would, I think, be going further than the law requires, to conclude this person by his former occupation, and by his present constrained residence in France, so as not to admit him to have taken himself out of the effect of supervening hostilities, by the means which he had used for his removal. On sufficient proof being made of the property, I shall be disposed to hold him entitled to restitution."[37]

In a note to this case, Sir *C. Robinson* states that the situation of British subjects wishing to remove from the enemy's country on the event of a war, but prevented by the sudden occurrence of hostilities from taking measures sufficiently early to obtain restitution, formed not unfrequently a case of considerable hardship in the prize court. He advises persons so situated, on their actual removal, to make application to government for a special pass, rather than to trust valuable property to the effect of a mere intention to remove, dubious as that intention may frequently appear under the circumstances that prevent it from being carried into execution. And Sir *W. Scott*, in the case of the *Dree Gebroeders*, observes, " that pretences of withdrawing funds are, at all times, to be watched with considerable jealousy; but when the transaction appears to have been conducted *bonâ fide* with that view, and to be directed only to the removal of property, which the

[36] Robinson's Adm. Rep. vol. v. p. 60.   The Diana.
[37] Robinson's Adm. Rep. vol. v. p. 91.

accidents of war may have lodged in the belligerent country, cases of this kind are entitled to be treated with some
indulgence." But in a subsequent case, where an indulgence
was allowed by the court for the withdrawal of British property under peculiar circumstances, he intimated that the
decree of restitution in that particular case was not to be understood as in any degree relaxing the necessity of obtaining
a license wherever property is to be withdrawn from the
enemy's country.[38]

The same principles as to the effect of domicil or commer- Decisions
cial inhabitancy in the enemy's country were adopted by the of the
American
prize tribunals of the United States during the late war with courts.
Great Britain. The rule was applied to the case of native
British subjects, who had emigrated to the United States long
before the war, and became naturalized citizens under the
laws of the Union, as well as to native citizens residing in
Great Britain at the time of the declaration. The naturalized
citizens in question had, long prior to the declaration of war,
returned to their native country, where they were domiciled
and engaged in trade at the time the shipments in question
were made. The goods were shipped before they had a
knowledge of the war. At the time of the capture, one of
the claimants was yet in the enemy's country, but had, since
he heard of the capture, expressed his anxiety to return to
the United States, but had been prevented by various causes
set forth in his affidavit. Another had actually returned some
time after the capture, and a third was still in the enemy's
country.

In pronouncing its judgment in this case, the Supreme
Court stated that, there being no dispute as to the facts upon
which the domicil of the claimants was asserted, the questions of law to be considered were two: *First*, by what
means and to what extent a national character may be impressed upon a person, different from that which permanent
allegiance gives him? and, *secondly*, what are the legal consequences to which this acquired character may expose him,

[38] Robinson's Adm. Rep. vol. iv. p. 234; vol. v. p. 141. The Juffrow
Catharina.

in the event of a war taking place between the country of
his residence and that of his birth, or that in which he had
been naturalized?

Upon the first of these questions, the opinions of the text
writers and the decisions of the British courts of prize, already cited, were referred to; but it was added, that in deciding whether a person has obtained the right of an acquired
domicil, it was not to be expected that much, if any assistance, should be derived from mere elementary writers on the
law of nations. They can only lay down the general principles of law, and it becomes the duty of courts of justice to
establish rules for the proper application of those principles.
The question whether the person to be affected by the right
of domicil has sufficiently made known his intention of fixing
himself permanently in the foreign country, must depend
upon all the circumstances of the case. If he has made no
express declaration on the subject, and his secret intention is
to be discovered, his *acts* must be attended to as affording the
most satisfactory evidence of his intention. On this ground
the courts of England have decided, that a person who re-
moves to a foreign country, settles himself there, and engages
in the trade of the country, furnishes by these acts such
evidences of an intention permanently to reside there, as to
stamp him with the national character of the state where he
resides. In questions on this subject, the chief point to be
considered is the *animus manendi;* and courts are to devise
such reasonable rules of evidence as may establish the fact
of intention. If it sufficiently appears that the intention of
removing was to make a permanent settlement, or for an indefinite time, the right of domicil is acquired by residence
even of a few days. This was one of the rules of the British prize courts, and it appeared to be perfectly reasonable.
Another was that a neutral or subject, found residing in a
foreign country, is presumed to be there *animo manendi;* and
if a state of war should bring his national character into
question, it lies upon him to explain the circumstances of his
residence. As to some other rules of the prize courts of
England, particularly those which fix the national character

of a person on the ground of constructive residence or the peculiar nature of his trade, the court was not called upon to give an opinion at that time; because in the present case it was admitted that the claimants had acquired a right of domicil in Great Britain at the time of the breaking out of the war between that country and the United States.

The next question was, what are the consequences to which this acquired domicil may legally expose the person entitled to it, in the event of a war taking place between the government under which he resides and that to which he owes permanent allegiance. A neutral, in this situation, if he should engage in open hostilities with the other belligerent, would be considered and treated as an enemy. A citizen of the other belligerent could not be so considered, because he could not, by any act of hostility, render himself, strictly speaking, an enemy, contrary to his permanent allegiance; but although he cannot be considered an enemy in the strict sense of the word, yet he is deemed such with reference to the seizure of so much of his property concerned in the enemy's trade as is connected with his residence. It is found adhering to the enemy; he is himself adhering to the enemy, although not criminally so, unless he engages in acts of hostility against his native country, or perhaps refuses, when required by his country, to return. The same rule as to property engaged in the commerce of the enemy, applies to neutrals, and for the same reason. The converse of this rule inevitably applies to the subject of a belligerent state domiciled in a neutral country: he is deemed a neutral by both belligerents, with reference to the trade which he carries on with the adverse belligerent, and with the rest of the world.

But this national character which a man acquires by residence may be thrown off at pleasure by a return to his native country, or even by turning his back on the country in which he resided, on his way to another. The reasonableness of this rule can hardly be disputed. Having once acquired a national character by residence in a foreign country, he ought to be bound by all the consequences of it until he has thrown it off, either by an actual return to his native country, or to that where he was naturalized, or by commencing his removal, *bonâ fide*, and without an intention of returning. If any thing short of actual removal be admitted to work a change in the national character acquired by residence, it seems perfectly reasonable that the evidence of a *bonâ fide* intention should be such as to leave no doubt of its sincerity. Mere declarations of such an intention ought never to be relied upon, when contradicted, or at least rendered doubtful, by a continuance of that residence which impressed the character. They may have been made to deceive; or if sincerely made, they may never be executed. Even the party himself ought not to be bound by them, because he may afterwards find reason to change his determination, and ought to be permitted to do so. But when he accompanies these declarations by acts which speak a language not to be mistaken, and can hardly fail to be consummated by actual removal, the strongest evidence is afforded which the nature of such a case can furnish. And is it not proper that the courts of a belligerent nation should deny to any person the right to use a character so equivocal as to put in his power whichever may best suit his purpose when it is called in question? If his property be taken trading with the enemy, shall he be allowed to shield it from confiscation, by alleging that he had intended to remove from the enemy's country to his own, then neutral, and therefore that as a neutral, the trade was to him lawful? If war exists between the country of his residence and his native country, and his property be seized by the former or by the latter, shall he be heard to say, in the former case, that he was a domiciled subject of the country of the captor, and in the latter that he was a native subject of the country of that captor also, because he had declared an intention to resume his native character, and thus to parry the belligerent rights of both? It was to guard against such inconsistencies, and against the frauds which such pretensions, if tolerated, would sanction, that the rule above-mentioned had been adopted. Upon what sound principle could a distinction be framed between the case of a neutral and the subject of one belligerent domiciled in the country of the other at the breaking out of the war ? The property of each found engaged in the commerce of their adopted country belonged to them before the war in their character of subjects of that country, so long as they continued to retain their domicil; and when war takes place between that country and any other, by which the two nations and all their subjects become enemies to each other, it follows that this property, which was once the property of a friend, belongs now to him who, in reference to that property, is an enemy.

This doctrine of the common law courts and prize tribunals of England is founded, like that mentioned under the first head, upon international law, and was believed to be strongly supported by reason and justice. And why, it might be confidently asked, should not the property of enemies' subjects be exposed to the law of reprisals and of war, so long as the owner retains his acquired domicil, or, in the words of Grotius, continues a permanent residence in the country of the enemy? They were before, and continue after the war, bound by such residence to the society of which they were members, subject to the laws of the state, and owing a qualified allegiance thereto. They are obliged to defend it, (with an exception of such subject with relation to his native country,) in return for the protection it affords them, and the privileges which the laws bestow upon them as subjects. The property of such persons, equally with that of the native subjects in their locality, is to be considered as the goods of the nation *in regard to other states*. It belongs in some sort to the state, from the right which the state has over the goods of its citizens, which make a part of the sum total of its riches, and augment its power. (*Vattel*, liv. i. ch. 14, § 182.) "In reprisals," continues the same author, "we seize on the property of the subject, just as on that of the sovereign; every thing that belongs to the nation is subject to reprisals, wherever it can be seized, with the exception of a deposite intrusted to the public faith." (Liv. ii. ch. 18, § 344.) Now if a permanent residence constitutes the

person a subject of the country where he is settled, so long
as he continues to reside there, and subjects his property to
the law of reprisals as a part of the property of the nation,
it would seem difficult to maintain that the same consequences would not follow in the case of an open and public
war, whether between the adopted and native countries of
persons so domiciled, or between the former and any other
nation.

If then nothing but an actual removal, or a *bonâ fide* beginning to remove, could change a national character acquired
by domicil; and if, at the time of the inception of the voyage, as well as at the time of capture, the property belonged
to such domiciled person, in his character of a subject; what
was there that did or ought to exempt it from capture by the
cruizers of his native country, if at the time of capture he
continues to reside in the country of the adverse belligerent?

It was contended that a native or naturalized subject of
one country who is surprised, in the country where he was
domiciled, by a declaration of war, ought to have time to
make his election to continue there, or to remove to the
country to which he owes a permanent allegiance; and that
until such election be made, his property ought to be protected from capture by the cruisers of the latter.   This doctrine
was believed to be as unfounded in reason and justice, as it
clearly was in law.   In the first place, it was founded upon
a presumption that the person will certainly remove before it
can possibly be known whether he may elect to do so or not.
It was said, that the presumption ought to be made, because
upon receiving information of the war it would be his duty
to return home.   This position was denied.   It was his duty
to commit no acts of hostility against his native country, and
to return to her assistance when required to do so; nor would
any just nation, regarding the mild principles of the law of
nations, require him to take arms against his native country,
or refuse permission to him to withdraw whenever he wished
to do so, unless under peculiar circumstances, which by such
removal at a critical period might endanger the public safety.
The conventional law of nations was in conformity with these

principles. It is not uncommon to stipulate in treaties that the subjects of each party shall be allowed to remove with their property, or to remain unmolested. Such a stipulation does not coerce those subjects to remove or remain. They are left free to choose for themselves; and when they have made their election, may claim the right of enjoying it under the treaty. But until the election is made, their former character continues unchanged. Until this election is made, if the claimant's property found upon the high seas engaged in the commerce of his adopted country, should be permitted by the cruisers of the other belligerent to pass free under a notion that he may elect to remove upon notice of the war, and should arrive safe ; what is to be done, in case the owner of it should elect to remain where he is? For if captured and brought immediately to adjudication, it must, upon this doctrine, be acquitted until the election to remain is made and known. In short, the point contended for would apply the doctrine of relation to cases where the party claiming the benefit of it may gain all and can lose nothing. If he, after the capture, should find it for his interest to remain where he is domiciled, his property embarked before his election was made is safe; and if he finds it best to return, it is safe of course. It is safe, whether he goes or stays. The doctrine producing such contradictory consequences was not only unsupported by any authority, but would violate principles long and well established in the prize courts of England, and which ought not, without strong reasons which may render them inapplicable to America, to be disregarded by the court. The rule there was, that the character of property during war cannot be changed *in transitu* by any act of the party, subsequent to the capture. The rule indeed went farther ; as to the correctness of which, in its greatest extension, no judgment needed then to be given : but it might safely be affirmed, that the change could not and ought not to be effected by an election of the owner and shipper, made subsequent to the capture, and more especially after a knowledge of the capture is obtained by the owner. Observe the consequences. The capture is made and known. The owner is allowed to deliberate whether it is his intention to remain a subject of his adopted, or of his native country. If the capture be made by the former, then he elects to become a subject of that country; if by the latter, then a subject of that. Could such a privileged situation be tolerated by either belligerent? Could any system of law be correct which places an individual, who adheres to one belligerent, and down to the period of his election to remove, contributes to increase her wealth, in so anomalous a situation as to be clothed with the privileges of a neutral as to both belligerents? This notion about a temporary state of neutrality impressed upon a subject of one of the belligerents, and the consequent exemption of his property from capture by either, until he has had notice of the war and made his election, was altogether a novel theory, and seemed from the course of the argument to owe its origin to a supposed hardship to which the contrary doctrine exposes him. But if the reasoning employed on the subject was correct, no such hardship could exist; for if before the election is made, his property on the ocean is liable to capture by the cruisers of his native and deserted country, it is not only free from capture by those of his adopted country, but is under its protection. The privilege is supposed to be equal to the disadvantage, and is therefore just. The double privilege claimed seems too unreasonable to be granted."[39]

§ 18.
Merchants
residing in
the east.
The national character of merchants residing in Europe and America is derived from that of the country in which they reside. In the eastern parts of the world, European persons, trading under the shelter and protection of the factories founded there, take their national character from that association under which they live and carry on their trade: this distinction arises from the nature and habits of the countries. In the western parts of the world, alien merchants mix in the society of the natives; access and intermixture are per-

[39] Cranch's Rep. vol. viii. p. 253. See other cases of Domicil in the American Prize Courts, Wheaton's Rep. vol. ii. Appendix, Note I. p. 27.

mitted, and they become incorporated to nearly the full extent. But in the east, from almost the oldest times, an immiscible character has been kept up; foreigners are not admitted into the general body and mass of the nation; they continue strangers and sojourners, as all their fathers were. Thus, with respect to establishments in Turkey, the British courts of prize, during war with Holland, determined that a merchant, carrying on trade at Smyrna, under the protection of the Dutch consul, was to be considered a Dutchman, and condemned his property as belonging to an enemy. And thus in China, and generally throughout the east, persons admitted into a factory are not known in their own peculiar national character; and not being permitted to assume the character of the country, are considered only in the character of that association or factory.

But these principles are considered not applicable to the vast territories occupied by the British in Hindostan; because, as Sir *W. Scott* observes, " though the sovereignty of the Mogul is occasionally brought forward for purposes of policy, it hardly exists otherwise than as a phantom: it is not applied in any way for the regulation of their establishments. Great Britain exercises the power of declaring war and peace, which is among the strongest marks of actual sovereignty; and if the high and empyrean sovereignty of the Mogul is sometimes brought down from the clouds, as it were, for the purposes of policy, it by no means interferes with the actual authority which that country, and the East India Company, a creature of that country, exercises there with full effect. Merchants residing there are hence considered as British subjects."[40]

In general, the national character of a person, as neutral or enemy, is determined by that of his domicil; but the property of a person may acquire a hostile character, independently of his national character, derived from personal residence. Thus the property of a house of trade established in

§ 19. House of trade in the enemy's country.

---

[40] Robinson's Adm. Rep. vol. iii. p: 12. The Indian Chief.

the enemy's country is considered liable to capture and condemnation as prize. This rule does not apply to cases arising
at the commencement of a war, in reference to persons who,
during peace, had habitually carried on trade in the enemy's
country, though not resident there, and are therefore entitled
to time to withdraw from that commerce. But if a person
enters into a house of trade in the enemy's country, or continues that connexion during the war, he cannot protect himself by mere residence in a neutral country.[41]

§ 20.
Converse
of the rule.
The converse of this rule of the British prize courts, which
has also been adopted by those of America, is not extended
to the case of a merchant residing in a hostile country, and
having a share in a house of trade in a neutral country. Residence in a neutral country will not protect his share in a
house established in the enemy's country, though residence in
the enemy's country will condemn his share in a house established in a neutral country. It is impossible not to see, in
this want of reciprocity, strong marks of the partiality towards
the interests of captors, which is perhaps inseparable from a
prize code framed by judicial legislation in a belligerent
country, and adapted to encourage its naval exertions.[42]

§ 21.
National
character
of ships.
So also, in general, and unless under special circumstances,
the character of ships depends on the national character of
the owner as ascertained by his domicil; but if a vessel is
navigating under the flag and pass of a foreign country, she
is to be considered as bearing the national character of the
country under whose flag she sails: she makes a part of its
navigation, and is in every respect liable to be considered as
a vessel of the country; for ships have a peculiar character
impressed upon them by the special nature of their documents, and are always held to the character with which they

[41] Robinson's Adm. Rep. vol. i. p. 1. The Vigilantia, Vol. ii. p. 255. The
Susa. Vol. iii. p. 41. The Portland. Vol. v. pp. 2, 97. The Jonge Clas-
sina. Wheaton's Rep. vol. i. p. 159. The Antonia Johanna. Vol. iv. p.
105. The Friendschaft.

[42] Mr. Chief Justice Marshall, Cranch's Rep. vol. viii. p. 253. The Venus.

are so invested, to the exclusion of any claims of interest which persons resident in neutral countries may actually have in them. But where the cargo is laden on board in time of peace, and documented as foreign property, in the same manner with the ship, with the view of avoiding alien duties, the sailing under the foreign flag and pass is not held conclusive as to the cargo. A distinction is made between the ship, which is held bound by the character imposed upon it by the authority of the government from which all the documents issue, and the goods, whose character has no such dependence upon the authority of the state. In time of war, a more strict principle may be necessary; but where the transaction takes place in peace, and without any expectation of war, the cargo ought not to be involved in the condemnation of the vessel, which, under these circumstances, is considered as incorporated into the navigation of that country whose flag and pass she bears.[43]

We have already seen that no commercial intercourse can be lawfully carried on between the subjects of states at war with each other, except by the special permission of their respective governments. As such intercourse can only be legalized in the subjects of one belligerent state by a license from their own government, it is evident that the use of such a license from the enemy must be illegal unless authorized by their own government; for it is the sovereign power of the state alone which is competent to act on the considerations of policy by which such an exception from the ordinary consequences of war must be controlled. And this principle is applicable not only to a license protecting a direct commercial intercourse with the enemy, but to a voyage to a country in alliance with the enemy, or even to a neutral port; for the very act of purchasing or procuring the license from the enemy is an intercourse with him prohibited by the laws of war: and even supposing it to be gra-

§ 22. Sailing under the enemy's license.

[43] Robinson's Adm. Rep. vol. i. p. 1. The Vigilantia. Vol. v. p. 161. The Vrow Anna Catharina. Dodson's Adm. Rep. vol. i. p. 131. The Success.

tuitously issued, it must be for the special purpose of further-
ing the enemy's interests, by securing supplies necessary to
prosecute the war, to which the subjects of the belligerent
state have no right to lend their aid by sailing under these
documents of protection.[44]

[44] Cranch's Rep. vol. viii. p. 181. The Julia. P. 203. The Aurora.
Wheaton's Rep. vol. ii. p. 143. The Ariadne. Vol. iv. p. 100. The Cale-
donia.

CHAPTER II.

RIGHTS OF WAR AS BETWEEN ENEMIES.

In general, it may be stated, that the rights of war, in re- §1.
spect to the enemy, are to be measured by the object of the Rights of war against
war. Until that object is attained, the belligerent has, an enemy.
strictly speaking, a right to use every means necessary to
accomplish the end for which he has taken up arms. We
have already seen that the practice of the ancient world,
and even the opinion of some modern writers on public law,
made no distinction as to the means to be employed for this
purpose. Even such institutional writers as *Bynkershoek* and
Wolf, who lived in the most learned and not least civilized
countries of Europe at the commencement of the eighteenth
century, assert the broad principle that every thing done
against an enemy is lawful; that he may be destroyed, though
unarmed and defenceless; that fraud, and even poison, may
be employed against him; and that an unlimited right is acquired by the victor to his person and property. Such, however, was not the sentiment and practice of enlightened
Europe at the period when they wrote; since *Grotius* had
long before inculcated milder and more humane principles,
which *Vattel* subsequently enforced and illustrated, and which
are adopted by the unanimous concurrence of all the publicists of the present age.[1]

The law of nature has not precisely determined how far §2.
an individual is allowed to make use of force, either to defend Limits to the rights
himself against an attempted injury, or to obtain reparation of war

---

[1] Bynkershoek, Quæst. Jur. Pub. lib. i. cap. 1.   Wolfius, Jus Gent. § 878.
Grotius, de Jur. Bel. ac Pac. lib. iii. cap. 4, §§ 5—7. Vattel, Droit des Gens,
liv. iii. ch. 8.

against the when refused by the aggressor, or to bring an offender to
persons of punishment. We can only collect, from this law, the general
an enemy.
rule, that such use of force as is necessary for obtaining these
ends is not forbidden. The same principle applies to the
conduct of sovereign states existing in a state of natural independence with respect to each other. No use of force is
lawful, except so far as it is necessary. A belligerent has,
therefore, no right to take away the lives of those subjects of
the enemy whom he can subdue by any other means. Those
who are actually in arms, and continue to resist, may be lawfully killed; but the inhabitants of the enemy's country who
are not in arms, or who, being in arms, submit and surrender
themselves, may not be slain, because their destruction is not
necessary for obtaining the just ends of war. Those ends
may be accomplished by making prisoners of those who are
taken in arms, or compelling them to give security that they
will not bear arms against the victor for a limited period, or
during the continuance of the war. The killing of prisoners
can only be justifiable in those extreme cases, where resistance on their part, or on the part of others who come to their
rescue, renders it impossible to keep them. Both reason and
general opinion concur in showing that nothing but the
strongest necessity will justify such an act.[2]

§ 3.   According to the law of war, as still practised by savage
Exchange   nations, prisoners taken in war are put to death. Among
of prison-
ers of war. the more polished nations of antiquity, this practice gradually
gave way to that of making slaves of them. For this, again,
was substituted that of ransoming, which continued through
the feudal wars of the middle age. The present usage of
exchanging prisoners was not firmly established in Europe
until some time in the course of the seventeenth century.
Even now this usage is not obligatory among nations who
choose to insist upon a ransom for the prisoners taken by
them, or to leave their own countrymen in the enemy's hands
until the termination of the war. Cartels for the mutual

[2] Rutherforth's Inst. b. ii. ch. 9, § 15.

exchange of prisoners of war are regulated by special convention between the belligerent states, according to their
respective interests and views of policy. Sometimes prisoners of war are permitted, by capitulation, to return to their
own country upon condition not to serve again during the
war, or until duly exchanged; and officers are frequently
released upon their parole, subject to the same condition.
Good faith and humanity ought to preside over the execution of these compacts, which are designed to mitigate the
evils of war without defeating its legitimate purposes. By
the modern usage of nations, commissaries are permitted to
reside in the respective belligerent countries, to negotiate
and carry into effect the arrangements necessary for this
object. Breach of good faith in these transactions can be
punished only by withholding from the party guilty of such
violation the advantages stipulated by the cartel; or, in cases
which may be supposed to warrant such a resort, by reprisals or vindictive retaliation.[3]

All the members of the enemy state may lawfully be treated as enemies in a public war; but it does not therefore follow, that all these enemies may be lawfully treated alike;
though we may lawfully destroy some of them, it does not
therefore follow that we may lawfully destroy all. For the
general rule derived from the natural law is still the same,
that no use of force against an enemy is lawful, unless it is
necessary to accomplish the purposes of war. The custom
of civilized nations, founded upon this principle, has therefore exempted the persons of the sovereign and his family,
the members of the civil government, women and children,
cultivators of the earth, artisans, labourers, merchants, men
of science and letters, and generally all other public or private individuals engaged in the ordinary civil pursuits of life,

§ 4.
Persons
exempt
from acts
of hosti-
lity.

[3] Grotius, de Jur. Bel. ac Pac. lib. iii. cap. 7, §§ 8, 9; cap. 11, §§ 9—13.
Vattel, Droit des Gens, liv. iii. ch. 8, § 153. Robinson's Adm. Rep. vol. iii.
Note, Appendix A. Correspondence between M. Otto, French Commissary
of Prisoners in England, and the British Transport Board, 1801. Annual
Register, vol. xliv. p. 265. (State Papers.)

from the direct effect of military operations, unless actually taken in arms, or guilty of some misconduct in violation of the usages of war by which they forfeit their immunity.[4]

§ 5.
Enemy's property, how far subject to capture and confiscation.

The application of the same principle has also limited and restrained the operations of war against the territory and other property of the enemy. From the moment one state is at war with another, it has, on general principles, a right to seize on all the enemy's property, of whatsoever kind and wheresoever found, and to appropriate the property thus taken to its own use or to that of the captors. By the ancient law of nations, even what were called *res sacræ* were not exempt from capture and confiscation. Cicero has conveyed this idea in his expressive metaphorical language, in the fourth Oration against Verres, where he says that " Victory made all the *sacred* things of the Syracusans *profane*." But by the modern usage of nations, which has now acquired the force of law, temples of religion, public edifices devoted to civil purposes only, monuments of art, and repositories of science, are exempted from the general operations of war. Private property on land is also exempt from confiscation, with the exception of such as may become booty in special cases, when taken from enemies in the field or in besieged towns, and of military contributions levied upon the inhabitants of the hostile territory. This exemption extends even to the case of an absolute and unqualified conquest of the enemy's country. In ancient times, both the moveable and immoveable property of the vanquished passed to the conqueror. Such was the Roman law of war, often asserted with unrelenting severity, and such was the fate of the Roman provinces subdued by the northern barbarians on the decline and fall of the western empire. A large portion, from one-third to two-thirds of the lands belonging to the vanquished provincials, was confiscated and partitioned among

---

[4] Rutherforth's Inst. b. ii. ch. 9, § 15. Vattel, Droit des Gens, liv. iii. ch. 8, §§ 145—147, 159. Kluber, Droit des Gens Moderne de l'Europe, pt. ii. tit. 2, sect. 2, ch. 1, §§ 245—247.

their conquerors. The last example in Europe of such a conquest was that of England by William of Normandy. Since that period, among the civilized nations of Christendom, conquest, even when confirmed by a treaty of peace, has been followed by no general or partial transmutation of landed property. The property belonging to the government of the vanquished nation passes to the victorious state, which also takes the place of the former sovereign in respect to the eminent domain. In other respects, private rights are unaffected by conquest.[5]

The exceptions to these general mitigations of the extreme rights of war, considered as a contest of force, all grow out of the same original principle of natural law which authorizes us to use against an enemy such a degree of violence, and such only, as may be necessary to secure the object of hostilities. The same general rule which determines how far it is lawful to destroy the persons of enemies will serve as a guide in judging how far it is lawful to ravage or lay waste their country. If this be necessary in order to accomplish the just ends of war, it may be lawfully done, but not otherwise. Thus, if the progress of an enemy cannot be stopped, nor our own frontier secured, or if the approaches to a town intended to be attacked cannot be made without laying waste the intermediate territory, the extreme case may justify a resort to measures not warranted by the ordinary purposes of war. If modern usage has sanctioned any other exceptions, they will be found in the right of reprisals or vindictive retaliation. The whole international code is founded upon reciprocity. The rules it prescribes are observed by one nation in confidence that they will be so by others. Where, then, the established usages of war are violated by an enemy, and there are no other means of restraining his excesses, retaliation may be justly resorted to by the suffering nation, in order

§ 6. Ravaging the enemy's territory, when lawful.

---

[5] Vattel, Droit des Gens, liv. iii. ch. 9, 13. Kluber, Droit des Gens Moderne de l'Europe, pt. ii. tit. 2, sect: 2, ch. 1, §§ 250—253: Martens, Précis, &c. liv. viii. ch. 4, §§ 279—282,

to compel the enemy to return to the observance of the law which he has violated.[6]

§ 7.
Distinction between private property, taken at sea, or on land.

The progress of civilization has slowly but constantly tended to soften the extreme severity of the operations of war by land; but it still remains unrelaxed in respect to maritime warfare, in which the private property of the enemy taken at sea or afloat in port is indiscriminately liable to capture and confiscation. This inequality in the operation of the laws of war, by land and by sea, has been justified by alleging the usage of considering private property, when captured in cities taken by storm, as booty; and the well-known fact that contributions are levied upon territories occupied by a hostile army in lieu of a general confiscation of the property belonging to the inhabitants; and that the objects of wars by land being conquest, or the acquisition of territory to be exchanged as an equivalent for other territory lost, the regard of the victor for those who are to be or have been his subjects, naturally restrains him from the exercise of his extreme rights in this particular; whereas the object of maritime wars is the destruction of the enemy's commerce and navigation, the sources and sinews of his naval power—which object can only be attained by the capture and confiscation of private property.

§ 8.
What persons are authorized to engage in hostilities against the enemy.

The effect of a state of war, lawfully declared to exist, is to place all the subjects of each belligerent power in a state of mutual hostility. The usage of nations has modified this maxim by legalizing such acts of hostility only as are committed by those who are authorized by the express or implied command of the state. Such are the regularly commissioned naval and military forces of the nation, and all others called out in its defence, or spontaneously defending themselves in case of urgent necessity, without any express authority for that purpose. *Cicero* tells us, in his *Offices*, that by the Roman

6 Vattel, liv. iii. ch. 8, § 142; ch. 9, §§ 166—173. Martens, Précis du Droit des Gens Moderne de l'Europe, liv. viii. ch. 4, §§ 272—280. Kluber, pt. ii. tit. 2, sect. 2, ch. 1, §§ 292—265.

fecial law, no person could lawfully engage in battle with the public enemy, without being regularly enrolled and taking the military oath. This was a regulation sanctioned both by policy and religion. The horrors of war would indeed be greatly aggravated, if every individual of the belligerent states was allowed to plunder and slay indiscriminately the enemy's subjects without being in any manner accountable for his conduct. Hence it is that in land wars, irregular bands of marauders are liable to be treated as lawless banditti, not entitled to the protection of the mitigated usages of war as practised by civilized nations.[7]

It must probably be considered as a remnant of the barbarous practices of those ages when maritime war and piracy were synonymous, that captures made by private armed vessels without a commission, not merely in self-defence, but even by attacking the enemy, are considered lawful, not indeed for the purpose of vesting the enemy's property thus seized in the captors, but to prevent their conduct from being regarded as piratical, either by their own government or by the other belligerent state. Property thus seized is condemned to the government as prize of war, or, as these captures are technically called, *Droits of Admiralty.* The same principle is applied to the captures made by armed vessels commissioned against one power, where war breaks out with another: the captures made from that other are condemned, not to the captors, but to the government.[8]

§ 9.
Non-commissioned captors.

The practice of cruising with private armed vessels commissioned by the state has been hitherto sanctioned by the laws of every maritime nation, as a legitimate means of destroying the commerce of an enemy. This practice has been

§ 10.
Privateers.

---

[7] Vattel, Droit des Gens, liv. iii. ch. 15, §§ 223—228. Kluber, Droit des Gens Moderne de l'Europe, § 267.

[8] Brown's Civ. and Adm. Law, vol. ii. p. 526, Appendix. Robinson's Adm. Rep. vol. iv. p. 72. The Abigail. Dodson's Adm. Rep. p. 397. The Georgiana. Sparks's Diplomatic Correspondence, vol. i. p. 443. Wheaton's, Rep. vol. ij. Appendix, Note I. p. 7.

justly arraigned as liable to gross abuses, as tending to encourage a spirit of lawless depredation, and as being in glaring contradiction to the more mitigated modes of warfare practised by land.   Powerful efforts have been made by humane and enlightened individuals to suppress it, as inconsistent with the liberal spirit of the age.   The treaty negotiated by Franklin between the United States and Prussia, in 1785, by which it was stipulated that, in case of war, neither power should commission privateers to depredate upon the commerce of the other, furnishes an example worthy of applause and imitation.   But this stipulation was not revived on the renewal of the treaty in 1799; and it is much to be feared that so long as maritime captures of private property are tolerated, this particular mode of injuring the enemy's commerce will continue to be practised, especially where it affords the means of countervailing the superiority of the public marine of an enemy.[9]

§ 11.
Title to
property
captured
in war.

The title to property lawfully taken in war may, upon general principles, be considered as immediately divested from the original owner, and transferred to the captor.   This general principle is modified by the positive law of nations, in its application both to personal and real property.   As to personal property or moveables, the title is, in general, considered as lost to the former proprietor as soon as the enemy has acquired a firm possession ; which, as a general rule, is considered as taking place after the lapse of twenty-four hours. The established usage of maritime nations has excepted from the operation of this rule the case of ships and goods captured at sea, the original title to which is not generally considered as completely divested until carried *infra præsidia*, and regularly condemned in a competent court of prize.   To such nations as do not acknowledge this rule, the principle of reciprocity or amicable retaliation is applied, by restoring the re-

---

[9] Vattel, liv. iii. ch. 15, § 229. Franklin's Works, vol. ii. pp. 447, 530. Edinburgh Review, vol. viii. pp. 13—15.   North American Review, vol. ii. (N. S.) pp. 166—196.

captured property of an ally in cases where the law of his own country would restore, upon the same terms of salvage, and condemning where it condemns. A neutral purchaser is, in all cases, required to produce a regular sentence of condemnation as evidence of his title against the claim of the original proprietor.[10]

The validity of maritime captures must be determined in a court of the captor's government, sitting either in his own country or in that of its ally. This rule of jurisdiction applies, whether the captured property be carried into a port of the captor's country, into that of an ally, or into a neutral port.

§ 12. Validity of maritime captures, determined in the courts of the captor's country.

Respecting the *first* case, there can be no doubt. In the *second* case, where the property is carried into the port of an ally, there is nothing to prevent the government of the country, although it cannot itself condemn, from permitting the exercise of that final act of hostility, the condemnation of the property of one belligerent to the other: there is a common interest between the two governments, and both may be presumed to authorize any measures conducing to give effect to their arms, and to consider each other's ports as mutually subservient. Such an adjudication is therefore sufficient in regard to property taken in the course of the operations of a common war. But where the property is carried into a *neutral* port, it may appear, on principle, more doubtful whether the validity of a capture can be determined even by a court of prize established in the captor's country; and the reasoning of Sir *W. Scott*, in the case of the *Henrick and Maria*, is certainly very cogent, as tending to show the irregularity of the practice; but he considered that the English court of admiralty had gone too far in its own practice of condemning captured vessels-lying in neutral ports to recall it to the proper purity of the original principle. In delivering the judg-

Condemnation of property lying in the ports of an ally.

Property carried into a neutral port.

---

[10] Grotius, de Jur. Bel. ac Pac. lib. iii. cap. 6, § 3; cap. 9, § 14. Kluber, Droit des Gens Moderne de l'Europe, § 254. Robinson's Adm. Rep. vol. i. p. 50. The Santa Cruz. P. 139. The Flad Oyen. Wheaton's Rep. vol. ii. Appendix, Note I. pp. 40—49; vol. iii. p. 73. The Star. P. 93, Note (*a*.)

ment of the court of appeals in the same case, Sir *William Grant* also held, that Great Britain was concluded by her own inveterate practice, and that neutral merchants were sufficiently warranted in purchasing under such a sentence of condemnation by the constant adjudications of the British tribunals. The same rule has been adopted by the supreme court of the United States, as being justifiable on principles of convenience to belligerents as well as neutrals; and though the prize was in fact within a neutral jurisdiction, it was still to be considered as under the control of the captor, whose possession is considered as that of his sovereign.[11]

§ 13.
Jurisdiction of the courts of the captor, how far exclusive. This jurisdiction of the national courts of the captor, to determine the validity of captures made in war under the authority of his government, is exclusive of the judicial authority of every other country, with two exceptions only:— 1. Where the capture is made within the territorial limits of a neutral state. 2. Where it is made by armed vessels fitted out within the neutral territory.[12]

In either of these cases, the judicial tribunals of the neutral state have jurisdiction to determine the validity of the captures thus made, and to vindicate its neutrality by restoring the property of its own subjects, or of other states in amity with it, to the original owners. These exceptions to the exclusive jurisdiction of the national courts of the captor have been extended by the municipal regulations of some' countries to the restitution of the property of their own subjects, in all cases where the same has been unlawfully captured, and afterwards brought into their ports; thus assuming to the neutral tribunal the jurisdiction of the question of prize or no prize, wherever the captured property is brought within the neutral territory. Such a regulation is contained in the marine ordinance of Louis XIV. of 1681, and its jus-

---

[11] Robinson's Adm. Rep. vol. iv. p. 43; vol. vi. p. 138, Note (*a*.) Bynkershoek, Quæst. Jur. Pub. lib. i. cap. 5. Duponceau's Transl. Note, p. 38. Kent's Commentaries on American Law, vol. i. p. 103.

[12] Wheaton's Rep. vol. iv. p. 298. The Estrella. Vol. vii. p. 283. The Santissima Trinidad.

tice is vindicated by *Valin,* upon the ground that this is done by way of compensation for the privilege of asylum granted to the captor and his prizes in the neutral port. There can be no doubt that such a condition may be expressly annexed by the neutral state to the privilege of bringing belligerent prizes into its ports, which it may grant or refuse at its pleasure, provided it be done impartially to all the belligerent powers; but such a condition is not implied in a mere general permission to enter the neutral ports. The captor who avails himself of such a permission does not thereby lose the military possession of the captured property, which gives to the prize courts of his own country exclusive jurisdiction to determine the lawfulness of the capture. This jurisdiction may be exercised either whilst the captured property is lying in the neutral port, or the prize may be carried thence *infra præsidia* of the captor's country where the tribunal is sitting. In either case, the claim of any neutral proprietor, even a subject of the state into whose ports the captured vessel or goods may have been carried, must, in general, be asserted in the prize court of the belligerent country, which alone has jurisdiction of the question of prize or no prize.[13]

This jurisdiction cannot be exercised by a delegated authority in the neutral country, such as a consular tribunal sitting in the neutral port, and acting in pursuance of instructions from the captor's state. Such a judicial authority in the matter of prize of war cannot be conceded by the neutral state to the agents of a belligerent power within its own territory, where even the neutral government itself has no right to exercise such a jurisdiction except in cases where its own neutral jurisdiction and sovereignty have been violated by the capture. A sentence of condemnation pronounced by a belligerent consul in a neutral port is therefore considered as insufficient to transfer the property in vessels

§ 14.
Condemnation by consular tribunal sitting in the neutral country.

---

[13] Valin, Comment. sur l'Ordon. de la Marine, liv. iii. tit. 9. Des Prises, art. 15, tom. ii. p. 274. Lampredi, Trattato del Commercio de' Popoli Neutrali in tempo di Guerra, p. 228.

or goods captured as prize of war and carried into such port for adjudication.[14]

§ 15.
Responsi-
bility of the
captor's go-
vernment
for the acts
of its com-
missioned
cruisers
and courts.
The jurisdiction of the court of the capturing nation is conclusive upon the question of property in the captured thing. Its sentence forecloses all controversy respecting the validity of the capture as between claimant and captors, and those claiming under them, and terminates all ordinary judicial inquiry upon the subject matter. Where the responsibility of the captors ceases, that of the state begins. It is responsible to other states for the acts of the captors under its commission, the moment these acts are confirmed by the definitive sentence of the tribunals which it has appointed to determine the validity of captures in war.

Unjust
sentence
of a foreign
court,
ground of
reprisals.
Grotius states that a judicial sentence, plainly against right, (*in re munime dubia*) to the prejudice of a foreigner, entitles his nation to obtain reparation by reprisals : " for the authority of the judge" (says he) " is not of the same force against strangers as against subjects. Here is the difference : subjects are bound up and concluded by the sentence of the judge, though it be unjust, so that they cannot lawfully oppose its execution, nor by force recover their own right, on account of the controlling efficacy of that authority under which they live. But strangers have coercive power," (*i. e.* of reprisals, of which the author is treating,) "though it be not lawful to use it so long as they can obtain their right in the ordinary course of justice."[15]

So also *Bynkershoek*, in treating the same subject, puts an unjust judgment upon the same footing with naked violence in authorizing reprisals on the part of the state whose subjects have been thus injured by the tribunals of another state. And *Vattel*, in enumerating the different modes in which justice may be refused so as to authorize reprisals, mentions "a judgment manifestly unjust and partial :" and though he states, what is undeniable, that the judgments of the ordinary

[14] Robinson's Adm. Rep. vol. i. p. 135. The Flad Oyen.
[15] Grotius, de Jur. Bel. ac Pac. lib. iii. cap. 2, § 5.

tribunals ought not to be called in question upon frivolous or
doubtful grounds, yet he is manifestly far from attributing to
them that sanctity which would absolutely preclude foreigners from seeking redress against them.[16]

These principles are sanctioned by the authority of numerous treaties between the different powers of Europe regulating the subject of reprisals, and declaring that they shall
not be granted unless in case of *the denial of justice.* An
unjust sentence must certainly be considered a denial of justice, unless the mere privilege of being heard before condemnation is all that is included in the idea of justice.

Even supposing that unjust judgments of municipal tribu- Distinction
nals do not form a ground of reprisals, there is evidently a between
municipal
wide distinction in this respect between the ordinary tribu- tribunals
nals of the state proceeding under the municipal law as their and courts
of prize.
rule of decision, and prize tribunals appointed by its authority, and professing to administer the law of nations to foreigners as well as subjects. The ordinary municipal tribunals
acquire jurisdiction over the person or property of a foreigner
by his consent, either *expressed* by his voluntarily bringing the
suit, or *implied* by the fact of his bringing his person or property within the territory. But when courts of prize exercise their jurisdiction over vessels captured at sea, the property of foreigners is brought by force within the territory of
the state by which those tribunals are constituted. By natural law, the tribunals of the captor's country are no more the
rightful exclusive judges of captures in war made on the high
seas from under the neutral flag, than are the tribunals of the
neutral country. The equality of nations would, on principle, seem to forbid the exercise of a jurisdiction thus acquired
by force and violence, and administered by tribunals which
cannot be impartial between the litigating parties, because
created by the sovereign of the one to judge the other. Such,
however, is the actual constitution of the tribunals in which
by the positive international law is vested the exclusive jurisdiction of prizes taken in war. But the imperfection of the

---

[16] Bynkershoek, Quæst. Jur. Pub.   Vattel, Droit des Gens.

voluntary law of nations, in its present state, cannot oppose
an effectual bar to the claim of a neutral government seeking
indemnity for its subjects who have been unjustly deprived
of their property under the erroneous administration of that
law. The institution of these tribunals, so far from exempt-
ing, or being intended to exempt, the sovereign of the belligerent nation from responsibility for the acts of his commissioned cruisers, is designed to ascertain and fix that responsibility. Those cruisers are responsible only to the sovereigns
whose commissions they bear. So long as seizures are regularly made upon apparent grounds of just suspicion, and followed by prompt adjudication in the usual mode, and until
the acts of the captors are confirmed by the sovereign in the
sentences of the tribunals appointed by him to adjudicate in
matters of prize, the neutral has no ground of complaint, and
what he suffers is the inevitable result of the belligerent right
of capture. But the moment the decision of the tribunal of
the last resort has been pronounced, (supposing it not to be
warranted by the facts of the case, and by the law of nations applied to those facts,) and justice has been thus finally
denied, the capture and the condemnation become the acts
of the state, for which the sovereign is responsible to the
government of the claimant.

There is nothing more irregular in maintaining that the sovereign is responsible towards foreign states for the acts of
his tribunals, than in maintaining that he is responsible for
his own acts, which, in the intercourse of nations, are constantly made the ground of complaint, of reprisals, and even
of war. No greater sanctity can be imputed to the proceedings of prize tribunals, even by the most extravagant theory
of the conclusiveness of their sentences, than is justly attributed to the acts of the sovereign himself. But those acts,
however binding upon his own subjects, if they are not conformable to the public law of the world, cannot be considered
as binding upon the subjects of other states. A wrong done
to them forms an equally just subject of complaint on the
part of their government, whether it proceeds from the direct
agency of the sovereign himself, or is inflicted by the instru-

mentality of his tribunals. The tribunals of a state are but a part, and only a subordinate part, of the government of that state. But the right of redress against injurious acts of the whole government, of the supreme authority, incontestably exists in foreign states, whose subjects have suffered by those acts. Much more clearly then must it exist when those acts proceed from persons, authorities, or tribunals, responsible to their own sovereign, but irresponsible to a foreign government otherwise than by its action on their sovereign.

These principles, so reasonable in themselves, are also supported by the authority of the writers on public law, and by historical examples.

" The exclusive right of the state to which the captors belong to adjudicate upon the captures made by them," says Rutherforth, is founded upon another," *i. e.* " its right to inspect into the conduct of the captors, both because they are members of it, and because it is responsible to all other states for what they do in war; since what they do in war is done either under its general or its special commission. The captors are therefore obliged, on account of the jurisdiction which the state has over their persons, to bring such ships or goods as they seize in the main ocean into their own ports, and they cannot acquire property in them until the state has determined whether they were lawfully taken or not. This right which their own state has to determine this matter is so far an exclusive one, that no other state can claim to judge of their conduct until it has been thoroughly examined into by their own; both because no other state has jurisdiction over their persons, and likewise because no other state is answerable for what they do. But the state to which the captors belong, whilst it is thus examining into the conduct of its own members, and deciding whether the ships or goods which they have seized are lawfully taken or not, is determining a question between its own members and the foreigners who claim the property: and this controversy did not arise within its own territory, but in the main ocean. The right, therefore, which it exercises, is not civil jurisdiction; and the civil law, which is peculiar to its own territory, is

not the law by which it ought to proceed. Neither the place
where the controversy arose, nor the parties who are concerned in it, are subject to this law. The only law by which
this controversy can be determined, is the law of nature,
applied to the collective bodies of civil societies, that is the
law of nations: unless indeed there have been any particular treaties made between the two states, to which the captors and the other claimants belong, mutually binding them
to depart from such rights as the law of nations would otherwise have supported. Where such treaties have been
made, they are a law to the two states, as far as they extend,
and to all the members of them in their intercourse with one
another. The state, therefore, to which the captors belong,
in determining what might or what might not be lawfully
taken, is to judge by these particular treaties, and by the
law of nations taken together. This right of the state, to
which the captors belong, to judge exclusively, is not a complete jurisdiction. The captors, who are its own members,
are bound to submit to its sentence, though this sentence
should happen to be erroneous, because it has a complete
jurisdiction over their persons. But the other parties to the
controversy, as they are members of another state, are only
bound to submit to its sentence so far as this sentence is
agreeable to the law of nations or to particular treaties: because it has no jurisdiction over them, either in respect of
their persons, or of the things that are the subject of the controversy. If justice therefore is not done them, they may
apply to their own state for a remedy; which may, consistently with the law of nations, give them a remedy either by
solemn war or reprisals. In order to determine when their
right to apply to their own state begins, we must inquire
when the exclusive right of the other state to judge in this
controversy ends. As this exclusive right is nothing else but
the right of the state, to which the captors belong, to examine into the conduct of its own members before it becomes
answerable for what they have done, such exclusive right
cannot end until their conduct has been thoroughly examined.
Natural equity will not allow that the state should be answera-

ble for their acts until those acts are examined by all the ways which the state has appointed for this purpose. Since, therefore, it is usual in maritime countries to establish not only inferior courts of marine to judge what is, and what is not lawful prize, but likewise superior courts of review to which the parties may appeal, if they think themselves aggrieved by the inferior courts; the subjects of a neutral state can have no right to apply to their own state for a remedy against an erroneous sentence of an inferior court, till they have appealed to the superior court, or to the several superior courts, if there are more courts of this sort than one, and till the sentence has been confirmed in all of them. For these courts are so many means appointed by the state, to which the captors belong, to examine into their conduct; and till their conduct has been examined by all these means, the state's exclusive right of judging continues. After the sentence of the inferior court has been thus confirmed, the foreign claimants may apply to their own state for a remedy, if they think themselves aggrieved: but the law of nations will not entitle them to a remedy unless they have been actually aggrieved. When the matter is carried thus far, the two states become the parties in the controversy. And since the law of nature, whether it is applied to individuals or civil societies, abhors the use of force till force becomes necessary, the supreme rulers of the neutral state, before they proceed to solemn war or to reprisals, ought to apply to the supreme rulers of the other state, both to satisfy themselves that they have been rightly informed, and likewise to try whether the controversy cannot be adjusted by more gentle methods."[17]

In the celebrated report made to the British government in 1753, upon the case of the reprisals granted by the king of Prussia on account of captures made by the cruisers of Great Britain of the property of his subjects, the exclusive jurisdiction of the captor's country over captures made in war by its commissioned cruisers, is asserted, and it is laid down that "the law of nations, founded upon justice, equity, conve-

---

[17] Rutherforth's Inst. vol. ii. b. ii. ch. 9, § 19.

nience, and the reason of the thing, does not allow of reprisals, except in case of violent injuries, directed or supported by the state, and justice absolutely denied *in re minime dubiâ*, by all the tribunals, and afterwards by the prince ;"—plainly showing that, in the opinion of the eminent persons by whom that paper was drawn up, if justice be denied, in a clear case, by all the tribunals, and afterwards by the prince, it forms a lawful ground of reprisals against the nation by whose commissioned cruisers and tribunals the injury is committed. And that *Vattel* was of the same opinion, is evident from the manner in which he quotes this paper to support his own doctrine, that the sentences of the tribunals ought not to be made the ground of complaint by the state against whose subjects they are pronounced, " *excepting* the case of a refusal of justice, palpable, and evident injustice, a manifest violation of rules and forms, &c."[18]

In the case above referred to, the king of Prussia (then neutral) had undertaken to set up within his own dominions a commission to re-examine the sentences pronounced against his subjects in the British prize courts, a conduct which is treated by the authors of the report to the British government as an innovation "which was never attempted in any country of the world before. Prize or no prize must be determined by courts of admiralty belonging to the power whose subjects made the capture." But the report proceeds to state that every foreign prince in amity has a right to demand that justice shall be done to his subjects in these courts according to the law of nations, or particular treaties, where they are subsisting. If *in re minime dubiâ*—these courts proceed upon foundations directly opposite to the law of nations, or subsisting treaties, the neutral state has a right to complain of such determination."

The king of Prussia did complain of the determinations of the British tribunals, and made reprisals by stopping the interest upon a loan due to British subjects and secured by hypothecation upon the revenues of Silesia, until he actually

---

[18] Vattel, Droit des Gens, liv. ii. ch. 7, § 85.

obtained from the British government an indemnity for the Prussian vessels unjustly captured and condemned. The proceedings of the British tribunals, though they were asserted by the British government to be the only legitimate mode of determining the validity of captures made in war, were not considered as excluding the demand of Prussia for redress upon the government itself. So also under the treaty of 1794 between the United States and Great Britain, a mixed commission was appointed to determine the claim of American citizens, arising from the capture of their property by British cruisers during the existing war with France, according to justice, equity, and the law of nations. In the course of the proceedings of this board objections were made on the part of the British government against the commissioners proceeding to hear and determine any case where the sentence of condemnation had been affirmed by the lords of appeal in prize causes, upon the ground that full and entire credit was to be given to their final sentence, inasmuch as according to the general law of nations it was to be presumed that justice had been administered by this the competent and supreme tribunal in matters of prize. But this objection was overruled by the board upon the grounds and principles already stated, and a full and satisfactory indemnity was awarded in many cases where there had been a final sentence of condemnation.

Many other instances might be mentioned of arrangements between states, by which mixed commissions have been appointed to hear and determine the claims of the subjects of neutral powers arising out of captures in war, not for the purpose of revising the sentences of the competent courts of prize as between the captors and captured, but for the purpose of providing an adequate indemnity between state and state, in cases where satisfactory compensation had not been received in the ordinary course of justice. Although the theory of public law treats prize tribunals established by and sitting in the belligerent country exactly as if they were established by and sitting in the neutral country, (i. e. conformably to the international law common to both,) yet it is well

known that in practice such tribunals do take for their guide
the prize ordinances and instructions issued by the belligerent
sovereign, without stopping to inquire whether they are consistent with the paramount rule. If, therefore, the final sentence of these tribunals were to be considered as absolutely
conclusive, so as to preclude all inquiry into their merits, the
obvious consequence would be to invest the belligerent state
with legislative power over the rights of neutrals, and to prevent them from showing that the ordinances and instructions under which the sentences have been pronounced are
repugnant to that law by which foreigners alone are bound.

These principles have received a recent confirmation in
the negotiation between the American and Danish governments respecting the captures of American vessels and cargoes made by the cruisers of Denmark during the last war
between that power and Great Britain. In the course of this
negotiation, it was objected by the Danish ministers that the
validity of these captures had been finally determined in the
competent prize court of the belligerent country, and could
not be again drawn in question. On the part of the American government, it was admitted that the jurisdiction of the
tribunals of the capturing nation was exclusive and complete
upon the question of prize or no prize, so as to transfer the
property in the things condemned from the original owner to
the captors, or those claiming under them; that the final
sentence of those tribunals is conclusive as to the change of
property operated by it, and cannot be again incidentally
drawn in question in any other judicial forum; and that it
has the effect of closing for ever all private controversy between the captors and the captured. The demand which
the United States made upon the Danish government was not
for a judicial revision and reversal of the sentences pronounced by its tribunals, but for the indemnity to which the
American citizens were entitled in consequence of the denial
of justice by the tribunal in the last resort, and of the responsibility thus incurred by the Danish government for the
acts of its cruisers and tribunals. The Danish government
was, of course, free to adopt any measures it might think

proper to satisfy itself of the injustice of those sentences, one of the most natural of which would be a re-examination and discussion of the cases complained of, conducted by an impartial tribunal under the sanction of the two governments, not for the purpose of disturbing the question of title to the specific property which had been irrevocably condemned, or of reviving the controversy between the individual captors and claimants which had been for ever terminated, but for the purpose of determining between government and government whether injustice had been done by the tribunals of one power against the citizens of the other, and of determining what indemnity ought to be granted to the latter.

The accuracy of this distinction was acquiesced in by the Danish ministers, and a treaty concluded, by which a satisfactory indemnity was provided for the American claimants.[19]

We have seen that a firm possession, or the sentence of a competent court, is sufficient to confirm the captor's title to personal property or moveables taken in war. A different rule is applied to real property, or immoveables. The original owner of this species of property is entitled to what is called the benefit of postliminy, and the title acquired in war must be confirmed by a treaty of peace before it can be considered as completely valid. This rule cannot be frequently applied to the case of mere private property, which by the general usage of modern nations is exempt from confiscation. It only becomes practically important in questions arising out of alienations of real property, belonging to the government, made by the opposite belligerent, while in the military occupation of the country. Such a title must be expressly confirmed by the treaty of peace, or by the general operation of the cession of territory made by the enemy in such treaty. Until such confirmation, it continues liable to be divested by the *jus postliminii*. The purchaser of any portion of the national domain takes it at the peril of being evicted by the original

§ 16.
Title to real property, how transferred in war,
Jus postliminii.

19 Martens, Nouveau Recueil, tom. viii. p. 350.

sovereign owner when he is restored to the possession of his dominions.[20]

§ 17.
Good faith
towards
enemies.

Grotius has devoted a whole chapter of his great work to prove, by the consenting testimony of all ages and nations, that good faith ought to be observed towards an enemy. And even *Bynkershoek*, who holds that every other sort of fraud may be practised towards him, prohibits perfidy, upon the ground that his character of enemy ceases by the compact with him, so far as the terms of that compact extend. " I allow of any kind of deceit," says he, " perfidy alone excepted, not because any thing is unlawful against an enemy, but because when our faith has been pledged to him, so far as the promise extends, he ceases to be an enemy." Indeed, without this mitigation, the horrors of war would be indefinite in extent, and interminable in duration. The usage of civilized nations has therefore introduced certain *commercia belli*, by which the violence of war may be allayed, so far as is consistent with its object and purposes, and something of a pacific intercourse may be kept up, which may lead, in time, to an adjustment of differences, and ultimately to peace.[21]

§ 18.
Truce or
armistice.

There are various modes in which the extreme rigour of the rights of war may be relaxed at the pleasure of the respective belligerent parties. Among these is that of a suspension of hostilities, by means of a truce or armistice. This may be either general or special. If it be general in its application to all hostilities in every place, and is to endure for a very long or indefinite period, it amounts in effect to a

---

[20] Grotius, de Jur. Bel. as Pac. lib. iii. cap. 6, § 4; cap. 9, § 13. Vattel, Droit des Gens, liv. iii. ch. 13, §§ 197—200, 210, 212. Kluber, Droit des Gens Moderne de l'Europe, §§ 256—258. Martens, Précis, &c. liv. viii. ch 4, § 282, *a*. Where the case of conquest is complicated with that of civil revolution, and a change of internal government recognised by the nation itself and by foreign states, a modification of the rule may be required in its practical application. Vide ante, pt. i. ch. 2.

[21] Bynkerstoek. Quæst. Jur. Pub. lib. i. cap. 1. Robinson's Adm. Rep. vol. iii. p. 139. The Daifje.

temporary peace, except that it leaves undecided the controversy in which the war originated. Such were the truces
formerly concluded between the Christian powers and the
Turks. Such, too, was the armistice concluded in 1609 between Spain and her revolted provinces in the Netherlands.
A partial truce is limited to certain places, such as the suspension of hostilities which may take place between two contending armies, or between a besieged fortress and the army
by which it is invested.[22]

The power to conclude a universal armistice or suspension
of hostilities is not necessarily implied in the ordinary official
authority of the general or admiral commanding in chief the
military or naval forces of the state. The conclusion of such
a general truce requires either the previous special authority
of the supreme power of the state, or a subsequent ratification by such power.[23]

§ 19.
Power to conclude an armis- tice.

A partial truce or limited suspension of hostilities may be
concluded between the military and naval officers of the respective belligerent states, without any special authority for
that purpose, where, from the nature and extent of their
commands, such an authority is necessarily implied as essential to the fulfilment of their official duties.[24]

A suspension of hostilities binds the contracting parties, and
all acting immediately under their direction, from the time it
is concluded; but it must be duly promulgated in order to
have the force of legal obligation with regard to the other
subjects of the belligerent states; so that if, before such notification, they have committed any act of hostility, they are
not penally responsible, unless their ignorance be imputable
to their own fault or negligence. But as the supreme power
of the state is bound to fulfil its own engagements, or those
made by its authority, express or implied, the government of

§ 20.
Period of its opera- tion.

[22] Vattel, Droit des Gens, liv. iii. ch. 16, §§ 235, 236.
[23] Grotius, de Jur. Bel. ac Pac. lib. iii. cap. 22, § 8. Barbeyrac's Note.
Vattel, Droit des Gens, liv. iii. ch. 16, §§ 233—238.
[24] Vide ante, pt. iii. ch. 2—Of Negotiations and Treaties.

the captor is bound, in the case of a suspension of hostilities by sea, to restore all prizes made in contravention of the armistice. To prevent the disputes and difficulties arising from such questions, it is usual to stipulate in the convention of armistice, as in treaties of peace, a prospective period within which hostilities are to cease, with a due regard to the situation and distance of places.[25]

§ 21.
Rules for interpreting conventions of truce.

Besides the general maxims applicable to the interpretation of all international compacts, there are some rules peculiarly applicable to conventions for the suspension of hostilities. The *first* of these peculiar rules, as laid down by Vattel, is that each party may do within his own territory, or within the limits prescribed by the armistice, whatever he could do in time of peace. Thus either of the belligerent parties may levy and march troops, collect provisions and other munitions of war, receive re-enforcements from his allies, or repair the fortifications of a place not actually besieged.

The *second* rule is, that neither party can take advantage of the truce to execute, without peril to himself, what the continuance of hostilities might have disabled him from doing. Such an act would be a fraudulent violation of the armistice. For example:—in the case of a truce between the commander of a fortified town and the army besieging it, neither party is at liberty to continue works, constructed either for attack or defence, or to erect new fortifications for such purposes. Nor can the garrison avail itself of the truce to introduce provisions or succours into the town, through passages or in any other manner which the besieging army would have been competent to obstruct and prevent had hostilities not been interrupted by the armistice.

The *third* rule stated by Vattel is rather a corollary from the preceding rules than a distinct principle capable of any separate application. As the truce merely suspends hostilities without terminating the war, all things are to remain in

[25] Grotius, de Jur. Bel. ac Pac. lib. iii. cap. 21, § 5. Vattel, Droit des Gens, liv. iii. ch. 16, § 239.

their antecedent state in the places, the possession of which was specially contested at the time of the conclusion of the armistice.

It is obvious that the contracting parties may, by express compact, derogate in any and every respect from these general conditions.

At the expiration of the period stipulated in the truce, hos- § 22. tilities recommence as a matter of course, without any new Recom-declaration of war. But if the truce has been concluded for mencefor an indefinite, or for a very long period, good faith and hu- hostilities manity concur in requiring previous notice to be given to the piration of enemy of an intention to terminate what he may justly re- truce. gard as equivalent to a treaty of peace. Such was the duty inculcated by the Fecial college upon the Romans at the expiration of a long truce which they had made with the people of Veii. That people had recommenced hostilities before the expiration of the time limited in the truce. Still it was held necessary for the Romans to send heralds and demand satisfaction before renewing the war.[26]

Capitulations for the surrender of troops, fortresses, and § 23. particular districts of country, fall naturally within the scope Capitula-tions for of the general powers intrusted to military and naval com- the sur-manders. Stipulations between the governor of a besieged render of place, and the general or admiral commanding the forces by fortresses. which it is invested, if necessarily connected with the sur-render, do not require the subsequent sanction of their re-spective sovereigns. Such are the usual stipulations for the security of the religion and privileges of the inhabitants, that the garrison shall not bear arms against the conquerors for a limited period, and other like clauses properly incident to the particular nature of the transaction. But if the com-mander of the fortified town undertake to stipulate for the perpetual cession of the place, or enter into other engage-

[26] Liv. Hist. lib. iv. cap. 30.

ments not fairly within the scope of his implied authority, his promise amounts to a mere *sponsion*.[27]

The celebrated convention made by the Roman consuls with the Samnites at the Caudine Forks was of this nature. The conduct of the Roman senate in disavowing this ignominious compact is approved by Grotius and Vattel, who hold that the Samnites were not entitled to be placed in *statu quo,* because they must have known that the Roman consuls were wholly unauthorized to make such a convention. This consideration seems sufficient to justify the Romans in acting on this occasion according to their uniform uncompromising policy by delivering up to the Samnites the authors of the treaty, and persevering in the war until this formidable enemy was finally subjugated.[28]

The convention concluded at Closter-Seven, during the seven years' war, between the Duke of Cumberland, commander of the British forces in Hanover, and Marshal Richelieu, commanding the French army, for a suspension of arms in the north of Germany, is one of the most remarkable treaties of this kind recorded in modern history. It does not appear, from the discussions which took place between the two governments on this occasion, that there was any disagreement between them as to the true principles of international law applicable to such transactions. The conduct, if not the language of both parties, implies a mutual admission that the convention was of a nature to require ratification as exceeding the ordinary powers of military commanders in respect to mere military capitulations. The same remark may be applied to the convention signed at El Arish in 1800 for the evacuation of Egypt by the French army; although the position of the two governments, as to the convention of Closter-Seven, was reversed in that of El Arish, the British government refusing in the first instance to permit the execution of the latter treaty upon the ground of the defect in Sir Sidney Smith's powers, and after the battle of Heliopolis insisting

---

[27] Vide ante, pt. iii. ch. 2, § 3.

[28] See the account given by Livy of this remarkable transaction.

upon its being performed by the French when circumstances had varied and rendered its execution no longer consistent with their policy and interest. Good faith may have characterized the conduct of the British government in this instance, as was strenuously insisted by ministers in the parliamentary discussions to which the treaty gave rise, but there is at least no evidence of perfidy on the part of General Kleber. His conduct may rather be compared with that of the Duke of Cumberland at Closter-Seven, (and it certainly will not suffer by the comparison,) in concluding a convention suited to existing circumstances, which it was plainly his interest to carry into effect when it was signed, and afterwards refusing to abide by it when those circumstances were materially changed. In these compacts, time is material: indeed it may be said to be of the very essence of the contract. If any thing occurs to render its immediate execution impracticable, it becomes of no effect, or at least is subject to be varied by fresh negotiation.[29]

Passports, safe-conducts, and licenses, are documents granted in war to protect persons and property from the general operation of hostilities. The competency of the authority to issue them depends on the general principles already noticed. This sovereign authority may be vested in military and naval commanders, or in certain civil officers, either expressly, or by inevitable implication from the nature and extent of their general trust. Such documents are to be interpreted by the same rules of liberality and good faith with other acts of the sovereign power.[30]

§ 24. Passports, safe conducts, and licenses.

Thus a license granted by the belligerent state to its own subjects, or to the subjects of its enemy, to carry on a trade interdicted by war, operates as a dispensation with the laws of war so far as its terms can fairly be construed to extend.

§ 25. Licenses to trade with the enemy.

[29] Flassan, Histoire de la Diplomatie Française, tom. vi. pp. 97—107. Annual Register, vol. i. pp. 209—213, 228—234; vol. xlii. p. [219,] pp. 223—233. State Papers, vol. xliii. pp. [28—34.]

[30] Grotius, de Jur. Bel. ac Pac. lib. iii. cap. 21, § 14. Vattel, Droit des Gens, liv. iii. ch. 17, §§ 265—277.

The adverse belligerent party may justly consider such documents of protection as *per se* a ground of capture and confiscation; but the maritime tribunals of the state, under whose
authority they are issued, are bound to consider them as lawful relaxations of the ordinary state of war.   A license is an
act proceeding from the sovereign authority of the state,
which alone is competent to decide on all the considerations
of political and commercial expediency, by which such an
exception from the ordinary consequences of war must be
controlled.   Licenses, being high acts of sovereignty, are
necessarily *stricti juris,* and must not be carried further than
the intention of the authority which grants them may be
supposed to extend.   Not that they are to be construed with
pedantic accuracy, or that every small deviation should
be held to vitiate their fair effect.   An excess in the quantity
of goods permitted might not be considered as noxious to any
extent, but a variation in their quality or substance might be
more significant, because a liberty assumed of importing one
species of goods, under a license to import another, might
lead to very dangerous consequences.   The limitations of
time, persons, and places, specified in the license, are also
material.   The great principle in these cases is, that subjects
are not to trade with the enemy, nor the enemy's subjects
with the belligerent state, without the special permission of
the government; and a material object of the control which
the government exercises over such a trade is, that it may
judge of the fitness of the persons, and under what restrictions of time and place such an exemption from the ordinary
laws of war may be extended.   Such are the general principles laid down by Sir *W. Scott* for the interpretation of
these documents: but *Grotius* lays down the general rule,
that safe-conducts, of which these licenses are a species, are
to be liberally construed; *laxa quam stricta interpretatio ad-
mittenda est.*   And during the last war licenses were eventu-
ally interpreted with great liberality in the British courts of
prize."[31]

    [31] Chitty's Law of Nations, ch. 7.   Kent's Comment. on American Law,
vol. i. p. 164, Note *a.*   2d Edit.

It was made a question in some cases in those courts, how far these documents could protect against British capture, on account of the nature and extent of the authority of the persons by whom they were issued. The leading case on this subject is that of the *Hope*, an American ship laden with corn and flour, captured whilst proceeding from the United States to the ports of the Peninsula occupied by the British troops, and claimed as protected by an instrument granted by the British consul at Boston, accompanied by a certified copy of a letter from the admiral on the Halifax station. In pronouncing judgment in this case, Sir *W. Scott* observed, that the instrument of protection, in order to be effectual, must come from those who have a competent authority to grant such a protection, but that the papers in question came from persons who were vested with no such authority. To exempt the property of enemies from the effect of hostilities is a very high act of sovereign authority: if at any time delegated to persons in a subordinate station, it must be exercised either by those who have a special commission granted to them for the particular business, and who in legal language are called *mandatories*, or by persons in whom such a power is vested in virtue of any situation to which it may be considered incidental. It was quite clear that no consul in any country, particularly in an enemy's country, is vested with any such power in virtue of his station. *Eæ rei non præponitur*, and, therefore, his acts in relation to it are not binding. Neither does the admiral, on any station, possess such authority. He has, indeed, power relative to the ships under his immediate command, and can restrain them from committing acts of hostility; but he cannot go beyond that—he cannot grant a safeguard of this kind beyond the limits of his own station. The protections, therefore, which had been set up did not result from any power incidental to the situation of the persons by whom they had been granted; and it was not pretended that any such power was specially intrusted to them for the particular occasion. If the instruments which had been relied upon by the claimants were to be considered as the naked acts of those persons, then they were, in every point

§ 26. Authority to grant licenses.

of view, totally invalid.   But the question was, whether the
British government had taken any steps to ratify these proceedings, and thus to convert them into valid acts of state;
for persons not having full power may make what in law are
termed *sponsiones*, or, in diplomatic language, treaties *sub spe
rati*, to which a subsequent ratification may give validity; *ra-
tihabitio mandato æquiparatur*.   The learned judge proceeded
to show, that the British government had confirmed the acts
of its officers by the order in council of the 26th October,
1813, and accordingly decreed restitution of the property.
In the case of the *Reward*, before the lords of appeal, the
principle of this judgment was substantially confirmed; but
in that of the *Charles*, and other similar cases, where certifi-
cates or passports of the same kind, signed by Admiral Saw-
yer, and also by the Spanish minister in the United States,
had been used for voyages from thence to the Spanish West
Indies, the lords of appeal held that these documents, not
being included within the terms of the confirmatory order in
council, did not afford protection.   In the cases of the passports granted by the British minister in the United States,
permitting American vessels to sail with provisions from
thence to the island of St. Bartholomew's, but not confirmed
by an order in council, the lords condemned in all the cases
not expressly included within the terms of the order in council by which certain descriptions of licenses granted by the
minister had been confirmed.[32]

§ 27.
Ransom of
captured
property.

The contract made for the ransom of enemy's property
taken at sea is generally carried into effect by a safe-conduct, granted by the captors, permitting the captured vessel
and cargo to proceed to a designated port within a limited
time.   Unless prohibited by the law of the captor's own country, this document furnishes a complete legal protection
against the cruisers of the same nation, or its allies, during
the period and within the geographical limits prescribed by
its terms.   This protection results from the general authority

[32] Dodson's Adm. Rep. vol. i. p. 226. The Hope. Ib. Appendix (D.)
Stewart's Vice-Adm. Rep. p. 367.

to capture which is delegated by the belligerent state to its commissioned cruisers, and which involves the power to ransom captured property when judged advantageous. If the ransomed vessel is lost by the perils of the sea before her arrival, the obligation to pay the sum stipulated for her ransom is not thereby extinguished. The captor guaranties the captured vessel against being interrupted in its course, or retaken by other cruisers of his nation, or its allies, but he does not ensure against losses by the perils of the seas. Even where it is expressly agreed that the loss of the vessel by these perils shall discharge the captured from the payment of the ransom, this clause is restrained to the case of a total loss on the high seas, and is not extended to shipwreck or stranding, which might afford the master a temptation fraudulently to cast away his vessel, in order to save the most valuable part of the cargo, and avoid the payment of the ransom. Where the ransomed vessel, having exceeded the time or deviated from the course prescribed by the ransom-bill, is retaken, the debtors of the ransom are discharged from their obligation, which is merged in the prize, and the amount is deducted from the net proceeds thereof, and paid to the first captor, whilst the residue is paid to the second captor. So if the captor, after having ransomed a vessel belonging to the enemy, is himself taken by the enemy, together with the ransom-bill, of which he is the bearer, this ransom-bill becomes a part of the capture made by the enemy; and the persons of the hostile nation, who were debtors of the ransom, are thereby discharged from their obligation. The death of the hostage taken for the faithful performance of the contract on the part of the captured does not discharge the contract; for the captor trusts to him as a collateral security only, and by losing it does not also lose his original security, unless there is an express agreement to that effect.[33]

Sir *William Scott* states, in the case of the *Hoop*, that as to ransoms, which are contracts arising *ex jure belli*, and tolerated as such, the enemy was not permitted to sue in the

[33] Pothier, Traité de Proprieté, Nos. 134—137. Valin, sur l'Ordonnance, liv. iii. tit. 9; des Prises, art. 19. Traité des Prises, ch. 11, Nos. 1—3,

British courts of justice in his own proper person for the pay-ment of the ransom, even before British subjects were pro-hibited by the statute 22 Geo. III. cap. 25, from ransoming enemy's property; but the payment was enforced by an ac-tion brought by the imprisoned hostage in the courts of his own country for the recovery of his freedom. But the effect of such a contract, like that of every other which may be lawfully entered between belligerents, is to suspend the cha-racter of enemy so far as respects the parties to the ransom-bill; and consequently the technical objection of the want of a *persona standi in judicio* cannot, on principle, prevent a suit being brought by the captor directly on the ransom-bill. And this appears to be the practice in the maritime courts of the European continent.[34]

[34] Robinson's Adm. Rep. vol. i. p. 201. The Hoop. See Lord Mansfield's judgment in the case of Ricord *v.* Bettenham, Burrow's Rep. p. 1734.

CHAPTER III.

RIGHTS OF WAR AS TO NEUTRALS.

THE right of every independent nation to remain at peace, § 1. whilst other nations are engaged in war, is an incontestable Rights and duties of attribute of sovereignty ; but it is obviously impossible that neutrality. neutral nations should be wholly unaffected by the existence of war between those with whom they continue to maintain the accustomed relations of friendship and commerce. The rights of neutrality bring with them corresponding duties. Among these duties is that of impartiality between the belligerent parties. The neutral is the common friend of both parties, and consequently is not at liberty to favour one party to the detriment of the other.[1]

There is, however, one very important exception arising § 2. out of antecedent engagements, by which the neutral may Neutrality modified be bound to one of the parties to the war. Thus the neu- by a limit- tral may be bound by treaty, previous to the war, to furnish ed alliance with one of one of the belligerent parties with a limited succour in mo- the belli- ney, troops, ships, or munitions of war, or to open his ports gerent to the armed vessels of his ally with their prizes. The ful- parties. filment of such an obligation does not necessarily forfeit his neutral character, nor render him the enemy of the other belligerent nation, because it does not render him the general associate of its enemy.[2]

How far a neutrality thus limited may be tolerated by the opposite belligerent must depend more upon considerations

---

[1] Bynkershoek, Quæst. Jur. Pub. lib. i. cap. 9.   Vattel, Droit des Gens, liv. iii. ch. 7, §§ 103—110.

[2] Vide ante, pt. iii. ch. 2, § 13.

of policy than of strict right. Thus where Denmark, in consequence of a previous treaty of defensive alliance, furnished limited succours in ships and troops to the Empress Catharine II. of Russia, in the war of 1788 against Sweden, the abstract right of the Danish court to remain neutral, except so far as regarded the stipulated succours, was scarcely contested by Sweden and the allied mediating powers. But it is evident from the history of these transactions, that if the war had continued, the neutrality of Denmark would not have been tolerated by these powers, unless she had withheld from her ally the succours stipulated by the treaty of 1773, or Russia had consented to dispense with its fulfilment.[3]

§ 3.
Qualified
neutrality,
arising out
of antece-
dent treaty
stipula-
tions, ad-
mitting the
armed ves-
sels and
prizes of
one belli-
gerent into
the neutral
ports,
whilst
those of the
other are
excluded.

Another case of qualified neutrality arises out of treaty stipulations antecedent to the commencement of hostilities, by which the neutral may be bound to admit the vessels of war of one of the belligerent parties, with their prizes, into his ports, whilst those of the other may be entirely excluded, or only admitted under limitations and restrictions. Thus by the treaty of amity and commerce of 1778, between the United States and France, the latter secured to herself two special privileges in the American ports :—1. Admission for her privateers, with their prizes, to the exclusion of her enemies. 2. Admission for her public ships of war, in case of urgent necessity, to refresh, victual, repair, &c., but not exclusively of other nations at war with her. Under these stipulations, the United States not being expressly bound to exclude the public ships of the enemies of France, granted an asylum to British vessels and those of other powers at war with her. Great Britain and Holland still complained of the exclusive privileges allowed to France in respect to her privateers and prizes, whilst France herself was not satisfied with the interpretation of the treaty by which the public ships of her enemies were admitted into the Ameri-

---

[3] Annual Register, vol. xxx. pp. 181, 182. State Papers, p. 292. Eggers, Lehen von Bernstorf, 2 abtheli. pp. 118—195,

can ports. To the former, it was answered by the American government that they enjoyed a perfect equality, qualified only by the exclusive admission of the privateers and prizes of France, which was the effect of a treaty made long before, for valuable considerations, not with a view to circumstances such as had occurred in the war of the French Revolution, nor against any nation in particular, but against all in general, and which might therefore be observed without giving just offence to any.[4]

On the other hand, the minister of France asserted the right of arming and equipping vessels for war, and of enlisting men, within the neutral territory of the United States. Examining this question under the law of nations and the general usage of mankind, the American government produced proofs from the most enlightened and approved writers on the subject, that a neutral nation must, in respect to the war, observe an exact impartiality towards the belligerent parties; that favours to the one, to the prejudice of the other, would import a fraudulent neutrality of which no nation would be the dupe; that no succour ought to be given to either, unless stipulated by treaty, in men, arms, or any thing else directly serving for war; that the right of raising troops being one of the rights of sovereignty, and consequently appertaining exclusively to the nation itself, no foreign power can levy men within the territory without its consent; that, finally, the treaty of 1778, making it unlawful for the enemies of France to arm in the United States, could not be construed affirmatively into a permission to the French to arm in those ports, the treaty being express as to the prohibition, but silent as to the permission.[5]

The rights of war can be exercised only within the territory of the belligerent powers, upon the high seas, or in a § 4. Hostilities within the

---

[4] Mr. Jefferson's Letter to Mr. Hammond and Mr. Van Berckel, Sept. 9, 1793. Waite's State Papers, vol. i. pp. 169, 172.

[5] Mr. Jefferson's Letter to Mr. G. Morris, Aug. 16, 1793. Waite's State Papers, vol. i. p. 140.

territory of territory belonging to no one.   Hence it follows that hostili-
the neutral ties cannot lawfully be exercised within the territorial juris-
state. diction of the neutral state which is the common friend of
both parties.[6]

§ 5.   This exemption extends to the passage of an army or fleet
Passage   through the limits of the territorial jurisdiction, which can
through
the neutral hardly be considered an innocent passage, such as one nation
territory. has a right to demand from another; and, even if it were
such an innocent passage, is one of those *imperfect* rights, the
exercise of which depends upon the consent of the proprietor, and which cannot be compelled against his will. It may
be granted or withheld, at the discretion of the neutral state;
but its being granted is no ground of complaint on the part
of the other belligerent power, provided the same privilege
is granted to him, unless there be sufficient reasons for withholding it.[7]

The extent of the maritime territorial jurisdiction of every
state bordering on the sea has already been described.[8]

§ 6.   Not only are all captures made by the belligerent cruisers
Captures
within the within the limits of this jurisdiction, absolutely illegal and
maritime   void, but captures made by armed vessels stationed in a bay
territorial
jurisdic-   or river, or in the mouth of a river, or in the harbour of a
tion, or by neutral state, for the purpose of exercising the rights of war
vessels
stationed   from this station, are also invalid. Thus where a British pri-
within it, vateer stationed itself within the river Mississippi, in the
or hover-
ing on the neutral territory of the United States, for the purpose of ex-
coasts.   ercising the rights of war from the river, by standing off and
on, obtaining information at the Balize, and overhauling vessels in their course down the river, and made the capture in

---

[6] Bynkershoek, Quæst. Jur. Pub. lib. i. cap. 8.   Martens, des Prises et
Reprises, ch. 2, § 18.

[7] Vide ante, pt. ii. ch. 4. Rights of Property.   Vattel, Droit des Gens,
liv. iii. ch. 7, §§ 119—131.   Grotius, de Jur. Bel. ac Pac. lib. ii. cap. 2, §
13.   Sir W. Scott, Robinson's Adm. Rep. vol. iii. p. 353.

[8] Vide ante, pt. ii. ch. 4. Rights of Property.

question within three English miles of the alluvial islands formed at its mouth, restitution of the captured vessel was decreed by Sir *W. Scott.* So also where a belligerent ship, lying within neutral territory, made a capture with her boats out of the neutral territory, the capture was held to be invalid; for though the hostile force employed was applied to the captured vessel lying out of the territory, yet no such use of a neutral territory for the purposes of war is to be permitted. This prohibition is not to be extended to *remote* uses, such as procuring provisions and refreshments, which the law of nations universally tolerates; but no *proximate* acts of war are in any manner to be allowed to originate on neutral ground.[9]

Although the immunity of the neutral territory from the exercise of any act of hostility is generally admitted, yet an exception to it has been attempted to be raised in the case of a hostile vessel met on the high seas and pursued; which it is said may, in the pursuit, be chased within the limits of a neutral territory. The only text writer of authority who has maintained this anomalous principle is *Bynkershoek.* He admits that he had never seen it mentioned in the writings of the publicists, or among any of the European nations, the Dutch only excepted; thus leaving the inference open, that even if reasonable in itself, such a practice never rested upon authority, nor was sanctioned by general usage. The extreme caution, too, with which he guards this license to belligerents, can hardly be reconciled with the practical exercise of it; for how is an enemy to be pursued in a hostile manner within the jurisdiction of a friendly power, without imminent danger of injuring the subjects and property of the latter? *Dum fervet opus*—in the heat and animation excited against the flying foe, there is too much reason to presume that little regard will be paid to the consequences that may

§ 7. Vessels chased into the neutral territory, and there captured.

[9] The Anna, Nov. 1805. Robinson's Adm. Rep. vol. v, p. 373. The Twee Gebroeders, July, 1800. Vol. iii. p. 162.

ensue to the neutral. There is, then, no exception to the rule, that every voluntary entrance into neutral territory, with hostile purposes, is absolutely unlawful. " When the fact is established," says Sir *W. Scott*, " it overrules every other consideration. The capture is done away; the property must be restored, notwithstanding that it may actually belong to the enemy."[10]

§ 8.
Claim on the ground of violation of neutral territory must be sanctioned by the neutral state.
Though it is the duty of the captor's country to make restitution of the property thus captured within the territorial jurisdiction of the neutral state, yet it is a technical rule of the prize court to restore to the individual claimant, in such a case, only on the application of the neutral government whose territory has been thus violated. This rule is founded upon the principle that the neutral state alone has been injured by the capture, and that the hostile claimant has no right to appear for the purpose of suggesting the invalidity of the capture.[11]

§ 9.
Restitution by the neutral state of property captured within its jurisdiction, or otherwise in violation of its neutrality.
Captures within the places called the *King's Chambers.*
Where a capture of enemy's property is made within neutral territory, or by armaments unlawfully fitted out within the same, it is the right as well as the duty of the neutral state, where the property thus taken comes into its possession, to restore it to the original owners. This restitution is generally made through the agency of the courts of admiralty and maritime jurisdiction. Traces of the exercise of such a jurisdiction are found at a very early period in the writings of Sir Leoline Jenkins, who was judge of the English high court of admiralty in the reigns of Charles II. and James II. In a letter to the king in council, dated Oct. 11, 1675, relating to a French privateer seized at Harwich with her prize, (a Hamburg vessel bound to London,) Sir Leoline states several questions arising in the case, among which was, " Whether this Hamburgher, being taken within one of your

---

[10] Robinson's Adm. Rep. vol. v. p. 15.   The Vrow Anna Catharina.
[11] Robinson's Adm. Rep. vol. iii. Note.   Case of the Etrusco.

Majesty's chambers, and being bound for one of your ports, ought not to be set free by your Majesty's authority, notwithstanding he were, if taken upon the high seas out of those chambers, a lawful prize. I do humbly conceive he ought to be set free, upon a full and clear proof that he was within one of the king's chambers at the time of the seizure, which he in his first memorial sets forth to have been eight leagues at sea over against Harwich. King James (of blessed memory) his direction, by proclamation, March 2, 1604, being that all officers and subjects, by sea and land, shall rescue and succour all merchants and others, as shall fall within the danger of such as shall await the coasts, in so near places to the hinderance of trade outward and homeward; and all foreign ships, when they are within the king's chambers, being understood to be within the places intended in those directions, must be in safety and indemnity, or else when they are surprised must be restored to it, otherwise they have not the protection worthy of your Majesty, and of the ancient reputation of those places. But this being a point not lately settled by any determination, (that I know of, in case where the king's chambers precisely, and under that name, came in question,) is of that importance as to deserve your Majesty's declaration and assertion of that right of the crown by an act of state in council, your Majesty's coasts being now so much infested with foreign men of war, that there will be frequent use of such a decision."[12]

Whatever doubts there may be as to the extent of the territorial jurisdiction thus asserted as entitled to the neutral immunity, there can be none as to the sense entertained by this eminent civilian as to the right and the duty of the neutral sovereign to make restitution where his territory is violated.

When the maritime war commenced in Europe in 1793, the American government, which had determined to remain neutral, found it necessary to define the extent of the line of

Extent of the neutral jurisdiction along

[12] Life and Works of Sir L. Jenkins, vol. ii. p. 727.

the coasts and within the bays and rivers. territorial protection claimed by the United States on their coasts, for the purpose of giving effect to their neutral rights and duties. It was stated on this occasion that governments and writers on public law had been much divided in opinion as to the distance from the sea coast within which a neutral nation might reasonably claim a right to prohibit the exercise of hostilities. The character of the coast of the United States, remarkable in considerable parts of it for admitting no vessels of size to pass near the shore, it was thought would entitle them in reason to as broad a margin of protected navigation as any nation whatever. The government, however, did not propose, at that time, and without amicable communications with the foreign powers interested in that navigation, to fix on the distance to which they might ultimately insist on the right of protection. President *Washington* gave instructions to the executive officers to consider it as restrained, for the present, to the distance of one sea league, or three geographical miles, from the sea-shores. This distance, it was supposed, could admit of no opposition, being recognised by treaties between the United States, and some of the powers with whom they were connected in commercial intercourse, and not being more extensive than was claimed by any of them on their own coasts. As to the bays and rivers, they had always been considered as portions of the territory, both under the laws of the former colonial government and of the present union, and their immunity from belligerent operations was sanctioned by the general law and usage of nations. The 25th article of the treaty of 1794, between Great Britain and the United States, stipulated that "neither of the said parties shall permit the ships or goods belonging to the citizens or subjects of the other, to be taken within cannon shot of the coast, nor in any of the bays, ports, or rivers of their territories, by ships of war, or others, having commissions from any prince, republic, or state whatever. But in case it should so happen, the party whose territorial rights shall thus have been violated, shall use his utmost endeavours to obtain from the offending party full and ample satisfaction for the vessel or vessels so taken, whether the same be vessels of war or merchant vessels." Previously to this treaty with Great Britain the United States were bound by treaties with three of the belligerent nations, (France, Prussia, and Holland,) to protect and defend, " by all the means in their power," the vessels and effects of those nations in their ports or waters, or on the seas near their shores, and to recover and restore the same to the right owner when taken from them. But they were not bound to make compensation if *all the means in their power* were used, and failed in their effect. Though they had, when the war commenced, no similar treaty with Great Britain, it was the President's opinion that they should apply to that nation the same rule which, under this article, was to govern the others abovementioned; and even extend it to captures made on the high seas, and brought into the American ports, if made by vessels which had been armed within them. In the constitutional arrangement of the different authorities of the American federal Union, doubts were at first entertained whether it belonged to the executive government, or the judiciary department, to perform the duty of inquiring into captures made within the neutral territory, or by armed vessels originally equipped, or the force of which had been augmented within the same, and of making restitution to the injured party. But it has been long since settled that this duty appropriately belongs to the federal tribunals acting as courts of admiralty and maritime jurisdiction.[13]

It has been judicially determined that this peculiar jurisdiction to inquire into the validity of captures made in violation of the neutral immunity will be exercised only for the

§ 10. Limitations of the neutral ju-

[13] Mr. Jefferson's Letter to M. Genet, Nov. 8, 1793. Waite's State Papers, vol. vi. p. 195. Opinion of the Attorney-General on the capture of the British ship Grange, May 14, 1793. Ibid. vol. i. p. 75. Mr. Jefferson's Letter to Mr. Hammond, Sept. 5, 1723. Waite's State Papers, vol. i. p. 165. Wheaton's Reports, vol. iv. p. 65, Note a.

risdiction
to restore
in cases of
illegal cap-
ture.

purpose of restoring the specific property, when voluntarily brought within the territory, and does not extend to the infliction of vindictive damages, as in ordinary cases of maritime injuries.   And it seems to be doubtful whether this jurisdiction will be exercised where the property has been once carried *infra præsidia* of the captor's country, and there regularly condemned in a competent court of prize.   However this may be in cases where the property has come into the hands of a *bonâ fide* purchaser, without notice of the unlawfulness of the capture, it has been determined that the neutral court of admiralty will restore it to the original owner, where it is found in the hands of the captor himself claiming under the sentence of condemnation.   But the illegal equipment will not affect the validity of a capture, made after the cruise, to which the outfit had been applied, is actually terminated.[14]

§ 11.
Right of
asylum in
neutral
ports de-
pendent on
the consent
of the neu-
tral state.

An opinion is expressed by some text writers that belligerent cruisers not only are entitled to seek an asylum and hospitality in neutral ports, but have a right to bring in and sell their prizes within those ports.   But there seems to be nothing in the established principles of public law which can prevent the neutral state from withholding the exercise of this privilege impartially from all the belligerent powers, or even from granting it to one of them, and refusing it to others, where stipulated by treaties existing previous to the war. The usage of nations, as testified in their marine ordinances, sufficiently shows that this is a rightful exercise of the sovereign authority, which every state possesses, to regulate the police of its own sea-ports, and to preserve the public peace within its own territory.   But the absence of a positive prohibition implies a permission to enter the neutral ports for these purposes.[15]

[14] Wheaton's Rep. vol. v. p. 385.   The Amistad de Rues, vol. viii. p. 108; vol. ix. p. 658; vol. vii. p. 519.   The Santissima Trinidad.

[15] Bynkershoek, Quæst. Jur. Pub. lib. i. cap. 15.   Vattel, liv. iii. ch. 7, § 132.   Valin, Comm. sur l'Ordonn. de la Marine, tom. ii. p. 272.

Vattel states that the impartiality, which a neutral nation ought to observe between the belligerent parties, consists of two points. 1. To give no assistance where there is no previous stipulation to give it; nor voluntarily to furnish troops, arms, ammunition, or any thing of direct use in war. "I do not say *to give assistance equally,* but *to give no assistance;* for it would be absurd that a state should assist at the same time two enemies. And besides, it would be impossible to do it with equality: the same things, the like number of troops, the like quantity of arms, of munitions, &c. furnished under different circumstances, are no longer equivalent succours. 2. In whatever does not relate to the war, the neutral must not refuse to one of the parties, merely because he is at war with the other, what she grants to that other."[16]

§ 12.
Neutral
impartiali-
ty, in what
it consists.

These principles were appealed to by the American government, when its neutrality was attempted to be violated on the commencement of the European war in 1793, by arming and equipping vessels, and enlisting men within the ports of the United States by the respective belligerent powers to cruise against each other. It was stated that if the neutral power might not, consistently with its neutrality, furnish men to either party for their aid in war, as little could either enrol them in the neutral territory. The authority both of *Wolfius* and *Vattel* was appealed to in order to show that the levying of troops is an exclusive prerogative of sovereignty, which no foreign power can lawfully exercise within the territory of another state without its express permission. The testimony of these and other writers on the law and usage of nations was sufficient to show that the United States, in prohibiting all the belligerent powers from equipping, arming, and manning vessels of war in their ports, had exercised a right and a duty with justice and moderation. By their treaties with several of the belligerent powers, which formed part of the law of the land, they had established a state of

§ 13.
Arming
and equip-
ping ves-
sels, and
enlisting
men within
the neutral
territory,
by either
bellige-
rent, un-
lawful.

---

[16] Droit des Gens, liv. iii. ch. 7, § 104.

peace with them. But without appealing to treaties, they
had established a state of peace with them. But without appealing to treaties, they were at peace with them all by the
law of nature; for, by the natural law, man is at peace
with man, till some aggression is committed, which, by the
same law, authorizes one to destroy another, as his enemy.
For the citizens of the United States, then, to commit mur-
ders and depredations on the members of other nations, or to
combine to do it, appeared to the American government as
much against the laws of the land as to murder or rob, or
combine to murder or rob, their own citizens; and as much
to require punishment, if done within their limits, where
they had a territorial jurisdiction, or on the high seas, where
they had a personal jurisdiction, that is to say, one which
reached their own citizens only; this being an appropriate
part of each nation, on an element where each has a common jurisdiction."[17]

§ 14.
Prohibi-
tion en-
forced by
municipal
statutes.

The same principles were afterwards consigned to the
forms of a law of congress passed in 1794, and revised and
re-enacted in 1818, by which it is declared to be a misde-
meanor for any person, within the jurisdiction of the United
States, to augment the force of any armed vessel belonging
to one foreign power at war with another power, with whom
they are at peace; or to prepare any military expedition
against the territories of any foreign nation with whom they
are at peace; or to hire or enlist troops or seamen for foreign
military or naval service; or to be concerned in fitting out
any vessel, to cruise or commit hostilities in foreign service,
against a nation at peace with them; and the vessel, in this
latter case, is made subject to forfeiture. The president is
also authorized to employ force to compel any foreign vessel
to depart, which, by the law of nations or treaties, ought not
to remain within the United States, and to employ generally

[17] Mr. Jefferson's Letter to M. Genet, June 17, 1793. American State
Papers, vol. i. p. 155.

the public force in enforcing the duties of neutrality prescribed by the law.[18]

The example of America was soon followed by Great Bri-   Foreign
tain, in the act of parliament 59 Geo. III. ch. 69, entitled,   Enlistment
                                                                 Act.
" An Act to prevent the Enlisting or Engagement of His Majesty's Subjects to serve in Foreign Service, and the Fitting
Out or Equipping in His Majesty's Dominions Vessels for
Warlike Purposes, without His Majesty's License." The
previous statutes, 9 and 29 Geo. II., enacted for the purpose
of preventing the formation of Jacobite armies in France and
Spain, annexed capital punishment as for a felony to the offence of entering the service of a foreign state. The 59 Geo.
III. ch. 69, commonly called the Foreign Enlistment Act,
provided a less severe punishment, and also supplied a defect
in the former law, by introducing after the words " king,
prince, state, or potentate," the words " colony or district
assuming the powers of a government," in order to reach
the case of those who entered the service of unacknowledged
as well as of acknowledged states. The act also provided
for preventing and punishing the offence of fitting out armed
vessels, or supplying them with warlike stores, upon which
the former law had been entirely silent.

In the debates which took place in parliament upon the
enactment of the last-mentioned act in 1819, and on the motion for its repeal in 1823, it was not denied by Sir *J. Mackintosh* and other members who opposed the bill, that the
sovereign power of every state might interfere to prevent its
subjects from engaging in the wars of other states, by which
its own peace might be endangered, or its political and commercial interests affected. It was, however, insisted that
the principles of neutrality only required the British legislature to maintain the laws in being, but could not command
it to change any law, and least of all to alter the existing
laws for the evident advantage of one of the belligerent parties. Those who assisted insurgent states, however merito-

---

[18] Kent's Comment. on American Law, vol. i. p. 123. 2d Ed.

rious the cause in which they were engaged, were in a much
worse situation than those who assisted recognised governments, as they could not lawfully be reclaimed as prisoners
of war, and might, as engaged in what was called rebellion,
be treated as rebels.   The proposed new law would go to
alter the relative risks, and operate as a law of favour to one
of the belligerent parties.   To this argument it was replied
by Mr. *Canning*, that when peace was concluded between
Great Britain and Spain in 1814, an article was introduced
into the treaty by which the former power stipulated not to
furnish any succours to what were then denominated the revolted colonies of Spain.   In process of time, as those colonies became more powerful, a question arose of a very difficult nature, to be decided on a due consideration of their *de
jure* relation to Spain on the one hand, and their *de facto* independence on the other.   The law of nations afforded no
precise rule as to the course which, under circumstances so
peculiar as the transition of colonies from their allegiance to
the parent state, ought to be pursued by foreign powers.
It was difficult to know how far the statute law or the
common law was applicable to colonies so situated.   It became necessary, therefore, in the act of 1819, to treat the
colonies as actually independent of Spain; and to prohibit mutually and with respect to both, the aid which had
been hitherto prohibited with respect to one only.   It
was in order to give full and impartial effect to the provisions of the treaty with Spain, which prohibited the exportation of arms and ammunition to the colonies, but did not prohibit their exportation to Spain, that the act of parliament
declared that the prohibition should be mutual.   When,
however, from the tide of events flowing from the proceedings of the congress of Verona, war became probable between
France and Spain, it became necessary to review these relations.   It was obvious that if war actually broke out, the
British government must either extend to France the prohibition which already existed with respect to Spain, or re-

move from Spain the prohibition to which she was then subject, provided they meant to place the two countries on an
equal footing. So far as the exportation of arms and ammunition was concerned, it was in the power of the crown
to remove any inequality between the belligerent parties,
simply by an order in council. Such an order was consequently issued, and the prohibition of exporting arms and
ammunition to Spain was removed. By this measure, the
British government offered a guarantee of their *bonâ fide*
neutrality. The mere appearance of neutrality might have
been preserved by the extension of the prohibition to France,
instead of the removal of the prohibition from Spain; but it
would have been a prohibition of words only, and not at all
in fact, for the immediate vicinity of the Belgic ports to
France would have rendered the prohibition of direct exportation to France totally nugatory. The repeal of the act of
1819 would have, not the same, but a correspondent effect
to that which would have been produced by an order in
council prohibiting the exportation of arms and ammunition
to France. It would be a repeal in words only as respects
France, but in fact respecting Spain; and would occasion an
inequality of operation in favour of Spain, inconsistent with
an impartial neutrality. The example of the American government was referred to, as vindicating the justice and
policy of preventing the subjects of a neutral country from
enlisting in the service of any belligerent power, and of prohibiting the equipment in its ports of armaments in aid of
such power. Such was the conduct of that government
under the presidency of Washington, and the secretaryship
of Jefferson; and such was more recently the conduct of the
American legislature in revising their neutrality statutes in
1818, when the congress extended the provisions of the act
of 1794 to the case of such unacknowledged states as the
South American colonies of Spain, which had not been provided for in the original law.[19]

---

[19] Annual Register, vol. lxi. p. 71. Canning's Speeches, vol. iv. p. 150;
vol. v. p. 34.

§ 15.
Immunity
of the
neutral
territory,
how far it
extends to
neutral
vessels on
the high
seas.

The unlawfulness of belligerent captures made within the territorial jurisdiction of a neutral state is incontestably established on principle, usage, and authority. Does this immunity of the neutral territory from the exercise of acts of hostility within its limits extend to the vessels of the nation on the high seas, and without the jurisdiction of any other state?

We have already seen that both the public and private vessels of every independent nation on the high seas, and without the territorial limits of any other state, are subject to the municipal jurisdiction of the state to which they belong.[20] This jurisdiction is exclusive only so far as respects offences against the municipal laws of the state to which the vessel belongs. It excludes the exercise of the jurisdiction of every other state under its municipal laws, but it does not exclude the exercise of the jurisdiction of other nations as to crimes under international law, such as piracy and other offences, which all nations have an equal right to judge and to punish. Does it, then, exclude the exercise of the belligerent right of capturing enemy's property?

This right of capture is confessedly such a right as may be exercised within the territory of the belligerent state, within the enemy's territory, or in a place belonging to no one: in short, in any place except the territory of a neutral state. Is the vessel of a neutral nation on the high seas such a place?

Distinction
between
public and
private
vessels.

A distinction has been here taken between the public and the private vessels of a nation. In respect to its *public* vessels, it is universally admitted that neither the right of visitation and search, of capture, nor any other belligerent right, can be exercised on board such a vessel on the high seas. A public vessel, belonging to an independent sovereign, is exempt from every species of visitation and search, even within the territorial jurisdiction of another state: à *fortiori*, must it be exempt from the exercise of belligerent rights on the ocean, which belongs exclusively to no one nation?[21]

---

[20] Vide ante, pt. ii. ch. 2, § 11.   [21] Ibid.

In respect to *private* vessels, it has been said, the case is different. They form no part of the neutral territory, and when within the territory of another state are not exempt from the local jurisdiction. That portion of the ocean which is temporarily occupied by them forms no part of the neutral territory; nor does the vessel itself, which is a moveable thing, the property of private individuals, form any part of the territory of that power to whose subjects it belongs. The jurisdiction which that power may lawfully exercise over the vessel on the high seas is a jurisdiction over the persons and property of its citizens: it is not a territorial jurisdiction. Being upon the ocean, it is a place where no particular nation has jurisdiction, and where, consequently, all nations may equally exercise their international rights.[22]

Whatever may be the true original abstract principle of natural law on this subject, it is undeniable that the constant usage and practice of belligerent nations, from the earliest times, have subjected enemy's goods in neutral vessels to capture and condemnation as prize of war. This constant and universal usage has only been interrupted by treaty stipulations, forming a temporary conventional law between the parties to such stipulations.[23]

§ 16. Usage of nations subjecting enemy's goods in neutral vessels to capture.

The regulations and practice of certain maritime nations, at different periods, have not only considered the *goods* of an enemy laden in the ships of a friend liable to capture, but have doomed to confiscation the neutral *vessel* on board of

§ 17. Neutral vessels laden with enemy goods sub-

---

[22] Rutherforth's Inst. vol. ii. b. ii. ch. 9, § 19. Azuni, Diritto Maritimo, pt. ii. ch. 3, art. 2. Letter of American Envoys at Paris to M. de Talleyrand, Jan. 17, 1798. Waite's American State Papers, vol. iv. p. 34.

[23] Consolato del Mare, cap. 273. Albericus Gentilis, Hisp. Advoc. lib. i. cap. 27. Grotius, de Jur. Bel. ac Pac. lib. iii. cap. 6, §§ 6, 26; cap. 1, § 5, Note 6. Bynkershoek, Quæst. Jur. Pub. lib. i. cap. 14. Vattel, Droit des Gens, liv. iii. ch. 7, § 115. Heineccius, de Nav. ob. vect. cap. 2, § 9. Loccenius, de Jure del Marit. lib. ii. cap. 4, § 12. Azuni, del Diritto Marit. pt. ii. ch. 3, art. 1, 2.

ject to con-
fiscation by
the ordi-
nances
of some
states.
which these goods were laden. This practice has been sought to be justified upon a supposed analogy with that provision of the Roman law which involved the vehicle of prohibited commodities in the confiscation pronounced against the prohibited goods themselves.[24]

Thus by the marine ordinance of Louis XIV. of 1681, all vessels laden with enemy's goods are declared lawful prize of war. The contrary rule had been adopted by the preceding prize ordinances of France, and was again revived by the règlement of 1744, by which it was declared that "in case there should be found on board of neutral vessels, of whatever nation, goods or effects belonging to his Majesty's enemies, the goods or effects shall be good prize, and the vessels shall be restored." *Valin*, in his commentary upon the ordinance, admits that the more rigid rule, which continued to prevail in the French prize tribunals from 1681 to 1744, was peculiar to the jurisprudence of France and Spain; but that the usage of other nations was only to confiscate the goods of the enemy.[25]

§ 18.
Goods of a
friend on
board the
ships of an
enemy,
Although by the general usage of nations, independently of treaty stipulations, the goods of an enemy found on board the ships of a friend are liable to capture and condemnation, yet the converse rule, which subjects to confiscation the goods of a friend on board the vessels of an enemy, is manifestly contrary to reason and justice. It may, indeed, afford, as *Grotius* has stated, a presumption that the goods are enemy's property; but it is such a presumption as will readily yield to contrary proof, and not of that class of presumptions which the civilians call *presumptiones juris et de jure*, and which are conclusive upon the party.

liable to
confisca-
tion by the
prize code
of some
nations.
But however unreasonable and unjust this maxim may be, it has been incorporated into the prize code of certain nations, and enforced by them at different periods. Thus by the

---

[24] Barbeyrac, Note to Grotius, lib. iii. cap. 6, § 6, Note 1.

[25] Valin, Comm. liv. iii. tit. 9. Des Prises, art. 7.

French ordinances of 1538, 1543, and 1584, the goods of a friend laden on board the ships of an enemy are declared good and lawful prize. The contrary was provided by the subsequent declaration of 1650; but by the marine ordinance of Louis XIV. of 1681, the former rule was again established. *Valin* and *Pothier* are able to find no better argument in support of this rule, than that those who lade their goods on board an enemy's vessels thereby favour the commerce of the enemy, and by this act are considered in law as submitting themselves to abide the fate of the vessel; and *Valin* asks, " How can it be that the goods of friends and allies found in an enemy's ship should not be liable to confiscation, whilst even those of subjects are liable to it ?" To which *Pothier* himself furnishes the proper answer: that in respect to goods, the property of the king's subjects, in lading them on board an enemy's vessels, they contravene the law which interdicts to them all commercial intercourse with the enemy, and deserve to lose their goods for this violation of the law.[26]

The fallacy of the argument by which this rule is attempted to be supported consists in assuming, what requires to be proved, that by the act of lading his goods on board an enemy's vessel the neutral submits himself to abide the fate of the vessel; for it cannot be pretended that the goods are subjected to capture and confiscation *ex re*, since their character of neutral property exempts them from this liability. Nor can it be shown that they are thus liable *ex delicto*, unless it be first proved that the act of lading them on board is an offence against the law of nations. It is therefore with reason that *Bynkershoek* concludes that this rule, where merely established by the prize ordinances of a belligerent power cannot be defended on sound principles. Where, indeed, it is made by special compact the equivalent for the converse maxim, that *free ships make free goods*, this relaxation of belligerent pretensions may be fairly coupled with a correspondent con-

---

[26] Valin, Comm. liv. iii. tit. 9. Des Prises, art. 7. Pothier Traité de Propriété, No. 96.

cession by the neutral, that *enemy ships should make enemy goods*. These two maxims have been, in fact, commonly thus coupled in the various treaties on this subject, with a view to simplify the judicial inquiries into the proprietary interest of the ship and cargo, by resolving them into the mere question of the national character of the ship.

§ 19.
The two maxims, of *free ships free goods*, and *enemy ships enemy goods*, not necessarily connected.
The two maxims are not, however, inseparable. The primitive law, independently of international compact, rests on the simple principle that war gives a right to capture the goods of an enemy, but gives no right to capture the goods of a friend. The right to capture an enemy's property has no limit but that of the *place* where the goods are found, which, if neutral, will protect them from capture. We have already seen that a neutral vessel on the high seas is not such a place. The exemption of neutral property from capture has no other exceptions than those arising from the carrying of contraband, breach of blockade, and other analogous cases, where the conduct of the neutral gives to the belligerent a right to treat his property as enemy's property. The neutral flag constitutes no protection to an enemy's property, and the belligerent flag communicates no hostile character to neutral property. States have changed this simple and natural principle of the law of nations, by mutual compact, in whole or in part, according as they believed it to be for their interest; but the one maxim, that *free ships make free goods*, does not necessarily imply the converse proposition, that *enemy ships make enemy goods*. The stipulation that neutral bottoms shall make neutral goods, is a concession made by the belligerent to the neutral, and gives to the neutral flag a capacity not given to it by the primitive law of nations. On the other hand, the stipulation subjecting neutral property found in the vessel of an enemy to confiscation as prize of war, is a concession made by the neutral to the belligerent, and takes from the neutral a privilege he possessed under the pre-existing law of nations; but neither reason nor usage

render the two concessions so indissoluble that the one cannot exist without the other.

It was upon these grounds that the Supreme Court of the United States determined that the treaty of 1795, between them and Spain, which stipulated that free ships should make free goods, did not necessarily imply the converse proposition, that enemy ships should make enemy goods, the treaty being silent as to the latter; and that, consequently, the goods of a Spanish subject found on board the vessel of an enemy of the United States were not liable to confiscation as prize of war. And although it was alleged that the prize law of Spain would subject the property of American citizens to condemnation when found on board the vessels of her enemy, the court refused to condemn Spanish property found on board a vessel of their enemy upon the principle of reciprocity; because the American government had not manifested its will to retaliate upon Spain; and until this will was manifested by some legislative act, the court was bound by the general law of nations constituting a part of the law of the land.[27]

The conventional law in respect to the rule now in question has fluctuated, at different periods, according to the fluctuating policy and interests of the different maritime states of Europe. It has been much more flexible than the consuetudinary law; but there is a great preponderance of modern treaties in favour of the maxim, *free ships free goods*, sometimes, but not always, connected with the correlative maxim, *enemy ships enemy goods;* so that it may be said that, for two centuries past, there has been a constant tendency to establish by compact the principle that the neutrality of the ship should exempt the cargo, even of enemy's property, from capture and confiscation as prize of war. Among the earliest examples of such a stipulation is that contained in the capitulation granted by the Ottoman Porte, in 1604, to

§ 20. Conventional law as to *free ships free goods.*

---

[27] Cranch's Rep. vol. ix. p. 388. The Nereide.

Henry IV. of France, which has been since followed in all
the conventions between the different nations of Christendom
and the Mohammedan powers, such as Turkey and the Barbary States. Under these treaties, the flag and pass are
made conclusive of the national character both as to ship
and cargo.[28]

It became, at an early period, an object of interest with
Holland, a great commercial and navigating country, whose
permanent policy was essentially pacific, to obtain a relax·
ation of the severe rules which had been previously observed
in maritime warfare. The States-General of the United
Provinces having complained of the provisions in the French
ordinance of Henry II. 1538, a treaty of commerce was
concluded between France and the Republic in 1646, by
which the operation of the ordinance, so far as respected the
capture and confiscation of neutral vessels for carrying enemy's property, was suspended; but it was found impossible
to obtain any relaxation as to the liability to capture of enemy's property in neutral vessels. The Dutch negotiator in
Paris, in his correspondence with the grand pensionary De
Witt, states that he had obtained the "repeal of the pretended French law, *que robe d'ennemi confisque celle d'ami ;* so
that if, for the future, there should be found in a free Dutch
vessel effects belonging to the enemies of France, these
effects alone will be confiscable, and the ship with the other
goods will be restored; for it is impossible to obtain the
twenty-fourth article of my Instructions, where it is said that
the freedom of the ship ought to free the cargo, even if belonging to an enemy." This latter concession the United
Provinces obtained from France by the treaty of alliance of
1662, and the commercial treaty signed at the same time
with the peace at Nimeguen in 1678, confirmed by the treaty
of Ryswick in 1697. The rule of *free ships free goods* was
coupled, in these treaties, with its correlative maxim, *enemy*

[28] Flassan, Histoire de la Diplomatie Française, tom. ii. p. 226. Azuni,
Dirs Marit. pt. ii. ch. 3, art. 1, § 8.

ships enemy goods. The same concession was obtained by Holland from England, in 1668 and 1674, as the price of an alliance between the two countries against the ambitious designs of Louis XIV. These treaties gave rise, in the war which commenced in 1756 between France and Great Britain, to a very remarkable controversy between the British and Dutch governments, in which it was contended on the one side that Great Britain had violated the rights of neutral commerce, and on the other that the States-General had not fulfilled the guarantee which constituted the equivalent for the concession made to the neutral flag in derogation of the pre-existing law of nations.[29]

The principle that the character of the vessel should determine that of the cargo was adopted by the treaties of Utrecht of 1713, subsequently confirmed by those of 1721 and 1739, between Great Britain and Spain, by the treaty of Aix-la-Chapelle in 1748, and of Paris in 1763, between Great Britain, France, and Spain.

Such was the state of the consuetudinary and conventional law prevailing among the different maritime powers of Christian Europe, and between them and that set of nations who profess the Mohammedan religion, when the declaration of independence by the British North American colonies gave rise to a maritime war between France and Great Britain. With a view to conciliate those powers which remained neutral in this war, the cabinet of Versailles issued, on the 26th of July, 1778, an ordinance or instruction to the French cruisers, prohibiting the capture of neutral vessels, even when bound to or from enemy ports, unless laden in whole or in

Armed neutrality of 1780.

[29] Dumont, Corps Diplomatique, tom. vi. pt. i. p. 342. Flassan, Histoire de la Diplomatie Française, tom. iii. p. 451. A pamphlet was published on the occasion of this controversy between the British and Dutch governments, by the elder Lord Liverpool, (then Mr. Jenkinson,) entitled, "A Discourse on the Conduct of Great Britain in respect to Neutral Nations during the present War," which contains a very full and instructive discussion of the question of neutral navigation, both as resting on the primitive law of nations and on treaties. London, 8vo. 1757. 2d Ed. 1794; 3d Ed. 1801.

part with contraband articles destined for the enemy's use;
reserving the right to revoke this concession, unless the enemy should adopt a reciprocal measure within six months.
The British government, far from adopting any such measure, issued in March, 1780, an order in council suspending
the special stipulations respecting neutral commerce and navigation contained in the treaty of alliance of 1674, between
Great Britain and the United Provinces, upon the alleged
ground that the States-General had refused to fulfil the reciprocal conditions of the treaty.   Immediately after this order
in council, the Empress Catharine II. of Russia communicated
to the different belligerent and neutral powers the famous
declaration of neutrality, the principles of which were acceded to by France, Spain, and the United States of America, as belligerents, and by Denmark, Sweden, Prussia, Holland, the Emperor of Germany, Portugal, and Naples, as
neutral powers.   By this declaration, which afterwards became the basis of the armed neutrality of the Baltic powers,
the rule that free ships make free goods was adopted, without the previously associated maxim that enemy ships should
make enemy goods.   The court of London answered this
declaration by appealing to the "principles generally acknowledged as the law of nations, being the only law between
powers where no treaties subsist;" and to the "tenor of its
different engagements with other powers, where those engagements had altered the primitive law by mutual stipulations, according to the will and convenience of the contracting parties."   Circumstances rendered it convenient for
the British government to dissemble its resentment towards
Russia and the other northern powers, and the war was terminated without any formal adjustment of this dispute between Great Britain and the other members of the armed
neutrality.[30]

[30] Flassan, Diplomatie Française, tom. vii. pp. 183, 273. Annual Register, vol. xxiii. p. 205. State Papers, pp. 345—356; vol. xxiv. p. 300.
State Papers.

By the treaties of peace concluded at Versailles in 1783, between Great Britain, France and Spain, the treaties of Utrecht were once more revived and confirmed. This confirmation was again reiterated in the commercial treaty of 1786, between France and Great Britain, by which the two kindred maxims were once more associated. In the negotiations at Lisle in 1797, it was proposed by the British plenipotentiary, Lord Malmesbury, to renew all the former treaties between the two countries confirmatory of those of Utrecht. This proposition was objected to by the French ministers, for several reasons foreign to the present subject; to which Lord Malmesbury replied that these treaties were become the law of nations, and that infinite confusion would result from their not being renewed. It is probable, however, that his Lordship meant to refer to the territorial arrangements rather than to the commercial stipulations contained in these treaties. Be this as it may, the fact is, that they were not renewed, either by the treaty of Amiens in 1802, or by that of Paris in 1814.

During the protracted wars of the French revolution all the belligerent powers began by discarding in practice, not only the principles of the armed neutrality, but even the generally received maxims of international law by which the rights of neutral commerce in time of war had been previously regulated. "Russia," says Von Martens, "made common cause with Great Britain and with Prussia, to induce Denmark and Sweden to renounce all intercourse with France, and especially to prohibit their carrying goods to the country. The incompatibility of this pretension with the principles established by Russia in 1780, was veiled by the pretext that in a war like that against revolutionary France, the rights of neutrality did not come in question." France, on her part, revived the severity of her ancient prize code, by decreeing, not only the capture and condemnation of the goods of her enemies found on board neutral vessels, but even of the vessels themselves laden with goods of British growth, produce, and manufacture. But in the further progress of

Armed
neutrality
of 1800.

the war, the principles which had formed the basis of the armed neutrality of the northern powers in 1780, were revived by a new maritime confederacy between Russia, Denmark, and Sweden, formed in 1800, to which Prussia acceded. This league was soon dissolved by the naval power of Great Britain and the death of the Emperor Paul; and the principle now in question was expressly relinquished by Russia by the convention signed at St. Petersburgh in 1801, between that power and the British government, and subsequently acceded to by Denmark and Sweden. In 1807, in consequence of the stipulations contained in the treaty of Tilsit between Russia and France, a declaration was issued by the Russian court, in which the principles of the armed neutrality were proclaimed anew, and the convention of 1801 was annulled by the Emperor Alexander. In 1812, a treaty of alliance against France was signed by Great Britain and Russia; but no convention respecting the freedom of neutral commerce and navigation has been since concluded between these two powers.

The international law of Europe adopted by America, and modified by treaty.

Without entering into the abstract question, how far the ancient international law, by which the intercourse of the maritime states of Europe has been so long regulated, is binding upon the new communities which have sprung up in the western hemisphere, it may be sufficient to observe that it was certainly considered by the United States as obligatory upon them during the war of their revolution. During that war, the American courts of prize acted upon the generally received principles of European public law, that enemy's property in neutral vessels was liable to, whilst neutral property in an enemy's vessels was exempt from, confiscation; until Congress issued an ordinance recognising the maxims of the armed neutrality of 1780, upon condition that they should be reciprocally acknowledged by the other belligerent powers. In the instructions given by Congress in 1784 to their ministers appointed to treat with the different European courts, the same principles were proposed as the basis of negotiation by which the independence of the United States was to be recognised. During the wars of the French revolution, the United States being neutral, admitted that the immunity of their flag did not extend to cover enemy's property, as a principle founded in the customary law and established usage of nations, though they sought every opportunity of substituting for it the opposite maxim of *free ships free goods*, by conventional arrangements with such nations as were disposed to adopt that amendment of the law. In the course of the correspondence which took place between the minister of the French republic and the government of the United States, the latter affirmed that it could not be doubted that, by the general law of nations, the goods of a friend found in the vessel of an enemy are free, and the goods of an enemy found in the vessel of a friend are lawful prize. It was true, that several nations, desirous of avoiding the inconvenience of having their vessels stopped at sea, over-hauled, carried into port, and detained, under pretence of having enemy's goods on board, had, in many instances, introduced by special treaties, the principle, that enemy ships should make enemy goods, and friendly ships friendly goods; a principle much less embarrassing to commerce, and equal to all parties in point of gain and loss: but this was altogether the effect of particular treaty, controlling in special cases the general principle of the law of nations, and therefore taking effect between such nations only as have so agreed to control it. England had generally determined to adhere to the rigorous principle, having in no instance, so far as was recollected, agreed to the modification of letting the property of the goods follow that of the vessel, except in the single one of her treaties with France. The United states had adopted this modification in their treaties with France, with the United Netherlands, and with Prussia; and, therefore, as to those powers, American vessels covered the goods of their enemies, and the United States lost their goods when in the vessels of the enemies of those powers. With Great Britain, Spain, Portugal, and Austria, the United States had then no treaties; and therefore had nothing to oppose them in acting

according to the general law of nations, that enemy goods
are lawful prize though found in the ships of a friend. Nor
was it perceived that France could, on the whole, suffer, for
though she lost her goods in American vessels, when found
therein by England, Spain, Portugal, or Austria; yet she
gained American goods when found in the vessels of England, Spain, Portugal, Austria, the United Netherlands, or
Prussia: and as the Americans had more goods afloat in the
vessels of those six nations, than France had afloat in their
vessels, France was the gainer, and they the losers, by the
principle of the treaty between the two countries. Indeed
the United States were losers in every direction of that principle; for when it worked in their favour, it was to save the
goods of their friends; when it worked against them, it was
to lose their own, and they would continue to lose whilst it
was only partially established. When they should, have
established it with all nations, they would be in a condition
neither to gain nor lose, but would be less exposed to vexatious searches at sea. To this condition the United States
were endeavouring to advance; but as it depended on the
will of other nations, they could only obtain it when others
should be ready to concur.[31]

By the treaty of 1794 between the United States and
Great Britain, article 17, it was stipulated that vessels, captured on suspicion of having on board enemy's property or
contraband of war, should be carried to the nearest port for
adjudication, and that part of the cargo only which consisted
of enemy's property, or contraband for the enemy's use made
prize, and the vessels be at liberty to proceed with the re-
mainder of her cargo. In the treaty of 1778, between France
and the United States, the rule of *free ships free goods* had
been stipulated; and, as we have already seen, France complained that her goods were taken out of American vessels

---

[31] Mr. Jefferson's Letter to M. Genet, July 24, 1793. Waite's State Papers, vol. i. p. 134. See also President Jefferson's Letter to Mr. R. R.
Livingston, American Minister at Paris, Sep. 9, 1801. Jefferson's Memoirs,
vol. iii. p. 489.

without resistance by the United States, who, it was alleged, had abandoned, by their treaty with Great Britain, their antecedent engagements to France, recognising the principles of the armed neutrality.

To these complaints, it was answered by the American government that when the treaty of 1778 was concluded, the armed neutrality had not been formed, and consequently the state of things on which that treaty operated was regulated by the pre-existing law of nations, independently of the principles of the armed neutrality. By that law, free ships did not make free goods, nor enemy ships enemy goods. The stipulation therefore in the treaty of 1778 formed an exception to a general rule which retained its obligation in all cases where not changed by compact. Had the treaty of 1794 between the United States and Great Britain not been formed, or had it entirely omitted any stipulation on this subject, the belligerent right would still have existed. The treaty did not concede a new right, but only mitigated the practical exercise of a right already acknowledged to exist. The desire of establishing universally the principle, that neutral ships should make neutral goods, was felt by no nation more strongly than by the United States. It was an object which they kept in view, and would pursue by such means as their judgment might dictate. But the wish to establish a principle was essentially different from an assumption that it is already established. However solicitous America might be to pursue all proper means tending to obtain the concession of this principle by any or all of the maritime powers of Europe, she had never conceived the idea of obtaining that consent by force. The United States would only arm to defend their own rights: neither their policy nor their interests permitted them to arm in order to compel a surrender of the rights of others.[32]

[32] Letter of the American Envoys at Paris, Messrs. Marshall, Pinkney, and Geary, to M. de Talleyrand, Jan. 17, 1798. Waite's State Papers, vol. iv. pp. 38—47.

The principle of *free ships free goods*, had been stipulated by the treaty of 1785, between the United States and Prussia. On the expiration of this convention in 1799, a new treaty was negotiated, which contains the following article :— " Experience having proved that the principle adopted in the 12th article of the treaty of 1785, according to which free ships make free goods, has not been sufficiently respected during the two last wars, and especially in that which still continues, the two contracting parties propose, after the return of a general peace, to agree, either separately between themselves, or jointly with other powers alike interested, to concert with the great maritime powers of Europe such arrangements and such permanent principles as may serve to consolidate the liberty and safety of neutral navigation and commerce in future wars. And if in the interval either of the contracting parties should be engaged in a war, to which the other should remain neutral, the ships of war and privateers of the belligerent power shall conduct themselves towards the vessels of the neutral power, as favourably as the course of the war then existing may permit, observing the principles and rules of the law of nations as generally acknowledged."

During the war which commenced between the United States and Great Britain in 1812, the prize courts of the former uniformly enforced the generally acknowledged rule of international law, that enemy's goods in neutral vessels are liable to capture and confiscation, except as to such powers with whom the American government had stipulated by subsisting treaties the contrary rule, that free ships should make free goods.

In their recent negotiations with the newly established republics of South America, the United States proposed the establishment of the principle of *free ships free goods*, as between all the powers of the North and South American continents. It was declared that the rule of public law,— that the property of an enemy is liable to capture in the vessels of a friend,—has no foundation in natural right, and, though it be the established usage of nations, rests entirely on the abuse of force. No neutral nation, it was said, was bound to submit to the usage; and though the neutral may have yielded at one time to the practice, it did not follow that the right to vindicate by force the security of the neutral flag at another, was thereby permanently sacrificed. But the neutral claim to cover enemy's property was conceded to be subject to this qualification; that a belligerent may justly refuse to neutrals the benefit of this principle, unless admitted also by their enemy for the protection of the same neutral flag. It is accordingly stipulated, in the treaty between the United States and the republic of Columbia, that the rule of *free ships free goods* should be understood " as applying to those powers only who recognise this principle; but if either of the two contracting parties shall be at war with a third, and the other neutral, the flag of the neutral shall cover the property of enemies whose governments acknowledge the same principle, and not of others." The same restriction of the rule had been previously incorporated into the treaty of 1819, between the United States and Spain.[33]

The general freedom of neutral commerce with the respective belligerent powers is subject to certain exceptions. Among these is the trade with the enemy in certain articles called contraband of war. The almost unanimous authority of elementary writers, of prize ordinances, and of treaties, agrees to enumerate among these all warlike instruments, or materials by their own nature fit to be used in war. Beyond these, there is some difficulty in reconciling the conflicting authorities derived from the opinions of publicists, the fluctuating usage among nations, and the text of various conventions designed to give to that usage the fixed form of positive

§ 21.
Contraband of war.

---

[33] Mr. Secretary Adams's Letter to Mr. Anderson, American minister to the republic of Columbia, 27th of May, 1823. For the practice of the prize court, as to the allowance or refusal of freight on enemies' goods taken on board neutral ships, and on neutral goods found on board an enemy's ship, see Wheaton's Rep. vol. ii. Appendix, Note I. pp. 54—56.

law. *Grotius,* in considering this subject, makes a distinction between those things which are useful only for the purposes of war, those which are not so, and those which are
susceptible of indiscriminate use in war and in peace. The
first, he agrees with all other text writers in prohibiting neutrals from carrying to the enemy, as well as in permitting
the *second* to be so carried; the *third* class, such as money,
provisions, ships, and naval stores, he sometimes prohibits,
and at others permits, according to the existing circumstances
of the war. *Vattel* makes somewhat of a similar distinction,
though he includes timber and naval stores among those articles which are particularly useful for the purposes of war,
and always liable to capture as contraband; and considers
provisions as such only under certain circumstances, " when
there are hopes of reducing the enemy by famine." *Bynkershoek* strenuously contends against admitting into the list of
contraband articles those things which are of promiscuous
use in peace and war. He considers the limitation assigned
by Grotius to the right of intercepting them, confining it to
the case of necessity, and under the obligation of restitution
or indemnification, as insufficient to justify the exercise of the
right itself. He concludes that the materials out of which
contraband articles may be formed are not themselves contraband; because if all the materials may be prohibited, out
of which something may be fabricated that is fit for war, the
catalogue of contraband goods will be almost interminable,
since there is hardly any kind of material out of which something, at least, fit for war may not be fabricated. The interdiction of so many articles would amount to a total interdiction of commerce, and might as well be so expressed. He
qualifies this general position by stating that it may sometimes happen that materials for building ships are prohibited,
" if the enemy is in great need of them, and cannot well
carry on the war without them." On this ground he justifies
the edict of the States-General of 1657 against the Portuguese, and that of 1652 against the English, as exceptions to
the general rule that materials for ship-building are not con-

traband. He also states that "provisions are often excepted" from the general freedom of neutral commerce "when the enemies are besieged by our friends, or are *otherwise* pressed by famine."[34]

Valin and *Pothier* both concur in declaring that provisions (*munitions de bouche*) are not contraband by the prize law of France, or the common law of nations, unless in the single case where they are destined to a besieged or blockaded place.[35]

As to naval stores, Sir *W. Scott*, laying down the doctrine of their being liable to seizure as contraband in their own nature, when going to the enemy's use, under the modern law of nations, observes that formerly, when the hostilities of Europe were less naval than they have since become, they were of a disputable nature, and perhaps continued so at the time of making the treaty between England and Sweden in 1661, or at least at the time of making the treaty which is the basis of it, that of 1656. And *Valin*, in his commentary upon the marine ordinance of Louis XIV., by which only munitions of war were declared to be contraband, says: "In the war of 1700, pitch and tar were comprehended in the list of contraband, because the enemy treated them as such, except when found on board Swedish ships, these articles being of the growth and produce of their country. In the treaty of commerce concluded with the king of Denmark, by France, the 23d of August, 1742, pitch and tar were also declared contraband, together with resin, sail-cloth, hemp and cordage, masts, and ship timber. Thus, as to this matter, there is no fault to be found with the conduct of the English, except where it contravenes particular treaties; for in law these things are now contraband, and have been so since the beginning of the present century, which was not

Naval stores, how far contraband.

---

[34] Grotius, de Jur. Bel. ac Pac. lib. iii. cap. 1, § 5. Rutherforth's Inst. b. ii. ch. 9, § 19. Vattel, liv. iii. ch. 7, § 112. Bynkershoek, Quæst. Jur. Pub. lib. i. cap. 9, 10.

[35] Valin, Comm. sur l'Ordonn. liv. iii. tit. 9; des Prises, art. 11. Pothier, de Propriété, No. 104.

the case formerly, as it appears by ancient treaties, and particularly that of St. Germain, concluded with England in 1677; the fourth article of which expressly provides, that the trade in all these articles shall remain free, as well as in every thing necessary to human nourishment, with the exception of places besieged or blockaded."[36]

By the treaty of navigation and commerce of Utrecht, between Great Britain and France, renewed and confirmed by the treaty of Aix-la-Chapelle in 1748, by the treaty of Paris in 1763, by that of Versailles in 1783, and by the commercial treaty between France and Great Britain of 1786, the list of contraband is strictly confined to munitions of war; and naval stores, provisions, and all other goods which have not been worked into the form of any instrument or furniture for warlike use, by land or by sea, are expressly excluded from this list. The subject of the contraband character of naval stores continued a vexed question, between Great Britain and the Baltic powers, throughout the whole of the eighteenth century. Various relaxations in favour of the extreme belligerent pretension on this subject had been conceded in favour of the commerce in articles the peculiar growth and production of these states, either by permitting them to be freely carried to the enemy's ports, or by mitigating the original penalty of confiscation, on their seizure, to the milder right of preventing the goods being carried to the enemy, and applying them to the use of the belligerent, on making a pecuniary compensation to the neutral owner. This controversy was at last terminated by the convention between Great Britain and Russia, concluded in 1801, to which Denmark and Sweden subsequently acceded. By the third article of this treaty, which is literally copied from the treaties of armed neutrality of 1780 and 1800, the list of contraband is confined to munitions of war, excluding naval stores, without " prejudice to the particular stipulations of one or the other crown with other powers, by which objects of similar kind should be reserved, provided or permitted."

[36] Valin, Comm. sur l'Ordonn. liv. iii. tit. 9; des Prises, art. 11.

The object of this convention is declared in its preamble to be the settlement of the differences between the contracting parties, which had grown out of the armed neutrality by " an invariable determination of their principles upon the rights of neutrality in their application to their respective monarchies;" which object was accomplished by the northern powers yielding to the rule of *free ships free goods*, whilst Great Britain conceded the points asserted by them as to contraband, blockades, and the coasting and colonial trade.[37]

The doctrine of the British prize courts as to provisions and naval stores becoming contraband, independently of special treaty stipulations, is laid down very fully by Sir *W. Scott*, in the case of the *Jonge Margaretha*. He there states that the catalogue of contraband had varied very much, and sometimes in such a manner as to make it difficult to assign the reason of the variations, owing to particular circumstances, the history of which had not accompanied the history of the decisions. In 1673, when many unwarrantable rules were laid down by public authority respecting contraband, it was expressly asserted by a person of great knowledge and experience in the English admiralty, that by its practice, *corn, wine,* and *oil*, were liable to be deemed contraband. In much later times, many sorts of provisions, such as butter, salted fish, and rice, has been condemned as contraband. The modern established rule was, that generally they are not contraband, but may become so under circumstances arising out of the peculiar situation of the war, or the condition of the parties engaged in it. Among the causes which

Provisions and naval stores, when contraband.

---

[37] See a pamphlet, entitled, " Substance of the Speech delivered by Lord Grenville in the House of Lords, Nov. 13, 1801," in which his lordship reasoned to show that the convention abandoned the maritime rights, previously asserted by Great Britain against the armed neutrality; that it not only formed a new conventional law between the contracting parties, but contained a recognition of universal and pre-existing rights which could not justly be refused by them to other states. For the very lame and unsuccessful replies made by the able speakers who entered the lists against him, see Annual Register for 1802, ch. 4.

tend to prevent provisions from being treated as contraband, one is that they are of the growth of the country which exports them. Another circumstance to which some indulgence, by the practice of nations is shown, is when the articles are in their native and unmanufactured state. Thus iron is treated with indulgence, though anchors and other instruments fabricated out of it are directly contraband. Hemp is more favourably considered than cordage; and wheat is not considered so noxious a commodity as any of the final preparations of it for human use. But the most important distinction is, whether the articles are destined for the ordinary uses of life or for military use. The nature and quality of the port to which the articles were going, is a test of the matter of fact on which the distinction is to be applied. If the port is a general commercial port, it shall be understood that the articles were going for civil use, although occasionally a frigate or other ships of war may be constructed in that port. On the contrary, if the great predominant character of a port be that of a port of naval equipment, it shall be intended that the articles were going for military use, although merchant ships resort to the same place, and although it is possible that the articles might have been applied to civil consumption; for it being impossible to ascertain the final application of an article *ancipitis usus*, it is not an injurious rule which deduces both ways the final use from the immediate destination; and the presumption of a hostile use, founded on its destination to a military port, is very much inflamed, if at the time when the articles were going, a considerable armament was notoriously preparing, to which a supply of those articles would be eminently useful."[38]

Articles of promiscuous use becoming contraband when destined to a port of naval equipment.
The distinction, under which articles of promiscuous use are considered as contraband, when destined to a port of naval equipment, appears to have been subsequently abandoned by Sir *W. Scott*. In the case of the *Charlotte*, he states that "the character of the port is immaterial, since naval stores, if they are to be considered as contraband, are so, without

[38] Robinson's Adm. Rep. vol. i. p. 192,

reference to the nature of the port, and equally, whether bound to a mercantile port only, or to a port of naval military equipment. The consequences of the supply may be nearly the same in either case. If sent to a mercantile port, they may then be applied to immediate use in the equipment of privateers, or they may be conveyed from the mercantile to the naval port, and there become subservient to every purpose to which they could have been applied if going directly to a port of naval equipment."[39]

The doctrine of the English court of admiralty, as to provisions becoming contraband, under certain circumstances of war, was adopted by the British government in the instructions given to their cruisers on the 8th June, 1793, directing them to stop all vessels, laden wholly or in part with corn, flour, or meal, bound to any port in France, and to send them into a British port to be purchased by government, or to be released on condition that the master should give security to dispose of his cargo in the ports of some country in amity with his Britannic Majesty. This order was justified upon the ground, that by the modern law of nations, all provisions are to be considered contraband, and as such, liable to confiscation, wherever the depriving an enemy of these supplies is one of the means intended to be employed for reducing him to terms. The actual situation of France, (it was said,) was notoriously such as to lead to the employing this mode of distressing her by the joint operations of the different powers engaged in the war; and the reasoning which the text writers apply to all cases of this sort, was more applicable to the present case, in which the distress resulted from the unusual mode of war adopted by the enemy himself, in having armed almost the whole labouring class of the French nation, for the purpose of commencing and supporting hostilities against almost all European governments; but this reasoning was most of all applicable to a trade, which was in a great measure carried on by the then actual rulers of France, and was

Provisions becoming contraband under certain circumstances of the war.

[30] Robinson's Adm. Rep. vol. v. p. 305.

no longer to be regarded as a mercantile speculation of individuals, but as an immediate operation of the very persons
who had declared war and were then carrying it on against
Great Britain.[40]

This reasoning was resisted by the neutral powers, Sweden, Denmark, and especially the United States. The American government insisted that when two nations go to war,
other nations, who choose to remain at peace, retain their
natural right to pursue their agriculture, manufacture, and
other ordinary vocations; to carry the produce of their industry for exchange to all countries, belligerent or neutral, as
usual; to go and come freely without injury or molestation;
in short, that the war among others should be, for neutral
nations, as if it did not exist. The only restriction to this
general freedom of commerce, which had been submitted to
by nations at peace, was that of not furnishing to either party
implements merely of war, nor any thing whatever to a place
blockaded by its enemy. These implements of war had
been so often enumerated in treaties under the name of contraband as to leave little question about them at that day.
It was sufficient to say that corn, flour, and meal, were not
of the class of contraband, and consequently remained articles of free commerce. The state of war then existing between Great Britain and France furnished no legitimate right
to either of these belligerent powers to interrupt the agriculture of the United States, or the peaceable exchange of their
produce with all nations. If any nation whatever had the
right to shut against their produce all the ports of the earth
except her own, and those of her friends, she might shut
these also, and thus prevent altogether the export of that
produce.[41]

In the treaty subsequently concluded between Great Britain and the United States on the 19th. November, 1794, it
was stipulated, (article 18,) that under the denomination of
contraband should be comprised all arms and implements

---

[40] Mr. Hammond's Letter to Mr. Jefferson, 12th Sept. 1793.
[41] Mr. Jefferson's Letter to Mr. T. Pinkney, 7th Sept. 1793.

serving for the purposes of war, " and also timber for ship-building, tar or rosin, copper in sheets, sails, hemp, and cord-age and generally whatever may serve directly to the equip-ment of vessels, unwrought iron and fir planks only except-ed." The article then goes on to provide that " whereas *the difficulty of agreeing on the precise cases, in which alone provi-sions and other articles, not generally contraband, may be regard-ed as such,* renders it expedient to provide against the incon-veniences and misunderstandings which might thence arise; it is further agreed, that whenever any such articles, so be-coming contraband according to the existing law of nations, shall for that reason be seized, the same shall not be confis-cated; but the owners thereof shall be speedily and com-pletely indemnified; and the captors, or in their default, the government under whose authority they act, shall pay to the masters or owners of such vessels the full value of all such articles, with a reasonable mercantile profit thereon, together with the freight, and also the demurrage incident to such de-tention."

The instructions of June, 1793, had been revoked previous to the signature of this treaty; but before its ratification the British government issued, in April, 1795, an order in council instructing its cruisers to stop and detain all vessels laden wholly or in part with corn, flour, meal, and other articles of provisions, and bound to any port in France, and to send them to such ports as might be most convenient, in order that such corn, &c. might be purchased on behalf of government. *British provision order of April, 1795.*

This last order was subsequently revoked, and the ques-tion of its legality became the subject of discussion before the mixt commission constituted under the treaty to decide upon the claims of American citizens by reason of irregular or illegal captures and condemnations of their vessels and other property, under the authority of the British govern-ment. The order in council was justified upon two grounds:—

1. That it was made when there was a prospect of re-ducing the enemy to terms by famine, and that in such a state of things, provisions bound to the ports of the enemy became

so far contraband, as to justify Great Britain in seizing them upon the terms of paying the invoice price, with a reasonable mercantile profit thereon, together with freight and demurrage.

2. That the order was justified by *necessity*, the British nation being at that time threatened with a scarcity of the articles directed to be seized.

The first of these positions was rested not only upon the general law of nations, but upon the above quoted article of the treaty between Great Britain and America.

The evidence adduced of this supposed law of nations was principally the following loose passage of *Vattel:* " Commodities particularly useful in war, and the carrying of which to an enemy is prohibited, are called contraband goods. Such are arms, ammunition, timber for ship-building, every kind of naval stores, horses, and even provisions, in certain junctures, when we have hopes of reducing the enemy by famine."[42]

In answer to this authority, it was stated that it might be sufficient to say that it was, at best, equivocal and indefinite, as it did not designate what the junctures are in which it might be held that " there are hopes of reducing the enemy by famine;" that it was entirely consistent with it, to affirm, that these hopes must be built upon an obvious and palpable chance of effecting the enemy's reduction by this obnoxious mode of warfare, and that no such chance is by the law of nations admitted to exist except in certain defined cases, such as the actual siege, blockade, or investment of particular places. This answer would be rendered still more satisfactory by comparing the above quoted passage with the more precise opinions of other respectable writers on international law, by which might be discovered that which Vattel does not profess to explain—the combination of circumstances to which his principle is applicable or is intended to be applied.

But there was no necessity for relying wholly on this answer, since Vattel would himself furnish a pretty accurate

[42] Droit des Gens, liv. iii. ch. 7, § 112.

commentary on the vague text which he had given. The only instance put by this writer which came within the range of his general principle, was that which he, as well as Grotius, had taken from Plutarch. "Demetrius," as *Grotius* expressed it, "held Attica by the sword. He had taken the town of Rhamnus, *designing a famine in Athens*, and had almost accomplished his design, when a vessel laden with provisions attempted to relieve the city." *Vattel* speaks of this as of a case in which provisions were contraband, (section 17,) and although he did not make use of this example for the declared purpose of rendering more specific the passage above cited, yet as he mentions none other to which it can relate, it is strong evidence to show that he did not mean to carry the doctrine of special contraband farther than that example would warrant.

It was also to be observed, that in sect. 113, he states expressly that all contraband goods, (including, of course, those becoming so by reason of the junctures of which he had been speaking at the end of sect. 112,) are to be confiscated. But nobody pretended that Great Britain could rightfully have *confiscated* the cargoes taken under the order of 1795; and yet if the seizures made under that order fell within the opinion expressed by Vattel, the confiscation of the cargoes seized would have been justifiable. It had long been settled that all contraband goods are subject to forfeiture by the law of nations, whether they are so in their own nature, or become so by existing circumstances; and even in early times, when this rule was not so well established, we find that those nations who sought an exemption from forfeiture, never claimed it upon grounds peculiar to any description of contraband, but upon general reasons embracing all cases of contraband whatsoever. As it was admitted, then, that the cargoes in question were not subject to forfeiture as contraband, it was manifest that the juncture which gave birth to the order in council could not have been such a one as Vattel had in view; or in other words, that the cargoes were not become contraband at all within the true meaning of his principle, or within any principle known to the general law of nations.

The authority of Grotius was also adduced as countenancing this position.

Grotius divides commodities into three classes, the first of which he declares to be plainly contraband; the second plainly not so; and as to the third, he says: " In tertio illo genere usus ancipitis, distinguendus erit belli status. Nam si tueri me non possum nisi quæ mittuntur intercipiam, necessitas, ut alibi exposuimus, jus dabit, sed sub onere restitutionis, nisi causa alia accedat." This " causa alia " is afterwards explained by an example, " ut si oppidum obsessum tenebam, si portus clausos, et jam deditio aut pax expectabitur."

This opinion of Grotius as to the third class of goods did not appear to proceed at all upon the notion of contraband, but simply upon that of a pure necessity on the part of the capturing belligerent. He does not consider the right of seizure as a means of effecting the reduction of the enemy, but as the indispensable means of our own defence. He does not state the seizure upon any supposed illegal conduct in the neutral, in attempting to carry articles of the third class (among which provisions are included,) *not bound to a port besieged or blockaded*, to be lawful, when made with the mere view of annoying or reducing the enemy, but solely when made with a view to our own preservation or defence, under the pressure of that imperious and unequivocal necessity, which breaks down the distinctions of property, and upon certain conditions, revives the original right of using things as if they were in common.

This necessity he explains at large in his second book, (cap. ii. sec. 6,) and in the above recited passage he refers expressly to that explanation. In section 7, 8, and 9, he lays down the conditions annexed to this right of necessity: as, 1. It shall not be exercised until all other possible means have been used; 2. Nor if the right owner is under a like necessity; and, 3. Restitution shall be made as soon as practicable.

In his third book, (cap. xvii. sec. 1,) recapitulating what he had before said on this subject, Grotius further explains this doctrine of necessity, and most explicitly confirms the construction placed upon the above-cited texts. And *Rutherforth*, in commenting on Grotius, (lib. iii. cap. 1, sec. 5,) also explains what he there says of the right of seizing provisions upon the ground of necessity, and supposes his meaning to be that the seizure would not be justifiable in that view, " unless the exigency of affairs is such that we cannot possibly do without them."[43]

Bynkershoek also confines the right of seizing goods, not generally contraband of war, (and provisions among the rest,) to the above-mentioned cases.[44]

It appeared, then, that so far as the authority of text writers could influence the question, the order in council of 1795 could not be rested upon any just notion of contraband; nor could it, in that view, be justified by the reason of the thing or the approved usage of nations.

If the mere hope, however apparently well founded, of annoying or reducing an enemy by intercepting the commerce of neutrals in articles of provision, (which in themselves are no more contraband than ordinary merchandise,) to ports not besieged or blockaded, would authorize that interruption, it would follow that a belligerent might at any time prevent, without a siege or blockade, all trade whatsoever with its enemy; since there is at all times reason to believe that a nation, having little or no shipping of its own, might be so materially distressed by preventing all other nations from trading with it, that such prevention might be a powerful instrument in bringing it to terms. The principle is so wide in its nature that it is, in this respect, incapable of any boundary. There is no solid distinction, in this view of the principle, between provisions and a thousand other articles. Men must be clothed as well as fed; and even the privation of the conveniences of life is severely felt by those to whom habit

[43] Rutherforth's Inst. vol. ii. b. ii. ch. 9, § 19.

[44] Bynkershoek, Quæst. Jur. Pub. lib. i. cap. 9.

has rendered them necessary. A nation, in proportion as it can be debarred its accustomed commercial intercourse with other states, must be enfeebled and impoverished; and if it is allowable to a belligerent to violate the freedom of neutral commerce in respect to any one article not contraband *in se*, upon the expectation of annoying the enemy, or bringing him to terms by a seizure of that article, and preventing its reaching his ports, why not upon the same expectation of annoyance cut off, as far as possible by captures, all communication with the enemy, and thus strike at once effectually at his power and resources?

As to the 18th article of the treaty of 1794, between the United States and Great Britain, it manifestly intended to leave the question where it found it; the two contracting parties, not being able to agree upon a definition of the cases in which provisions and other articles not generally contraband might be regarded as such, (the American government insisting on confining it to articles destined to a place actually besieged, blockaded, or invested, whilst the British government maintained that it ought to be extended to all cases where there is an expectation of reducing the enemy by famine,) concurred in stipulating that " whenever any such articles, so becoming contraband, *according to the existing law of nations*, shall for that reason be seized, the same shall not be confiscated," but .he owners should be completely indemnified in the manner provided for in the article. When the law of nations existing at the time the case arises pronounces the articles contraband, they may for that reason be seized; when otherwise, they may not be seized. Each party was thus left as free as the other to decide whether the law of nations, in the given case, pronounced them contraband or not, and neither was obliged to be governed by the opinion of the other. If one party, on a false pretext of being authorized by the law of nations, made a seizure, the other was at full liberty to contest it, to appeal to that law, and, if he thought fit, to resort to reprisals and war.

As *to* the second ground upon which the order in council,

was justified, *necessity*, Great Britain being, as alleged, at the time of issuing it, threatened with a scarcity of those articles directed to be seized, it was answered that it would not be denied that extreme necessity might justify such a measure. It was only important to ascertain whether that necessity then existed, and upon what terms the right it communicated might be carried into exercise.

Grotius and the other text writers on the subject concurred in stating that the necessity must be real and pressing, and that even then it does not confer a right of appropriating the goods of others until all other practicable means of relief have been tried and found inadequate. It was not to be doubted that there were other practicable means of averting the calamity apprehended by Great Britain. The offer of an advantageous market in the different ports of the kingdom was an obvious expedient for drawing into them the produce of other nations. Merchants do not require to be forced into a profitable commerce; they will send their cargoes where interest invites; and if this inducement is held out to them in time, it will always produce the effect intended. But so long as Great Britain offered less for the necessaries of life than could have been obtained from her enemy, was it not to be expected that neutral vessels should seek the ports of that enemy, and pass by her own? Could it be said, that under the mere apprehension (not under the actual experience) of scarcity, she was authorized to have recourse to the forcible means of seizing provisions belonging to neutrals, without attempting those means of supply which were consistent with the rights of others, and which were not incompatible with the exigency? After this order had been issued and carried into execution, the British government did what it should have done before: it offered a bounty upon the importation of the articles of which it was in want. The consequence was that neutrals came with these articles, until at length the market was found to be overstocked. The same arrangement, had it been made at an earlier period, would have rendered wholly useless the order of 1795.

Upon these grounds, a full indemnification was allowed by the commissioners, under the seventh article of the treaty of 1794, to the owners of the vessels and cargoes seized under the orders in council, as well for the loss of a market as for the other consequences of their detention.[45]

§ 22.
Transportation of military persons and despatches in the enemy's service.

Of the same nature with the carrying of contraband goods is the transportation of military persons or despatches in the service of the enemy.

A neutral vessel which is used as a transport for the enemy's forces is subject to confiscation if captured by the opposite belligerent. Nor will the fact of her having been impressed by violence into the enemy's service exempt her. The master cannot be permitted to aver that he was an involuntary agent. Were an act of force exercised by one belligerent power on a neutral ship or person to be considered a justification for an act contrary to the known duties of the neutral character, there would be an end of any prohibition under the law of nations to carry contraband, or to engage in any other hostile act. If any loss is sustained in such a service, the neutral yielding to such demands must seek redress from the government which has imposed the restraint upon him.[46] As to the number of military persons necessary to subject the vessel to confiscation, it is difficult to define, since fewer persons of high quality and character may be of much more importance than a much greater number of persons of lower condition. To carry a veteran general, under some circumstances, might be a much more noxious act than the conveyance of a whole regiment. The consequences of such assistance are greater, and therefore the belligerent has a stronger right to prevent and punish it; nor is it material, in the judgment of the prize court, whether the master be ignorant of the character of the service on which he is engaged. It is deemed sufficient if there has

[45] Proceedings of the Board of Commissioners under the seventh article of the treaty of 1794. MS. Opinion of Mr. W. Pinkney, case of the Neptune.

[46] Robinson's Adm. Rep. vol. iv. p. 256. The Carolina.

been an injury arising to the belligerent from the employment in which the vessel is found. If imposition be prac-
tiséd, it operates as force; and if redress is to be sought
against any person, it must be against those who have, by
means either of compulsion or deceit, exposed the property
to danger; otherwise such opportunities of conveyance
would be constantly used, and it would be almost impossible
in the greater number of cases to prove the privity of the
immediate offender.[47]

The fraudulently carrying the despatches of the enemy
will also subject the neutral vessel, in which they are transported, to capture and confiscation. The consequences of
such a service are indefinite, infinitely beyond the effect of
any contraband that can be conveyed. The carrying of two
or three cargoes of military stores," says Sir *W. Scott,* " is
necessarily an assistance of a limited nature; but in the
transmission of despatches may be conveyed the entire plan
of a campaign, that may defeat all the plans of the other
belligerent in that quarter of the world. It is true, as it has
been said, that *one ball* might take off a Charles the XIIth,
and might produce the most disastrous effects in a campaign;
but that is a consequence so remote and accidental, that in
the contemplation of human events it is a sort of evanescent
quantity of which no account is taken; and the practice has
been, accordingly, that it is in considerable quantities only
that the offence of contraband is contemplated. The case of
despatches is very different: it is impossible to limit a letter
to so small a size as not to be capable of producing the most
important consequences. It is a service, therefore, which,
in whatever degree it exists, can only be considered in one
character—as an act of the most hostile nature. The offence
of fraudulently carrying despatches in the service of the
enemy being, then, greater than that of carrying contraband
under any circumstances, it becomes absolutely necessary, as
well as just, to resort to some other penalty than that inflicted
in cases of contraband. The confiscation of the noxious ar-

[47] Robinson's Adm. Rep. vol. vi. p. 430. The Orozembo.

ticle, which constitutes the penalty in contraband, where the vessel and cargo do not belong to the same person, would be ridiculous when applied to *despatches*. There would be *no* freight dependent on their transportation, and therefore this penalty could not, in the nature of things, be applied. The vehicle in which they are carried must, therefore, be confiscated."[48]

But carrying the despatches of an ambassador or other public minister of the enemy, resident in a neutral country, is an exception to the reasoning on which the above general rule is founded. " They are despatches from persons who are, in a peculiar manner, the favourite object of the protection of the law of nations, residing in the neutral country for the purpose of preserving the relations of amity between that state and their own government. On this ground, a very material distinction arises, with respect to the right of furnishing the conveyance. The neutral country has a right to preserve its relations with the enemy, and you are not at liberty to conclude that any communication between them can partake, in any degree, of the nature of hostility against you. The limits assigned to the operations of war against ambassadors, by writers on public law, are, that the belligerent may exercise his right of war against them, wherever the character of hostility exists : he may stop the ambassador of his enemy on his passage ; but when he has arrived in the neutral country, and taken on himself the functions of his office, and has been admitted in his representative character, he becomes a sort of *middle man*, entitled to peculiar privileges, as set apart for the preservation of the relations of amity and peace, in maintaining which, all nations are, in some degree, interested. If it be argued that he retains his national character unmixed, and that even his residence is considered as a residence in his own country ; it is answered, that this is a fiction of law, invented for his further protection only, and as such a fiction, it is not to be extended beyond the reasoning on which it depends. It was intended as

[48] Robinson's Adm. Rep. vol. vi. p. 440. The Atalanta.

a privilege; and cannot be urged to his disadvantage. Could it be said that he would, on that principle, be subject to any of the rights of war in the neutral territory? Certainly not: he is there for the purpose of carrying on the relations of peace and amity, for the interests of his own country primarily, but, at the same time, for the furtherance and protection of the interest which the neutral country also has in the continuance of those relations. It is to be considered also with regard to this question, what may be due to the convenience of the neutral state; for its interest may require that the intercourse of correspondence with the enemy's country should not be altogether interdicted. It might be thought to amount almost to a declaration, that an ambassador from the enemy shall not reside in the neutral state, if he is declared to be debarred from the only means of communicating with his own. For to what useful purpose can he reside there, without the opportunity of such a communication? It is too much to say that all the business of the two states shall be transacted by the minister of the neutral state resident in the enemy's country. The practice of nations has allowed to neutral states the privilege of receiving ministers from the belligerent powers, and of an immediate negotiation with them."[49]

In general, where the ship and cargo do not belong to the same person, the contraband articles only are confiscated, and the carrier-master is refused his freight, to which he is entitled upon innocent articles which are condemned as enemy's property. But where the ship and the innocent articles of the cargo belong to the owner of the contraband, they are all involved in the same penalty. And even where the ship and the cargo do not belong to the same person, the carriage of contraband, under the fraudulent circumstances of false papers and false destination, will work a confiscation of the ship as well as the cargo. The same effect has likewise been held

§ 23. Penalty for the carrying of contraband.

---

[49] Sir W. Scott, Robinson's Adm. Rep. vol. vi. p. 461. The Carolina.

to be produced by the carriage of contraband articles in a ship, the owner of which is bound by the express obligation of the treaties subsisting between his own country and the capturing country, to refrain from carrying such articles to the enemy.   In such a case, it is said that the ship throws off her neutral character, and is liable to be treated at once as an enemy's vessel, and as a violator of the solemn compacts of the country to which she belongs.[50]

The general rule as to contraband articles, as laid down by Sir *W. Scott*, is, that the articles must be taken *in delicto*, in the actual prosecution of the voyage to an enemy's port. "Under the present understanding of the law of nations, you cannot generally take the proceeds in the return voyage. From the moment of quitting port on a hostile destination, indeed, the offence is complete, and it is not necessary to wait till the goods are actually endeavouring to enter the enemy's port; but beyond that, if the goods are not taken *in delicto*, and in the actual prosecution of such a voyage, the penalty is not now generally held to attach."[51]   But the same learned judge applied a different rule in other cases of contraband, carried from Europe to the East Indies, with false papers and false destination, intended to conceal the real object of the expedition, where the return cargo, the proceeds of the outward cargo taken on the return voyage, was held liable to condemnation.[52]

[50] Robinson's Adm. Rep. vol. i. p. 91.   The Ringende Jacob.   P. 244. The Sarah Christina.   P. 288. The Mercurius. Vol. iii. p. 217. The Franklin. Vol. iv. p. 69. The Edward.   Vol. vi. p. 125. The Ranger. Vol. iii. p. 295. The Neutralitet.

As to how far the ship-owner is liable for the act of the master in cases of contraband, see Wheaton's Rep. vol. ii. Appendix, Note I. pp. 37, 38.

[51] Robinson's Adm. Rep. vol. iii. p. 168. The Ionina.

[52] Ibid. vol. ii. p. 343.   The Rosalie and Betty.   Vol. iii. p. 122.   The Nancy.   The soundness of these last decisions may be well questioned; for in order to sustain the penalty, there must be, on principle, a *delictum* at the moment of seizure.   To subject the property to confiscation whilst the offence no longer continues, would be to extend it indefinitely, not only to the return voyage, but to all future cargoes of the vessel, which would thus never be purified from the contagion communicated by the contraband articles.

Although the general policy of the American government, in its diplomatic negotiations, has aimed to limit the catalogue of contraband by confining it strictly to munitions of war, excluding all articles of promiscuous use, a remarkable case occurred during the late war between Great Britain and the United States, in which the supreme court of the latter appears to have been disposed to adopt all the principles of Sir W. Scott as to provisions becoming contraband under certain circumstances. But as that was not the case of a cargo of *neutral* property, supposed to be liable to capture and confiscation as contraband of war, but of a cargo of *enemy's* property going for the supply of the enemy's naval and military forces, and clearly liable to condemnation, the question was, whether the neutral master was entitled to his freight as in other cases of the transportation of innocent articles of enemy's property; and it was not essential to the determination of the case to consider under what circumstances articles *anticipitis usus* might become contraband. Upon the actual question before the court, it seems there would have been no difference of opinion among the American judges in the case of an ordinary war; all of them concurring in the principle, that a neutral, carrying supplies for the enemy's naval or military forces, does, under the mildest interpretation of international law, expose himself to the loss of freight. But the case was that of a Swedish vessel, captured by an American cruiser, in the act of carrying a cargo of British property, consisting of barley and oats, for the supply of the allied armies in the Spanish peninsula, the United States being at war with Great Britain, but at peace with Sweden and the other powers allied against France. Under these circumstances a majority of the judges were of the opinion that the voyage was illegal, and that the neutral carrier was not entitled to his freight on the cargo condemned as enemy's property.

It was stated in the judgment of the court, that it had been solemnly adjudged in the British prize courts, that being engaged in the transport service of the enemy, or in the conveyance of military persons in his employment, or the carrying of despatches, are acts of hostility which subject the property to confiscation. In these cases, the fact that the voyage was to a neutral port was not thought to change the character of the transaction. The principle of these determinations was asserted to be, that the party must be deemed to place himself in the service of the enemy state, and to assist in warding off the pressure of the war, or in favouring its offensive projects. Now these cases could not be distinguished, in principle, from that before the court. Here was a cargo of provisions exported from the enemy's country, with the avowed purpose of supplying the army of the enemy. Without this destination, they would not have been permitted to be exported at all. It was vain to contend that the direct effect of the voyage was not to aid the British hostilities against the United States. It might enable the enemy indirectly to operate with more vigour and promptitude against them, and increase his disposable force. But it was not the effect of the particular transaction which the law regards : it was the general tendency of such transactions to assist the military operations of the enemy, and to tempt deviations from strict neutrality. The destination to a neutral port could not vary the application of this rule. It was only doing that indirectly, which was directly prohibited. Would it be contended that a neutral might lawfully transport provisions for the British fleet and army, while it lay at Bordeaux preparing for an expedition to the United States? Would it be contended that he might lawfully supply a British fleet stationed on the American coast? An attempt had been made to distinguish this case from the ordinary cases of employment in the transport service of the enemy, upon the ground that the war of Great Britain against France was a war distinct from that against the United States; and that Swedish subjects had a perfect right to assist the British arms in respect to the former, though not to the latter. But the court held, that whatever might be the right of the Swedish sovereign, acting under his own

authority, if a Swedish vessel be engaged in the actual service of Great Britain, or in carrying stores for the exclusive
use of the British armies, she must, to all intents and purposes, be deemed a British transport. It was perfectly immaterial in what particular enterprise those armies might, at
the time, be engaged; for the same important benefits were
conferred upon the enemy of the United States, who thereby
acquired a greater disposable force to bring into action against
them. In the *Friendship*, (6 *Rob.* 420,) Sir *W. Scott*, speaking
on this subject, declared that "it signifies nothing, whether
the men so conveyed are to be put into action on an immediate expedition or not. The mere shifting of drafts in
detachments, and *the conveyance of stores* from one place to
another, is an ordinary employment of a transport vessel, and
it is a distinction totally unimportant whether this or that case
may be connected with the *immediate active* service of the
enemy. In removing forces from distant settlements, there
may be no intention of immediate action; but still the general
importance of having troops conveyed to places where it is
convenient that they should be collected, either for present
or future use, is what constitutes the object and employment
of transport vessels." It was obvious that the learned judge
did not deem it material to what places the stores might be
destined; and it must be equally immaterial, what is the immediate occupation of the enemy's force. That force was
always hostile to America, be it where it might. To-day it
might act against France, to-morrow against the former
country; and the better its commissary department was supplied, the more life and activity was communicated to all its
motions. It was not therefore material whether there was
another distinct war, in which the enemy of the United States
was engaged, or not. It was sufficient, that his armies were
every where their enemies; and every assistance offered to
them must directly or indirectly, operate to their injury.

The court was therefore of opinion that the voyage, in
which the vessel was engaged, was illicit, and inconsistent
with the duties of neutrality, and that it was a very lenient

administration of justice to confine the penalty to a mere denial of freight.[53]

It had been contended in argument in the above case that the exportation of grain from Ireland being generally prohibited, a neutral could not lawfully engage in that trade during war, upon the principle of what has been called the "Rule of the War of 1756," in its application to the colonial and coasting trade of an enemy not generally open in time of peace. The court deemed it unnecessary to consider the principles on which that rule is rested by the British prize courts, not regarding them as applicable to the case in judgment. But the legality of the rule itself has always been contested by the American government, and it appears in its origin to have been founded upon very different principles from those which have more recently been urged in its defence. During the war of 1756, the French government, finding the trade with their colonies almost entirely cut off by the maritime superiority of Great Britain, relaxed their monopoly of that trade, and allowed the Dutch, then neutral, to carry on the commerce between the mother country and her colonies, under special licenses or passes, granted for this particular purpose, excluding, at the same time, all other neutrals from the same trade. Many Dutch vessels so employed were captured by the British cruisers, and, together with their cargoes, were condemned by the prize courts, upon the principle that by such employment, they were, in effect, incorporated into the French navigation, having adopted the commerce and character of the enemy, and identified themselves with his interests and purposes. They were, in the judgment of these courts, to be considered like transports in the enemy's service, and hence liable to capture and condemnation, upon the same principle with property condemned for carrying military persons or despatches. In these cases, the property is considered, *pro hac vice*, as enemy's property, as so completely identified with his interests as to acquire a

[53] Wheaton's Rep. vol. i. p. 382. The Commercen.

hostile character. So, where a neutral is engaged in a trade, which is exclusively confined to the subjects of any country, in peace and in war, and is interdicted to all others, and cannot at any time be avowedly carried on in the name of a foreigner, such a trade is considered so entirely national, that it must follow the hostile situation of the country.[54] There is all the difference between this principle and the more modern doctrine, which interdicts to neutrals, during war, all trade not open to them in time of peace, that there is between the granting by the enemy of special licenses to the subjects of the opposite belligerent, protecting their property from capture in a particular trade, which the policy of the enemy induces him to tolerate, and a general exemption of such trade from capture. The former is clearly cause of confiscation, whilst the latter has never been deemed to have such an effect. The Rule of the War of 1756 was originally founded upon the former principle: it was suffered to lay dormant during the war of the American revolution: and when revived at the commencement of the war against France in 1793, was applied, with various relaxations and modifications, to the prohibition of all neutral traffic with the colonies and upon the coasts of the enemy. The principle of the rule was frequently vindicated by Sir *W. Scott*, in his masterly judgments in the High Court of Admiralty, and in the writings of other British publicists of great learning and ability. But the conclusiveness of their reasonings was ably contested by different American and other foreign writers, and failed to procure the acquiescence of neutral powers in this prohibition of their trade with the enemy's colonies. The question continued a fruitful source of contention between Great Britain and those powers until they became her allies or enemies at the close of the war; but its practical importance will probably be hereafter much

[54] Robinson's Adm. Rep. vol. ii. p. 52. The Princessa. Vol. iv. p. 118. The Anna Catharina. P. 121. The Rendesborg. Vol. v. p. 150. The Vrow Anna Catharina. Wheaton's Rep. vol. ii. Appendix, p. 29.

diminished by the revolution which has since taken place in
the colonial system of Europe.[55]

§ 25.
Breach of
blockade.

Another exception to the general freedom of neutral commerce in time of war is to be found in the trade to ports
or places besieged or blockaded by one of the belligerent
powers.

The more ancient text writers all require that the siege or
blockade should actually exist, and be carried on by an adequate force, and not merely declared by proclamation, in order to render commercial intercourse with the port or place
unlawful on the part of neutrals. Thus *Grotius* forbids the
carrying any thing to besieged or blockaded places, "*if* it
might impede the execution of the belligerent's lawful designs, and if the carriers might have known of the siege or
blockade; as in the case of a town actually invested or a
port closely blockaded, and when a surrender or peace is
already expected to take place."[56] And *Bynkershoek,* in
commenting upon this passage, holds it to be "unlawful
to carry any thing, whether contraband or not, to a place
thus circumstanced, since those who are within may be compelled to surrender, not merely by the direct application of
force, but also by the want of provisions and other necessaries. If, therefore, it should be lawful to carry to them
what they are in need of, the belligerent might thereby be
compelled to raise the siege or blockade, which would be
doing him an injury, and therefore unjust. And because it
cannot be known what articles the besieged may want, the
law forbids, in general terms, carrying *any thing* to them;
otherwise disputes and altercations would arise to which
there would be no end."[57]

[55] Wheaton's Rep. vol. i.   Appendix, Note iii.

[56] "*Si juris mei executionem rerum subvectio impedieret, idque scire po-
tuerit qui advexit, ut si* OPPIDUM OBSESSUM TENEBAM, *si* PORTUS CLAUSOS, *et
jam deditio aut pax expectabitur,*" &c.   Grotius, de Jur. Bel. ac Pac. lib. iii.
cap. 1, sec. 5, Note 3.

[57] Bynkershoek, Quæst. Jur. Pub. lib. i, cap. 11.   Duponceau's Transl.
p. 82.

Bynkershoek appears to have mistaken the true sense of the above-cited passage from Grotius, in supposing that the latter meant to require, as a necessary ingredient in a strict blockade, that there should be an expectation of peace or of a surrender, when in fact he merely mentions that as an example by way of putting the strongest possible case. But that he concurred with Grotius in requiring a strict and actual siege or blockade, where a town is actually invested with troops, or a port closely blockaded by ships of war, (*oppidum obsessum, portus clausos,*) is evident from his .subsequent remarks in the same chapter upon the decress of the States-General against those who should carry any thing to the Spanish camp, the same not being then actually besieged. He holds the decrees to be perfectly justifiable, so far as they prohibited the carrying of contraband of war to the enemy's camp, but as to other things, whether they were or were not lawfully prohibited, depends entirely upon the circumstance of the place being besieged or not." So also, in commenting upon the decree of the States-General of the 26th June, 1630, declaring the ports of Flanders in a state of blockade, he states that this decree was for some time not carried into execution by the actual presence of a sufficient naval force, during which period certain neutral vessels trading to those ports were captured by the Dutch cruisers; and that part of their cargoes only which consisted of contraband articles was condemned, whilst the residue was released with the vessels. " It has been asked," says he, " by what law the contraband goods were condemned under those circumstances, and there are those who deny the legality of their condemnation. It is evident, however, that whilst those coasts were guarded in a lax or remiss manner, the law of blockade, by which all neutral goods going to or coming from a blockaded port may be lawfully captured, might also have been relaxed; but not so the general law of war, by which contraband goods, when carried to an enemy's port, even though not blockaded, are liable to confiscation."

What things must be proved to constitute a violation of blockade.

To constitute a violation of blockade, says Sir *W. Scott,* " three things must be proved: 1st, the existence of an actual blockade; 2dly, the knowledge of the party supposed to have offended; and, 3dly, some act of violation, either by going in or coming out with a cargo laden after the commencement of blockade."[58]

Actual presence of the blockading force.

1. The definition of a lawful maritime blockade requiring the actual presence of a sufficient force, stationed at the entrance of the port, sufficiently near to prevent communication, as given by the text writers, is confirmed by the authority of numerous modern treaties, and especially by the convention of 1801 between Great Britain and Russia, intended as a final adjustment of the disputed points of maritime law which had given rise to the armed neutrality of 1780 and of 1801.[59]

The only exception to the general rule, which requires the actual presence of an adequate force to constitute a lawful blockade, arises out of the circumstances of the occasional temporary absence of the blockading squadron, produced by accident, as in the case of a storm, which does not suspend the legal operation of the blockade. The law considers an attempt to take advantage of such an accidental removal, a fraudulent attempt to break the blookade.[60]

Knowledge of the party.

2. As a proclamation, or general public notification, is not of itself sufficient to constitute a legal blockade, so neither can a knowledge of the existence of such a blockade be imputed to the party *merely* in consequence of such a proclamation or notification. Not only must an actual blockade exist, but a knowledge of it must be brought home to the party, in order to show that it has been violated.[61] As, on the one

[58] Robinson's Adm. Rep. vol. i. p. 92. The Betsey.

[59] The 3d art. sect. 4, of this convention, declares, " That in order to determine what characterizes a blockaded port, that denomination is given only where there is, by the disposition of the power which attacks it with ships stationary, or sufficintly near, an evident danger in entering."

[60] Robinson's Adm. Rep. vol. i. p. 154. The Columbia.

[61] Ibid. p. 93. The Betsey.

hand, a declaration of blockade which is not supported by the fact cannot be deemed legally to exist, so on the other hand, the fact, duly notified to the party on the spot, is of itself sufficient to affect him with a knowledge of it; for public notifications between governments can be meant only for the information of individuals; but if the individual is personally informed, that purpose is still better obtained than by a public declaration.[62] Where the vessel sails from a country lying sufficiently near to the blockaded port to have constant information of the state of the blockade, whether it is continued or is relaxed, no special notice is necessary; for the public declaration in this case implies notice to the party after sufficient time has elapsed to receive the declaration at the port whence the vessel sails.[63] But where the country lies at such a distance that the inhabitants cannot have this constant information, they may lawfully send their vessels conjecturally, upon the expectation of finding the blockade broken up, after it has existed for a considerable time. In this case, the party has a right to make a fair inquiry whether the blockade be determined or not, and consequently cannot be involved in the penalties affixed to a violation of it, unless, upon such inquiry, he receives notice of the existence of the blockade."[64]

" There are," says Sir *W. Scott,* " two sorts of blockade: one by the *simple fact* only, the other by a notification accompanied with the fact. In the former case, when the fact ceases otherwise than by accident or the shifting of the wind, there is immediately an end of the blockade; but where the fact is accompanied by a public notification from the government of a belligerent country to neutral governments, I apprehend, *primâ facie,* the blockade must be supposed to exist till it has been publicly repealed. It is the duty, undoubtedly, of a belligerent country which has made the notification of blockade, to notify in the same way, and imme-

[62] Robinson's Adm. Rep. p. 83. The Mercurdus.
[63] Ibid. vol. ii. p. 131. The Jonge Petronella. P. 298. The Calypso.
[64] Ibid. vol. i. p. 332. The Betsey.

diately, the discontinuance of it: to suffer the fact to cease, and to apply the notification again, at a distant time, would be a fraud on neutral nations, and a conduct which we are not to suppose that any country would pursue. I do not say that a blockade of this sort may not in any case expire *de facto;* but I say such a conduct is not hastily to be presumed against any nation ; and, therefore, till such a case is clearly made out, I shall hold that a blockade by notification is *primâ facie,* to be presumed to continue till the notification is revoked."[65] And in another case, he says : " The effect of a notification to any foreign government would clearly be to include all the individuals of that nation ; it would be nugatory if individuals were allowed to plead their ignorance of it ; it is the duty of foreign governments to communicate the information to their subjects, whose interests they are bound to protect. I shall hold, therefore, that a neutral master can never be heard to aver against a notification of blockade that he is ignorant of it. If he is really ignorant of it, it may be a subject of representation to his own government, and may raise a claim of compensation from them, but it can be no plea in the court of a belligerent. In the case of a blockade *de facto* only, it may be otherwise ; but this is a case of a blockade by notification. Another distinction between a notified blockade and a blockade existing *de facto* only, is, that in the former the act of sailing for a blockaded place is sufficient to constitute the offence. It is to be presumed that the notification will be formally revoked, and that due notice will be given of it ; till that is done, the port is to be considered as closed up ; and from the moment of quitting port to sail on such a destination, the offence of violating the blockade is complete, and the property engaged in it subject to confiscation. It may be different in a blockade existing *de facto* only : there no presumption arises as to the continuance, and the ignorance of the party may be admitted as an excuse for sailing on a doubtful and provisional destination."[66]

[65] Robinson's Adm. Rep. vol. i. p. 171. The Neptunus.
[66] Ibid. vol. ii. p. 112. The Neptunus, Hempel.

A more definite rule as to the notification of an existing blockade has been frequently provided by conventional stipulations between different maritime powers. Thus by the 18th article of the treaty of 1794, between Great Britain and the United States, it was declared—" That whereas it frequently happens that vessels sail for a port or place belonging to an enemy, without knowing that the same is either besieged, blockaded, or invested, it is agreed that every vessel so circumstanced may be turned away from such port or place; but she shall not be detained, nor her cargo, if not contraband, be confiscated, unless, after notice, she shall again attempt to enter; but she shall be permitted to go to any other port or place she may think proper." This stipulation, which is equivalent to that contained in previous treaties between Great Britain and the Baltic powers, having been disregarded by the naval authorities and prize courts in the West Indies, the attention of the British government was called to the subject by an official communication from the American government. In consequence of this communication, instructions were sent out in the year 1804, by the Board of Admiralty, the naval commanders and judges of the vice-admiralty courts, not to consider any blockade of the French West-India islands as existing, unless in respect to particular ports which were actually invested; and then not to capture vessels bound to such ports, unless they should previously have been warned not to enter them. The stipulation in the treaty intended to be enforced by these instructions seems to be a correct exposition of the law of nations, and is admitted by the contracting parties to be a correct exposition of that law, or to constitute a rule between themselves in place of it. Neither the law of nations nor the treaty admits of the condemnation of a neutral vessel for the mere intention to enter a blockaded port, unconnected with any fact. In the above cited cases, the fact of sailing was coupled with the intention, and the condemnation was thus founded upon a supposed actual breach of the blockade. Sailing for a blockaded port, knowing it to be blockaded, was there construed into an attempt to enter that port, and was therefore adjudged a breach of blockade from the departure of the vessel. But the fact of clearing out for a blockaded port is, in itself, innocent, unless it be accompanied with a knowledge of the blockade. The right to treat the vessel as an enemy is declared by *Vattel*, (liv. iii. sect. 177,) to be founded on the *attempt* to enter; and certainly this attempt must be made by a person knowing the fact. The import of the treaty, and of the instructions issued in pursuance of the treaty, is that a vessel cannot be placed in the situation of one having a notice of the blockade, until she is warned off. They gave her a right to inquire of the blockading squadron if she had not previously received this warning from one capable of giving it, and consequently dispensed with her making that inquiry elsewhere. A neutral vessel might thus lawfully sail for a blockaded port, knowing it to be blockaded; and being found sailing towards such port would not constitute an attempt to break the blockade, unless she should be actually warned off.[67]

Where an enemy's port was declared in a state of blockade by notification, and at the same time when the notification was issued, news arrived that the blockading squadron had been driven off by the superior force of the enemy, the blockade was held by the prize court to be null and defective from the beginning, in the main circumstance that is essentially necessary to give it legal operation; and that it would be unjust to hold neutral vessels to the observance of a notification, accompanied by a circumstance that defeated its effect. This case was, therefore, considered as independent of the presumption arising from notification in other instances; the notification being defeated, it must have been shown that the actual blockade was again resumed, and the vessel would have been entitled to a warning, if any such blockade had existed when she arrived off the port. The mere act of sail-

[67] Cranch's Rep. vol. iv. p. 185. Fitzsimmons *v.* the Newport Insurance Company. Mr. Merry's Letter to Mr. Secretary Madison, 12th April, 1804. Wheaton's Rep. vol. iii. Appendix, p. 11.

ing for the port, under the dubious state of the actual blockade at the time, was deemed insufficient to fix upon the
vessel the penalty for breaking the blockade.[68]

In the above case, a question was raised whether the notification which had issued was not still operative; but the
court was of opinion that it could not be so considered, and
that a neutral power was not obliged, under such circumstances, to presume the continuance of a blockade, nor to
act upon a supposition that the blockade would be resumed
by any other competent force. But in a subsequent case,
where it was suggested that the blockading squadron had
actually returned to its former station off the port, in order
to renew the blockade, a question arose whether there had
been that notoriety of the fact, arising from the operation of
time or other circumstances, which must be taken to have
brought the existence of the blockade to the knowledge of
the parties. Among other modes of resolving this question,
a prevailing consideration would have been the length of
time, in proportion to the distance of the country from which
the vessel sailed. But as nothing more came out in evidence
than that the squadron came off the port on a certain day, it
was held that this would not restore a blockade which had
been thus effectually raised, but that it must be renewed
again, by notification, before foreign nations could be affected
with an obligation to observe it. The squadron might return
off the port with different intentions. It might arrive there
as a fleet of observation merely, or for the purpose of only a
qualified blockade. On the other hand, the commander might
attempt to connect the two blockades together; but this is
what could not be done; and in order to revive the former
blockade, the same form of communication must have been
observed *de novo* that is necessary to establish an original
blockade.[69]

3. Besides the knowledge of the party, some act of viola- Some act
tion is essential to a breach of blockade, as either going in or of violation.

[68] Robinson's Adm. Rep. vol. vi. p. 65. The Triheten.
[69] Ibid. vol. vi. p. 112. The Hoffnung.

coming out of the port with a cargo laden after the commencement of the blockade.[70]

Thus by the edict of the States-General of Holland of
1630, relative to the blockade of the ports of Flanders, it was
ordered that the vessels and goods of neutrals which should
be found going in or coming out of the said ports, or so near
thereto as to show beyond a doubt that they were endeavouring to run into them; or which from the documents on
board should appear bound to the said ports, although they
should be found at a distance from them, should be confiscated, unless they should, voluntarily, before coming in sight of
or being chased by the Dutch ships of war, change their intention, while the thing was yet undone, and alter their course.
Bynkershoek, in commenting upon this part of the decree, defends the reasonableness of the provision which affects vessels
*found so near to the blockaded ports as to show beyond a doubt
that they were endeavouring to run into them*, upon the ground
of legal presumption, with the exception of extreme and well-
proved necessity only. Still more reasonable is the infliction
of the penalty of confiscation, where the intention is expressly
avowed by the papers found on board. The third article of
the same edict also subjected to confiscation such vessels and
their cargoes as should come out of the said ports, not having
been forced into them by stress of weather, although they
should be captured at a distance from them, unless they had,
after leaving the enemy's port, performed their voyage to a
port of their own country, or to some other neutral or free
port, in which case they should be exempt from condemnation; but if, in coming out of the said ports of Flanders, they
should be pursued by the Dutch ships of war, and chased into
another port, such as their own, or that of their destination,
and found on the high seas coming out of *such port*, in that
case they might be captured and condemned. Bynkershoek
considers this provision as distinguishing the case of a vessel
having broken the blockade, and afterwards terminated her
voyage by proceeding voluntarily to her destined port, and

[70] Robinson's Adm. Rep. vol. i. p. 93. The Betsey.

that of a vessel chased and compelled to take refuge; which latter might still be captured after leaving the port in which she had taken refuge. And in conformity with these principles is the more modern law and practice.[71]

With respect to violating a blockade by coming out with a cargo, the time of shipment is very material, for although it might be hard to refuse a neutral liberty to retire with a cargo already laden, and by that act already become neutral property; yet, after the commencement of a blockade, a neutral cannot be allowed to interpose in any way to assist the exportation of the property of the enemy.[72] A neutral ship departing can only take away a cargo *bonâ fide* purchased and delivered before the commencement of the blockade; if she afterwards take on board a cargo, it is a violation of the blockade. But where a ship was transferred from one neutral merchant to another in a blockaded port, and sailed out in ballast, she was determined not to have violated the blockade.[73] So where goods were sent into the blockaded port before the commencement of the blockade, but re-shipped by order of the neutral proprietor as found unsaleable, during the blockade, they were held entitled to restitution. For the same rule which permits neutrals to withdraw their vessels from a blockaded port, extends also, with equal justice, to merchandise sent in before the blockade, and withdrawn *bonâ fide* by the neutral proprietor.[74]

After the commencement of a blockade, neutral is no longer at liberty to make any purchase in that port. Thus where a ship which had been purchased by a neutral of the enemy in a blockaded port, and sailed on a voyage to the neutral country, had been driven by stress of weather into a bellige-

[71] Bynkershoek, Quæst. Jur. Pub. lib. i. cap. 11. Robinson's Adm. Rep. vol. ii. p. 128. The Welvaart van Pillaw. Vol. iii. p. 147. The Juffrow Maria Schroeder.

[72] Robinson's Adm. Rep. vol. i. p. 93. The Betsey.

[73] Ibid. vol. i. p. 150. The Vrouw Judith.

[74] Ibid. vol. iv. p. 89. The Potsdam. Wheaton's Rep. vol. iii. p. 183. Olivera *v.* Union Insurance Company.

rent port, where she was seized, she was held liable to condemnation under the general rule. That the vessel had been purchased out of the proceeds of the cargo of another vessel, was considered as an unavailing circumstance on a question of blockade. If the ship has been purchased in a blockaded port, *that* alone is the illegal act, and it is perfectly immaterial out of what funds the purchase was effected. Another distinction taken in argument was, that the vessel had terminated her voyage, and therefore that the penalty would no longer attach. But this was also overruled, because the port into which she had been driven was not represented as forming any part of her original destination. It was therefore impossible to consider this accident as any discontinuance of the voyage, or as a defeasance of the penalty which had been incurred.

A maritime blockade is not violated by sending goods to the blockaded port, or by bringing them from the same, through the interior canal navigation or land carriage of the country. A blockade may be of different descriptions. A mere maritime blockade, effected by a force operating only at sea, can have no operation upon the interior communications of the port. The legal blockade can extend no further than the actual blockade can be applied. If the place be not invested on the land side, its interior communications with other ports cannot be cut off. If the blockade be rendered imperfect by this rule of construction, it must be ascribed to its physical inadequacy by which the extent of its legal pretensions is unavoidably limited.[75] But goods shipped in a river, having been previously sent in lighters along the coast from the blockaded port, with the ship under charter-party proceeding also from the blockaded port in ballast to take them on board, were held liable to confiscation. This case is very different from the preceding, because there the communication had been by inland navigation, which was in no manner, and in no part of it, subject to the blockade.[76]

[75] Edwards's Adm. Rep. p. 32. The Comet.
[76] Robinson's Adm. Rep. vol. iii. p. 297.   Vol. iv. p. 65.   The Stert.

The offence incurred by a breach of blockade generally remains during the voyage; but the offence never travels on with the vessel further than to the end of the return voyage, although if she is taken in any part of that voyage, she is taken *in delicto*. This is deemed reasonable, because no other opportunity is afforded to the belligerent cruisers, to vindicate the violated law. But where the blockade has been raised between the time of sailing and the capture, the penalty does not attach; because the blockade being gone, the necessity of applying the penalty to prevent future transgression no longer exists. When the blockade is raised, a veil is thrown over every thing that has been done, and the vessel is no longer taken *in delicto*. The *delictum* may have been completed at one period, but it is by subsequent events done away.[77]

The right of visitation and search of neutral vessels at sea is a belligerent right essential to the exercise of the right of capturing enemy's property, contraband of war, and vessels committing a breach of blockade. Even if the right of capturing enemy's property be ever so strictly limited, and the rule of *free ships free goods* be adopted, the right of visitation and search is essential in order to determine whether the ships themselves are neutral and documented as such according to the law of nations and treaties; for, as *Bynkershoek* observes, "it is lawful to detain a neutral vessel, in order to ascertain, not by the flag merely, which may be fraudulently assumed, but by the documents themselves on board, whether she is really neutral." Indeed it seems that the practice of maritime captures could not exist without it. Accordingly the text writers generally concur in recognising the existence of this right.[78]

§ 26. Right of visitation and search.

[77] Robinson's Adm. Rep. vol. ii. p. 128. The Welvaart van Pillaw. Vol. vi. p. 387. The Lisette. As to how far the act of the master binds the shipowner in cases of breach of blockade, see the cases collected in Wheaton's Reports, vol. ii. Appendix, pp. 36—40.

[78] Bynkershoek, Quæst. Jur. Pub. lib. i. cap. 14. Vattel, Droit des Gens, liv. iii. ch. 7, § 114. Martens, Précis, &c. liv. viii. ch. 7, §§ 317, 321. Ga-

The international law on this subject is ably summed up by
Sir *W. Scott* in the case of the *Maria*, where the exercise of
the right was attempted to be resisted by the interposition of
a convoy of Swedish ships of war. In delivering the judgment of the High Court of Admiralty in that memorable case,
this learned civilian lays down the three following principles
of law:—

1. That the right of visiting and searching merchant-ships
on the high seas, whatever be the ships, the cargoes, or the
destinations, is an incontestable right of the lawfully commissioned cruisers of a belligerent nation. "I say, be the ships,
the cargoes, and the destination what they may, because till
they are visited and searched, it does not appear what the
ships, or the destination are; and it is for the purpose of ascertaining these points that the necessity of this right of visitation and search exists. This right is so clear in principle
that no man can deny it who admits the right of maritime
capture; because if you are not at liberty to ascertain by sufficient inquiry whether there is property that can legally be
captured, it is impossible to capture. Even those who contend for the inadmissible rule that *free ships make free goods*,
must admit the exercise of this right at least for the purpose
of ascertaining whether the ships are free ships or not. The
right is equally clear in practice; for practice is uniform and
universal upon the subject. The many European treaties
which refer to this right, refer to it as pre-existing, and
merely regulate the exercise of it. All writers upon the law
of nations unanimously acknowledge it, without the exception
even of *Hubner* himself, the great champion of neutral privileges."

2. That the authority of the neutral sovereign being forcibly interposed cannot legally vary the rights of a lawfully
commissioned belligerent cruiser. "Two sovereigns may
unquestionably agree, if they think fit, as in some late in-

liani, dei Doveri de' Principi Neutrali, &c. p. 458. Lampredi, Del Commercio de' Popoli Neutrali, &c. p. 185. Kluber, Droit des Gens Moderne
de l'Europe, § 293.

stances they have agreed, by special covenant, that the presence of one of their armed ships along with their merchant-
ships shall be mutually understood to imply that nothing is
to be found in that convoy of merchant-ships inconsistent with
amity or neutrality; and if they consent to accept this pledge,
no third party has a right to quarrel with it, any more than
any other pledge which they may agree mutually to accept.
But surely no sovereign can legally compel the acceptance
of such a security by mere force. The only security known
to the law of nations upon this subject, independently of all
special covenant, is the right of personal visitation and search,
to be exercised by those who have the interest in making it."

3. That the penalty for the violent contravention of this
right is the confiscation of the property so withheld from visitation and search. "For the proof of this I need only refer
to *Vattel*, one of the most correct and certainly not the least
indulgent of modern professors of public law. In book iii.
c. 7, sect. 114, he expresses himself thus:—' On ne peut em-
pêcher le transport des effets de contrebande, si l'on ne visite
pas les vaisseaux neutres. On est donc en droit de les visiter.
Quelques nations puissantes ont refusé en différents temps de
se soumettre à cette visite. Aujourd'hui un vaisseau neutre,
qui refuseroit de souffrir la visite, se feroit condamner par cela
seul, comme étant de bonne prise.' Vattel is here to be considered not as a lawyer merely delivering an opinion, but as
a witness asserting a fact—the fact that such is the existing
practice of modern Europe. Conformably to this principle
we find in the celebrated French ordinance of 1681, now in
force, article 12, 'That every vessel shall be good prize in
case of resistance and combat;' and *Valin*, in his smaller
Commentary, p. 81, says expressly, that although the expression is in the conjunctive, yet that the *resistance alone is sufficient*. He refers to the Spanish ordinance, 1718, evidently
copied from it, in which it is expressed in the disjunctive, 'in
case of resistance *or* combat.' And recent instances are at
hand and within view, in which it appears that Spain continues to act upon this principle. The first time it occurs to

my notice on the inquiries I have been able to make in the institutes of our own country respecting matters of this nature, except what occurs in the Black Book of the Admiralty, is in the order of council, 1664, art. 12, which directs, ' That when any ship, met withal by the royal navy or other ship commissionated, shall fight or make resistance, the said ship and goods shall be adjudged lawful prize.' A similar article occurs in the proclamation of 1672. I am therefore warranted in saying that it was the rule and the undisputed rule of the British Admiralty. I will not say that that rule may not have been broken in upon in some instances by considerations of comity or of policy, by which it may be fit that the administration of this species of law should be tempered in the hands of those tribunals which have a right to entertain and apply them; for no man can deny that a state may recede from its extreme rights, and that its supreme councils are authorized to determine in what cases it may be fit to do so, the particular captor having in no case any other right and title than what the state itself would possess under the same facts of capture. But I stand with confidence upon all principles of reason,—upon the distinct authority of Vattel,—upon the institutes of other great maritime countries, as well as those of our own country, when I venture to lay it down that, by the law of nations, as now understood, a deliberate and continued resistance to search, on the part of a neutral vessel, to a lawful cruiser, is followed by the legal consequence of confiscation."[79]

The judgment of condemnation pronounced in this case was followed by the treaty of armed neutrality entered into by the Baltic powers in 1800, which league was dissolved by the death of the emperor Paul, and the points in the controversy between those powers and Great Britain were finally adjusted by the convention of 5th June, 1801. By the 4th article of this convention, the right of search as to merchant vessels sailing under neutral convoy was modified, by limiting

---

[79] Robinson's Adm. Rep. vol. i. p. 340. The Maria.

it to public ships of war of the belligerent party, excluding private armed vessels. Subject to this modification, the pretensions of resisting by means of convoy the exercise of the belligerent right of search, was surrendered by Russia and the other northern powers, and various regulations provided to prevent the abuse of that right to the injury of neutral commerce. As has already been observed, the object of this treaty is expressly declared by the contracting parties in its preamble to be the settlement of the differences which had grown out of the armed neutrality by " an invariable determination of their principles upon the rights of neutrality in their application to their respective monarchies." The 8th article also provides that the principles and measures adopted by the present act shall be alike applicable to all the maritime wars in which one of the two powers may be engaged whilst the other remains neutral. These stipulations shall consequently be regarded as permanent, and shall serve as a constant rule for the contracting parties in matters of commerce and navigation."[80]

In the case of the *Maria*, the resistance of the convoying ship was held to be a resistance of the whole fleet of merchant vessels under convoy, and subjected the whole to confiscation. This was a case of neutral property condemned for an attempted resistance by a neutral armed vessel to the exercise of the right of visitation and search by a lawfully commissioned belligerent cruiser. But the forcible resistance by an enemy master will not, in general, affect neutral property laden on board an enemy's merchant vessel; for an

§ 27.
Forcible resistance by an enemy master.

[80] The question arising out of the case of the Swedish convoy gave rise to several instructive polemic essays. The judgment of Sir W. Scott was attacked by Professor J. F. W. Schlegel, of Copenhagen, in a Treatise on the Visitation of Neutral Ships under Convoy, transl. London, 1801; and vindicated by Dr. Croke in "Remarks on M. Schlegel's Work," 1801. See also "Letters of Sulpicius on the Northern Confederacy," London, 1801. "Substance of the Speech of Lord Grenville in the House of Lords, Nov. 13, 1801." London, 1802.

attempt on his part to rescue his vessel from the possession
of the captor is nothing more than the hostile act of a hostile
person, who has a perfect right to make such an attempt.

" If a *neutral* master," says Sir *W. Scott*, " attempts a rescue, or to withdraw himself from search, he violates a duty
which is imposed upon him by the law of nations, to submit
to search, and to come in for inquiry as to the property of the
ship or cargo ; and if he violates this obligation by a recur-
rence to force, the consequence will undoubtedly reach the
property of his owner ; and it would, I think, extend also
to the whole property intrusted to his care, and thus fraudulently attempted to be withdrawn from the operation of the
rights of war. With an *enemy* master, the case is very different : no duty is violated by such an act on his part—*lupum
auribus teneo,* and if he can withdraw himself, he has a right
so to do."[81]

§ 28.
Right of a
neutral to
carry his
goods in
an *armed*
enemy
vessel.
The question how far a neutral merchant has a right to
lade his goods on board an armed enemy vessel, and how far
his property is involved in the consequences of resistance
by the enemy master, was agitated both in the British and
American prize courts during the last war between Great
Britain and the United States. In a case adjudged by the
supreme court of the United States in 1815, it was determined that a neutral had a right to charter and lade his
goods on board a belligerent armed merchant ship, without
forfeiting his neutral character, unless he actually concurred
and participated in the enemy master's resistance to capture.[82] Cotemporaneously with this decision of the American court, Sir *W. Scott* held directly the contrary doctrine,
and decreed salvage for the recapture of neutral Portuguese
property previously taken by an American cruiser from on
board an armed British vessel, upon the ground that the
American prize courts might justly have condemned the

[81] Robinson's Adm. Rep. vol. v. p. 232. The Catharina Elizabeth.
[82] Cranch's Rep. vol. ix. p. 388. The Nereide.

property.[83]   In reviewing its former decision, in a subsequent
case adjudged in 1818, the American court confirmed it,
and, alluding to the decision in the English high court of admiralty, stated, that if a similar case should again occur in
that court, and the decisions of the American court should in
the mean time have reached that learned judge, he would be
called upon to acknowledge that the danger of condemnation in the United States courts was not as great as he had
imagined.   In determining the last-mentioned case, the
American court distinguished it both from those where neutral vessels were condemned for the unneutral act of the
convoying vessel, and those where neutral vessels had been
condemned for placing themselves under enemy's convoy.
With regard to the first class of cases, it was well known
that they originated in the capture of the Swedish convoy at
the time when Great Britain had resolved to throw down
the glove to all the world, on the contested principles of the
northern maritime confederacy.   But, independently of this,
there were several considerations which presented an obvious
distinction between both classes of cases and that under consideration.   A convoy was an association for a hostile object.
In undertaking it, a state spreads over the merchant vessels
an immunity from search which belongs only to a national
ship; and by joining a convoy, every individual vessel puts
off her pacific character, and undertakes for the discharge
of duties which belong only to the military marine. If, then,
the association be voluntary, the neutral, in suffering the fate
of the entire convoy, has only to regret his own folly in wed-
ding his fortune to theirs; or if involved in the resistance of
the convoying ship, he shares the fate to which the leader
of his own choice is liable in case of capture.[84]

The Danish government issued, in 1810, an ordinance re-   § 29.
lating to captures, which declared to be good and lawful   Neutral vessels un-

[83] Dodson's Adm. Rep. vol. i. p. 443.   The Fanny.
[84] Wheaton's Rep. vol. iii. p. 409.   The Atalanta.

der ene-
my's con-
voy liable
to capture? prize " such vessels as, notwithstanding their flag is considered neutral, as well with regard to Great Britain as the
powers at war with the same nation, still, either in the Atlantic or Baltic, have made use of English convoy." Under
this ordinance, many American neutral vessels were captured,
and, with their cargoes, condemned in the Danish prize
courts for offending against its provisions. In the course of
the discussions which subsequently took place between the
American and Danish governments respecting the legality
of these condemnations, the principles upon which the ordinance was grounded were questioned by the United States
government as inconsistent with the established rules of international law. It was insisted that the prize ordinances of
Denmark, or of any other particular state, could not make or
alter the general law of nations, nor introduce a new rule
binding on neutral powers. The right of the Danish monarch to legislate for his own subjects and his own tribunals,
was incontestable ; but before his edicts could operate upon
foreigners carrying on their commerce upon the seas, which
are the common property of all nations, it must be shown
that they were conformable to the law by which all are
bound. It was, however, unnecessary to suppose, that in
issuing these instructions to its cruisers, the Danish government intended to do any thing more than merely to lay down
rules of decision for its own tribunals, conformable to what
that government understood to be just principles of public
law. But the observation became important when it was
considered that the law of nations nowhere existed in a written code accessible to all, and to whose authority all de-
ferred ; and that the present question regarded the application of a principle (to say the least) of doubtful authority, to
the confiscation of neutral property for a supposed offence
committed, not by the owner, but by his agent the master,
without the knowledge or orders of the owner, under a belligerent edict, retrospective in its operation, because unknown
to those whom it was to affect.

The principle laid down in the ordinance, as interpreted

by the Danish tribunals, was that the fact of having navigated under enemy's convoy is, *per se*, a justifiable cause, not of capture merely, but of condemnàtion, in the courts of the other belligerent; and *that*, without inquiring into the proofs of proprietary interest, or the circumstances and motives under which the captured vessel had joined the convoy, or into the legality of the voyage, or the innocence of her conduct in other respects. A belligerent pretension so harsh, apparently so new, and so important in its consequences, before it could be assented to by neutral states, must be rigorously demonstrated by the authority of the writers on public law, or shown to be countenanced by the usage of nations. Not one of the numerous expounders of that law even mentioned it; no belligerent nation had ever before acted upon it; and still less could it be asserted that any neutral nation had ever acquiesced in it. Great Britain, indeed, had contended that a neutral state had no right to resist the exercise of the belligerent claim of visitation and search by means of convoys *consisting of its own ships of war*. But the records even of the *British* courts of admiralty might be searched in vain for a precedent to support the principle maintained by Denmark, that the mere fact of having sailed under belligerent convoy is, in all cases and under all circumstances, conclusive cause of condemnation.

The American vessels in question were engaged in their accustomed lawful trade, between Russia and the United States; they were unarmed, and made no resistance to the Danish cruisers; they were captured on the return voyage, after having passed up the Baltic and been subjected to examination by the Danish cruisers and authorities, and were condemned under an edict which was unknown, and consequently, as to them, did not exist when they sailed from Cronstadt, and which, unless it could be strictly shown to be consistent with the pre-existing law of nations, must be considered as an unauthorized measure of retrospective legislation. To visit upon neutral merchants and mariners extremely penal consequences from an act, which they had

reason to believe to be innocent at the time, and which is not
pretended to be forbidden by a single treaty or writer upon
public law, by the general usage of nations, or even by the
practice of any one belligerent, or the acquiescence of any
one neutral state, must require something more than a mere
resort to the supposed analogy of other acknowledged principles of international law, but from which it would be vain
to attempt to deduce that now in question as a corollary.

Being found in company with an enemy's convoy might, indeed, furnish a *presumption* that the captured vessel and cargo
belonged to the enemy, in the same manner as goods taken
in an enemy's vessel are presumed to be enemy's property
until the contrary is proved; but this presumption is not of
that class of presumptions called *presumptiones juris et de
jure*, which are held to be conclusive upon the party, and
which he is not at liberty to controvert. It is a slight presumption only, which will readily yield to countervailing
proof. One of the proofs which, in the opinion of the American negotiator, ought to have been admitted by the prize
tribunal to countervail this presumption, would have been
evidence that the vessel had been compelled to join the convoy; or that she had joined it, not to protect herself from
examination by Danish cruisers, but against others, whose
notorious conduct and avowed principles rendered it certain
that captures by them would inevitably be followed by condemnation. It followed, then, that the simple fact of having
navigated under British convoy could be considered as a
ground of suspicion only, warranting the captors in sending
in the captured vessel for further examination, but not constituting in itself a conclusive ground of confiscation.

Indeed it was not perceived how it could be so considered,
upon the mere ground of its interfering with the exercise of
the belligerent pretensions of visitation and search, by a state
which, when neutral, had asserted the right of protecting its
private commerce against belligerent visitation and search
by armed convoys of its own public ships.

Nor could the consistency of the Danish government, in

this respect, be vindicated, by assuming a distinction between the doctrine maintained by Denmark, when neutral, against Great Britain, from that which she sought, as a belligerent, to enforce against America. Why was it that navigating under the convoy of a *neutral* ship of war was deemed a conclusive cause of condemnation ? It was because it tended to impede and defeat the belligerent right of search—to render every attempt to exercise this lawful right a contest of violence—to disturb the peace of the world, and to withdraw from the proper forum the determination of such controversies by forcibly preventing the exercise of its jurisdiction.

The mere circumstance of sailing in company with a *belligerent* convoy had no such effect ; being an *enemy*, the belligerent had *a right to resist.* The masters of the vessels under his convoy could not be involved in the consequences of that resistance, because they were neutral, and had not actually participated in the resistance. They could no more be involved in the consequences of a resistance by the belligerent, which is his own lawful act, than is the neutral shipper of goods on board a belligerent vessel for the resistance of the master of that vessel, or the owner of neutral goods found in a belligerent fortress for the consequences of its resistance.

The right of capture in war extends only to things actually belonging to the enemy, or such as are considered as constructively belonging to him, because taken in a trade prohibited by the laws of war, such as contraband, property taken in breach of blockade, and other analogous cases ; but the property now in question was neither constructively nor actually the property of the enemy of Denmark. It was not pretended that it was actually his property, and it could not be shown to have been constructively his. If, indeed, these American vessels had been armed; if they had thus contributed to augment the force of the belligerent convoy ; or if they had actually participated in battle with the Danish cruisers,—they would justly have fallen by the fate of war, and the voice of the American government would never have been raised in their favour. But they were, in fact, unarmed merchantmen; and far from increasing the force of the British convoying squadron, their junction tended to weaken it by expanding the sphere of its protecting duty; and instead of participating in the enemy's resistance, in fact there was no battle and no resistance, and the merchant vessels fell a defenceless prey to the assailants.

The illegality of the act on the part of the neutral masters, for which the property of their owners had been confiscated, must then be sought for in a higher source, and must be referred back to the circumstance of *their joining the convoy.* But why should this circumstance be considered illegal any more than the fact of a neutral taking shelter in a belligerent port, or under the guns of a belligerent fortress which is subsequently invested and taken? The neutral cannot, indeed, seek to escape from visitation and search by *unlawful* means, either of force or fraud; but if, by the use of any lawful and innocent means, he may escape, what is to hinder his resorting to such means for the purpose of avoiding a proceeding so vexatious? The belligerent cruisers and prize courts had not always been so moderate and just as to render it desirable for the neutral voluntarily to seek for an opportunity of being examined and judged by them. Upon the supposition, indeed, that justice was administered promptly, impartially, and purely in the prize tribunals of Denmark, the American ship masters could have had no motive to avoid an examination by Danish cruisers, since their proofs of property were clear, their voyages lawful, and they were not conscious of being exposed to the slightest hazard of condemnation in these tribunals. Indeed some of these vessels had been examined on their voyage up the Baltic, and acquitted by the Danish courts of admiralty. Why, then, should a guilty motive be imputed to them, when their conduct could be more naturally explained by an innocent one? Surely, in the multiplied ravages to which neutral commerce was then exposed on every sea, from the sweeping decrees of confiscation fulminated by the great belligerent powers, the conduct of these parties might be sufficiently accounted for, without resorting to the supposition that they meant to resist or even to evade the exercise of the belligerent rights of Denmark.

Even admitting, then, that the neutral American had no right to put himself under convoy in order to avoid the exercise of the right of visitation and search by a *friend*, as Denmark professed to be, he had still a perfect right to defend himself against his *enemy*, as France had shown herself to be, by her conduct and the avowed principles upon which she had declared open war against all neutral trade. Denmark had a right to capture the commerce of her enemy, and for that purpose to search and examine vessels under the neutral flag, whilst America had an equal right to protect her commerce against French capture by all the means allowed by the ordinary laws of war between enemies. The exercise of this perfect right could not legally be affected by the circumstance of the war existing between Denmark and England, or by the alliance between Denmark and France. America and England were at peace. The alliance between Denmark and France was against England, not against America; and the Danish government, which had refused to adopt the decrees of Berlin and Milan as the rule of its conduct towards neutrals, could not surely consider it culpable on the part of the American ship masters to have defended themselves against the operation of these decrees by every means in their power. If the use of any of these means conflicted in any degree with the belligerent rights of Denmark, that was an incidental consequence, which could not be avoided by the parties without sacrificing their incontestable right of self-defence.

But it might perhaps be said, that as resistance to the right of search is, by the law and usage of nations, a substantive ground of condemnation *in the case of the master of a single ship*, still more must it be so, where *many vessels are associated* for the purpose of defeating the exercise of the same right.

In order to render the two cases stated perfectly analogous, there must have been an actual resistance on the part of the vessels in question, or at least on the part of the enemy's fleet, having them at the time under its protection, so as to connect them inseparably with the acts of the enemy. Here was no *actual* resistance on the part of either, but only a *constructive* resistance on the part of the neutral vessels, implied from the fact of their having joined the enemy's convoy. This however was, at most, a *mere intention to resist*, never carried into effect, which had never been considered, in the case of a single ship, as involving the penalty of confiscation. But the resistance of the master of a single ship, which is supposed to be analogous to the case of convoy, must refer to a *neutral* master, whose resistance would, by the established law of nations, involve both ship and cargo in the penalty of confiscation. The same principle would not, however, apply to the case of an *enemy*-master, who has an incontestable right to resist his enemy, and whose resistance could not affect the *neutral owner of the cargo*, unless he was on board, and actually participated in the resistance. Such was, in a similar case, the judgment of Sir W. Scott. So also the right of a neutral to transport his goods on board even of an *armed* belligerent vessel was solemnly affirmed by the decision of the highest judicial tribunal in the United States during the late war with Great Britain, after a most elaborate discussion, in which all the principles and analogies of public law bearing upon the question were thoroughly examined and considered.

The American negotiator then confidently relied upon the position assumed by him—that the entire silence of all the authoritative writers on public law, as to any such exception to the general freedom of neutral navigation, laid down by them in such broad and comprehensive terms, and of every treaty made for the special purpose of defining and regulating the rights of neutral commerce and navigation, constituted of itself a strong negative authority to show that no such exception exists, especially as that freedom is expressly extended to every case which has the slightest resemblance to that in question. It could not be denied that the goods of a friend, found in an enemy's fortress, are exempt from confiscation as prize of war; that a neutral may lawfully carry his goods in an armed belligerent ship; that the neutral shipper of goods on board an enemy's vessel, (armed or unarmed,) is not responsible for the consequences of resistance by the enemy-master. How then could the neutral owner, both of ship and cargo, be responsible for the acts of the belligerent convoy, under the protection of which his property had been placed, not by his own immediate act, but by that of the master proceeding without the knowledge or instructions of the owner?

Such would certainly be the view of the question, even applying to it the largest measure of belligerent rights ever assumed by any maritime state. But when examined by the milder interpretations of public law, which the Danish government, in common with the other northern powers of Europe, had hitherto patronised, it would be found still more clear of doubt. If, as Denmark had always insisted, a neutral might lawfully arm himself against all the belligerents; if he might place himself under the convoying force of his own country, so as to defy the exercise of belligerent force to compel him to submit to visitation and search on the high seas; the conduct of the neutral Americans who were driven to take shelter under the floating fortresses of the enemy of Denmark, not for the purpose of resisting the exercise of her belligerent rights, but to protect themselves against the lawless violence of those, whose avowed purpose rendered it certain, that, notwithstanding this neutrality, capture would inevitably be followed by condemnation, would find its complete vindication in the principles which the publicists and statesmen of that country had maintained in the face of the world. Had the American commerce in the Baltic been placed under the protection of the public ships of war of the United States, as it was admitted it might have been, the belligerent rights

of Denmark would have been just as much infringed as they
were by what actually happened. In that case, the Danish
cruisers must, upon Danish principles, have been satisfied
with the assurance of the commander of the American convoying squadron, as to the neutrality of the ships and cargoes sailing under his protection. But that assurance could
only have been founded upon their being accompanied with
the ordinary documents found on board of American vessels,
and issued by the American government upon the representa-
tions and proofs furnished by the interested parties. If these
might be false and fraudulent in the one case, so might they
be in the other, and the Danish government would be equally
deprived of all means of examining their authenticity in both.
In the one, it would be deprived of those means by its own
voluntary acquiescence in the statement of the commander
of the convoying squadron, and in the other by the presence
of a superior enemy's force, preventing the Danish cruisers
from exercising their right of search. This was put for the
sake of illustration, upon the supposition that the vessels under
convoy had escaped from capture; for upon that supposition
only could any *actual* injury have been sustained by Denmark
as a belligerent power. Here they were captured without
any hostile conflict, and the question was, whether they were
liable to confiscation for having navigated under the enemy's
convoy, notwithstanding the neutrality of the property and
the lawfulness of their voyage in other respects.

Even supposing then that it was the intention of the American ship-masters in sailing with the British convoy, to
escape from Danish as well as French cruisers, that intention
had failed of its effect; and it might be asked what belligerent right of Denmark had been practically injured by such
an abortive attempt? If any, it must be the right of visitation and search. But that right is not a substantive and independent right, with which belligerents are invested by the
law of nations for the purpose of wantonly vexing and inter-
rupting the commerce of neutrals. It is a right growing out
of the greater right of capturing enemy's property, or con-

traband of war, and to be used, as means to an end, to enforce the exercise of that right. Here the actual exercise
of the right was never in fact opposed, and no injury had
accrued to the belligerent power. But it would perhaps be
said, that it might have been opposed and actually defeated,
had it not been for the accidental circumstance of the separation of these vessels from the convoying force, and that
the entire commerce of the world with the Baltic Sea might
thus have been effectually protected from Danish capture.
And it might be asked in reply, what injury would have resulted to the belligerent rights of Denmark from that circumstance? If the property were neutral, and the voyage lawful, what injury would result from the vessels escaping from
examination? On the other hand, if the property were enemy's property, its escape must be attributed to the superior
force of the enemy, which, though a *loss*, could not be an
injury of which Denmark would have a lawful right to complain. Unless it could be shown that a neutral vessel navigating the seas is bound *to volunteer to be searched* by the belligerent cruisers, and that she had no right to avoid search
by any means whatever, it was apparent that she might avoid
it by any means not unlawful. Violent resistance to search,
rescue after seizure, fraudulent spoliation or concealment of
papers, are all avowedly unlawful means, which, unless, ex-
tenuated by circumstances, may justly be visited with the
penalty of confiscation. Those who alleged that sailing
under belligerent convoy was also attended with the same
consequences, must show it, by appealing to the oracles of
public law, to the text of treaties, to some decision of an international tribunal, or to the general practice and understanding of nations.

The negotiation finally resulted in the signature of a treaty
in 1830, between the United States and Denmark, by which
the latter power stipulated to indemnify the American claimants generally for the seizure of their property by the payment of a fixed sum *en bloc*, leaving it to the American government to apportion it by commissioners appointed by itself,

and authorized to determine "according to the principles of justice, equity, and the law of nations," with a declaration that the convention, having no other object than to terminate all the claims, "can never hereafter be invoked, by one party or the other, as a precedent or rule for the future."[85]

[85] Martens, Nouveau Recueil, tom. viii. p. 350.

CHAPTER IV.

TREATY OF PEACE.

THE power of concluding peace, like that of declaring war, depends upon the municipal constitution of the state. These authorities are generally associated.   In unlimited monarchies, both reside in the sovereign; and even in limited or constitutional monarchies, each may be vested in the crown. Such is the British constitution, at least in form; but it is well known, that in its practical administration the real power of making war actually resides in the parliament, without whose approbation it cannot be carried on, and which body has consequently the power of compelling the crown to make peace, by withholding the supplies necessary to prosecute hostilities.   The American constitution vests the power of declaring war in the two houses of congress, with the assent of the president.   By the forms of the constitution, the president has the exclusive power of making treaties of peace, which, when ratified with the advice and consent of the senate, become the supreme law of the land, and have the effect of repealing the declaration of war and all other laws of congress, and of the several states which stand in the way of their stipulations.   But the congress may at any time compel the president to make peace, by refusing the means of carrying on war.   In France the king has, by the express terms of the constitutional charter, power to declare war, to make treaties of peace, of alliance, and of commerce; but the real power of making both peace and war resides in the chambers, which have the authority of granting or refusing the means of prosecuting hostilities.

§ 1. Power of making peace dependent on the municipal constitution.

§ 2.
Power of
making
treaties of
peace li-
mited in its
extent.
The power of making treaties of peace, like that of making other treaties with foreign states, is, or may be, limited in its extent by the national constitution. We have already seen that a general authority to make treaties of peace necessarily implies a power to stipulate the conditions of peace; and among these may properly be involved the cession of the public territory and other property, as well as of private property included in the eminent domain. If, then, there be no limitation expressed in the fundamental laws of the state, or necessarily implied from the distribution of its constitutional authorities, on the treaty-making power in this respect, it necessarily extends to the alienation of public and private property, when deemed necessary for the national safety or policy.[1]

The duty of making compensation to individuals, whose private property is thus sacrificed to, the general welfare, is inculcated by publicists as correlative to the sovereign right of alienating those things which are included in the eminent domain; but this duty must have its limits. No government can be supposed to be able, consistently with the welfare of the whole community, to assume the burden of losses produced by conquest, or the violent dismemberment of the state. Where, then, the cession of territory is the result of coercion and conquest, forming a case of imperious necessity beyond the power of the state to control, it does not impose any obligation upon the government to indemnify those who may suffer a loss of property by the cession.[2]

The fundamental laws of most free governments limit the treaty-making power in respect to the dismemberment of the state, either by an express prohibition or by necessary implication from the nature of the constitution. Thus, even under the constitution of the old French monarchy, the States-General of the kingdom declared that Francis I. had no power

[1] Vide ante, pt. iii. ch. 2, Rights of Negotiation and Treaties, § 6.
[2] Grotius, de Jur. Bel. ac Pac. lib. iii. cap. 20, § 7. Vattel, Droit des Gens, liv. i. ch. 20, § 244; liv. iv. ch. 2, § 12. Kent's Comment. on American Law, vol. i. p. 179. 2d Ed.

to dismember the kingdom, as was attempted by the treaty of Madrid concluded by that Monarch; and that not merely upon the ground that he was a prisoner, but that the assent of the nation represented in the States-General was essential to the validity of the treaty.　The cession of the province of Burgundy was therefore annulled, as contrary to the fundamental laws of the kingdom; and the provincial states of that duchy, according to Mezeray, declared that " never having been other than subjects of the crown of France, they would die in that allegiance; and if abandoned by the king, they would take up arms, and maintain by force their independence, rather than pass under a foreign dominion." But when the ancient feudal constitution of France was gradually abolished by the disuse of the States-General, and the absolute monarchy became firmly established under Richelieu and Louis XIV., the authority of ceding portions of the public territory as the price of peace passed into the hands of the king, in whom all the other powers of government were concentrated.　The different constitutions established in France subsequently to the revolution of 1789, limited this authority in the hands of the executive in various degrees.　The provision in the constitution of 1795, by which the recently conquered countries on the left bank of the Rhine were annexed to the French territory, became an insuperable obstacle to the conclusion of peace in the conferences at Lisle.　By the constitutional charter of 1830 the king is invested with the power of making peace, without any limitation of this authority other than that which is implied in the general distribution of the constitutional powers of the government.　Still it is believed that, according to the general understanding of French publicists, the assent of the chambers, clothed with the forms of a legislative act, is considered essential to the ultimate validity of a treaty ceding any portion of the national territory.　The extent and limits of the territory being defined by the municipal laws, the treaty-making power is not considered sufficient to repeal those laws.

In Great Britain, the treaty-making power, as a branch of the regal prerogative, has in theory no limits; but it is practically limited by the general controlling authority of parliament, whose approbation is necessary to carry into effect a treaty by which the existing territorial arrangements of the empire are altered.

In confederated governments, the extent of the treaty-making power in this respect must depend upon the nature of the confederation. If the union consists of a system of confederated states, each retaining its own sovereignty complete and unimpaired, it is evident that the federal head, even if invested with the general power of making treaties of peace for the confederacy, cannot lawfully alienate the whole or any portion of the territory of any member of the union, without the express assent of that member. Such was the theory of the ancient Germanic constitution: the dismemberment of its territory was contrary to the fundamental laws and maxims of the empire; and such is believed to be the actual constitution of the present Germanic confederation. This theory of its public law has often been compelled to yield in practice to imperious necessity, such as that which forced the cession to France of the territories belonging to the states of the empire on the left bank of the Rhine, by the treaty of Luneville in 1800. Even in the case of a supreme federal government or composite state, like that of the United States of America, it may perhaps be doubted how far the mere general treaty-making power vested in the federal head necessarily carries with it that of alienating the territory of any member of the union without its consent.

§ 3.
Effects of
a treaty of
peace.
The effect of a treaty of peace is to put an end to the war, and to abolish the subject of it. It is an agreement to waive all discussion concerning the respective rights and claims of the parties, and to bury in oblivion the original causes of the war. It forbids the revival of the same war by resuming hostilities for the original cause which first kindled it, or for whatever may have occurred in the course of

it. But the reciprocal stipulation of perpetual peace and amity between the parties does not imply that they are never again to make war against each other for any cause whatever. The peace relates to the war which it terminates: and is perpetual, in the sense that the war cannot be revived for the same cause. This will not, however, preclude the right to claim and resist, if the grievances which originally kindled the war be repeated,—for that would furnish a new injury and a new cause of war equally just with the former. If an abstract right be in question between the parties, on which the treaty of peace is silent, it follows, that all previous complaints and injury, arising under such claim, are thrown into oblivion, by the *amnesty,* necessarily implied, if not expressed: but the claim itself is not thereby settled either one way or the other. In the absence of express renunciation or recognition, it remains open for future discussion. And even a specific arrangement of a matter in dispute, if it be special and limited, has reference only to that particular mode of asserting the claim, and does not preclude the party from any subsequent pretensions to the same thing on other grounds. Hence the utility in practice of requiring a general renunciation of all pretensions to the thing in controversy, which has the effect of precluding for ever the assertion of the claim in any mode.[3]

The treaty of peace does not extinguish claims founded upon debts contracted or injuries inflicted previously to the war, and unconnected with its causes, unless there be an express stipulation to that effect. Nor does it affect private rights acquired antecedently to the war, or private injuries unconnected with the causes which produced the war. Hence debts previously contracted between the respective subjects, though the remedy for their recovery is suspended during the war, are revived on the restoration of peace, unless actually confiscated in the mean time in the rigorous exercise of the strict rights of war, contrary to the milder

---

[3] Vattel, Droit des Gens, liv. iv. ch. 2, §§ 19—21.

practice of recent times. There are even cases where debts contracted, or injuries committed, between the respective subjects of the belligerent nations during the war, may become the ground of a valid claim, as in the case of ransom-bills, and of contracts made by prisoners of war for subsistence, or in the course of trade carried on under a license. In all these cases the remedy may be asserted subsequently to the peace.[4]

§ 4.
Uti possi-detis the basis of every treaty of peace unless the contrary be expressed.

The treaty of peace leaves every thing in the state in which it found it, unless there be some express stipulation to the contrary. The existing state of possession is maintained, except so far as altered by the terms of the treaty. If nothing be said about the conquered country or places, they remain with the conqueror, and his title cannot afterwards be called in question. During the continuance of the war, the conqueror in possession has only a usufructuary right, and the latent title of the former sovereign continues, until the treaty of peace, by its silent operation, or express provisions, extinguishes his title for ever.[5]

The restoration of the conquered territory to its original sovereign by the treaty of peace carries with it the restoration of all persons and things, which have been temporarily under the enemy's dominion, to their original state. This general rule is applied without exception to real property or immoveables. The title acquired in war to this species of property, until confirmed by a treaty of peace, confers a mere temporary right of possession. The proprietary right cannot be transferred by the conqueror to a third party, so as to entitle him to claim against the former owner on the restoration of the territory to the original sovereign. If, on the other hand, the conquered territory is ceded by the

4 Kent's Comment. vol. i. p. 169. 2d Ed.

5 Grotius, de Jur. Bel. ac Pac. lib. iii. cap. 6, §§ 4, 5. Vattel, Droit des Gens, liv. iii. ch. 13, §§ 197, 198. Martens, Précis du Droit des Gens, liv. iii. ch. 4, § 282. Kluber, Droit des Gens Moderne de l'Europe, §§ 254—259.

treaty of peace to the conqueror, such an intermediate transfer is thereby confirmed, and the title of the purchaser becomes valid and complete. In respect to personal property,
or moveables, a different rule is applied. The title of the
enemy to things of this description is considered complete
against the original owner after twenty-four hours' possession, in respect to booty on land. The same rule was formerly considered applicable to captures at sea: but the
more modern usage of maritime nations requires a formal
sentence of condemnation as prize of war in order to preclude
the right of the original owner to restitution on payment of
salvage. But since the *jus postliminii* does not, strictly
speaking, operate after the peace, if the treaty of peace contains no express stipulation respecting captured property, it
remains in the condition in which the treaty finds it, and is
thus tacitly ceded to the actual possessor. The *jus postliminii* is a right which belongs exclusively to a state of war;
and therefore a transfer to a neutral, before the peace, even
without a judicial sentence of condemnation, is valid, if there
has been no recovery or recapture before the peace. The
intervention of peace covers all defects of title, and vests a
lawful possession in the neutral, in the same manner as it
quiets the title of the hostile captor himself.[6]

A treaty of peace binds the contracting parties from the
time of its signature. Hostilities are to cease between them
from that time, unless some other period be provided in the
treaty itself. But the treaty binds the subjects of the belligerent nations only from the time it is notified to them. Any
intermediate acts of hostility committed by them, before it
was known, cannot be punished as criminal acts, though it
is the duty of the state to make restitution of the property
seized subsequently to the conclusion of the treaty: and, in
order to avoid disputes respecting the consequences of such

§ 5.
From what
time the
treaty of
peace com-
mences its
operation.

---

[6] Vattel, liv. iii. ch. 14, §§ 209, 212, 216. Robinson's Adm. Rep. vol. vi.
p. 45. The Parissima Conception. P. 138. The Sophia.

acts, it is usual to provide in the treaty itself the periods at which hostilities are to cease in different places. *Grotius* intimates an opinion that individuals are not responsible, even *civiliter*, for hostilities thus continued after the conclusion of peace, so long as they are ignorant of the fact, although it is the duty of the state to make restitution wherever the property has not been actually lost or destroyed.   But the better opinion seems to be that wherever a capture takes place at sea, after the signature of the treaty of peace, mere ignorance of the fact will not protect the captor from civil responsibility in damages; and that, if he acted in good faith, his own government must protect him and save him harmless. When a place or country is exempted from hostility by articles of peace, it is the duty of the state to give its subjects timely notice of the fact; and it is bound in justice to indemnify its officers and subjects, who act in ignorance of the fact.   In such a case it is the actual wrong-doer who is made responsible to the injured party, and not the superior commanding officer of the fleet, unless he be on the spot, and actually participating in the transaction.   Nor will damages be decreed by the prize court, even against the actual wrong-doer, after the lapse of a great length of time.[7]

When the treaty of peace contains an express stipulation that hostilities are to cease in a given place at a certain time, and a capture is made previous to the expiration of the period limited, but with a knowledge of the peace on the part of the captor, the capture is still invalid: for since constructive knowledge of the peace, after the periods limited in the different parts of the world, renders the capture void, much more ought actual knowledge of the peace to produce that effect.   It may, however, be questionable whether any thing short of an official notification from his own government would be sufficient in such a case to affect the captor with the legal consequences of actual knowledge.   And where a capture was made by an American cruiser of a British vessel,

---

[7] Robinson's Adm. Rep. vol. i. p. 121.   The Mentor.

before the period fixed for the cessation of hostilities by the
treaty of Ghent in 1814, and in ignorance of the fact,—but
the prize had not been carried *infra præsidia* and condemned,
and while at sea was recaptured by a British ship of war
after the period fixed for the cessation of hostilities, but without knowledge of the peace,—it was judicially determined
that the possession of the vessel by the American cruiser was
a lawful possession, and that the British recaptor could not
after the peace lawfully use force to devest this lawful possession. The restoration of peace put an end from the time
limited to all force; and then the general principle applied,
that things acquired in war remain, as to title and possession,
precisely as they stood when the peace took place. The
uti possidetis is the basis of every treaty of peace, unless the
contrary be expressly stipulated. Peace gives a final and
perfect title to captures without condemnation, and as it
forbids all force, it destroys all hope of recovery as much as
if the captured vessel was carried *infra præsidia* and judicially condemned.[8]

Things stipulated to be restored by the treaty are to be
restored in the condition in which they were first taken, unless there be an express provision to the contrary; but this
does not refer to alterations which have been the natural
effect of time, or of the operations of war. A fortress or town
is to be restored as it was when taken, so far as it still remains in that condition when the peace is concluded. There
is no obligation to repair, as well as restore a dismantled fortress, or a ravaged territory. The peace extinguishes all
claim for damages done in war, or arising from the operations
of war. Things are to be restored in the condition in which
the peace found them; and to dismantle a fortification or
waste a country after the conclusion of peace, and previously
to the surrender, would be an act of perfidy. If the con-

§ 6.
In what
condition
things
taken are
to be re-
stored.

[8] Valin, Traité des Prises, ch. iv. §§ 4, 5. Emérigon, Traité d'Assurance,
ch. 12, § 19. Merlin, Répertoire de Jurisprudence, tom. ix. tit. Prise Maritime, § 5. Kent's Comment. vol. i. p. 173.

queror has repaired the fortifications, and re-established the
place in the state it was in before the siege, he is bound to
restore it in the same condition. But if he has constructed
new works, he may demolish them: and, in general in order
to avoid disputes, it is advisable to stipulate in the treaty precisely in what condition the places occupied by the enemy
are to restored.[9]

§ 7.
Breach of
the treaty.
The violation of any one article of the treaty is a violation
of the whole treaty; for all the articles are dependent on
each other, and one is to be deemed a condition of the other.
A violation of any single article abrogates the whole treaty,
if the injured party elects so to consider it. This may, however, be prevented by an express stipulation, that if one article be broken, the others shall nevertheless continue in full
force. If the treaty is violated by one of the contracting
parties, either by proceedings incompatible with its general
spirit, or by a specific breach of any one of its articles, it becomes not absolutely void, but voidable at the election of the
injured party. If he prefers not to come to a rupture, the
treaty remains valid and obligatory. He may waive or remit the infraction committed, or he may demand a just satisfaction.[10]

§ 8.
Disputes
respecting
its breach,
how ad-
justed.
Treaties of peace are to be interpreted by the same rules
with other treaties. Disputes respecting their meaning or
alleged infraction may be adjusted by amicable negotiation
between the contracting parties, by the mediation of friendly
powers, or by reference to the arbitration of some one power
selected by the parties. This latter office has recently been
assumed, in several instances, by the five great powers of
Europe, with the view of preventing the disturbance of the
general peace by a partial infraction of the territorial arrangements stipulated by the treaties of Vienna, in conse-

[9] Vattel, Droit des Gens, liv. iv. ch. 3, § 31.
[10] Grotius, de Jur. Bel. ac Pac. lib. ii. cap. 15, § 15; lib. iii. cap. 19, § 14.
Vattel, liv. iv. ch. 4, §§ 47, 48, 54.

quence of the internal revolutions which have taken place in some of the states constituted by those treaties. Such are the protocols of the conference of London, by which a suspension of hostilities between Holland and Belgium has been enforced, and terms of separation between the two countries proposed, which, when accepted by both, are to form the basis of a permanent peace. The objections to this species of interference, and the difficulty of reconciling it with the independence of the smaller powers, are obvious; but it is clearly distinguishable from that general right of superintendence over the internal affairs of other states, asserted by the powers who were the original parties to the Holy Alliance, for the purpose of preventing changes in their municipal constitutions not proceeding from the voluntary concession of the reigning sovereign, or supposed in their consequences, immediate or remote, to threaten the social order of Europe. The proceedings of the conference treat the revolution, by which the union between Holland and Belgium established by the congress of Vienna, had been dissolved, as an irrevocable event, and confirm the independence, neutrality, and state of territorial possessions of Belgium, upon the conditions contained in the treaty of the 15th November, 1831, between the five powers and that kingdom, subject to such modifications as may ultimately be the result of direct negotiations between the North Netherlands and Belgium.

THE END.

www.ingramcontent.com/pod-product-compliance
Lightning Source LLC
Chambersburg PA
CBHW032341280326
41935CB00008B/414